HEARING BY EYE II

Hearing by Eye II

Advances in the Psychology of Speechreading and Auditory-visual Speech

edited by

Ruth Campbell
Barbara Dodd
Denis Burnham

Psychology Press
a member of the Taylor & Francis group

Psychology Press Ltd, Publishers
27 Church Road
Hove
East Sussex, BN3 2FA
UK

British Library Cataloguing in Publication Data

A catalogue record for this book is available from the British Library

ISBN 0-86377-502-0

Typeset by DP Photosetting, Aylesbury, Bucks.
Printed and bound in the United Kingdom by
T J International Ltd, Padstow

Contents

v

List of Contributors

Jésus Alegria Laboratoire de Psychologie Expérimentale, Université libre de Bruxelles, C.P. 191, 50, avenue Franklin Roosevelt, B-1050 Brussels, Belgium

Anne-Catherine Bachoud-Levi Service de Neurologie, Hôpital Henri-Mondor, 51 Avenue du M. de Lattre-de-Tassigny, 94010 Créteil cedex-Paris, France

Linda Bement National Technical Institute for the Deaf, Rochester Institute of Technology, 52 Lomb Memorial Drive, Rochester, NY 14623, USA

Lynne E. Bernstein Spoken Language Processes Laboratory, House Ear Institute, Los Angeles, California, USA

Peter Blamey Department of Otolaryngology, University of Melbourne, 384–388 Albert Street, East Melborne, Victoria 3002, Australia

Michael Brooke Media Technology Research Centre, Department of Mathematical Sciences, University of Bath, Bath BA2 7AY, UK

Denis Burnham School of Psychology, University of New South Wales, Sydney, 2052, Australia

Ruth Campbell Department of Human Communication Science, University College London, Chandler House, 2 Wakefield Street, London WC1 1PG, UK

Brigitte Charlier Laboratoire de Psychologie Expérimentale, Université libre de Bruxelles, C.P. 191, 50, avenue Franklin Roosevelt, B-1050 Brussels, Belgium

Beatrice de Gelder Department of Psychology, Tilburg University, PO Box 90153, 500 LE Tilburg, The Netherlands

Marilyn E. Demorest Department of Psychology, University of Maryland Baltimore County, Baltimore, Maryland, USA

Barbara Dodd Department of Speech, University of Newcastle upon Tyne, UK

Pierre Escudier Institut de la Communication Parlée, 46 Av Félix-Viallet, 38031 Grenoble Cedex 1, France

Kerry P. Green   Psychology Department, P.O. Box 210068, University of Arizona, Tucson, AZ 85721, USA

Catherine Hage   Laboratoire de Psychologie Expérimentale, Université libre de Bruxelles, C.P. 191, 50, avenue Franklin Roosevelt, B-1050 Brussels, Belgium

Timothy R. Jordan   School of Psychology, University of St Andrews, St Andrews, Fife, KY16 9JU, Scotland

Dominique LePoutre   National Technical Institute for the Deaf, Rochester Institute of Technology, 52 Lomb Memorial Drive, Rochester, NY 14623, USA

Jacqueline Leybaert   Laboratoire de Psychologie Expérimentale, Université libre de Bruxelles, C.P. 191, 50, avenue Franklin Roosevelt, B-1050 Brussels, Belgium

Björn Lyxell   Department of Education and Psychology, Linköping University, S-581 83, Linköping, Sweden

Beth McIntosh   Department of Speech Pathology and Audiology, School of Health and Rehabilitation Sciences, The University of Queensland, Brisbane, Australia

Marc Marschark   National Technical Institute for the Deaf, Rochester Institute of Technology, 52 Lomb Memorial Drive, Rochester, NY 14623, USA

Kevin G. Munhall   Department of Psychology, Queen's University, Kingston, Ontario, Canada K7L 3N6

Michael Oerlemans   Department of Otolaryngology, University of Melbourne, 384–388 Albert Street, East Melborne, Victoria 3002, Australia

Jordi Robert-Ribes   CSIRO Division of Information Technology, Bldg E6B Macquarie University, North Ryde, NSW 2113, Australia

Jerker Rönnberg   Department of Education and Psychology, Linköping University, S-581 83, Linköping, Sweden

Lawrence D. Rosenblum   Department of Psychology, University of California, Riverside, CA 92521, USA

Helena M. Saldaña   Spoken Language Processes Laboratory, House Ear Institute, Los Angeles, California, USA

Stefan Samuelsson   Department of Education and Psychology, Linköping University, S-581 83, Linköping, Sweden

Jean-Luc Schwartz   Institut de la Communication Parlée, 46 Av Félix-Viallet, 38031 Grenoble Cedex 1, France

Paul C. Sergeant   School of Psychology, University of St Andrews, St Andrews, Fife, KY16 9JU, Scotland

Paula E. Tucker   Spoken Language Processes Laboratory, House Ear Institute, Los Angeles, California, USA

Eric Vatikiotis-Bateson   ATR Human Information Processing Research Laboratories, Kyoto, Japan 619-02

Jean Vroomen   Department of Psychology, Tilburg University, PO Box 90153, 500 LE Tilburg, The Netherlands

Lynn Woodhouse   Department of Speech Pathology and Audiology, School of Health and Rehabilitation Sciences, The University of Queensland, Brisbane, Australia

Introduction

Ruth Campbell *Department of Human Communication Science, University College London, UK*

Barbara Dodd *Department of Speech, University of Newcastle upon Tyne, UK*

Denis Burnham *Department of Psychology, University of New South Wales, Sydney, Australia*

They not only speak, write and understand what is written, but if he that speaks looks towards them, and modifies his organs by distinct and full utterance, they know so well what is spoken that it is an expression scarcely figurative to say they hear with the eye
— p. 125 of *Journey to the Western Islands of Scotland*, Samuel Johnson, Folio Society edition, 1990 (after Boswell's Journal of a tour in the Hebrides, 1775)

Ten years ago *Hearing By Eye* was published (Dodd & Campbell, 1987). As far as we knew, it was the first edited book on the psychology of lipreading to focus on lipreading in hearing people rather than the uses of lipreading in deafness. In planning the book we were concerned that, despite the importance of lipreading as the primary mode of speech input for deaf and hard-of-hearing people, it had been overlooked within theoretical psycho-linguistics and speech science. In setting out the book, we learned more about how speechreading may be implicated in developing a theory of spoken language comprehension (Summerfield); of possible integration metrics for vision and hearing (Massaro); of the role of seen speech in the development of language in deaf children (Dodd) and in blind children (Mogford, Mills), and of its uses as hearing fails (Gailey). In people who hear and see perfectly well there were further intriguing studies—seeing the speaker's mouth movements aids comprehension even with good auditory input (Reisberg et al.) and short-term memory for seen speech resembles that for heard speech more than anything else (Campbell, Gathercole), and lipreading can be usefully investigated in patients with neuropsychological impairment (Campbell).

All of this seemed bookworthy, but what has happened since to justify a new volume? One change is indicated in the subtitle of the present book: "speechreading" has replaced "lipreading" as the accepted term for reading speech from facial actions. At the most literal level, this change in terminology recognises that the process relies on more than the lips. Not only is the visibility of teeth and tongue important (Summerfield et al., 1989), but face actions away from the mouth area may contribute to speech perception (see Munhall & Vatikiotis-Bateson, this volume). It also carries the implication that whatever is read from these actions is indeed natural speech rather than a more arcane code. This is important for a number of reasons. One reason is that it suggests we should seek the roots of individual variability in speechreading within speech-based skills, albeit delivered by the eye, rather than in something new and special. Dodd et al.'s, Bernstein et al.'s, and Rönnberg et al.'s chapters in this volume endorse this view in different ways, and offer some detailed insights into such individual differences in both deaf and hearing people. A second implication is in relation to speechreading in people born deaf and who have sign as an early-acquired language. As Marschark et al.'s chapter shows, face-actions have a special role in sign, and these do not overlap with those of speech. A bilingual person with profound prelingual deafness can develop two distinct languages by sight—a sign language, such as ASL or BSL and a spoken language, such as English or French. In both of these, face actions have a role, but such actions signify quite different things, just as the word "pain" refers to something different in English and in French.

The idea of speechreading as a natural aspect of speech perception is in some ways more problematic than the earlier term. If we "read speech" then speech cannot be explained on the basis of auditory events alone. The McGurk illusion (McGurk & MacDonald, 1976; MacDonald & McGurk, 1978) brings this insight home vividly. This illusion is of a "new" speech sound, such as "da" being uttered when one hears one sound ("ba") dubbed onto a seen utterance ("ga").The illusion is immediate and mandatory. For the perceiver it can be direct demonstration—an existence proof—that the immediate perception of speech, while phenomenologically "in the ear", need not be entirely auditory in its origins. McGurk illusions have become something of a research topic in their own right, and their boundary conditions enable us to understand more of their workings (Jordan & Sergeant, this volume). They also help us to understand how vision influences audition at the segmental (phonetic) level. An integrated percept that takes accounts of events at the ear and the eye itself raises important questions: how is the integration of vision and audition achieved in formal terms (Schwartz, Robert-Ribes & Escudier's chapter), in experimental terms

(Green's chapter; Burnham's chapter), and in biological terms (Campbell's chapter)?

One evolving consensus is that *an amodal representational space* may be required as the functional substrate for phonetic perception, whether by ear or by eye. The precise parameters for auditory and for visual information would be set by exposure—by ear and by eye—to the native language. The importance of developmental and cross-linguistic investigations is then to indicate with greater precision just which parameters these are and the time course of their stabilisation (Burnham). If phonetic perception is intrinsically amodal, it may develop in profoundly prelingually deaf as in hearing people, although the weights on the parameters for visual and for auditory information may differ greatly between the groups. "May", we write, not "must". Although some born-deaf people do acquire the native spoken language very well indeed by eye (Bernstein, Demorest & Tucker's chapter), many do not. Without hearing, the visible contrasts of speech can be hard to acquire. One reason is that in order for the contrasts (e.g. between "bin" and "pin") to be perceived, they must be meaningful—phonetic development is driven by phonological (language-specific) requirements. If the child is in difficulties trying to identify the object of speech he or she will be unlikely to tune into the phonetic contrasts that signal such relevant distinctions ... and show corresponding delay in language acquisition. The great advantage of sign as a language medium is that the phonology of the language—the language-specific segmental structure—is fully available to the deaf child. Can the phonology of the *spoken* language be delivered to the deaf child, too?

Cornett's cued speech system (Cornett, 1967) is designed to do just this. It uses manual cues to distinguish speech actions that look very similar but which are different acoustically. So it can be used to disambiguate (again) "pin" and "bin" in speaking English. First reports on the effectiveness of cued-speech were muted, but it seems that in these early studies little attempt was made to use it as a primary language medium, immersing the child in a rich language environment. Recent studies using such cues accompanying speechread phonetic information show that receptive phonology can develop in the deaf to similar levels of discrimination as those in hearing children. Behavioural testing of the deaf children with cued speech *as a first language* described in Leybaert et al.'s chapter suggests that their "inner ear" is pretty much like that of a hearing French-speaking child when it comes to reading, writing and remembering speech.

Cued speech delivers *phonological*, not (transformed) auditory information to the deaf person. A different approach to augmentation is to deliver the missing auditory information directly to an intact sensorium. Tactile stimulation (Oerlemans & Blamey's chapter) is one such mode, auditory cochlear implants (Tyler et al., 1995) another. In both cases current technology can preprocess the auditory signal to deliver an information-rich, speech-structured input to a receptor system that can respond effectively (skin, intact auditory nerve). The further development and use of such patterned aids is becoming more widespread. There is a large-scale natural experiment underway already as many deaf, deafened and hard-of-hearing people are recruited into such programmes. In 10 years or so we may be able to gain a clearer idea of the extent to which such aids work to recover speech-distinctive signals (in postlingually deafened people) and to what extent they may be used by prelingually deaf people—both children in the process of acquiring language and adults who had been prelingually deaf. In doing so, we will glean further insights into the key contrastive elements (and their disposition) that are required for effective spoken language learning.

Technology has made other advances. In the last 10 years computer-based speech recognition and production have become increasingly feasible. This is important for practical reasons, such as the development of efficient telecommunications systems, as well as theoretical ones. Engineers are now aware that making speech visible as facial actions not only offers interesting engineering challenges in visual animation (Terzopoulos & Waters, 1990), but has direct consequences on the intelligibility and informativeness of the message. Computational engineering has enabled working models to be built and tested. Brooke's chapter outlines one simple image-based model that speechreads well with limited image-processing resources. The key to the success of this model is a neural-net algorithm (HMM-based) that learns quickly to classify seen speech sounds presented as short facial animations. Do these models give us useful clues for understanding human spee-chreading skills? They could do: they can suggest just which visual aspects of the seen speech event are particularly important for driving the classification function, as well as illuminating the developmental question—what needs to be in place before learning (exposure) starts and what comprises the most efficacious learning environment?

The machine model described by Brooke uses the image sequences of a speaking face to guide its classifications. How important are the dynamic, rather than the visual-form aspects of speechreading? This has been a relatively underexplored question until very recently, although at least one demonstration, that of Green and Miller (1985) had shown that perceived seen speech rate could alter the perception of a heard speech syllable. Munhall and Vatikiotis-Bateson's chapter brings new insights to this area. Rosenblum and Saldaña's chapter adapts the paradigm developed by Johansson (1973) to explore the dynamic nature of speechreading directly. Johansson showed that it was easy to perceive whole-body actions from animated film clips of points illuminated on the joints—with no other visible form information. A range of other explorations of such point-light displays followed, including demonstrations that manual signs could be perceived by this means even when the form of the hands was invisible (Tartter & Knowlton, 1981; Poizner, Bellugi & Lutes-Driscoll 1981) Rosenblum and colleagues illuminated a speaking face with point-lights over the lower face and teeth and have shown such displays are "speechreadable". In addition to its theoretical insights, this suggests a means for delivering seen speech to the deafblind or in conditions of poor illumination. The point-light demonstrations also suggest a rather different theme for exploring how acquired damage to the neural systems that support vision can affect speechreading. The visual agnosic patient BC cannot identify a pictured face but shows some spared speechreading abilities (De Gelder, Vroomen & Bachoud-Levi's chapter). Could these be due to spared visual pathways for the detection of visual motion? Campbell's chapter, meanwhile, confirms that speechreading in general does not localise in a clearly predictable way to one or other cortical hemisphere; but suggests that some left hemisphere structures may, nevertheless, be more crucial for phonetic classification. Studies of the cortical localisation of speechreading in deaf people are sparse and important comparisons between the localisation of speech and of sign in native users of each of these visual languages are still to be done.

The contributors to this volume have different interests and backgrounds that have been brought to bear on two questions: how does the perception of audio-visual speech work and how does silent speechreading relate to this? Despite differences of approach, there are a number of common themes. First, auditory-visual integration seems to happen early—both in developmental and in information-processing terms. Second, speechreading can deliver speech in a relatively direct fashion to the language user, both in terms of neurological structures and psychological function. Third, time-varying (dynamic) properties of seen speech afford important clues to understanding seen speech processing. These may be in addition to time-invariant ones. We know more about how speechreading may be effectively supplemented and how it accesses higher cognitive abilities even when the segmental structure is incomplete. Perhaps when *Hearing by Eye III* appears, some of the current arguments and ideas will have been surpassed. We are sure, however, that these findings will start to impact on important developments in practical areas of language understanding, including automatic speech recognition and the use of augmenting aids for hearing loss and to make an irreducible mark on theories of language structure and process.

REFERENCES

Cornett, O. (1967). Cued Speech. *American Annals of the Deaf, 112,* 3–13.

Dodd, B. & Campbell, R. (Eds) (1987). *Hearing by eye: The psychology of lip-reading.* Hove, UK: Lawrence Erlbaum Associates Ltd.

Green, K.P. & Miller, J.L. (1985). On the role of visual rate information in phonetic perception. *Perception and Psychophysics, 38,* 269–76.

Johansson, G. (1973). Visual perception of biological motion and a model for its analysis. *Perception and Psychophysics, 14,* 201–11.

MacDonald, J. & McGurk, H. (1978). Visual influences on speech perception. *Perception and Psychophysics, 24,* 253–7.

McGurk, H. & MacDonald, J. (1976). Hearing lips and seeing voices. *Nature, 264,* 746–8.

Poizner, H., Bellugi, U. & Lutes-Driscoll, V. (1981). Perception of American sign language in dynamic point-light displays. *Journal of Experiential Psychology: HPP, 7,* 430–40.

Summerfield, A.Q., MacLeod, P., McGrath, M. & Brooke, N.M. (1989). Lips, teeth, and the benefits of lipreading. In A.W. Young and A.W. Ellis (Eds), *Handbook of research on face processing.* Amsterdam: North Holland, pp. 223–33.

Tartter, V.C. & Knowlton, K.C. (1981). Perception of sign language from an array of 27 moving dots. *Nature, 289,* 676–8.

Terzopoulos D. & Waters, K. (1990). Physically-based facial modelling, analysis and animation. *Journal of Visualisation and Computer Animation, 1,* 73–80.

Tyler, R.S., Louder, M.W., Parkinson, A.J., Woodworth, C.G. & Gantz, B.J. (1995). Performance of adult ineraid and nucleus cochlear implant patients after 3.5 years of use. *Audiology, 34,* 135–44.

AUDIO-VISUAL SPEECH PROCESSING: IMPLICATIONS FOR THEORIES OF SPEECH PERCEPTION

The use of auditory and visual information during phonetic processing: implications for theories of speech perception

Kerry P. Green   *University of Arizona, Tucson, USA*

INTRODUCTION

It has been well-documented that visual information from a talker's mouth and face play a role in the perception and understanding of spoken language (for reviews, see Summerfield, 1987; Massaro, 1987). Much of this research has examined the benefit that the visual information provides to the recognition of speech presented under noisy situations in normal hearing adults (e.g. Sumby & Pollack, 1954). A study by McGurk and MacDonald (1976) was the first to demonstrate that visual information plays a role in the perception of clear, unambiguous speech tokens. They dubbed auditory syllables consisting of labial consonants such as /ba/ onto a videotape of a talker saying different syllables such as /ga/. When observers watched and listened to the videotape, they heard the talker saying a syllable like /da/ or /ða/. However, when asked to face away from the video monitor and just listen to the videotape, they heard the auditory tokens correctly. This type of stimulus has been termed a "fusion token", because the response suggests a blending or fusing of the place information from the two modalities. A second type of token consisting of an auditory /ga/ dubbed onto a visual articulation of /ba/ was often perceived as /bga/. Such stimuli are referred to as "combination tokens", because the response reflects a combining of the information from the two modalities.

Since the findings of McGurk and MacDonald (1976; MacDonald & McGurk, 1978), the McGurk effect has been used extensively as a behavioural tool to examine the processes involved in the integration of information from the auditory and visual modalities during speech perception. A number of studies have been conducted in an attempt to shed light on four different issues concerning the integration of auditory and visual phonetic information. The first issue concerns the various stimulus factors that influence the McGurk effect. One approach to understanding the integration processes is to examine the boundary conditions under which integration does and does not occur. For example, a comparison of this research with other auditory-visual phenomena (e.g. the ventriloquism effect), has led some researchers to suggest that the integration of auditory and visual speech information may be accomplished by a module specific to the processing of speech (Radeau, 1994).

A second issue concerns the level of phonetic processing at which the auditory and visual information are integrated to produce the effect, and whether the information from the two modalities is processed independently or interactively. Since the phonetic information is presented to the perceptual system in separate modalities, the auditory and visual information will be processed separately at least in the early stages of processing (e.g., Roberts & Summerfield, 1981; Saldaña & Rosenblum, 1994). However, at some point during phonetic perception, the two sources of information are combined to influence the phonetic outcome. The main question addressed by many of these studies is whether the information is combined at an early or late stage of phonetic processing. A related question of interest is whether there is any interaction between the two sources of information prior to their integration.

A third important issue concerns the effect of language or developmental experience on the McGurk effect. Currently, there is debate as to whether the ability to discriminate different phonetic categories reflects the initial capacity of the perceptual system at birth, or is the result of experience with a particular language along with the operation of perceptual learning mechanisms (e.g. Pisoni, Lively & Logan, 1994). In a similar manner, researchers have questioned whether the ability to integrate phonetic information from the auditory and visual modalities requires experience watching the movement of talkers' mouths while at the same time hearing a speech utterance (Diehl & Kluender, 1989). Recent studies examining the McGurk effect in young infants and children (e.g. Rosenblum, Smuckler & Johnson, 1997; Massaro et al., 1986) as well as cross-linguistically (Massaro et al., 1993; Sekiyama & Tohkura, 1993) are attempts to address this issue (for a review see Burnham, this volume).

The fourth issue that researchers have investigated is the underlying neurological systems involved in the integration of auditory and visual speech information. Some studies have examined the integration of auditory and visual speech in patients with damage to either the right or left cerebral hemispheres (Campbell et al., 1990) as well as the hemispheric lateralization of the McGurk effect in normal adults (Baynes, Funnell & Fowler, 1994). Others have employed various types of sophisticated imaging techniques to view the activation of the brain under different types of unimodal and bimodal speech conditions (Sams et al., 1991; Campbell, 1996). The intent of such studies is to determine the various types of cognitive processes that might be involved in the processing and integration of phonetic information from the auditory and visual modalities. The results from the different studies addressing the four issues have important implications for theories of speech perception which must account for how and when the information from the two modalities is integrated during speech processing. Moreover, since the auditory signal by itself provides sufficient information for accurate speech perception under most conditions, a good theory should also provide an account of why the two signals are combined.

In this chapter, I will describe studies that examine the level of processing at which the auditory and visual information are integrated, as well as the effect of developmental experience. In the second section, I review some of the research examining the effect of visual influences on phonetic processing of the auditory signal, while in the third section I examine the effect of developmental experience on the McGurk effect. The fourth section discusses the implications of the various studies with respect to theories of speech perception.

VISUAL INFLUENCES ON PHONETIC PERCEPTION

Although the McGurk effect demonstrates an influence of visual information on phonetic perception, it does not isolate the stage of phonetic processing at which the visual and auditory information are combined. The visual information could be combined after the extraction of phonetic prototypes from the auditory signal and act as a kind of visual bias on the phonetic decision of the auditory information. This would be a post-phonetic access approach to the integration of the auditory and visual information. A second possibility is that the visual and auditory information are mapped onto the prototype at the same level of phonetic processing, referred to by some as a "late integration" approach (Robert-Ribes, Schwartz & Escudier, 1995). In one version of this approach, Massaro's Fuzzy Logic Model of Perception (FLMP), separate evaluations of the different dimensions in each modality are extracted independently and then mapped onto the phonetic prototypes (Massaro, 1987). In this model, there is no interaction of the auditory and visual dimensions until the information is mapped onto the prototypes. An alternative version of a late integration approach is to have the separate evaluations along certain dimensions be made contingent upon the evaluations along other dimensions (e.g. Crowther & Batchelder, 1995). This type of model, termed "conditionally independent" (CI), would allow for early interaction among the auditory and visual information, even though the integration of information itself occurs late. Finally, a third possibility is that the visual and auditory information are combined before the information from either modality is mapped onto the phonetic prototypes, usually referred to as "early integration" (Robert-Ribes, Schwartz & Escudier, 1995; see Schwartz, Robert-Ribes & Escudier, this volume).[1]

In an attempt to examine these different possibilities, my colleagues and I have been investigating how conflicting visual information influences the phonetic processing of the auditory speech signal. One of our earliest studies examined whether a change in the perceived place of articulation resulting from the McGurk effect influenced the processing of other dimensions of the auditory signal such as voice-onset-time (VOT) (Green & Kuhl, 1989). Previous studies had shown that the voicing boundary along a VOT continuum ranging from a voiced to voiceless stop consonant varied as a function of the place of articulation of the consonant. A bilabial continuum typically produces a boundary at a relatively short VOT value while an alveolar continuum produces a moderate and a velar continuum a relatively long VOT boundary (Lisker & Abramson, 1970; Miller, 1977). Green and Kuhl (1989) investigated whether the perception of voicing was made with respect to the place of articulation resulting from the combined auditory and visual information in the McGurk effect, or based solely on the place value of the auditory token. An auditory /ibi–ipi/ continuum was dubbed onto a sequence of visual /igi/ tokens and presented to subjects in an auditory-visual (AV) and an auditory-only (AO) condition. Due to the McGurk effect, the AV tokens were perceived as ranging from /idi/ to /iti/.

The results from this experiment (shown in Figure 1) revealed a significant shift in the percentage of voiced responses for the AV condition (e.g. /d/) relative to the AO (e.g. /b/) even though the auditory tokens were identical in the two conditions. This shift indicates that the McGurk effect can impact on the phonetic processing of other dimensions of the auditory signal. The fact that the voicing boundary is modified as a function of the combined auditory and visual place information demonstrates that the visual information does not serve to simply "bias" the phonetic decision made on the basis of the auditory information. One can imagine such bias occurring to change the perceived place decision of an auditory token, especially if that token were somewhat ambiguous with respect to place of articulation. But, to change the voicing decision as well would require a reanalysis of the voicing information. From this it can be concluded that the auditory and visual information are combined by the time a phonetic decision is made, ruling out the possibility of a post-phonetic integration of the auditory and visual information.

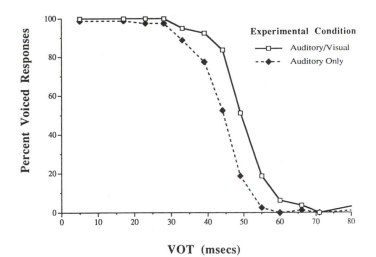

FIG. 1.   Per cent of voiced responses for the /ibi-ipi/ continuum under the auditory-visual and auditory-only conditions

Other studies have investigated whether the perception of speech is influenced by the surrounding speech context. Such influences, usually referred to as "context effects", have often been interpreted as revealing the operation of an early interaction of complex cues during speech perception (Repp, 1982). Overall, two kinds of context effects have been investigated with respect to the auditory-visual perception of speech. One kind consists of nonphonetic contextual information, such as changes in speaking rate or talker characteristics. These contexts influence the phonetic interpretation of speech without providing direct information about segmental identity (Miller, 1981; for a review, see Johnson, 1990). A second kind of context effect involves the influence of neighbouring segments on the phonetic interpretation of a target phoneme. For example, the type of vowel following a consonant influences the interpretation of a preceding fricative (Mann & Repp, 1980). Such phonetic context effects are usually thought to reflect the tacit knowledge of coarticulatory effects from speech production during phonetic perception (Repp, 1982), although other interpretations are possible (Diehl, Kluender & Walsh, 1990).

Two studies have examined whether nonphonetic contextual information in the visual modality, such as information for speaking rate or talker characteristics, influence phonetic processing. Green and Miller (1985) examined whether visual rate information influences the voicing boundary along a /bi–pi/ continuum. Previous research had shown the perception of voicing to be influenced by the speaking rate of the auditory token: fast tokens produced a shorter VOT boundary than slow tokens did (Green &

Miller, 1985; Summerfield, 1981). Green and Miller (1985) dubbed tokens from an auditory /bi–pi/ continuum spoken at a medium rate of speech onto visual articulations of /bi/ and /pi/ spoken at fast and slow rates of speech. They found a shift in the VOT boundary as a function of whether the same auditory tokens were paired with either the fast or the slow visual tokens. This finding demonstrates that visual rate information, like auditory rate information, plays a role in the perception of voicing.[2]

In another study, Strand and Johnson (1996) examined whether the auditory distinction between /s/ and /ʃ/ would be influenced by visual information for talker gender. Previous research had shown that the spectra of the frication noise corresponding to /s/ and /ʃ/ varies with gender characteristics. The overall spectrum is shifted towards higher frequencies for female relative to male talkers (Schwartz, 1968). More important, Mann and Repp (1980) found that the category boundary separating /s/ and /ʃ/ is influenced by the gender characteristics of the talker saying the following vowel (Mann & Repp, 1980). Following Mann and Repp (1980), Strand and Johnson (1996) first constructed "sod" to "shod" continua with vowel characteristics corresponding to either a male or a female talker. In an auditory-only presentation, they also found a reliable shift in the /s–ʃ/ category boundary as a function of the gender characteristics of the vowel. Next, they created an auditory continuum varying from "sod" to "shod" that was ambiguous with respect to the gender of the talker in both F0 and formant frequency values. These tokens were dubbed onto a male or a female face saying either "sod" or "shod" and presented to subjects in an auditory-visual condition. Strand and Johnson found a significant shift in the /s–ʃ/ category boundary for the auditory tokens dubbed onto a male face relative to the same auditory tokens dubbed onto a female face. Their findings demonstrate that gender characteristics from the talker's face can influence the interpretation of auditory frication noise.

Phonetic context effects are situations in which the perception of target phoneme is influenced by the surrounding phonetic context. Two recent studies have provided evidence for such effects between the auditory and visual modalities. Green and Gerdeman (1995) investigated whether the McGurk effect was influenced by a mismatch in the vowel context following the consonant. Previous studies had shown the perceptual system to be sensitive to a mismatch in the coarticulatory information between a consonant and its following vowel. Creating such a mismatch disrupts the coarticulatory information and increases the time needed to classify the consonant (Whalen, 1984). Green and Gerdeman examined whether the perceptual system was sensitive to a mismatch in coarticulatory information when it occurs cross-modally. Auditory /ba/ and /bi/ tokens were dubbed onto visual /gi/ and /ga/ tokens respectively to create McGurk fusion stimuli that conflicted not only in the initial consonant, but also in the following vowel. When the vowels were congruent, the McGurk effect was relatively strong (75%). When the AV tokens were incongruent with respect to the vowel information, there was a reliable decrease in the size of the McGurk effect (44%). Thus, the observers were sensitive to the coarticulatory information between a consonant and its following vowel when integrating the auditory and visual signals.

In phonetic context effects, the change in perception is usually in accord with the coarticulatory influences of the surrounding context on a target phoneme during production. For example, Mann (1980) has shown that the location of the category boundary along a /da–ga/ continuum varied as a function of whether the tokens were preceded by either /al/ or /ar/. Moreover, the shift in the boundary was consistent with the coarticulatory effects of a preceding /l/ or /r/ on the production of /d/ and /g/. The congruence between production and perception is taken as support for the notion that listeners use tacit knowledge of coarticulation during speech perception (Repp, 1982).

Norrix and Green (1996) investigated whether context effects can occur when the phonetic context is presented in just one modality (the visual) while the relevant segmental information is presented in another modality (the auditory). There were three different parts to the study. The first part consisted of a production experiment in which the impact of the preceding bilabial stop consonant /b/ on the production of /r/ and /l/ in stop clusters such as /ibri/ and /ibli/ was examined. The bilabial context resulted in a significant reduction in the onset frequency of the second formant (F2) for /l/ and the onset frequency of the third formant (F3) for /r/, as well as a significant increase in the slope of F2 for /l/ (see Table 1). These results demonstrated coarticulatory influences from a preceding bilabial stop consonant on the production of /l/ and /r/ in a stop cluster. Moreover, they raised the question of whether the perceptual system was sensitive to such coarticulatory effects during speech perception.

In order to answer this question, an AO experiment was conducted in which an auditory /ili–iri/ continuum was synthesized by raising the onset frequency of F3. In addition, a single /ibi/ token was also synthesized. From these tokens, three different types of stimuli were constructed. The first consisted of a diotic presentation of the /iri–ili/ tokens over headphones (same token simultaneously presented to both ears). For the second type, a bilabial release burst and its following aspiration were added into the waveform of each /r–l/ token, just before the onset of the formant transitions characterizing the consonant. These tokens were also presented diotically. Due to the presence of the release burst however, they were all perceived as ranging from /ibri–ibli/. For the third type of stimuli, each member of the /iri–ili/ continuum was paired with the auditory /ibi/ token. A member of the /iri–ili/ continuum was presented to just one ear while the /ibi/ was simultaneously presented to the other ear in a dichotic presentation. These tokens were also perceived as ranging from /ibri–ibli/. As in the AO experiment, listeners identified whether the test syllable contained an /r/ or an /l/.

Raising the onset frequency of F3 resulted in a consistent change in the identification of the diotic /iri–ili/ tokens (see Figure 2). More important, the dichotic /ibri–ibli/ tokens shifted the identification function and the /r–l/ boundary towards a lower F3 onset frequency relative to the /iri–ili/ tokens. This shift was consistent with the production data which showed that /r/ is produced with a lower F3 onset frequency when it is preceded by a bilabial stop consonant. Finally, the diotic /iri–ili/ tokens with the release burst and aspiration did not produce a shift in the /r–l/ identification function relative to the unaltered /iri–ili/ tokens, even though they were perceived as ranging from /ibri–ibli/. A follow-up experiment indicated that listeners perceived no difference in the overall "goodness" of the stop consonant in the two types of /ibri–ibli/ stimuli. Thus, there was compensation for a preceding bilabial context on the perception of /r/ and /l/ only when there was a more complete specification of the bilabial token in the auditory signal as in the dichotic condition. The addition of the acoustic correlate of the stop consonant release burst was not enough to produce a shift in the /r–l/ category boundary, although it was enough to signal the presence of a bilabial stop consonant.

The findings from the AO experiment raised a question about what would happen when the information for the bilabial context was specified only in the visual signal while the relevant segmental information for /r–l/ was presented in the auditory signal. In a medial context, this combination produces a strong impression of a bilabial stop consonant, even though there is no auditory information for the bilabial token. One possibility was that the visual signal would provide information about coarticulation that could be taken into account during speech perception. That is, the visual bilabial information might be extracted and used to influence the analysis of

TABLE 1
Mean formant frequency values (Hz) associated with the initial onset of /r/ and /l/ in different context, as well as the formant transition rates (Hz/ms)
(A ** indicates a significant difference, p. <.05)

	F2 Onset Frequency	F3 Onset Frequency	F2 Slope	F3 Slope
/iri/	1401	2167	13.1	12.25
/ibri/	1405	2058	10.9	11.82
Difference	−4.0	109**	2.3	−.43
/ili/	1601	2794	13.6	2.2
/ibli/	1333	2731	17.1	6.2
Difference	268**	63	−3.5**	−4.0

the various acoustic characteristics of the /iri–ili/ tokens in a coarticulatory manner. As with the dichotic condition in the AO experiment, this AV condition should produce a shift in the /r–l/ boundary relative to the /iri–ili/ tokens presented diotically without any visual information. An alternative possibility is that the visual context would produce no shift in the /r–l/ boundary because the visual information, although creating the impression of a bilabial stop, provided no actual acoustic evidence for the stop. This would be analogous to the /iri–ili/ tokens with the stop burst in the AO experiment which also produced the perception of a bilabial stop but produced no shift in the /r–l/ boundary.

In the third part of the study, subjects were presented with the stimuli under two conditions: AO and AV. In the AO condition, they heard the /iri–ili/ series with no burst (previously discussed). In the AV condition, each of these tokens was paired with a visual /ibi/ articulation. As in the previous AO experiment, the subjects identified whether the tokens contained an /r/ or an /l/. The results of this experiment demonstrated a clear shift in the /r–l/ identification function for the AV relative to the AO condition (see Figure 3). The change in the /r–l/ boundary was of comparable magnitude and direction as found in the previous AO experiment between the dichotic /ibri–ibli/ and diotic /iri–ili/ stimuli. A visual-only experiment ruled out the possibility that the shift in the /r–l/ boundary occurred simply because the visual /ibi/ looked like more like an /l/ than an /r/. This experiment indicated that no such bias existed in the perception of the visual /ibi/ tokens.

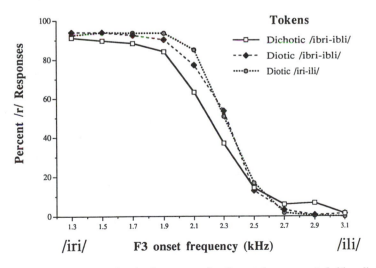

FIG. 2.   Per cent /r/ responses for the three types of auditory tokens presented either diotically or dichotically

One question raised by this study concerns the level of processing at which the coarticulatory information influences the processing of the segmental information for /r–l/ distinction. One possibility is that there is late integration of the auditory and visual information. According to such an approach, the coarticulatory compensation would result from inhibitory and excitatory connections among the different phonetic representations that are activated when the auditory and visual information are mapped onto the phonetic prototypes. For example, because of the coarticulatory effects of the bilabial stop consonant /b/ on /r/ and /l/ in a stop cluster, activation of the /b/ representation by the auditory or the visual information would result in some inhibition of the /r/ representation and excitation of the /l/ representation. This would result in a shift in the /r–l/ boundary towards more /l/ responses in both the AV condition, and the dichotic /ibri–ibli/ condition in the AO experiment. However, such an approach would also predict that a shift would occur whenever there was sufficient information to activate the bilabial stop consonant representation. The diotic /ibri–ibli/ condition however, indicates that this is not always the case and creates a problem for a late integration account of these findings.

The alternative possibility is early integration of the coarticulatory influences of the visual information. With early integration, the visual bilabial would provide the perceptual system with coarticulatory information about some articulatory characteristics such as the rate of change in the oral cavity. This information could then be used to adjust the derived characteristics of the auditory signal that differentiate /r/ and /l/, such as F3 onset frequency or the slope of F2 at an early level of processing, prior to the mapping of the information onto phonetic representations. Such an account is consistent with the findings from the AO experiment because it would predict that compensation would only occur when there was some kind of articulatory evidence for the rate of change in the oral cavity, regardless of whether this evidence came from the auditory or the visual modality. Since the diotic /ibri–ibli/ tokens in the AO experiment contained no such information, compensation would not be expected to occur even though there is the percept of a bilabial stop consonant. Taken together, the AV and AO experiments provide clear evidence of cross-modal coarticulatory effects. Moreover, they are consistent with the notion that the auditory and visual information interact at an early level of phonetic processing before the information is mapped onto the underlying phonetic representations (for more details, see Green, 1996).

To summarize, a number of studies have provided evidence of interactions between the auditory and visual modalities during phonetic perception. Many of these findings indicate that such interactions occur prior to phonetic categorization (Green & Miller, 1985; Strand & Johnson, 1996; Norrix & Green, 1996). These demonstrations are problematic for late-

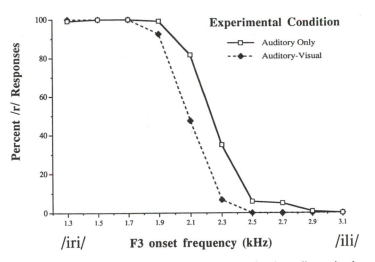

FIG. 3.   Per cent /r/ responses for the /iri–ili/ continuum under the auditory-visual condition (perceived as /ibri–ibli/) versus the auditory-only condition (perceived as /iri–ili/).

integration models which assume that the auditory and visual information are evaluated separately and interact only when the information is mapped onto phonetic prototypes (see Massaro, 1987).

An alternative late-integration approach that might account for many of these findings is a CI model in which the information from the two modalities is evaluated separately, but in a conditionally-independent manner. A CI model has been shown to produce a better account than FLMP for the interaction between two different acoustic dimensions used in consonant and vowel perception (Crowther & Batchelder, 1995). Moreover, the model is consistent with the findings of Green and Kuhl (1991) which showed the phonetic information in the auditory and visual modalities is processed in a dependent or interactive manner. A CI model would have the advantage of not requiring a transformation of the information from one sensory modality into a metric compatible with dimensions in another modality. Instead, the psychological space in which phonetic prototypes are represented might encompass a number of different dimensions including auditory, visual and tactile with some of the dimensions being conditionally-related.

Finally, the results from the studies described above are consistent with the view that the auditory and visual information are integrated at an early stage of processing before the extraction of phonetic prototypes (Summerfield, 1987; Robert-Ribes, Schwartz & Escudier, 1995). According to this view, the information from the two modalities is transformed and combined into a single underlying metric that is then mapped onto phonetic representations. Two metrics that have been considered are based on either auditory or gestural properties (Summerfield, 1987; Robert-Ribes, Schwartz & Escudier, 1995). Of these two metrics, a gesturally-based metric seems to offer the best possibility of accounting for the cross-modal phonetic effects demonstrated by Norrix and Green (1996, see Green, 1996) as well as other auditory-visual phenomena (Robert-Ribes, Schwartz & Escudier, 1995).

THE ROLE OF EXPERIENCE

One question that a theory of speech perception has to account for is why the auditory and visual information are combined during phonetic perception. In some theories, the visual information plays a role because of an association between the visual articulatory characteristics and their respective phonetic representations that result from watching mouths move while hearing speech (Diehl & Kluender, 1989). For such theories, experience is the major factor in accounting for the ability to use both auditory and visual information for speech perception. For other theories, the auditory and visual information are combined because both signals provide information about a common event: the articulatory gestures used to produce speech. Two such gestural theories include the motor theory of speech perception (Liberman & Mattingly, 1985) and the ecological approach (Best, 1995; Fowler, 1986; Fowler & Rosenblum, 1991). Although the two gestural theories differ on other issues, neither requires the learning of the associations between the auditory and visual characteristics in order to account for the integration of the bimodal information. If learning is necessary to acquire the associations between the auditory and visual phonetic information, then developmental differences should arise according to the degree to which visual information influences speech perception. For example, young infants ought to get little or no McGurk effect because they are still in the process of forming their phonological prototypes and have had little opportunity to correlate visual characteristics with auditory speech sounds. However, as children get older, the visual information ought to have a greater impact, resulting in stronger McGurk effects.

The original study by McGurk and MacDonald (1976) examined children as well as adults and revealed an increase in the magnitude of the McGurk effect with age: young children (ages 3–5) produced relatively smaller effects than older children (ages 7–8), who, in turn, produced smaller effects than adults. This finding has since been replicated by several more recent studies (Boliek et al., 1996; Desjardins, Rogers & Werker, in press; Hockley & Polka, 1994; Massaro, 1984), providing further support for a learning or associationist account of why visual articulatory gestures play a role in the auditory perception of speech. However, there are several considerations which suggest caution in accepting such a conclusion.

First, there is considerable variation in the magnitude of the McGurk effect found in young children across different studies that probably reflects different task and stimulus factors. For example, Desjardins et al. (in press) used a procedure that was more suited to engaging young children in an experimental task and obtained robust McGurk effects in 4-year-old children (67%) relative to adults (83%). Desjardins et al. (in press) raise the question of whether the smaller McGurk effects found in previous studies with children of a comparable age might be attributed in part to the type of testing procedures used. Boliek et al. (1996) found that simply using a different voice with the same face can have a significant impact on the magnitude of the McGurk effect in young children. They created two different sets of McGurk tokens by dubbing a female and a male voice onto the same female face. When the AV tokens were presented to young children (ages 6–8), the male voice produced a much stronger McGurk effect (79%) than the female voice (28%).[3] Older children (ages 9–12) showed a similar pattern of responses, although the difference between the two types of stimuli was much smaller (98% versus 83% for the male and female voices respectively). Thus, both younger and older children get robust McGurk effects even when there is an incongruency in the gender characteristics between the face and the voice (for a similar finding with adults, see Green et al., 1991). What is interesting is that the same visual tokens produced large and small McGurk effects in the young children as a function of the characteristics of the auditory token. If the younger children were having difficulty associating the visual gestures with underlying representations due to a lack of experience, then they should have exhibited relatively weak McGurk effects for the same visual articulations regardless of the auditory token used. Instead, studies like Boliek et al. (1996) show that changing the voice can sometimes result in substantial increases in the McGurk effect for young children.[4] Thus, not all studies of young children show evidence of small McGurk effects, although it is the case that the younger children have smaller effects relative to older children or adults.

A second consideration is that the ability to detect the correspondence between visual and auditory speech events is present at 4 months of age and maybe even as early as 1 month of age (Kuhl & Meltzoff, 1982; Walton & Bower, 1993). The fact that infants were able to match up the visual articulations with some form of representation of the auditory signal indicates an initial capacity for lipreading in young infants. Moreover, several recent studies have demonstrated that infants as young as 5 months of age show evidence of a McGurk effect (Burnham, this volume; Burnham & Dodd, 1996; Desjardins & Werker, 1996; Rosenblum, Schmuckler & Johnson, in press). For example, Rosenblum et al. (in press) used a habituation-of-looking paradigm to determine whether 5-month-old infants detected the difference between a congruent auditory-visual (AV) token consisting of auditory /va/–visual /va/, and incongruent tokens consisting of auditory /ba/–visual /va/ and auditory /da/–visual /va/. Their infants showed recovery from habituation when an AV stimulus was presented that was both acoustically and perceptually different from the habituation stimulus (auditory /da/–visual /va/ perceived as "da"), and no recovery when the AV stimulus was acoustically different but perceptually similar (auditory /ba/–visual /va/ perceived as "va"). This study shows that infants have the capacity to actually integrate the phonetic information from the two modalities in a manner similar to adults.

Despite such findings, the results from the infant studies do not completely discount the possibility that experience or learning play a role in forming links between the visual articulations and the underlying representations. By the age of 5 months, infants have had considerable experience listening to, and presumably watching, speech. It is possible that the experience acquired during the first few months is enough to lay down the basic associations between the visual articulations and developing phonetic prototypes. Future studies might address this possibility in a couple of different ways. One approach would be to examine even younger infants to determine if they show evidence of a McGurk effect. However, such attempts will be hampered by the methodological difficulties of getting responses from infants at younger ages (although see Werner & Marean, 1991). An alternative approach might be to examine the McGurk effect in normal hearing infants that have had reduced exposure to auditory-visual speech (e.g. normal hearing infants born to deaf parents who are native users of sign language). If early experience is important for associating the visual articulations with developing phonetic representations, then such infants ought to show reduced evidence of McGurk effects compared to other infants.[5]

Finally, it is worth noting that the methodologies used in the infant studies only indicate whether infants have a McGurk type percept and are, therefore, capable of integrating auditory and visual information. To date, no studies have attempted to compare the size of the McGurk effect in infants with older children or adults to determine if infants have smaller effects than older children or adults. One reason why such comparisons haven't been performed is that the task used for looking at auditory-visual speech perception in infants, the habituation-of-looking paradigm, is quite different from the tasks used with children and adults. Developing a task that can be used to investigate auditory-visual speech perception across the lifespan (e.g. Werker, 1994) would be useful in determining whether experience serves to strengthen the association between visual articulations and phonetic representations (see Burnham, this volume).

A third consideration is that there is little evidence that the amount of experience or training improves the way visual articulations are associated or mapped onto phonetic representations. For many individuals who become hearing-impaired after acquiring language, lipreading (or speech-reading) becomes an important mode for language reception. Given the larger amount of motivation and experience of these individuals to speechread, as well as potential feedback when they misinterpret a talker's utterances, one might expect experience to play a large role in improving the mapping between the visual articulations and underlying phonetic representations. However, research shows that there is considerable variation in the ability of hearing-impaired individuals to speechread and the variation shows little correlation with experience (Jeffers & Barley, 1971). In fact, the range of variation is comparable to that found in normal-hearing individuals, suggesting that motivation or explicit experience has little impact on this ability. This is further supported by the fact that specific training on speechreading usually shows little improvement (except for an increase in general linguistic or communication strategies) even when the training is specifically designed to enhance the visual articulatory-to-phonetic associations (e.g. Gagné, Dinon & Parsons, 1991).

The few studies that have shown a benefit from training on lipreading have typically used the same talker or a limited phonetic context (Massaro, Cohen & Gesi, 1993; Walden et al., 1977). It is still unknown whether such improvements will generalize to other talkers or contexts.[6] Such a generalization should occur if the experience actually improves the mapping between abstract visual articulations and phonetic representations. Thus, the benefits that arise from training on lipreading may be specific to a particular talker or phonetic environment, or involve the improvement of general communication strategies.

Neither training nor experience, therefore, provide a suitable account of the wide variation in lipreading skills across both hearing-impaired and normal hearing subjects. Since there is a correlation between lipreading skills and the use of visual information during speech perception (Massaro et al. 1986; MacLeod & Summerfield, 1990), whatever accounts for the variation in lipreading skills will most likely account for the variation in the ability to use visual information during normal speech perception (Summerfield, 1991). What then accounts for such variation? Typical measures of education, training, experience, verbal/language skills show little correlation with lipreading skill (Jeffers & Barley, 1971). However, a number of studies have found a correlation between lipreading ability and visual evoked potentials (VEPs) (although see Rönnberg et al., 1989), suggesting that the ability to lipread is a function of the speed of processing in the visual system (for a review see Summerfield, 1991). Future studies might investigate whether particular components of the VEP waveforms correlate with the size of the McGurk effect in individuals and whether experience (either explicit training or developmental) influences such VEP components.

In summary, there is only limited evidence that children are learning to associate visual articulations with phonological representations. Young children and even infants are capable of integrating the phonetic information from the auditory and visual modalities, and there is little evidence that training or experience improves the mapping between visual articulations and the underlying phonetic representations. The question still remains however, as to why age differences in the McGurk effect occur between children and adults. Two possible answers come to mind, based upon the existing data. First, the finding of a correlation between VEPs and lipreading raises the possibility that some of the increase in the McGurk effect that occurs as children get older may be a function of development or maturation. Exactly what such development might entail is not quite clear, although it may be part of the same mechanism(s) that results in a sensitive period for the acquisition of the phonetics and phonology of a second language (e.g. Flege, 1995).

Another possibility is that age and experience may alter the way in which children use various dimensions of the auditory signal. Young children weight certain auditory dimensions differently than adults (Morrongiello et al., 1984; Nittrouer & Studdert-Kennedy, 1987). Green and Norrix (1997) have shown that the deletion of certain place cues influences the McGurk effect more than others. Their findings indicate that in adults, some auditory place cues such as the release burst and aspiration have a smaller impact on the McGurk percept than the formant transitions. Perhaps as children age, they alter their perceptual weighting of the different place cues, putting a greater emphasis on those dimensions that are more directly influenced by the visual articulations. Thus, the age effects that do occur with the McGurk effect, may be the result of how children weight the underlying auditory dimensions of the speech signal. Note that in this account, experience plays a role. However, the effect of experience is not to create associations between visual articulations or features and the underlying phonetic representations; rather, it may enable the child to differentiate the auditory (and perhaps visual) cues that play a critical role in distinguishing different phonetic elements. This may consist of a rescaling of the underlying psychological space in which phonetic representations are differentiated (e.g. Nosofsky, 1988).

Such an account may also explain some of the impact of language background on the McGurk effect. Recently, Sekiyama and Tohkura (1993) have provided evidence of a weaker McGurk effect in Japanese listeners compared to American listeners (see also Kuhl et al., 1994). They argue that the small McGurk effects for the Japanese reflect cultural differences that result in reduced use of visual information. However, Massaro et al. (1993) provide evidence that the way in which the visual and auditory information are processed and integrated are the same for Japanese, Spanish, and American English speakers. In their study, differences in the McGurk effect across different languages were due to the different phonetic representations contained in the languages. It may be the case that language background also affects the weighting of various cues in the auditory signal (e.g. Simon & Fourcin, 1978). As with young children, the different weightings may be reflected in the degree to which auditory cues to place of articulation interact with the visual place information.

IMPLICATIONS FOR THEORIES OF SPEECH PERCEPTION

The studies described in the two previous sections point out two important findings. First, they indicate that the auditory and visual information interact at a prephonetic level of processing. Whether this interaction implies integration or simply a conditionally-independent analysis of the auditory and visual information remains to be seen. Second, they show that experience does play a role in the McGurk effect. However, the current data suggest that experience does not increase the association between visual articulations and phonetic representations per se. Rather, experience may alter the weights of the various auditory and visual dimensions, thereby influencing the integration of the cross-modal information.

These findings have implications for theories of speech perception and, in particular, the debate surrounding the objects (or primitives) of speech perception, much of which has focused on whether the objects are auditory or gestural in nature (Best, 1995; Diehl & Kluender, 1989; Fowler, 1986; Fowler & Rosenblum, 1991; Liberman & Mattingly, 1985). For gestural theories, the objects of speech perception are the intended articulatory gestures used in speech production (Liberman & Mattingly, 1985; Fowler, 1986). For auditory theories, the objects are the auditory qualities of the phonetic segments (Diehl & Kluender, 1989). Gestural theories make no distinction with regard to the level of processing at which the auditory and visual information interact, and both the gestural and the motor theory could accommodate early or late integration of the information. The situation is somewhat different for many auditory theories which typically assume that the auditory and visual information are combined at the phonetic level of processing. For example, in their auditory enhancement hypothesis, Diehl and Kluender (1989) propose that listeners are primarily sensitive to the auditory qualities of phonetic segments and it is these qualities that define the multidimensional phonetic space. Visual characteristics are mapped into this space by their association with specific phonetic representations.

While early integration of the auditory and visual information is more consistent with gestural theories than with current auditory theories, it is not incompatible with auditory theories. It is possible to have an auditory theory with early integration in which the visual articulations are associated with auditory cues rather than phonetic representations. The outcome of such an association would be a value along an auditory-based metric. A problem arises, however, when accounting for why a particular visual gesture (e.g. rapid opening of the oral cavity) is associated with one auditory cue (e.g. the F2 transition) and not another (e.g. the F1 transition) when there is no overt awareness of the separate auditory cues in the speech signal. It may be that the perceptual system "knows" what visual articulations go with what auditory cues, although the theory has to account for where such knowledge comes from.

An alternative possibility is that the correlation between the visual articulation and a particular auditory cue may be large enough to overcome the correlations with other co-occurring auditory cues in a process known as "unsupervised learning" (Kluender, 1994). However, such correlations are derived from experience and the studies summarized show little evidence that experience is necessary for establishing them. Thus, the effect of experience seems to be more consistent with gestural theories than with current auditory theories, although gestural theories still have to account for why the McGurk effect is slightly stronger in older children and adults compared to younger children.

In summary, the McGurk effect has become a useful tool with which to examine the processing of phonetic information from the auditory and visual modalities, as well as the integration of the bimodal information. Studies of the McGurk effect have provided insight into how the information from the two modalities may combine, as well as the level of processing at which the integration occurs. Moreover, studies of the effect of experience on the McGurk effect raise questions about why the two sources of information are combined in the first place, since the auditory signal by itself is usually sufficient to provide accurate speech understanding in many listening situations. Future studies will provide insight into the neural mechanisms underlying the McGurk effect and other auditory-visual speech phenomena (e.g. Sams et al., 1991). By examining such data with regard to various theories of speech perception, it should be possible to attain a more complete understanding of how and why auditory and visual information are used in spoken-language processing.

ACKNOWLEDGEMENTS

Preparation of this chapter has been supported in part by Research and Training Grant P60-DC-01409 from the National Institutes on Deafness and Other Communication Disorders. Thanks go to Kathy Fohr for her help in conducting several of the experiments described in this chapter. Also, special thanks to Linda Norrix and Mary Zampini for their comments, insights and discussion of the research and issues described here, as well as their comments and those of the editors of the book, Ruth Campbell, Denis Burnham and Barbara Dodd, on previous versions of this chapter. Correspondence can be addressed to Kerry P. Green, Psychology Department, University of Arizona, Tucson, AZ 85721. Electronic mail can be sent to kgreen@u.arizona.edu.

NOTES

1. Currently, there is no agreement as to the kind of representation onto which the auditory and visual information are first mapped. One possibility is that the information is mapped onto phonetic representations which are used to extract phonemic representations (or prototypes). Alternatively, the information could be mapped directly onto phonemic representations (or syllabic) (see Massaro, 1987). With regard to the issue of early versus late integration, the difference between these two levels is irrelevant. Early integration is considered to occur before phonemic or phonetic processing while late integration is considered to be the stage at which the information is first mapped onto some kind of linguistic (either phonetic, phonemic or syllabic) representation. In this chapter, the phrases "phonetic processing" or "phonetic representations" will refer to this later stage of processing without being specific to the particular type of representation that is involved.

2. Munhall et al. (1996) have shown that a mismatch in speaking rate between the auditory and visual modalities reduces the magnitude of the McGurk effect, suggesting that rate information plays more than a normalizing role in the extraction of phonetic information from the auditory and visual modalities.

3. The McGurk effect in this study is defined as the number of responses that did not correspond to the auditory portion of the McGurk fusion tokens (e.g. the number of non /b/ responses). The response categories were limited in this study.

4. This is assuming that the auditory tokens are equivalent with respect to their overall phonetic quality. It is possible that the auditory tokens from the female talker were simply more "ambiguous" than the tokens from the male talker. The stronger links between the visual information and the phonetic representations in the older children resulting from experience would account for the greater influence of the visual on the more ambiguous auditory token. However, both sets of auditory tokens were identified at greater than 92% accuracy by adult listeners, suggesting that there was little difference in overall ambiguity of the different auditory tokens that would account for the difference in the magnitude of the McGurk effects for the younger children.

5. Fowler and Dekle (1991) took a similar approach in their study of tactile-auditory interactions during speech perception. They used the Tadoma method to present the tactile information for articulatory gestures along with the conflicting auditory signal and found a reliable influence of the tactile information on the perception of the auditory, similar to an auditory-visual McGurk effect. Since their subjects never had any experience with perceiving speech using their hands and fingers, they argued that their findings were not due to experience per se (see Best, 1995).

6. A similar issue arises with respect to the acquisition of foreign phonetic contrasts during the acquisition of a second language (see Lively, Logan & Pisoni, 1993).

REFERENCES

Baynes, K., Funnell, M.G. & Fowler, C.A. (1994). Hemispheric contributions to the integration of visual and auditory information in speech perception. *Perception and Psychophysics*, 55, 633–41.

Best, C.T. (1995). A direct realist view of cross-language speech perception. In W. Strange (Ed.), *Speech Perception and Linguistic Experience: Issues in Cross-Language Research* (pp. 171–204). Baltimore: York Press.

Boliek, C., Green, K.P., Fohr, K. & Obrzut, J. (1996). Auditory-visual perception of speech in children with learning disabilities: The McGurk effect. Annual meeting of the International Neuropsychological Society, Chicago.

Burnham, D. & Dodd, B. (1996). Auditory-visual speech perception as an automatic process: The fusion effect in human infants and across languages. In D. Stork & M.E. Hennecke (Eds), *Speech Reading by Humans and Machines*. Berlin: Springer-Verlag.

Campbell, R. (1996). Seeing speech in space and time: Psychological and neurological findings. *Proceedings ICSLP*, Philadelphia, pp. 1493–6.

Campbell, R., Garwood, J., Franklin, S., Howard, D., Landis, T. & Regard, M. (1990). Neuropsychological studies of auditory-visual fusion illusions: Four case studies and their implications. *Neuropsychologia*, 28, 787–802.

Crowther, C.S. & Batchelder, W.H. (1996). Multinomial models of speech perception. *Journal of the Acoustical Society of America*, 97, 3362.

Desjardins, R.N. & Werker, J.F. (1995). 4-month-old infants notice both auditory and visual components of speech. American Psychological Society, June.

Desjardins, R.N., Rogers, J. & Werker, J.F. (in press). An exploration of why preschoolers perform differently than do adults in audiovisual speech perception tasks.

Diehl, R.L. & Kluender, K.R. (1989). On the objects of speech perception. *Ecological Psychology*, 1, 121–44.

Diehl, R.L., Kluender, K.R. & Walsh, M.A. (1990). Some auditory bases of speech perception and production. In W.A. Ainsworth (Ed.), *Advances in Speech, Hearing, and Language Processing*, London: JAI Press (pp. 243–68).

Flege, J.E. (1995). Second language speech learning: Theory, findings, and problems. In W. Strange (Ed.), *Speech Perception and Linguistic Experience. Issues in Cross-Language Research* (pp. 233–72). Baltimore: York Press, pp. 233–272.

Fowler, C.A. (1986). An event approach to the study of speech perception from a direct-realist perspective. *Journal of Phonetics*, 14, 3–28.

Fowler, C.A. & Dekle, D.J. (1991). Listening with eye and hand: Cross-modal contributions to speech perception. *Journal of Experimental Psychology: Human Perception and Performance*, 17, 816–828.

Fowler, C.A. & Rosenblum, L.D. (1991). The perception of phonetic gestures. In I.G. Mattingly & M. Studdert-Kennedy (Eds), *Modularity and the Motor Theory of Speech Perception*. Hillsdale, NJ: Lawrence Erlbaum Associates Inc.

Gagné, J-P., Dinon, D. & Parsons, J. (1991). An evaluation of CAST: A Computer-Aided Speechreading Training program. *Journal of Speech and Hearing Research*, 34, 213–21.

Green, K.P. (1996). Studies of the McGurk effect: Implications for theories of speech perception. *Proceedings ICSLP*, Philadelphia, pp. 1652–5.

Green, K.P. & Gerdeman, A. (1995). Cross-modal discrepancies in coarticulation and the integration of speech information: The McGurk effect with mismatched vowels. *Journal of Experimental Psychology: Human Perception and Performance*, 25, 1409–26.

Green, K.P. and Kuhl, P.K. (1989). The role of visual information in the processing of place and manner features in speech perception. *Perception and Psychophysics*, 45, 34–42.

Green, K.P. and Kuhl, P.K. (1991). Integral processing of visual place and auditory voicing information during phonetic perception. *Journal of Experimental Psychology: Human Perception and Performance*, 17, 278–88.

Green, K.P., Kuhl, P.K., Meltzoff, A.N. & Stevens, E.B. (1991). Integrating speech information across talkers, gender, and sensory modality: Female faces and male voices in the McGurk effect. *Perception and Psychophysics*, 50, 524–36.

Green, K.P. & Miller, J.L. (1985) On the role of visual rate information in phonetic perception. *Perception and Psychophysics*, 38, 269–76.

Green, K.P., & Norrix, L.W. (1997). Acoustic cues to place of articulation and the McGurk effect: The role of release bursts, aspiration, and format transitions. *Journal of Speech, Language and Hearing Research, 40*, 646–665.

Hockley, S.N. & Polka, L. (1994). A developmental study of audio-visual speech perception using the McGurk paradigm. *Journal of the Accoustical Society of America, 96*, 3309.

Jeffers, J. & Barley, M. (1971). *Speechreading (Lipreading)*. Springfield: Thomas.

Johnson, K. (1990). Contrast and normalization in vowel perception. *Journal of Phonetics, 18*, 229–54.

Kluender, K.R. (1994). Speech perception as a tractable problem in cognitive science. In M.A. Gernsbacher (Ed.), *Handbook of Psycholinguistics*. Academic Press: San Diego.

Kuhl, P.K. & Meltzoff, A. (1982). The bimodal perception of speech in infancy. *Science, 218*, 1138–41.

Kuhl, P.K., Tsuzaki, M., Tohkura, Y. & Meltzoff, M.N. (1994). Human processing of auditory-visual information in speech perception: potential for multimodal human-machine interfaces. In *Proceedings of the International Conference on Spoken Language Processing*, Kyoto (pp. 539–42).

Liberman, A.M. & Mattingly, I.G. (1985). The motor theory of speech perception revised. *Cognition, 21*, 1–36.

Lisker, L. & Abramson, A.S. (1970). The voicing dimension: Some experiments in comparative phonetics. In *Proceedings of the Sixth International Congress of Phonetic Sciences*. Prague: Academia.

Lively, S.E., Logan, J.S. & Pisoni, D.B. (1993). Training Japanese listeners to identify English /r/ and /l/ II: The role of phonetic environment and talker variability in learning new perceptual categories. *Journal of the Acoustical Society of America, 94*, 1242–55.

MacDonald, J. & McGurk, H. (1978). Visual influences on speech perception processes. *Perception and Psychophysics, 24*, 253–7.

McGurk, H. & MacDonald, J. (1976). Hearing lips and seeing voices. *Nature, 264*, 746–8.

MacLeod, A. & Summerfield, A.Q. (1990). A procedure for measuring auditory and audio-visual speech-reception thresholds for sentences in noise: Rationale, evaluation, and recommendations for use. *British Journal of Audiology, 24*, 29–43.

Mann, V.A. (1980). Influence of preceding liquid on stop consonant perception. *Perception and Psychophysics, 28*, 407–12.

Mann, V.A. & Repp, B.H. (1980). Influence of vocalic context on perception of the [ß]–[s] distinction. *Perception and Psychophysics, 28*, 213–28.

Massaro, D.W. (1984). Children's perception of visual and auditory speech. *Child Development, 55*, 1777–88.

Massaro, D.W. (1987). *Speech perception by ear and eye: A paradigm for Psychological Inquiry*. Hillsdale, NJ: Lawrence Erlbaum Associates Inc.

Massaro, D.W., Cohen, M.M. & Gesi, A.T. (1993). Long-term training, transfer, and retention in learning to lipread. *Perception and Psychophysics, 53*, 549–62.

Massaro, D.W., Cohen, M.M., Gesi, A., Heredia, R. & Tsuzaki, M. (1993). Bimodal speech perception: an examination across languages. *Journal of Phonetics, 21*, 445–78.

Massaro, D.W., Thompson, L.A., Barron, B. & Laren, E. (1986). Developmental changes in visual and auditory contributions to speech perception. *Journal of Experimental Child Psychology, 41*, 93–113.

Miller, J.L. (1977). Nonindependence of feature processing in initial consonants. *Journal of Speech and Hearing Research, 20*, 510–18.

Miller, J.L. (1981). Effects of speaking rate on segmental distinctions. In P.D. Eimas & J.L. Miller (Eds), *Perspectives on the Study of Speech*. Hillsdale, N.J.: Lawrence Erlbaum Associates Inc.

Morrongiello, B.A., Robson, R.C., Best, C.T. & Clifton, R.K. (1984). Trading relations in the perception of speech by 5-year-old children. *Journal of Experimental Child Psychology*, *37*, 231–50.

Munhall, K., Gribble, P., Sacco, L. & Ward, M. (1996). Temporal constraints on the McGurk effect. *Perception and Psychophysics*, *58*, 351–62.

Nittrouer, S. & Studdert-Kennedy, M. (1987). The role of coarticulatory effects in the perception of fricatives by children and adults. *Journal of Speech and Hearing Research*, *30*, 319–29.

Norrix, L.W. & Green, K.P. (1996). Auditory-visual context effects on the perception of /r/ and /l/ in a stop cluster. Binannual meeting of the Acoustical Society of America, Spring, Indianapolis.

Nosofsky, R.M. (1988). Similarity, frequency, and category representation. *Journal of Experimental Psychology: Learning, Memory and Cognition*, *14*, 54–65.

Pisoni, D.B., Lively, S.E. & Logan, J.S. (1994). Perceptual learning of nonnative speech contrasts: Implications for theories of speech perception. In J.C. Goodman & H.C. Nusbaum (Eds), *The Development of Speech Perception* (pp. 121–66). Cambridge, MA: MIT Press.

Radeau, M. (1994). Auditory-visual spatial interaction and modularity. *Current Psychology of Cognition*, *13*, 3–51.

Repp, B.H. (1982). Phonetic trading relations and context effects: New experimental evidence for a speech mode of perception. *Psychological Bulletin*, *92*, 81–110.

Robert-Ribes, J., Schwartz, J.L. & Escudier, P. (1995). "A comparison of models for fusion of the auditory and visual sensors in speech perception". *Artificial Intelligence Review*, *9*, 323–46.

Roberts, M. & Summerfield, A. (1981). Audio-visual presentation demonstrates that selective adaptation in speech perception is purely auditory. *Perception and Psychophysics*, *30*, 309–14.

Rönnberg, J., Arlinger, S., Byxell, B. & Kinnefords, C. (1989). Visual evoked potentials: Relation to adult speechreading and cognitive function. *Journal of Speech and Hearing Research*, *32*, 725–35.

Rosenblum, L.D., Schmuckler, M.A. & Johnson, J.A. (1997). The McGurk effect in infants. *Perception and Psychophysics*, *59*, 347–57.

Saldaña, H.M. & Rosenblum, L.D. (1994). Selective adaptation in speech perception using a compelling audio-visual adaptor. *Journal of the Acoustical Society of America*, *95*, 3658–65.

Sams, M., Aulanko, R., Hämäläinen, M., Hari., R., Lounasmaa, O.V., Lu, S-T. & Simola, J. (1991). Seeing speech: visual information from lip movements modifies activity in the human auditory cortex. *Neuroscience Letters*, *127*, 141–5.

Sekiyama, K. & Tohkura, Y. (1993). Inter-language differences in the influence of visual cues in speech perception. *Journal of Phonetics*, *21*, 427–44.

Simon, C. & Fourcin, A.J. (1978). Cross-language study of speech-pattern learning. *Journal of the Acoustical Society of America*, *63*, 925–35.

Strand, E.A. and Johnson, K. (1996) Gradient and visual speaker normalization in the perception of fricatives. In D. Gibbon (Ed.) *Natural Language Processing and Speech Technology*. Results of the 3rd KONVENS Conference, Bielefeld, October 1996. Berlin: Mouton de Gruyter.

Sumby, W.H. & Pollack, I. (1954). Visual contributions to speech intelligibility in noise. *Journal of the Acoustical Society of America*, *26*, 212–15.

Summerfield, A.Q. (1981). Articulatory rate and perceptual constancy in phonetic perception. *Journal of Experimental Psychology: Human Perception and Performance*, *7*, 1074–95.

Summerfield, A.Q. (1987). Some preliminaries to a comprehensive account of audio-visual speech perception. In B. Dodd & R. Campbell (Eds), *Hearing by Eye: The Psychology of Lipreading*. Hove, UK: Lawrence Erlbaum Associates Ltd.

Summerfield, A.Q. (1991). Visual perception of phonetic gestures. In I.G. Mattingly & M. Studdert-Kennedy (Eds). *Modularity and the Motor Theory of Speech Perception.* Hillsdale, N.J.: Lawrence Erlbaum Associates Inc.

Walden, B.E., Prosek, R.A., Montgomery, A.A., Scherr, C.K. & Jones, C.J. (1977). Effects of training on the visual recognition of consonants. *Journal of Speech and Hearing Research, 20,* 130–45.

Walton, G. & Bower, T.G.R. (1993). Amodal representation of speech in infants. *Infant Behavior and Development, 16,* 233–43.

Werker, J.F. (1994). Cross-language speech perception: Development change does not involve loss. In J.C. Goodman & H.C. Nusbaum (Eds), *The Development of Speech Perception* (pp. 93–120), Cambridge, MA: MIT Press.

Werner, L.A. & Marean, G.C. (1991). Methods for estimating infant thresholds. *Journal of the Acoustical Society of America, 90,* 1867–75.

Whalen, D.H. (1984). Subcategorical phonetic mismatches slow phonetic judgments. *Perception and Psychophysics, 35,* 49–64.

CHAPTER TWO

Language specificity in the development of auditory-visual speech perception

Denis Burnham *Department of Psychology, University of New South Wales, Sydney, Australia*

AUDITORY AND AUDITORY-VISUAL SPEECH PERCEPTION ACROSS LANGUAGES

Newborn infants have a seemingly universal ability to perceive just about any phone or contrast of phones in any of the world's languages, and are thus ideally equipped to learn whatever language they happen to hear around them. From this initial state, speech perception becomes specifically tuned to the ambient native language, such that the fluent language user's perceptual ability for native phones is considerably better than for non-native phones (Burnham, 1986). The composition and size of the subset of native phones will differ depending on the particular language that language-users hear around them (Maddieson, 1984). So mature speakers of different languages structure their perception of speech in specifically different ways. In this chapter, both developmental and cross-language research will be examined in order to ascertain how the mature language-user arrives at this specialised state.

Speech perception is the product of both auditory and visual information, as many chapters in this book demonstrate. Understanding the manner in which auditory and visual speech information is integrated, how such integration might develop, and how it might be affected by specific linguistic experience, is essential for comprehensive models of speech perception and speech perception development. Thus, in this chapter developmental and cross-language processes in both auditory and auditory-visual speech perception will be examined. Relevant new data will be presented. As there has been much more research conducted on auditory than on auditory-visual speech perception, the state of knowledge of the former will aid in the identification of empirical and theoretical lacunae in the latter, and in speculation about the processes involved in auditory-visual speech perception and its development.

LANGUAGE SPECIFICITY IN AUDITORY SPEECH PERCEPTION

The phonemes of a particular language are always a subset of the phonetic and articulatory possibilities of the world's languages (Maddieson, 1984). How does the developing child deal with the specific phonology of the language around them? How does adult speech perception differ from infant and child speech perception?

The initial state and development of the auditory system

By the beginning of the third trimester of pregnancy the human auditory system is functional, it being the first sensory system to develop fully (Bredberg, 1985). Moreover, the unborn child can hear aspects both of the immediate intra-uterine and of the extra-uterine world, the latter being mediated by the low-pass filter of the mother's womb (Querleu & Renard, 1981; Querleu et al., 1988).

Peripheral auditory mechanisms are physiologically mature at birth (Bredberg, 1968) and newborns' relatively sophisticated auditory abilities bear witness to this. Auditory cortex maturation, however, proceeds relatively slowly: myelinisation of the primary auditory cortex begins around 3 months but myelin is not present throughout all layers of the cortex until 2 years (Gibson, 1981), and myelinisation is not complete until around 3–4 years (Yakovlev & Lecours, 1967). Thus, it appears there is early functional maturity of auditory abilities at birth, but that more complex abilities may take some time to develop.

The development of auditory speech perception

Newborn infants' speech perception abilities are extremely well developed even at birth (for a review see Burnham, 1986). Infants are highly proficient at discriminating pairs of consonants differing on single phonetic features (Eimas et al., 1971; Burnham, Earnshaw & Clark, 1991; Eimas, 1975; Eilers, Wilson & Moore, 1977; Eilers & Minifie, 1975). Moreover, this discrimination occurs not only for native phonemes but also for phonetic distinctions not phonologically relevant in the surrounding language environment (Lasky et al., 1975; Streeter, 1976; Aslin et al., 1981; Best, McRoberts & Sithole, 1988). Despite this seeming universality, specific phonetic factors appear to affect early discriminative abilities, e.g., fricatives are relatively difficult to discriminate (Holmberg, Morgan & Kuhl, 1977; Eilers & Minifie, 1975), and it appears that at least some phonetic distinctions are based on underlying strengths and constraints of the human auditory system (Miller et al., 1976; Pisoni, 1977; Jusczyk et al., 1980). Turning to the perception of vowels, it appears that vowels are discriminated at a young age by infants (Kuhl et al., 1992), and that this ability may be constrained and guided by pre-set language-general phonetic values (Polka, 1995; Polka & Bohn, 1996).

Modulation of speech perception occurs in the first year after birth. For consonants this modulation is first evident at 7–11 months, when sensitivity to non-native consonant contrasts is gradually attenuated (Werker et al., 1981; Werker & Tees, 1983, 1984a; Werker & Lalonde, 1988), while developmental loss for non-native vowel contrasts may occur even earlier, around 4 months (Kuhl et al., 1992; Polka & Werker, 1994; Polka & Bohn, 1996). Modulation of ability for suprasegmentals, such as stress and intonation patterns, also occurs early in development, with quite marked perceptual drift towards the speech patterns present in the infant's immediate (ambient) language environment (Jusczyk et al., 1992; Jusczyk, Cutler & Redanz, 1993; Jusczyk et al., 1993; Hirsh-Pasek et al., 1987). These findings of early modulation of ability for vowels and prosody have been taken to reflect a periodicity bias in infancy (Cutler, 1994; Cutler & Mehler, 1993): although newborn infants may discriminate almost any consonant contrast experimenters wish to test them on, it is quite possible that in their natural speech environment in which there is a variety of information, they selectively attend to periodic information rather than to discrete consonant contrasts.

It might be thought that this early loss of perceptual ability for non-native contrasts locks the developing child into perceiving and producing just the language(s) they hear around them. However, this is not true: young children can learn foreign languages with relative ease, and so can adults, albeit perhaps not so easily. The developmental loss of speech perception abilities in the first year is in fact not a loss but a re-organisation (Werker, 1994). This re-organisation is neither absolute nor permanent: It is mitigated by phonetic, phonological, and linguistic factors, and each of these is discussed below.

With regard to phonetic factors, in the Robust and Fragile (RAF) model Burnham claims that the degree to which the perception of consonant contrasts is attenuated depends upon their psychoacoustic salience: "fragile" contrasts tend to be attenuated early in the first year, while more "robust" contrasts are attenuated later (Burnham 1986; Burnham et al., 1996). As an example of the latter, it has been found that English Language

Environment (ELE) infants' perception of a non-native bilabial stop voicing contrast, the prevoiced [b] versus the unvoiced unaspirated [p] (both perceived as the phoneme /b/ in English), continues to improve from infancy until 2–4 years. However, it *is* sharply attenuated at 6 years, in contrast to the perception of a similar *native* voicing contrast, the [p] versus the unvoiced aspirated [pʰ] (perceived as /b/ and /p/ in English), which improves monotonically from infancy right through to 8 years. Burnham suggests that the perceptual attenuation for the non-native contrast at 6 years is due to a phonological bias in children caused by the onset of reading—a task that requires that perceptual differences between allophones are ignored in order for efficient and automatic phoneme-to-grapheme mapping to occur ([b] and [p] onto "b" in this case). This claim is substantiated by findings that, for the aforementioned bilabials (Burnham, 1986) and other voicing contrasts (Burnham et al., in preparation), the degree of children's phonological bias (towards relevant and away from irrelevant contrasts) is positively related to their level of reading ability. Interestingly, perceptual ability for these robust but irrelevant non-native contrasts re-emerges at 8 years, by which stage reading skills have presumably become more automatic and less controlled (Burnham, 1986; Burnham et al., in preparation). Thus, both the timing and degree of perceptual loss for non-native contrasts depends to some extent on phonetic considerations.

Phonological considerations, in particular the relationship between the phonemes of the perceiver's first (L1) and second (L2) language, are also important. In her Perceptual Assimilation Model (PAM), Best (1993, 1994, 1995a,b) outlines a number of perceptual assimilation patterns. For example, the Ethiopian ejectives [p'] and [t'] are perceived by ELE listeners to be highly similar to English [pʰ] and [tʰ]. This is a Two-Category (TC) assimilation pattern that results in good discrimination. In this pattern, phoneme categories from the native language are used to structure language representations found in foreign languages or perhaps even unfamiliar dialects. Another case is that of Zulu click contrasts: Best has found that ELE listeners cannot assimilate either sound of a click contrast into their native phonemic space, and adults report that clicks do not sound like speech. Consequently, these sounds can be discriminated by attending to acoustic differences, with discriminability depending on their psychoacoustic salience (Best, McRoberts & Sithole, 1988). Such patterns aid in the explanation of adults' L2 perceptual abilities which fall neither into the early-attenuated pattern (e.g. Werker et al., 1981) nor into the robust attenuated-late category (Burnham, 1986).

The example of Zulu clicks shows that when the usual linguistic mode of processing speech is suspended and conditions favour an acoustic or phonetic mode, then perceptual ability may improve. There are two ways in which the mode of processing speech can be manipulated experimentally: by reducing memory load or by disengagement of the linguistic processing mode which is assumed to be engaged automatically when listening to language. With regard to memory load, Werker and her colleagues (Werker & Logan, 1985; Werker & Tees, 1984b) have shown that with training and/ or reduction of the inter-stimulus-interval (ISI) in a two-sound discrimination task, adults can perceive various non-native speech contrasts. The reduction of the ISI allows discrimination by acoustic or phonetic matching, without the need to store information for longer periods in phonologically-determined categories. With regard to the disengagement of linguistic processing, this can be effected either by changing the nature of the stimulus, or by changing listeners' beliefs about the nature of the stimulus. An example of changing the physical nature of the stimulus is the study of English language speakers' perception of Thai tones by Burnham et al. (1996). They found that English speakers perceived non-native lexical tone contrasts significantly better when the tones were presented in non-speech formats— as filtered speech or as musical sounds, than as speech. An example of changing the listeners' beliefs about the stimulus is the study by Thein-Tun and Burnham (Thein-Tun & Burnham, 1994), who presented adults and children with sine-wave analogues in a cue trading paradigm. Subjects who were instructed that the sounds were "computer sounds" showed less cue trading (a distinctly linguistic phenomenon) than subjects told that the sounds were "speech sounds".

The fact that experimental manipulations can change listeners' processing from a phonemic to a phonetic mode of processing suggests that the latter is readily available though not always apparent. This is underlined by Mann's (1986) study of the effect of preceding /l/ or /r/ on the categorical identification of a synthetic /da/–/ga/ continuum. English listeners make more /ga/ identifications when exemplars along this continuum are preceded by /al/ than when they are preceded by /ar/; that is preceding continuum exemplars by /l/ or by /r/ differentially affect the perceiver's category boundary. Mann (1986) used this effect to test English listeners, and also Japanese listeners, for whom the /l/–/r/ distinction is phonologically irrelevant. Japanese listeners showed the same category boundary shifts as English listeners, despite their inability to perceive the /l/–/r/ distinction. This shows that Japanese listeners have a *phonetic* sensitivity to distinctions that are not phonemically available or relevant, and also suggests that phonetic-level information constantly underlies speech perception abilities even when this is not immediately apparent.

Together this research shows that, while there is early attenuation of perceptual ability for phonologically-irrelevant speech sounds, this attenuation is by no means absolute or permanent. The nature, degree, and timing of the attenuation is affected by phonetic, phonological, and linguistic factors. That is, the degree to which the ambient language affects auditory speech perception depends upon the nature of the actual sounds, whether the sounds are perceived to be native or non-native, and whether the sounds are perceived to be speech or non-speech. It remains to be seen whether similar factors are at play in auditory-visual speech perception.

LANGUAGE SPECIFICITY IN AUDITORY-VISUAL SPEECH PERCEPTION

Initial state and development of the visual system

In contrast to the auditory system, the peripheral visual system is often claimed to be relatively immature at birth (Abramov et al., 1982). However, both peripheral and central development are complete by 4–5 months, and this is accompanied by rapid development over the first 3 months of such abilities as accommodation (Banks, 1980), convergence (Aslin, 1977), acuity (Dobson & Teller, 1978), and facial recognition (Maurer, 1985; Yin, 1978). In fact, the visual abilities of young infants are surprisingly good, and their ability to perceive faces and visual speech may not necessarily be deficient.

Infants' visual *abilities* appear to be relatively unrestricted by object distance (Burnham & Day, 1979). However, their visual *attention* appears to be restricted to within about 1 metre in the central area of the fronto-parallel plane (McKenzie & Day, 1972; Tronick, 1972; de Schonen et al., 1978). These restrictions are less severe when objects are rendered more interesting through movement (Ihsen & Day, 1981). There is also some indication of infants' selective perception of faces and face-like configurations (Morton & Johnson, 1991). Thus, infants' visual perception of speech directed to them, usually in near space in the central field, would appear to be relatively unrestricted.

The emergence of auditory-visual integration

Cortical association areas begin to develop at around 4 months (Gibson, 1981; Yakovlev & Lecours, 1967). Visual abilities involving these areas, for example eye blink to impending collision (Pettersen, Yonas & Fisch, 1980) and visual-tactile transfer (Rose, Gottfried & Bridger, 1978, 1979), appear to follow a maturational course of development, whereas for other abilities, such as visual recognition memory, there appears to be some interplay of maturational and experiential factors (Rose, 1980).

It appears that maturation, in the form of development of the cortical association areas, is important in the emergence of the auditory-visual abilities involved in auditory localisation and the precedence effect. Auditory localisation (AL), looking towards the source of eccentrically-presented sounds, is operational at birth (Field et al., 1980; Muir & Field, 1979), but in a simple reflexive form, in which the visual response is slow and ballistic—

infants listen, look, *and* see. Later, over the 1–3 month period, the frequency and accuracy of this AL reflex wanes (though it never completely disappears) and then re-emerges around 4 months in a swifter, more accurate, form. The response then appears to be more cognitively based and to take into account the visual source of sounds—infants listen and look *to* see (Field et al., 1980; Muir, 1985; Muir, Clifton & Clarkson, 1989).

In the precedence effect (PE), produced by a slight temporal asynchrony between sounds presented from two laterally-located sources, the listener perceives a single sound to originate from the leading source. Animal studies suggest that visual response to the auditory PE (turning to the leading source) involves and requires cortical maturation (Cranford & Oberholtzer, 1976; Cranford et al., 1971; Whitfield et al., 1972; Whitfield et al., 1978; Hochster & Kelly, 1981; for a review, see Burnham et al., 1993). Behavioural studies with human infants bear this out: in contrast to the reflexive form of AL, visual response to the PE is not evident in human newborns (Clifton et al., 1981) and only emerges around 4 months at the same time as the more cognitively-based AL emerges (Muir et al., 1989). Studies with full- and preterm infants show that this late emergence of the PE in infancy is a product of maturation not experience (Burnham et al., 1993). Thus, at least in the case of the visual localisation of auditory sources (in both AL and the PE), it seems that auditory-visual functioning relies on maturational processes (perhaps those involved in the development of cortical association areas) evident in behaviour around 4 months of age.

The development of auditory-visual speech perception

There are three main ways in which auditory and visual speech information may interact:

1. information from one modality may *enhance* information in, or *direct* attention to, the other modality
2. information from the two modalities may be *matched* by the perceiver
3. information from the two modalities may be *integrated* by the perceiver.

The degree to which infants achieve these three tasks and the age at which they do so is important for understanding how the ambient language may affect auditory-visual speech perception development.

Facilitation of face perception by voice information

Most face perception studies concern infants' recognition of their mother's face. Very few of these provide evidence that infants younger than

3 months can spontaneously discriminate the mother's and a stranger's face on the basis of visual information alone. Those that do have often been marred by confounding factors. For example, while Carpenter (1974a) found that infants as young as 2 weeks fixated their mother's face longer than a female stranger's face, the scorers were not blind to which face was being presented to the infant, and only a single female stranger's face was used, irrespective of the characteristics of the mother's face (Melhuish, 1982). In other studies, the mother's live face was paired with three-dimensional mannequins, thus introducing various confounding visual cues (Carpenter, 1974b; Carpenter et al., 1970). In addition, possible olfactory cues for mother recognition (Cernoch & Porter, 1985) were not controlled (Field et al., 1984; Masi & Scott, 1983). (For a review, see Burnham, 1993.)

The studies of greatest validity are longitudinal studies in which discrimination at older but not younger ages has been found: mother/stranger facial discrimination has been found at 4 months but not at 1 or 2 months (Fitzgerald, 1968), at 4 and 5 months but not at 1 month (Nottle, 1980), and at 5 months but not at 1 or 3 months (Sherrod, 1979). Bernard and Ramey (1977) found an increase in facial discrimination ability from 4–6 months, and Kaitz et al. (1985), studying infants from 1 to 27 weeks, found the onset of consistent mother/stranger discrimination emerged at 13–15 weeks. Thus, it seems that infants only develop the ability to discriminate mother and stranger visually by around 3 months. This conclusion is consistent with findings of infants' increasingly more detailed visual exploration of the features of geometric figures (Salapatek, 1975) and faces (Maurer & Salapatek, 1976) at 2 months, but inconsistent with parents' reports that their infants recognise them soon after birth.

Following such parental reports and indications from previous studies that voice information may facilitate face discrimination (Laub, 1973; Laub & McClusky, 1974; Culp, 1974; Spelke & Owsley, 1979; Bigelow, 1977), Burnham (1993) investigated the effect of voices on infants' mother/stranger face recognition. Voices were found to facilitate mother/stranger face recognition even in 1-month-old infants, well below the age at which infants discriminate faces on the basis of visual information alone and before the cortical association areas appear to develop. Such counter-intuitive findings may suggest either that fledgling face perception abilities are enhanced by attention to lip movements and/or by attention to voice information. Unravelling these options, Burnham (1993) conducted further studies in which just the lip movements or just the voices were presented to aid simultaneous face recognition. These studies revealed that 1-month-olds' recognition of faces was facilitated by lip movements alone, but not voices, whereas 3-month-olds' recognition of faces was facilitated by voices alone, but not lip movements. Thus, for 1-month-old infants, facilitation of facial recognition by speech is not an auditory-visual phenomenon: it is accounted for by visual, not auditory effects, just as infants' visual attention to objects beyond near space may be attracted by stimulus movement (Burnham & Day, 1979; Ihsen & Day, 1981, see earlier section on initial state and development of the visual system, p.32). For 3-month-olds, however, it seems that auditory-visual perceptual abilities have begun to emerge.

Matching face and voice information

Most studies on auditory-visual matching in infants use the matching method, in which a single auditory source is placed equidistant between two visual displays. Infants' relative preference for each of the two visual displays is then determined by recording the duration of visual fixation to each, while an auditory stimulus appropriate to just one of them is presented (Spelke, 1976).

Using this method, it has been found that infants perceive auditory-visual relationships in non-speech events by at least 3–4 months (Bahrick, Walker & Neisser, 1981; Bahrick, 1988; Spelke, 1976, 1979). With regard to speech events, Dodd (1979), using running speech, found that infants aged 10–20 weeks fixate a human speaker longer when lip movements and voice are temporally in, rather than out, of synchrony; and Burnham and Dodd (in preparation) have confirmed this under different conditions. Using isolated syllables, Kuhl and Meltzoff (1982, 1984) found that even when the onset and offset of a single vowel sound, either [i] or [a], is precisely coordinated with two simultaneously-presented sets of lip movements, one for [i] and one for [a], 4-month-old infants match the auditory presentation with the appropriate lip movements. This also occurs for other vowels, [i] and [u] (Kuhl & Meltzoff, 1988). As there are no temporal asynchrony cues to guide infants here, matching presumably occurs on the basis of structural correspondences between seen and heard speech. Furthermore, the results suggest that infants can visually discriminate between distinct vowels by at least 4 months of age. In a similar study with 6-month-olds, MacKain et al. (1983), using disyllables, e.g., /vava/ versus /zuzu/, found essentially the same results with the rider that the preference for matches over mismatches only emerged when fixations to the right of the two visual displays were considered, despite appropriate side counterbalancing and controls. The authors take this as evidence that there is left hemisphere specialisation in auditory-visual speech perception in infancy.

Infants' matching of faces and voices on the basis of gender also appears to emerge at around 4 months. Francis and McCroy (1983) found that 6- but not 3-month-olds fixate the face of the appropriate sex when either a female or male voice is presented. Walker-Andrews et al. (1991) also found that 6-month-old infants match faces and voices on the basis of gender whereas 3.5-month-old infants do not, with some ability for matching beginning at around 4 months. It is interesting in this regard that infants begin to categorise male and female voices some time before 6 months (Miller, 1983), while gender-based categorisation of faces does not emerge until 7 months (Cohen & Strauss, 1979). Again, as in the case of facilitation of mother/stranger face recognition (Burnham, 1993), auditory abilities appear to precede and perhaps guide visual abilities.

A single study has been conducted on the language specificity of lips–voice matching. Dodd and Burnham (1988) showed ELE infants two faces presented side-by-side, one miming a Greek passage and the other miming a semantically-equivalent English passage. On one trial the appropriate Greek soundtrack was played from a source mid-way between the two faces and on another the appropriate English soundtrack was played. A no-soundtrack control trial was also presented. In the first experiment, 10-week-old ELE infants were tested. The proportion of time they spent fixating the English mimer in the three conditions is shown in Table 2. Although 9 of the 12 infants had equal or greater English mimer preference scores on English than Greek soundtrack trials, and the mean English mimer preference score was greater on English than Greek soundtrack trials, the standard deviations were relatively high, and the comparison between English and Greek soundtrack trials was not significant, $t(11) = 0.16$. At 10 weeks, therefore, infants do not show a reliable preference for either of the face–voice matches. Older, 20-week infants were then tested. Now, 11 of the 12 infants had equal or higher English preference scores on the English soundtrack than the Greek soundtrack trial, and the difference in preference scores was significant, $t(11) = 11.33 \, p < .01$. Therefore, 20-week-old infants match face and voice in their familiar language (68.4% preference), but not in an unfamiliar language (51.0% preference). This study confirms that the ability to match face and voice emerges sometime between 3 and 5 months. Further, the results suggest that the matching of voice and lip movements is affected by the specific articulatory-acoustic associations of the infant's native language environment. Unfortunately no developmental studies with infants younger than 3 months have been conducted to investigate when such matching abilities may emerge. Notwithstanding the absence of such

TABLE 2
10 and 20-week old infants' attention to native and foreign language mimers

		No soundtrack	Preference for English mimer English soundtrack	Greek soundtrack
10-week-olds	Mean	54.4%	67.9%	62.5%
	sd	(37.7)	(36.2)	(31.5)
20-week-olds	Mean	56.8%	68.4%	51.0%
	sd	(28.1)	(23.4)	(22.4)

studies, it would appear that auditory-visual matching abilities are based on the maturation of underlying structures, as it has been found that 3, 5-, and 7-month-old full-term, but not pre-term, infants are able to match a voice with the appropriate lip movements (Pickens et al., 1994).

Given these results, a likely course of development emerges. There appears to be some auditory-visual abilities present before 3 months, but these are either reflexive in nature (as in the case of AL), or actually based on *visual* information (as in the case of facilitation of face perception by lip movements). So, to date, there is no evidence for true auditory-visual speech perception abilities before the age of 3 months. True auditory-visual matching appears to require relatively sophisticated associative functions which only mature at around 3 months. This auditory-visual matching has less in common with the early reflexive form of AL than with the later form of AL and the PE, which appear to involve cortical rather than reflexive functioning. Once these auditory-visual abilities emerge at around 3 months, environmental variables, such as the ambient language, can have an effect. Thus, it is quite feasible that by the age of 3 months infants have developed a general ability to perceive structural correspondences between seen and heard speech (Kuhl & Meltzoff, 1982, 1984, 1988; MacKain et al., 1983), but that this is first and most evident in their native language. It remains for studies with infants younger than 3 months of age to elaborate the processes involved in the development of auditory-visual matching.

Integration of face and voice information

The evidence just presented demonstrates infants' *matching* of auditory and visual speech, but not their *integration* of auditory and visual speech. One elegant method by which this can be tested is with the McGurk effect, in which acoustic [ba] dubbed onto the lip movements for [ga] (designated A[ba]V[ga] hereafter), is perceived by adults as [da] or [ða] (as in them) (McGurk & McDonald, 1976). This shows that visual information is an integral part of speech perception, even when the speech is acoustically unambiguous. If young infants perceive the emergent [da] or [ða], then it could be the case that phonetic integration occurs developmentally prior to infants' speech perception becoming tuned to the ambient phonology. This would support speech perception models which claim that auditory-visual speech integration occurs at an early, phonetic level of processing (Green, 1996; Green, in this volume; Robert-Ribes, Schwartz & Escudier, 1995; Robert-Ribes et al., 1996; Burnham & Dodd, 1996), rather than at a late, post-categorical stage (Massaro, 1987, 1995, 1996).

Johnson, Rosenblum and Schmuckler (1995) investigated the McGurk effect in 5-month-old ELE infants. Following habituation of visual fixation to auditory-visual [va], infants were given three test trials: the original A[va]V[va], an A[ba]V[va] trial (perceived by adults as "va"), and an A[da]V[va] trial (perceived by adults as "da"). Test trials showed that the rate of re-habituation was slower for A[da]V[va] than for A[va]V[va] or A[ba]V[va], the latter two showing an equal rate of re-habituation. Thus, as is the case for adults, 5-month-old infants appear to perceive both A[ba]V[va] and A[va]V[va] as "va", while A[da]V[va] is presumably perceived as "da".

In a similar study, Desjardins and Werker (1996) investigated the McGurk effect in 4-month-old ELE infants. They found that infants habituated to auditory-visual [vi], showed no recovery of visual fixation when presented with A[bi]V[vi], suggesting that infants (both male and female) perceive A[bi]V[vi] as "vi", just as adults do. If this is so, then another group of infants habituated to auditory-visual [bi], should have shown recovery of visual fixation to A[bi]V[vi] in test trials. This was found to be the case, but only for female infants, suggesting that in this situation only 4-month-old girls are influenced by visual information.

Given that girls are often found to be more developmentally advanced around this age, the Desjardins and Werker (1996) female-specific 4-month-old results coupled with the Johnson, Rosenblum and Schmuckler (1995) pan-gender 5-month-old results suggests that it is just around these ages that auditory-visual abilities are emerging. However, with regard to auditory-visual integration, the results must be interpreted with caution. Although both studies demonstrate that infants *register* visual speech information, neither actually shows auditory-visual *integration* because the version of the McGurk effect used in both studies did not elicit a fused response, i.e. it did not involve the emergent perception of a third phone different from either the auditory or the visual component.

Burnham and Dodd (1996; Burnham, 1992) tested 4.5-month-old ELE infants on the traditional A[ba]V[ga] McGurk effect. In this, the expected percept is a fusion—[da] or [ða]—neither of which is equivalent to the auditory [ba] or visual [ga] component. Infants were presented with a live face which spoke only when they fixated it. In habituation the experimental group were presented with A[ba]V[ga] and the control group with matching A[ba]V[ba]. Both groups were then presented with three test trials: auditory-only [ba], [da] or [ða].

Fixation durations on the first two and the last two habituation trials are shown in Figure 4. The experimental group fixated the face longer in initial trials than the control group did, though fixation durations were equivalent by the end of habituation. This suggests that, initially, the experimental group infants perceived the mismatching A[ba]V[ga] to be more interesting or novel than the control group infants did perceiving the matching A[ba]V[ba]. Thus, it appears that at some level 4.5-month-old infants

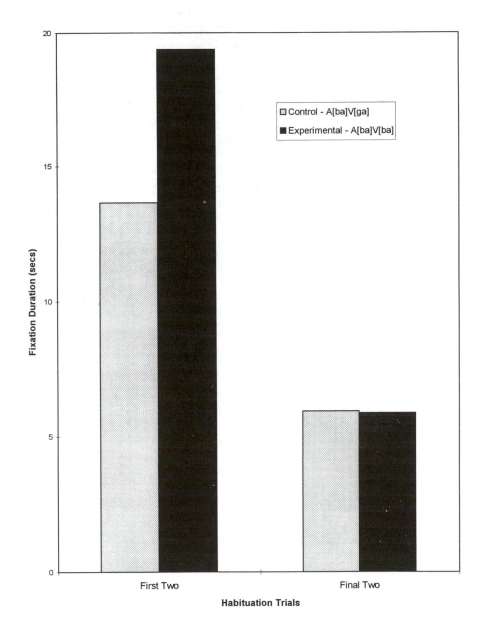

FIG. 4. Mean fixation duration at beginning and end of habituation trials.

register mismatching auditory and visual speech. The equivalent fixation durations at the end of habituation suggest that over trials experimental group infants were able to integrate the discrepant auditory and visual information. However, this can only be directly determined from the test trial data.

If experimental group infants had perceived a [da] or [ða] fusion then one of these sounds plus [ba] would appear novel to them, while if their perception was auditorily governed and [ba] was perceived, then both [da] and [ða], but not [ba], would appear novel. Control group infants' test responses should, of course, be governed by the familiarity of the percept of [ba]. Now from habituation to test trials there was a change of modality (from auditory-visual in habituation to auditory-alone in test trials), and such changes sometimes result in a familiarity preference rather than the usual novelty preference (Wagner & Sakovits, 1986; Walker-Andrews & Gibson, 1986; Burnham & Dodd, in press). Therefore, in test trials here it was unclear whether infants would look longer in order to hear novel or familiar sounds. To overcome this problem, we developed the Odd One Out Method in which two scores—an auditory score and a fusion score—are calculated for each individual infant to determine which best accounts for the range of each infant's fixation durations in the three test trials. As set out in the upper panel of Figure 2 (further details are given in Burnham & Dodd, 1996, in press) each score is based on the *absolute value* of the difference between the looking time for one stimulus and the mean looking time for the other two stimuli. As the absolute difference is used, the direction of the difference is not important, and the scores no longer reflect looking durations. Thus a high score does not mean that there is a high novelty preference. Rather, a high score means that that score accounts for a large proportion of the variance. Thus, it is the relationship between the scores which is important, and it is essential to include an experimental and control group for whom the predictions differ.

As set out in the hypotheses in the central panel of Figure 2, the experimental group, if they perceived a [da] or [ða] fusion from auditory [ba] and visual [ga], would be expected to have higher fusion scores than the control group, whereas the control group, who were presented with just auditory-visual matched [ba], would be expected to have higher auditory scores than the experimental group. As shown in the graph in the lower panel of Figure 2, this is exactly what happened, with the group by auditory/ fusion score interaction being statistically significant. These results show that 4.5-month-old infants perceive the McGurk effect, that is they integrate auditory and visual speech information as a fused percept.

The age at which auditory-visual integration first emerges is yet to be determined. The combined results of the Desjardins and Werker (1996) and Johnson et al. (1995) studies on the influence of visible speech suggest that the ability emerges between 4 and 5 months, and this is supported by our

Auditory Percept Score:
Percent range accounted for when the auditory stimulus, [ba], is taken as the odd one out.

Formula	Example
100 |[ba] - ½([da] + [ða])| / Range	100 | 8 - ½ (10 + 24) | /16 = 56%
	Auditory Score = 56%

Fused Percept Score:
Percent range accounted for when either of the possible fusion percepts, [da] or [ða], are taken as the odd one out. The fusion score used in analyses is the higher of the two.

Formula	Example
100 |[da] - ½([ba] + [ða])| / Range	100 | 10 - ½ (8 + 24) | /16 = 38%
or	**or**
100 |[ða] - ½([ba] + [da])| / Range	100 | 24 - ½ (8 + 10) | /16 = 94%
	Fusion Score = 94%

In the example, the fusion score (94%) is higher than the auditory score (56%), and so for this infant the fusion hypothesis is upheld. In practice, group statistics were conducted with two repeats, auditory and fusion scores, and two groups, experimental and control, for whom a different pattern of results are expected, as shown below.

Hypotheses:
If infants *do* perceive the McGurk effect then:

Fusion Score: Experimental should have higher scores than Control group	**E > C**
Auditory Score: Control should have higher scores than Experimental group	**C > E**

If infants *do not* perceive the McGurk effect then:

Fusion Score: Should not differ between control and experimental groups	**C = E**
Auditory Score: Should not differ between control and experimental groups	**C = E**

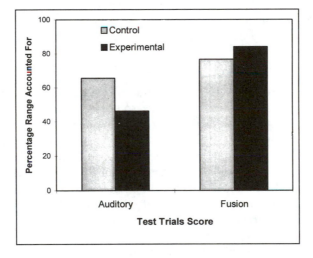

FIG. 5. Upper Panel: Formulae and calculation of auditory and fusion scores with an example for fixations of [ba] = 8 secs, [da] = 10 secs, [ða] = 24 secs (Range = 16).
Central Panel: Hypotheses for the Experimental and Control groups.
Lower Panel: Mean per cent range accounted for by auditory and fusion scores in the control and experimental groups.

results with 4.5-month-old infants. Earlier it was suggested that auditory-visual *matching* is unlikely to occur before the age of about 3 months because it involves relatively sophisticated cortical structures and cognitive functions. Does auditory-visual *integration* similarly require such structures and functions? If auditory-visual speech integration occurs at an early, phonetic level of processing (Green, 1996, in this volume; Robert-Ribes et al., 1995, 1996; Burnham & Dodd, 1996), then it could be predicted that it may be evident even earlier than 3 or 4 months. As research is lacking with younger infants, the answer to this question remains unanswered. However, convergent evidence about the level of processing involved in auditory-visual integration may be obtained from cross-language studies, to which we now turn.

Language specificity in adult auditory-visual speech perception

Studies on the incidence of the McGurk effect as a function of language background can be considered in three categories: *cross-cultural* studies, in which the incidence of the McGurk effect in different languages is examined in order to ascertain whether there are cross-cultural differences in cue weighting for auditory and visual speech components; *inter-lingual* studies, in which the effect of being presented with auditory-visual speech by speakers of a foreign language compared with one's native language is studied; and *cross-language* studies, in which differences between the phonologies of languages are used as a tool for investigating issues such as the manner and level of auditory-visual integration.

Cross-cultural auditory-visual speech perception

Many of the cross-cultural McGurk effect studies have investigated Japanese perceivers. In one study (Massaro et al., 1993) it is concluded that when language-specific phonetic repertoires, phonetic realisations of syllables, and phonotactic constraints are taken into account, the influence of visible speech is equivalent across American and Japanese perceivers. These results are taken to support the universal applicability of the Fuzzy Logical Model of Perception (FLMP). However, a series of studies by Sekiyama and her colleagues support the existence of cross-cultural differences between Japanese and English perceivers: Japanese subjects' final percept appears to be much less influenced by visual speech.

Sekiyama and Tohkura (1991) found that Japanese subjects' perception of dubbed McGurk syllables spoken by a Japanese speaker showed very little influence of visual information. However, Japanese subjects did increase their reliance on visual information when auditory noise was introduced. Similar visual facilitation in noise compared with no noise conditions was found by Sekiyama (1994) again with Japanese subjects, and by de Gelder and Vroomen (1992) with Chinese subjects. More recently, Sekiyama et al. (1995) found that under some conditions (when easy-to-lipread speakers are used or when speakers are instructed to lengthen their vowels) Japanese subjects' incorporation of visual cues is facilitated. Nevertheless, Japanese subjects generally show less robust McGurk effects than American subjects across a number of situations.

Sekiyama suggests two possible factors which may be operating here. First, that due to cultural politeness, Japanese tend not to look at the face of the speaker. Second, in Japanese there is less need to incorporate visual information because there are no consonant clusters, only five vowels, and no visually-distinct consonants such as /v/ or /ð/ (Sekiyama & Tohkura, 1993). More recent work provides further depth to this explanation. Sekiyama (Sekiyama, Tohkura, & Umeda 1996; Sekiyama, 1996) found that for Mandarin-speaking Chinese perceivers the McGurk effect is reduced even below the level of Japanese speakers. Sekiyama attributes this not only to cultural factors, but to the lexical tones used in Mandarin phonology, which possibly make attention to visual information even more superfluous than in Japanese. Perhaps a functional utility model for the effect of visual information could be proposed, in which the degree to which visual information is incorporated in speech perception depends on both the density of phonemes in the phonetic space of a particular language and the degree to which visual information is useful in disambiguating close phonetic neighbours. The development of theoretical models of this nature must await more systematic investigations of various particular languages, with known variations of phonology.

To return to the Japanese results, the relative contribution of cultural, phonological, or other factors to the reduced Japanese McGurk effect is as yet unclear. However, one fact is clear: Japanese subjects *do* perceive the visual information. Sekiyama (1994) found that Japanese subjects report auditory-visual discrepancy more than their American counterparts do, and that the incidence of such reports correlates negatively with the perception of the McGurk effect. Thus Japanese subjects *perceive* the visual information but appear not to *integrate* it as readily with the auditory information as their American counterparts do.

Inter-lingual auditory-visual speech perception

The results of Sekiyama's studies also bear on inter-lingual effects in the perception of auditory-visual speech. In addition to the increased use of visual information in noise-added, easy-to-read, and long vowel conditions (Sekiyama & Tohkura, 1991; Sekiyama, 1994; Sekiyama et al., 1995), Sekiyama has found that Japanese subjects incorporate visual information more when they listen to a foreign speaker. Sekiyama and Tohkura (1993) investigated American and Japanese subjects' perception of McGurk stimuli spoken by American and Japanese speakers in a 2 × 2 design. As in other studies, Japanese subjects generally showed less visual influence, but over and above this, both Japanese and American subjects demonstrated greater visual influence when presented with stimuli in the non-native language. Sekiyama and Tohkura (1993) explained this in terms of auditory ambiguity: when subjects hear phones that are phonemically relevant in their language but acoustically deviant, then any extra information that can be used will be used. Thus, visual information is incorporated to a greater extent by Americans listening to Japanese speech, and even by the visually-reticent Japanese when listening to American English. Kuhl et al. (1994) found a similar effect of non-native language on the reliance on visual cues by Japanese and American subjects and explained it in a similar fashion: while the non-native sounds fall within the same phone class as in their native language, perceivers detect the deviation of non-native speech tokens from native language prototypes. Thus, there is increased reliance on the visual signal in processing these discrepant auditory speech stimuli.

The importance of visual information in perceiving non-native speech has also been explored in a number of other L1/L2 contexts. First, although both Austrian and Hungarian subjects perceive McGurk effects spoken by an Austrian speaker, Grassegger (1995) found there were more McGurks (more visual influence) for the Hungarians. Second, de Gelder et al. (1995) found McGurk fusion effects in both Dutch and Cantonese language subjects presented with a Dutch speaker, but the incidence of visually-influenced blends was greater for the Cantonese. Finally, in a factorial study of German and Spanish perceivers and speakers, Fuster-Duran (1996) found that when given auditory-visual conflict in pairs of German words, e.g. "brat–Grad", or Spanish words, e.g. "napa–paca", Spanish and German subjects incorporated visual information more for foreign than for native auditory-visual words. Fuster-Duran also found a couple of interesting exceptions that support the Sekiyama and Tohkura (1993) auditory ambiguity explanation: Spanish subjects showed the weakest visual influence in "Bier–Gier" and "nein–Bein" pairs, presumably because both the auditory components in the pairs "Bier" and "nein" are German words known by most non-German speakers. Thus, the non-native influence on visual attention appears to be quite specific and immediate.

Cross-language auditory-visual speech perception

In what can be called "cross-language research", phonological differences are used to locate the basis of the McGurk effect and, thus, auditory-visual integration. In the first study of this nature, Werker, Frost and McGurk

(1992) paired auditory [ba] with visual [ba], [va], [ða], [da], [ʒa], or [ga] and asked ELE subjects and native French subjects with varying levels of English language proficiency for perceptual identifications. All these consonants are used in both languages, except [ð] which is not used in French. It was found that there were more [ða] identifications of A[ba]V[ða] by English than by French subjects, who tended to substitute [da] or [tʰa]. However, the frequency of [ða] identifications increased as a function of English language experience, suggesting some influence of phonology on auditory-visual speech perception. This influence could be perceptual: French subjects may, through their language experience, have a phonologically-determined *perceptual bias* against perceiving [ð]. However, it could equally be a post-perceptual labelling effect: French subjects may perceive [ð] just as often as their English-speaking counterparts but could have a phonologically-determined *response bias* against reporting their perceptual experience of [ð] as "th". While Werker, Frost and McGurk ensured that their French subjects could produce [ð] and also found no difference in French subjects' incidence of written and spoken "d" or "t" responses to acoustic-only [ð] presentations, it is nevertheless possible that there was a response bias against a phone not relevant in the perceivers' native phonology and orthography.

Burnham (1992; Burnham & Dodd, 1996) investigated the effect of phonology on auditory-visual speech perception in a study designed to overcome the confounding effect of response bias. A variant of the McGurk effect was used, in which auditory [m] paired with visual [ŋ], as in sing, tends to result in the perception of "n". The experimental design also exploited the fact that [ŋ] is used in both word-initial and word-final positions in Thai, but not in the word-initial position in English. Thai and English adults were presented with A[m]V[ŋ] either in syllable-initial or syllable-final position, as well as various other auditory-visual, auditory-only, and visual-only stimuli. This design overcomes any response-bias problems because the non-native phoneme is a *component* of the McGurk effect, rather than the expected fusion *response*. English speakers' perception in the initial position is the condition of interest. Due to the illegality of initial [ŋ] in English and the ambiguity of visual-only [ŋ] (since visual [ŋ] looks like visual [n]) (see Mills, 1987; Mills & Thiem, 1980), English subjects would be expected to respond "n" more often in the initial than in the final position for visual-only [ŋ] and matching auditory-visual [ŋ]. As can be seen in the first two rows of Table 3 this is indeed what happened. There were significant language background by position interactions for both visual-only [ŋ] and matching auditory-visual [ŋ] showing English subjects' greater tendency to respond "n" in the initial position as a result of visual ambiguity (69.6% versus 7.5%) and phonological bias (8.5% versus 0%) respectively.

Is such visual ambiguity and phonological bias carried over into the mismatching fusion? An analysis of the "n" responses to A[m]V[ŋ] shown in

TABLE 3
Mean per cent "n" responses (%) and reaction times in Msecs (RT) for all responses to
visual-only (VO) [ŋ], auditory-visual (AV) [ŋ], and A[m]V[ŋ] in initial and final positions
for English and Thai perceivers

| | Initial position | | | | Final position | | | |
| | English | | Thai | | English | | Thai | |
Stimulus	%	RT	%	RT	%	RT	%	RT
VO[ŋ]	69.6	1677	7.5	1458	58.7	1640	29.5	1456
AV[ŋ]	8.5	1399	0	1109	1.1	1486	2.2	1262
A[m]v[ŋ]	28.1	1505	20.9	1473	63.1	1538	56.2	1433

the last row of Table 3 revealed a generally greater percentage of "n" responses on final than initial consonants but no significant difference between English and Thai subjects, nor any English/Thai by initial/final interaction. Thus, despite the significantly greater phonological bias for initial auditory-visual [ŋ] and visual ambiguity for initial visual-only [ŋ] by English speakers, their frequency of "n" responses to A[m]V[ŋ] was not significantly greater than that of the Thais. The reaction time (RT) data support these results: despite generally longer RTs by English speakers than Thai speakers for visual-only and auditory-visual [ŋ] trials, there were no significant RT differences on A[m]V[ŋ] trials. So, despite other differences, the presence of the A[m]V[ŋ] McGurk in the initial position does not increase English speakers' relative processing time. As a result, the study shows that there was no effect of phonological bias on the McGurk effect: for the McGurks both the incidence of "n" responses and the RTs are unaffected by word position or native language. These results are consistent with the finding that pre-phonological infants perceive the McGurk effect (Johnson et al., 1995; Desjardins & Werker, 1996; Burnham, 1992, Burnham & Dodd, 1996) and with the notion that auditory and visual speech information is integrated at an early (phonetic) level of processing before phonological categorisation (Green, 1996, in this volume; Robert-Ribes et al., 1995; Robert-Ribes et al., 1996; Burnham & Dodd, 1996).

If auditory-visual speech perception indeed occurs phonetically, then phonetic manipulations should affect the resultant perception, irrespective of the phonological relevance of that perception. Green (Green, Kuhl & Meltzoff, 1988; Green et al., 1991; Green, 1996) has shown that the relative distribution of "d" and "th" responses to the traditional A[b]V[g] McGurk is changed when moving from an [a], as in "father", to [i], as in "feet", vowel context. English-speaking subjects' distribution of fusion responses to A[ba]V[ga] is 85% "tha" and 15% "da", while for A[bi]V[gi] it is 40% "thi" and 60% "di" (Green et al., 1988, 1991; Green, 1996). It can be reasoned that if the McGurk effect occurs phonetically, then this effect of vowel

context should be apparent whether the phonemes /d/ and /ð/ are phonologically relevant in the listener's language or not.

Burnham and Keane (1996) tested this hypothesis with Australian
English and with Japanese language environment subjects with three levels
of English ability: beginning, intermediate and advanced. As /ð/ is not used
in Japanese phonology, a response bias toward perceiving "d" rather than
"th" would be expected for Japanese subjects. As shown in Table 4(a),
Japanese listeners showed a bias to report "d" rather than "th" for
auditory-visual [ð], auditory-only [ð], and visual-only [ð], but this bias
decreased as a function of language experience. Whether this "d" bias in
Japanese perceivers is due to a perceptual bias or a response bias (see earlier
in this section with respect to the study by Werker et al., 1992) can only be
determined by inspection of the results on the McGurk trials.

The results for the McGurk stimulus, A[b]V[g], are shown in Table 4(b).
Two points are of interest. First, note that in the [a] vowel context English-
speaking subjects show more fusions (78.13%) than do Japanese listeners
(mean = 56.77%), and this difference was statistically significant. By contrast, in the [i] vowel context the number of fusion responses was statistically
equivalent between the English (78.13%) and Japanese (mean = 80.32%)
subjects. Thus, it is possible that the reduced visual influence for Japanese

TABLE 4a

Response bias for "th" versus "d" responses for Japanese and English speakers,
averaged across vowel contexts (AV = auditory-visual, AO = auditory-only,
VO = visual-only)

	Australian	Beginners	Japanese Intermediate	Advanced
% "th" responses for AV [ð]	100	81.25	89.06	97.66
for AO [ð]	96.09	53.90	65.62	78.12
for VO [ð]	96.87	84.37	75.00	90.62

TABLE 4b

For A[b]V[g], incidence of fusions responses, and in [a] and [i] vowel contexts of "th"
and "d" responses for Japanese and English speakers

	% Fusion responses [a]	[i]	[a] Vowel context % "d"	% "th"	[i] Vowel context % "d"	% "th"
Australian English	78.13	78.13	4.69	73.44	15.62	62.5
Japanese: beginners	56.25	80.47	26.56	29.69	56.25	24.22
Japanese: intermediate	47.66	82.81	30.47	17.19	51.56	31.25
Japanese: advanced	66.40	78.28	32.81	33.59	56.25	32.03

subjects obtained by Sekiyama and her colleagues may occur peculiarly in the [a] vowel context. This possibility needs to be investigated further.

The second point of interest in these results is the distribution of "d" and "th" responses to the fusion stimuli. Despite the bias by Japanese subjects towards responding "d" when presented with [ð] (see Table 4a), the cross-over effect for "d" versus "th" responses in the [a] and [i] vowel contexts was obtained, and was found to be statistically equivalent across the four language groups (see Table 4b). As with the results of the Thai study (Burnham, 1992; Burnham & Dodd, 1996), this result shows that auditory and visual speech information is initially integrated at a phonetic level of processing, free from phonological constraints. Any phonological constraints that influence subjects' responses must then occur post-phonetically on the resultant auditory-visual speech percept.

These results are consistent with other findings of pre-phonological integration of visual and auditory speech information in both infants (Johnson et al., 1995; Burnham, 1992; Burnham & Dodd, 1996) and adults (Robert-Ribes et al., 1995; Green et al., 1991; Green & Miller, 1985; Green & Kuhl, 1989; see also Green, this volume) and support the notion that auditory-visual integration occurs early in processing (Green, 1996, this volume; Robert-Ribes et al., 1995, 1996; Burnham & Dodd, 1996), rather than at a late post-categorical stage (Massaro, 1987, 1995, 1996). The processes involved are captured in what can be called the Phonetic Plus Post-Categorical (3PC) model of auditory-visual speech perception. In this, auditory-visual integration occurs in a common representational space with either a motoric (Robert-Ribes et al., 1995, 1996), articulatory/gestural (Liberman & Mattingly, 1985, 1989; Browman & Goldstein, 1992; Studdert-Kennedy & Goodell, 1992), or phonetic (Dodd & Burnham, 1988; Green & Kuhl, 1991) basis. Whatever the nature of this common metric, the important point is that auditory-visual integration occurs early and directly (in the Gibsonian sense), devoid of any influence of learned associations or phonological prototypes. What *does* occur late are post-categorical effects of native phonology, and cross-cultural and inter-lingual factors. Thus a distinction can be made between the *direct* McGurk effect (Phonetic-level auditory-visual integration), and the *reported* McGurk effect, additionally influenced by the later phonological (Post-Categorical) effects.

AUDITORY-VISUAL SPEECH PERCEPTION INTEGRATED

Language specificity in mature auditory-visual speech perception

The evidence just presented in the language specificity section shows that there are both language-specific and language-general aspects of mature auditory-visual speech perception. Before examining these, let us for a moment recall what has been found in auditory-only speech perception. By adulthood, auditory speech perception is specifically structured by the speaker's language environment. However, the language perceiver has not lost the ability to perceive non-native phones: under certain conditions, such as when short ISIs allow language-general phonetic processing, or when stimulus modifications allow the adoption of non-linguistic perceptual modes, unfamiliar L2 distinctions can be discriminated. With auditory-visual speech perception, although the findings are fewer, a parallel can be drawn. The cross-cultural and inter-lingual studies of auditory-visual speech perception inform us about the phonemic level of processing, at which the effects of phonological factors such as L1/L2 discordance (Sekiyama & Tohkura, 1993; Kuhl, et al., 1994), lexical status (Fuster-Duran, 1996), and stimulus characteristics such as noise (Sekiyama, 1994; de Gelder & Vroomen, 1992), visibility (Sekiyama et al., 1995), and vowel length (Sekiyama et al., 1995) are all apparent. On the other hand, the cross-language studies show that auditory-visual integration occurs at an earlier phonetic level of processing and that this integration is affected by phonetic factors such as vowel context (Burnham & Keane, 1996), and *not* phonemic factors such as phonological relevance (Burnham, 1992; Burnham & Dodd, 1996; Burnham & Keane, 1996). Thus, just as in Mann's (1986) auditory-only study (see the development of auditory speech perception section, p.31) in which Japanese listeners' sensitivity to the differential phonetic effects of /r/ and /l/ on subsequent consonants was revealed, the basically phonetic nature of auditory-visual speech integration can be revealed under appropriate circumstances. The 3PC model of auditory-visual speech perception, which holds that auditory-visual speech integration first occurs phonetically before phonological influences, is thus consistent with what we know about the perception of auditory-only speech. And the effects of learning a particular language are the same for both auditory-only and auditory-visual speech: phonological biases are established as a function of experience, but basic speech perception mechanisms are left unaltered. Thus the 3PC model could provide a stepping stone to an integrated model of speech perception, which embraces auditory-only, auditory-visual, and multimodal aspects of speech perception.

The effects of learning a particular language on auditory-only speech perception are clear from the research reported earlier. However, the similar issue concerning visual speech has not been addressed. Is visual speech organised in categories that show internal structure, that is, are there native language viseme prototypes? Can inter-linguistic differences in visual speech that are deviant from native visual prototypes be detected? For example, when native English speakers see unfamiliar lip-rounding by a native Swedish speaker speaking English, do they then make more use of the available auditory speech information? If so, then a good strategy might be to ignore or look away from the lip movements. Anecdotal evidence suggests that as a function of experience, speaker's lip and face movements become specifically tuned or adapted for speaking a particular L1. A likely corollary of this is that L2 speakers display a "visual accent", that is they may produce visual speech information that appears visually foreign to a native speaker. However, there appears to be no systematic research on these issues.

Similarly, very little research has been conducted on the possible changes that might occur to visual speech perception as a product of experience with a specific language. Some research has been conducted on the relative salience and perceptual discriminability of different visemes (Mills, 1987; Mills & Thiem, 1980; van Son et al., 1994), which echoes to some extent the work on psychoacoustic salience in auditory speech perception (see Burnham's studies in the earlier section on auditory speech perception, pp.29–30). However, there appears to be little, if any, research on the selective perception of native over non-native visemes (see Werker's auditory studies in the auditory speech perception section, pp.29 and 31), nor on how the similarity of L1 and L2 visemes may affect visual and auditory-visual speech perception (see Best's auditory-only studies in the earlier section on auditory speech perception, p.30). Campbell (this volume) cites studies that show that areas of primary auditory cortex respond specifically to visual speech movements, but not to "gurning" movements of the mouth that are unrelated to speech. If humans respond differently to visual speech and non-speech, then it is possible that the small differences between pseudospeech and speech conditions in the experiments Campbell reports may turn out to be systematically related to the detection and comparison of seen speech events to L1 phonemes. This speculation remains to be investigated.

The development of language specificity in auditory-visual speech perception

In auditory speech perception development the organism's initial state of pan-linguistic sensitivity begins to become tuned to the ambient language environment quite early in infancy. Is the same process involved in the development of auditory-visual speech perception? That is, are all possible visual manifestations of the world's phones initially perceived, with subsequent native language specialisation? Alternatively, must the developing infant learn to perceive particular visual dynamics, and then learn to associate these with particular phonemes? Or are the structural characteristics of articulatory gestures perceived directly by infants irrespective of sensory modality? Let us briefly review what is currently known about speech perception development in attempting to answer these questions.

The auditory system develops early and auditory information, especially speech, is available pre-natally. At birth, perception of auditory speech phones, both phonologically relevant and irrelevant, is extremely good. The visual system is operational at birth, especially for high contrast moving objects in central near space, such as faces, and acuity develops quickly over the first few months. It is unclear yet whether neonatal infants discriminate visually between speech phones, though this appears to be evident by at least the age of 4 months. One-month-old infants turn to the source of heard voices but once a face is fixated, lip movements (not voices) maintain infants' attention and facilitate visual recognition. Thus, lip movements are *perceived* by young infants, but the degree of *discrimination* between different speech gestures is not known. True auditory-visual speech perception becomes evident at around 3–4 months when voice information rather than lip movements facilitates face perception, when visible speech influences speech perception, and when matching of auditory and visual speech occurs. That matching occurs for 20- but not 10-week-old infants and for full- but not pre-term infants suggests that there is a strong maturational component in these developments.

It is possible that facilitation and matching, both emerging at around 3 months, rely on the same underlying processes, and that these are similar to those involved in the phonemic processing evident in language-specific auditory-only speech perception, and in cross-cultural and inter-lingual auditory-visual speech perception studies. With respect to auditory-visual integration, I have argued that this is a phonetic level phenomenon akin to that revealed in the cross-language studies. If so, then there is no reason, except perhaps maturational, why this may not be present in younger infants. Whether it is or not may depend to some extent upon the manner in which auditory-visual integration occurs in both infants and adults. The results presented here are consistent with the notion that auditory and visual speech information is coded in a common metric. The exact nature of this metric is unclear; however, if it is some sort of amodal code, e.g. motor or gestural, which does not rely upon specific experience, then in a Gibsonian (Gibson, 1969) or neo-Gibsonian (Bower, 1974) vein, there is no reason why it should not be available at birth. Thus the developmental arm of the 3PC (phonetic plus post-categorical) model would predict that phonetic amodal speech perception is present at birth, with post-categorical phonemic information affecting perception at a later stage. The developmental evidence presented in this chapter suggests that this might be as early as 3 months. Again there is a parallel with auditory-only speech perception, in which language-specific influences seem to emerge by 4 months (Kuhl et al., 1992).

Although the distinction between language-general phonetic and language-specific phonemic modes of auditory-visual speech perception is reminiscent of the auditory speech perception literature, it is unclear whether they involve the same process of development, that is universal perception followed by attenuation of the perception of non-native phonemes. Of critical importance here is whether infants can perceive visible speech articulations as specifically linguistic. We now know that adults perceive visible speech as speech, while non-speech mouth movements such as "gurning" are not perceived as speech (see Campbell, this volume). While there is evidence that 6-month-olds' auditory-visual matching for speech is a left hemisphere function (MacKain et al., 1983), it is not clear whether such specialisation *only* occurs for speech, nor how early this might occur. This needs to be investigated. Similarly, although some research has been conducted on the relative salience and discriminability of visemes in adults, the extent to which infants discriminate visemes is not known. Moreover, it is not known whether infants, or adults for that matter, reliably distinguish between visible articulations of native and non-native phonemes or whether L2 visemes are assimilated into L1 categories in the same manner as in auditory speech perception (Best, 1993, 1994, 1995a,b). If adults can make such distinctions, then it would be of great interest to know when such native language tuning becomes available to the developing language user.

Data from auditory-only speech perception development may for the moment inform us about visual speech perception development. Kuhl's data suggests that auditory-only prototypes based on the native language may begin to emerge at around 4–6 months (Kuhl et al., 1992). If so, then in situations in which auditory information discrepant with these prototypes is detected there would be a strong advantage in using available visual speech information to facilitate veridical speech perception. This could be seen as the beginning of the inter-lingual effect found with adults: whereas visual information is always incorporated phonetically when it is present, it becomes important in auditory-visual speech perception when non-native or unusual sounds are detected.[1] In terms of the 3PC model this could be seen as the initial emergence of post-categorical processes in auditory-visual speech perception. Note that this 3PC model is *prima facie* a serial processing model because such extra use of visual information must occur post-categorically after auditory-visual integration. Alternatively, this information could be simultaneously available if an interactive model of speech perception such as the TRACE model (McClelland & Elman, 1986) were adopted.

The effect of this heightened visual attention would be to increase the likelihood of correct perception when non-native, or perhaps even extra-dialectal or degraded auditory speech, is detected. As young infants have less phonologically specific experience than adults, then visual information should significantly aid them initially in veridical phonetic level speech perception and later phonemic level speech perception. Visual speech information is not only an integral part of speech perception, it is also adaptive and useful. It is lucky for us as a species that auditory-visual speech integration occurs so early in development and processing, so that it can foster native language acquisition and help us to understand non-native speakers.

NOTES

1. The opposite effect is also simultaneously possible: infants' visual perception of speech may gradually become tuned to the ambient language, such that visual differences between non-native articulations are not as easily discriminated as are similar differences in native articulations. If so, then the detection of L2 visual speech may result in greater attention to *auditory* speech.

ACKNOWLEDGMENTS

The writing of this chapter was supported by Australian Research Council large (A79601993) and small grants to the author. My appreciation to Vera Thomson for typing the initial draft; to Lynne-Maree Crain, Lynda Earnshaw, Susan Gibson, and Megan Smith for assistance with testing; to Sheila Keane for provocative discussions, stimulating suggestions, and interesting data; and to Elizabeth Francis and the other two editors of this volume, Ruth Campbell and Barbara Dodd, for extremely useful comments on the drafts.

REFERENCES

Abramov, L., Gordon, J., Hendrickson, A., Hainline, L., Dobson, V. & LaBossiere, E. (1982). The retina of the newborn infant. *Science, 217,* 265–7.

Aslin, R.N. (1977). Development of binocular vision in human infants. *Journal of Experimental Child Psychology, 23,* 133–50.

Aslin, R.N., Pisoni, D.B., Hennessy, B.L. & Perey, A.J. (1981). Discrimination of voice onset time by human infants: New findings and implications for the effects of early experience. *Child Development, 52,* 1135–45.

Bahrick, L.E. (1988). Intramodal learning in infancy: Learning on the basis of two kinds of invariant relations in audible and visible events. *Child Development, 59,* 197–209.

Bahrick, L.E., Walker, A.S. & Neisser, U. (1981). Selective looking by infants. *Cognitive Psychology, 13,* 377–90.

Banks, M.S. (1980). The development of visual accommodation in early infancy. *Child Development, 51,* 646–66.

Bernard, J.A. & Ramey, C.T. (1977). Visual regard of familiar and unfamiliar persons in the first six months of infancy. *Merrill-Palmer Quarterly, 23,* 121–7.

Best, C.T. (1993). The emergence of native language phonological influences in infants: A perceptual assimilation model. In J.C. Goodman & H.C. Nusbaum (Eds), *The Development of Speech Perception: The Transition from Speech Sounds to Spoken Words.* Cambridge MA: MIT Press.

Best, C.T. (1994). Emergence of language-specific constraints in perception of non-native speech: A window on early phonological development. In B. de Boysson-Bardies, S. de Schonen, P.W. Jusczyk, P. McNeilage & J. Morton (Eds), *Developmental Neurocognition: Speech and Face Processing in the First Year of Life.* NATO ASI series D: Behavioural and Social sciences, *69.* Dordrecht, Netherlands: Kluwer Academic Publishers.

Best, C.T. (1995a). A direct realist view of cross-language speech perception. In W. Strange (Ed.), *Speech Perception and Linguistic Experience*. Timonium, MD: York Press.

Best, C.T. (1995b). Learning to perceive the sound patterns of English. In C. Rovee-Collier & L. Lipsitt (Eds). *Advances in Infancy Research, 4*, 217–304.

Best, C.T., McRoberts, G.W. & Sithole, N.M. (1988). Examination of perceptual reorganization for nonnative speech contrasts: Zulu Click Discrimination by English speaking adults and infants. *Journal of Experimental Psychology: Human Perception and Performance, 14*, 345–60.

Bigelow, A. (1977). Infants' recognition of their mothers. Paper presented at the biennial meeting of the Society for Research in Child Development, March, New Orleans, USA.

Bower, T.G.R. (1974). The evolution of the sensory systems. In R.B. McLeod & L. Pick, Jr., (Eds.), *Perception: Essays in honor of James T. Gibson*. Ithaca: Cornell University Press.

Bredberg, G. (1968). Cellular pattern and nerve supply of the human organ of Corti. *Acta Otolaryngolica Supplementum, 236*, 1–135.

Bredberg, G. (1985). The anatomy of the developing ear. In S.E. Trehub & B. Schneider (Eds), *Auditory Development in Infancy*. New York: Plenum Press.

Browman, C.P. & Goldstein, L. (1992). Articulatory phonology: An overview. *Phonetica, 49*, 155–80.

Burnham, D. (1986). Developmental loss of speech perception: Exposure to and experience with a first language. *Applied Psycholinguistics, 7*, 206–40.

Burnham, D. (1992). Processing auditory-visual speech in infancy and across phonologies. *International Journal of Psychology, 27*, 59.

Burnham, D. (1993). Visual recognition of mother by young infants: Facilitation by speech. *Perception, 22*, 1133–53.

Burnham, D. & Day, R.H. (1979). Detection of color in rotating objects by infants and its generalization over changes in velocity. *Journal of Experimental Child Psychology, 28*, 191–204.

Burnham, D. & Dodd, B. (1996). Auditory-visual speech perception as a direct process: The McGurk effect in infants and across languages. In D. Stork and M. Hennecke (Eds), *Speechreading by Humans and Machines*. Berlin: Springer-Verlag.

Burnham, D. & Dodd, B. (in press). Familiarity and novelty performance in infants' auditory-visual speech perception: Problems, factors and a solution. In C. Rovee-Collier (Ed.), *Advances in Infancy Research, 12*.

Burnham, D. & Dodd, B. (in preparation). Infants' auditory-visual perception of speech in familiar and foreign languages.

Burnham, D. & Keane, S. (1996). Where does auditory-visual speech integration occur? Japanese speakers' perception of the McGurk effect as a function of vowel environment. In P. McCormack & A. Russell (Eds.), *Proceedings of the Sixth Australian International Conference on Speech Science and Technology* (pp.503–8).

Burnham, D., Earnshaw, L. & Clark J. (1991). Development of categorical identification of native and non-native bilabial stops: Infants, children and adults. *Journal of Child Language, 18*, 231–60.

Burnham, D., Earnshaw, L., O'Connor, G. & Clark, J. (in preparation). Native-language phonological bias in speech perception and its relation to the onset of reading.

Burnham, D., Francis, E., Webster, D., Luksaneeyanawin, S., Attapaiboon, C., Lacerda, F. & Keller, P. (1996). Perception of lexical tone across languages: Evidence for a linguistic mode of processing. *Proceedings of the Fourth International Conference on Spoken Language Processing*. Philadelphia, *4*, 2514–16.

Burnham, D., Taplin, J., Henderson-Smart, D., Earnshaw-Brown, L. & O'Grady, B. (1993). Maturation of precedence effect thresholds: Full-term and pre-term infants. *Infant Behavior and Development, 16*, 213–32.

Campbell, R. (this volume). How brains see speech: The cortical localisation of speechreading in hearing people. In R. Campbell, B. Dodd & D. Burnham (Eds). *Hearing by Eye II: Advances in the Psychology of Speechreading and Auditory-visual Speech*. Hove, UK: Psychology Press.

Carpenter, G.C. (1974a). Mother's face and the newborn. *New Scientist, 61,* 742–4.

Carpenter, G.C. (1974b). Visual regard of moving and stationary faces in early infancy. *Merrill-Palmer Quarterly, 20,* 181–94.

Carpenter, G.C., Tecce, J.J., Stechler, G. & Friedman, S. (1970). Differential visual behaviour to human and humanoid faces in early infancy. *Merrill-Palmer Quarterly, 16,* 91–108.

Cernoch, M.J. & Porter, R.H. (1985). Recognition of maternal axillary odors by infants. *Child Development, 56,* 1593–8.

Clifton, R.K., Morrongiello, B., Kulig, J. & Dowd, J. (1981). Newborns' orientation toward sound: Possible implications for cortical development. *Child Development, 52,* 833–8.

Cohen, L.B. & Strauss, M.S. (1979). Concept development in the human infant. *Child Development, 50,* 419–24.

Cranford, J.L. & Oberholtzer, M. (1976). Role of the neocortex in binaural hearing in the cat. II. The "precedence effect" in sound localization. *Brain Research, III,* 225–39.

Cranford, J., Ravizza, R., Diamond, I.T. & Whitfield, I.C. (1971). Unilateral ablation of the auditory cortex in the cat impairs complex sound localization. *Science, 172,* 286–8.

Culp, R.E. (1974). The use of the mother's voice to control infant attending behaviour. *Monographs of the Society for Research in Child Development, 39,* 42–51.

Cutler, A. (1994). Segmentation problems, rhythmic solutions. *Lingua, 92,* 81–104.

Cutler, A. & Mehler, J. (1993). The periodicity bias. *Journal of Phonetics, 21,* 103–8.

de Gelder, B., Bertelson, P., Vroomen, J. & Chen, H.C. (1995). Interlanguage differences in the McGurk effect for Dutch and Cantonese listeners. *Proceedings of the Fourth European Conference on Speech Communication and Technology* (pp. 1699–1702). Madrid.

de Gelder, B. & Vroomen, J. (1992). Auditory and visual speech perception in alphabetic and non-alphabetic Chinese-Dutch bilinguals. In R.J. Harris (Ed.), *Cognitive Processing in Bilinguals*. North Holland: Elsevier Science Publishers.

de Schonen, S., McKenzie, B., Maury, L. & Bresson, F. (1978). Central and peripheral object distances as determinants of the effective visual field in early infancy. *Perception, 7,* 499–506.

Desjardins, R.N. & Werker, J.F. (1996). 4-month-old female infants are influenced by visible speech. Poster presented at the International Conference of Infant Studies, Providence RI.

Dobson, V. & Teller, D.Y. (1978). Visual acuity in human infants: A review and comparison of behavioral and electrophysiological studies. *Vision Research, 18,* 1469–83.

Dodd, B. (1979). Lipreading in infants: Attention to speech presented in- and-out-of-synchrony. *Cognitive Psychology, 11,* 478–84.

Dodd, B. & Burnham, D. (1988). Processing speechread information. *Volta Review: New Reflections on Speechreading, 90,* 45–60.

Eilers, R.E. & Minifie, F.D. (1975). Fricative discrimination in early infancy. *Journal of Speech and Hearing Research, 18,* 158–67.

Eilers, R.E., Wilson, W.R. & Moore, J.M. (1977). Development of changes in speech discrimination in infants. *Journal of Speech and Hearing Research, 20,* 766–80.

Eimas, P.D. (1975). Auditory and phonetic coding of the cues for speech: Discrimination of the [r–l] distinction by young infants. *Perception and Psychophysics, 18,* 341–7.

Eimas, P.D., Siqueland, E.R., Jusczyk, P. & Vigorito, J. (1971). Speech perception in infants. *Science, 171,* 303–6.

Field, J., Muir, D., Pilon, R., Sinclair, M. & Dodwell, P. (1980). Infants' orientation to lateral sounds from birth to three months. *Child Development, 51,* 295–8.

Field, T.M., Cohen, D., Garcia, R. & Greenberg, R. (1984). Mother–stranger face discrimination by the newborn. *Infant Behavior and Development, 7,* 19–25.

Fitzgerald, H.E. (1968). Autonomic pupillary reflex activity during early infancy and its relation to social and non-social visual stimuli. *Journal of Experimental Child Psychology, 6*, 470–82.

Francis, P.L. & McCroy, G. (1983). Infants' bimodal recognition of human stimulus configurations. Paper presented at the biennial meeting of the Society for Research in Child Development, April, Detroit, USA.

Fuster-Duran, A. (1996). Perception of conflicting audio-visual speech: An examination across Spanish and German. In D.G. Stork & M.E. Hennecke (Eds), *Speechreading by Humans and Machines*. Berlin: Springer-Verlag.

Gibson, E.J. (1969). *Principles of perceptual learning and development.* New York: Appleton-Century-Crofts.

Gibson, K.R. (1981). Comparative neuro-ontogeny: Its implications for the development of human intelligence. In G. Butterworth (Ed.), *Infancy and Epistemology*. Brighton: Harvester Press.

Grassegger, H. (1995). McGurk effect in German and Hungarian listeners. *Proceedings of the International Congress of Phonetic Sciences, Stockholm, 4*, 210–13.

Green, K.P. (1996). The use of auditory and visual information in phonetic perception. In D.G. Stork & M.E. Hennecke (Eds), *Speechreading by Humans and Machines*. Berlin: Springer-Verlag.

Green, K.P. & Kuhl, P.K. (1989). The role of visual information in the processing of place and manner features in speech perception. *Perception and Psychophysics, 45*, 34–42.

Green, K.P. & Miller, J.L. (1985). On the role of visual rate information in phonetic perception. *Perception and Psychophysics, 38*, 269–76.

Green, K.P., Kuhl, P.K. & Meltzoff, A.N. (1988). Factors affecting the integration of auditory and visual information in speech: The effect of vowel environment. *Journal of the Acoustical Society of America, 84*, S155.

Green, K.P., Kuhl, P.K., Meltzoff, A.N. & Stevens, K.N. (1991). Integrating speech information across talkers, gender, and sensory modality: Female faces and male voices in the McGurk effect. *Perception and Psychophysics, 50*, 524–36.

Hirsh-Pasek, K., Kemler-Nelson, D.G., Jusczyk, P.W., Wright-Cassidy, K., Druss, B. & Kennedy, L. (1987). Clauses are perceptual units for young infants. *Cognition, 26*, 269–86.

Hochster, M.E. & Kelly, J.B. (1981). The precedence effect and sound localization by children with temporal lobe epilepsy. *Neuropsychologia, 19*, 49–55.

Holmberg, T.L., Morgan, K.A. & Kuhl, P.K. (1977). Speech perception in early infancy: Discrimination of fricative contrasts. Paper presented at the 94th meeting of the Acoustical Society of America, December, Miami Beach.

Ihsen, E. & Day, R.H. (1981). Infants' visual perception of moving objects at different distances. In A.R. Nesdale, C. Pratt, R. Grieve, J. Field, J. Illingworth & J. Hogben (Eds), *Advances in Child Development: Theory and Research*. Perth, Australia: National Conference on Child Development.

Johnson, J.A., Rosenblum, L.D. & Schmuckler, M.A. (1995). The McGurk effect in infants. *Journal of Acoustical Society of America, 97*, 2aSC7. 3286.

Jusczyk, P.W., Cutler, A. & Redanz, N.J. (1993). Infants' preference for the predominant stress patterns of English words. *Child Development, 23*, 648–54.

Jusczyk, P.W., Friederici, A.D., Wessells, J.M.I., Svenkerud, V. & Jusczyk, A.M. (1993). Infants' sensitivity to the sound patterns of native language words. *Journal of Memory and Language, 32*, 402–20.

Jusczyk, P.W., Hirsh-Pasek, K., Kemler-Nelson, D.G., Kennedy, L.J., Woodward, A. & Piwoz, J. (1992). Perception of acoustic correlates of major phrasal units by young infants. *Cognitive Psychology, 24*, 252–92.

Jusczyk, P.W., Pisoni, D.B., Walley, A. & Murray, J. (1980). Discrimination of relative onset of two-component tones by infants. *Journal of the Acoustical Society of America*, *67*, 262–70.

Kaitz, M., Shaviv, E., Greenwald, M., Blum, M. & Auerbach, J. (1985). At what age can a baby recognize mother's face? Unpublished manuscript, Psychology Department, Hebrew University, Jerusalem, Israel.

Kuhl, P.K. & Meltzoff, A.N. (1982). The bimodal perception of speech in infancy. *Science*, *218*, 1138–41.

Kuhl, P.K. & Meltzoff, A.N. (1984). The intermodal representation of speech in infants. *Infant Behavior and Development*, *7*, 361–81.

Kuhl, P.K. & Meltzoff, A.N. (1988). Speech as an intermodal object of perception. In A. Yonas (Ed.), *Perceptual Development in Infancy: The Minnesota Symposia on Child Psychology* (*20*, pp. 235–66). Hillsdale, NJ: Lawrence Erlbaum Associates Inc.

Kuhl, P.K., Tsuzaki, M., Tohkura, Y. & Meltzoff, A. (1994). Human processing of auditory-visual information in speech perception: Potential for multimodal human-machine interfaces. *Proceedings of the International Conference on Spoken Language Processing*, Tokyo, 1994, S11–4.1.

Kuhl, P.K., Williams, K.A., Lacerda, F., Stevens, K.N. & Lindblom, B. (1992). Linguistic experience alters phonetic perception in infants by 6 months of age. *Science*, *255*, 606–8.

Lasky, R.E., Syrdal-Lasky, A. & Klein, R.E. (1975). VOT discrimination by four to six and a half month old infants from Spanish environments. *Journal of Experimental Child Psychology*, *20*, 215–25.

Laub, K.W. (1973). Discrimination of mother from stranger by ten- and eleven-week-old infants. *Dissertation Abstracts International*, *34*, 6242–3.

Laub, K.W. & McClusky, K.A. (1974). Visual discrimination of social stimuli with and without auditory cues. *Society for Research in Child Development*, *39*, 92–104.

Liberman, A.M. & Mattingly, I.G. (1985). The motor theory of speech perception revised. *Cognition*, *21*, 1–36.

Liberman, A.M. & Mattingly, I.G. (1989). A specialization for speech perception. *Science*, *243*, 489–94.

McClelland, J.L. & Elman, J.L. (1986). The TRACE model of speech perception. *Cognitive Psychology*, *18*, 1–86.

McGurk H. & Buchanan, L. (1981). Bimodal speech perception: Vision and hearing. Unpublished manuscript, Department of Psychology, University of Surrey.

McGurk, H. & MacDonald J. (1976). Hearing lips and seeing voices. *Nature*, *264*, 746–8.

MacKain, K., Studdert-Kennedy, M., Spieker, S. & Stern, D. (1983). Infant intermodal speech perception is a left-hemisphere function. *Science*, *219*, 1347–8.

McKenzie, B.E. & Day, R.H. (1972). Object distance as a determinant of visual fixation in early infancy. *Science*, *178*, 1108–10.

Maddieson, I. (1984). *Patterns of Sounds*. Cambridge: Cambridge University Press.

Mann, V.A. (1986). Distinguishing universal and language-dependent levels of speech perception: Evidence of Japanese listeners' perception of English "l" and "r". *Cognition*, *24*, 169–96.

Masi, W. & Scott, K. (1983). Recognition of mothers' faces by term and pre-term infants. In T. Field & A. Sostek (Ed.), *Infants Born at Risk: Physiological Perception and Cognitive Processes*. New York: Grune and Stratton.

Massaro, D.W. (1987). *Speech Perception by Eye and Ear: The Psychology of Lipreading*. Hillsdale, NJ: Lawrence Erlbaum Associates Inc.

Massaro, D.W. (1995). Modelling the perception of bimodal speech. *Proceedings of the International Congress of Phonetic Sciences, Stockholm*, *3*, 106–13.

Massaro, D.W. (1996). Bimodal speech perception: A progress report. In D.G. Stork & M.E. Hennecke (Eds), *Speechreading by Humans and Machines*. Berlin: Springer-Verlag.

Massaro, D.W., Cohen, M.M., Gesi, A., Heredia, R. & Tsuzaki, M. (1993). Bimodal speech perception: An examination across languages. *Journal of Phonetics, 21,* 445–78.

Maurer, D. (1985). Infants' perception of facedness. In T. Field & N.A. Fox (Eds), *Social Perception in Infancy.* Norwood, NJ: Ablex.

Maurer, D. & Salapatek, P. (1976). Developmental changes in the scanning of faces by young infants. *Child Development, 47,* 523–7.

Melhuish, E.C. (1982). Visual attention to mother's and stranger's faces and facial contrast in 1-month-old infants. *Developmental Psychology, 18,* 229–31.

Miller, C.L. (1983). Developmental changes in male/female voice classification by infants. *Infant Behavior and Development, 6,* 313–30.

Miller, J.D., Weir, C.C., Pastore, R., Kelly, W.J. & Dooling, R.J. (1976). Discrimination and labelling of noise-buzz sequences with varying noise-lead times An example of categorical perception. *Journal of the Acoustical Society of America, 60,* 410–17.

Mills, A.E. (1987). The development of phonology in the blind child. In B. Dodd & R. Campbell (Eds), *Hearing by Eye: The Psychology of Lipreading.* Hove, UK: Lawrence Erlbaum Associates Ltd.

Mills, A.E. & Thiem, R. (1980). Auditory-visual fusions and illusions in speech perception. *Linguistische Berichte, 68/80,* 85–108.

Morton, J. & Johnson, M.H. (1991). CONSPEC, CONLERN and the development of face recognition in the infant. *Psychological Review, 98,* 164–81.

Muir, D. (1985). The development of infants' auditory spatial sensitivity. In S.E. Trehub & B. Schneider (Eds), *Auditory Development in Infancy.* New York: Plenum.

Muir, D. & Field, J. (1979). Newborn infants orient to sounds. *Child Development, 50,* 431–6.

Muir, D., Clifton, R.K. & Clarkson, M.G. (1989). The development of a human auditory localization response: A U-shaped function. *Canadian Journal of Psychology, 43,* 199–216.

Nottle, E. (1980). Visual facial discrimination of mother and female stranger by young infants. Unpublished honours thesis: Department of Psychology, Monash University.

Pettersen, L. Yonas, A. & Fisch, R.O. (1980). The development of blinking in response to impending collision in pre-term, full-term, and post-term infants. *Infant Behavior and Development, 3,* 155–65.

Pickens, J., Field, T., Nawrocki, T., Martinez, A., Soutullo, D. & Gonzalez, J. (1994). Full-term and pre-term infants' perception of face voice-voice synchrony. *Infant Behavior and Development, 17,* 447–55.

Pisoni, D.B. (1977). Identification and discrimination of the relative onset time of two component tones: Implications for voicing perception in stops. *Journal of the Acoustical Society of America, 61,* 1352–61.

Polka, L. (1995). Developmental patterns in infant speech perception. *Proceedings of the International Congress of Phonetic Sciences, Stockholm, 2,* 148–55.

Polka, L. & Bohn, O-S. (1996). A cross-language comparison of vowel perception in English-learning and German-learning infants. *Journal of the Acoustical Society of America, 100,* 577–92.

Polka, L. & Werker, J.F. (1994). Developmental changes in perception of nonnative vowel contrasts. *Journal of Experimental Psychology: Human Perception and Performance, 19,* 421–35.

Querleu, D. & Renard, X. (1981). Les perceptions auditives du fetus humain. *Medicine and Hygiene, 39,* 2101–10.

Querleu, D., Renard, X., Versyp, F., Paris-Delrue, L. & Crepin, G. (1988). Fetal hearing. *European Journal of Obstetrics and Gynaecology and Reproductive Biology, 29,* 191–212.

Robert-Ribes, J., Piquemal, M., Schwartz, J-L. & Escudier, P. (1996). Exploiting sensor fusion architectures and stimuli complementarity in AV speech recognition. In D.G. Stork & M.E. Hennecke (Eds), *Speechreading by Humans and Machines.* Berlin: Springer-Verlag.

Robert-Ribes, J., Schwartz, J-L., Escudier, P. (1995). Auditory, visual, and audiovisual vowel representations: Experiments and modelling. *Proceedings of the International Congress of Phonetic Sciences*, Stockholm, *3*, 114–21.

Rose, S.A. (1980). Enhancing visual recognition memory in pre-term infants. *Developmental Psychology*, *16*, 85–92.

Rose, S.A., Gottfried, A.W. & Bridger, W.H. (1978). Cross-modal transfer in infants: Relationship to prematurity and socioeconomic background. *Developmental Psychology*, *14*, 643–52.

Rose, S.A., Gottfried, A.W. & Bridger, W.H. (1979). Effects of haptic cues on visual recognition memory in full-term and pre-term infants. *Infant Behavior and Development*, *2*, 55–7.

Salapatek, P. (1975). Pattern perception in early infancy. In L.B. Cohen & P. Salapatek (Eds), *Infant Perception: From Sensation to Cognition Vol. 1: Basic Visual Processes*. Orlando, Fl: Academic Press.

Sekiyama, K. (1994). Differences in auditory-visual speech perception between Japanese and Americans: McGurk effect as a function of incompatibility. *Journal of the Acoustical Society of Japan*, *15*, 143–58.

Sekiyama, K. (1996). Cultural and linguistic factors in auditovisual speech processing: The McGurk effect in Chinese subjects. *Perception and Psychophysics*, *59*, 73.

Sekiyama, K. & Tohkura, Y. (1991). McGurk effect in non-English listeners: Few visual effects for Japanese subjects hearing Japanese syllables of high auditory intelligibility. *Journal of the Acoustical Society of America*, *90*, 1797–1805.

Sekiyama, K. & Tohkura, Y. (1993). Inter-language differences in the influence of visual cues in speech perception. *Journal of Phonetics*, *21*, 427–44.

Sekiyama, K., Braida, L.D., Nishino, K., Hayashi, M. & Tuyo, M.M. (1995). The McGurk effect in Japanese and American perceivers. *Proceedings of the International Congress of Phonetic Sciences*, Stockholm, *4*, 214–17.

Sekiyama, K., Tohkura, Y. & Umeda, M. (1996). A few factors which affect the degree of incorporating lip-read information into speech perception. *Proceedings of the Fourth International Conference on Spoken Language Processing*, Philadelphia, *3*, 1481–4.

Sherrod, L.R. (1979). Social cognition in infants: Attention to the human face. *Infant Behavior and Development*, *2*, 279–94.

Spelke, E. (1976). Infants' intermodal perception of events. *Cognitive Psychology*, *8*, 53–60.

Spelke, E.S. (1979). Perceiving bimodally specified events in infancy. *Developmental Psychology*, *15*, 626–36.

Spelke, E.S. & Owsley, C.J. (1979). Intermodal exploration and knowledge in infancy. *Infant Behavior and Development*, *2*, 13–27.

Streeter, L.A. (1976). Language perception of 2-month-old infants shows effects of both innate mechanisms and experience. *Nature*, *259*, 39–41.

Studdert-Kennedy, M. (1986). Development of the speech perceptuomotor system. In B. Lindblom & R. Zetterstrom (Eds), *Precursors of Early Speech*. New York: Stockton Press.

Studdert-Kennedy, M. & Goodell, E.W. (1992). Gestures, features and segments in early child speech. *Haskins Laboratories Status Report on Speech Perception*, *SR-111/112*, 89–102.

Summerfield, A.Q. (1987). Some preliminaries to a comprehensive account of audio-visual speech perception. In B. Dodd & R. Campbell (Eds), *Hearing by Eye: The Psychology of Lip-reading*. Hove, UK: Lawrence Erlbaum Associates Ltd.

Thein-Tun, U. & Burnham, D. (1994). The nature of information processing in speech perception. In R. Togneri (Ed.), *Proceedings of the Fifth Australian International Conference on Speech Science and Technology*, *2*, 430–5.

Tronick, E. (1972). Stimulus control and the growth of the infants' effective visual field. *Perception and Psychophysics*, *11*, 373–6.

van Son, N., Huiskamp, T.M., Bosman, A.J. & Smoorenburg, G.F. (1994). Viseme classifications of Dutch consonants and vowels. *Journal of the Acoustical Society of America, 96*, 1341–55.

Wagner, S.H. & Sakovits, L.J. (1986). A process analysis of infant visual and cross-modal recognition memory: Implications for an amodal code. In L. Lipsitt & C. Rovee-Collier (Eds), *Advances in Infancy Research, IV*. New Jersey: Ablex.

Walker-Andrews, A.S. & Gibson, E.J. (1986). What develops in bimodal perception? In L. Lipsitt & C. Rovee-Collier (Eds), *Advances in Infancy Research, IV*. New Jersey: Ablex.

Walker-Andrews, A.S., Bahrick, L.E., Raglioni, S.S. & Diaz, I. (1991). Infants' bimodal perception of gender. *Ecological Psychology, 3*, 55–75.

Werker, J.F. (1994). Cross-language speech perception: Developmental change does not involve loss. In J.C. Goodman & H.L. Nusbaum (Eds.), *The development of speech perception: The transition from speech sounds to spoken words*. Cambridge, MA: MIT Press.

Werker, J.F. & Lalonde, C.E. (1988). Cross-language speech perception: Initial capabilities and developmental change. *Developmental Psychology, 24*, 672–83.

Werker, J.F. & Logan, J.S. (1985). Cross-language evidence for three factors in speech perception. *Perception and Psychophysics, 37*, 35–44.

Werker, J.F. & Tees, R.C. (1983). Developmental changes across childhood in the perception of non-native speech sounds. *Canadian Journal of Psychology, 37*, 278–86.

Werker, J.F. & Tees (1984a). Cross language speech perception: Evidence for perceptual reorganization during the first year of life. *Infant and Behavior and Development, 7*, 49–63.

Werker, J.F. & Tees (1984b). Phonemic and phonetic factors in adult cross-language speech perception. *Journal of the Acoustical Society of America, 75*, 1866–78.

Werker, J.F., Frost, P. & McGurk, H. (1992). Cross-language influences on bimodal speech perception. *Canadian Journal of Psychology, 46*, 551–68.

Werker, J.F., Gilbert, J.H.V., Humphrey, K. & Tees, R.C. (1981). Development aspects of cross-language speech perception. *Child Development, 52*, 349–55.

Whitfield, I.C., Cranford, J., Ravizza R. & Diamond, I.T. (1972). Effects of unilateral ablation of auditory cortex in cat on complex sound localization. *Journal of Neurophysiology, 35*, 718–31.

Whitfield, I.C., Diamond, K., Chiveralls, K. & Williamson T.G. (1978). Some further observations on the effects of unilateral cortical ablation on sound localization in the cat. *Experimental Brain Research, 31*, 221–34.

Yakovlev, P. & Lecours, A. (1967). The myelogenetic cycles of regional maturation of the brain. In A. Minkowski (Ed.), *Regional Development of the Brain in Early Life*. Philadelphia: Davis.

Yin, R.K. (1978). Face perception: A review of experiments with infants, normal adults, and brain-injured persons. In R. Held, H.W. Leibowitz & H.-L. Teuber (Eds.), *Handbook of Sensory Physiology (8)* Berlin: Springer-Verlag.

CHAPTER THREE

Time-varying information for visual speech perception

Lawrence D. Rosenblum   *University of California, Riverside, California, USA*

Helena M. Saldaña   *House Ear Institute, Los Angeles, California, USA*

INTRODUCTION

In recent years, a number of theories of speechreading and audio-visual speech integration have been developed. Although many of these accounts give an adequate description of the processes used for visual speech recognition and integration, they often take as their starting point abstract descriptions of the information available to the system. We propose that the form of the information utilized by the system largely constrains the processes and should, therefore, be an important part of any theory of visual speech perception. We acknowledge the difficulty of identifying the metric of the source information and, therefore, set out to differentiate the type of information available in very broad strokes. At an elementary level, the information for visual speech perception can be described in two distinct ways. Information can be described as time-independent (static; pictorial) or time-varying (kinematic; dynamic).[1] In this chapter we will outline the evidence for both descriptions.

We believe that a consideration of visual speech information is not only important for those interested in speechreading, but also for researchers concerned with general auditory speech perception. In his influential chapter from the first volume of this series Summerfield wrote: "any comprehensive account of how speech is perceived should encompass audio-visual speech perception. The ability to see as well as hear has to be integral to the design, not merely a retro-fitted after-thought" (1987, p. 47). Since then, the issue of visual information in spoken language processing has received a great deal of interest from theorists typically interested in auditory speech perception. This is probably due to increasing evidence that language processing is a multi-modal affair. In addition to the now famous demonstration that visual information can influence heard speech (McGurk & McDonald, 1976), there is mounting evidence that listeners make use of visual information to increase speech intelligibility (for reviews, see MacLeod & Summerfield, 1987; Rosenblum, Johnson & Saldaña, 1996).

Another reason auditory speech researchers should be concerned with this issue is that it could allow them to gain perspective on how information is construed in a modality with (potentially) different spatial, temporal, and sensory characteristics. For example, whereas acoustic information is necessarily spread over time, visual information is often considered to be spread over space. This might imply that the information for the two modalities is of a different form. However, we will propose that the relevant forms of auditory and visual speech information are fundamentally the same in that both forms can and should be described as time-varying. This is not to say that speechreaders cannot make use of static/pictorial information. Rather, we believe that the primary information that is utilized by the system is time-varying in nature. Our argument will be built on recent research on visual speech perception conducted in our laboratory and others as well as analogous research in auditory speech and visual event perception.

TIME-INDEPENDENT AND TIME-VARYING VISUAL SPEECH INFORMATION

While there has been a great deal of research identifying the salient information for auditory speech, there has been relatively little work on visual speech information. Most descriptions of visual speech information have involved static facial positions, such as (visual information for) lip shape, place of cavity constriction, and visible teeth (Montgomery & Jackson, 1983; Petajan, 1984; Summerfield & McGrath 1984; McGrath, 1985; Massaro & Cohen, 1990; Braida, 1991). For example, Montgomery and Jackson (1983) described the visual information for vowels in terms of a scaling space representing the degree of lip spreading/rounding and tongue height. These features are statically defined in that they can be captured in a still photograph. This description of features also assumes that the goal of vowel production is to approximate steady-state articulator positions. In a subsequent section, we will discuss how this assumption has been discredited from the perspective of auditory speech perception.

We can think of two reasons why most existent descriptions of visual speech are based on time-independent facial forms. First, visual speech information is conveyed by the face. Intuition, as well as research, suggests that we perceive faces by recognizing static features. Evidence shows that the shape and configuration of the eyes, nose, and mouth, as well as the skin tone, hair, and the overall shape of the face, can be used for face recognition (for a review, see Bruce, 1988). Second, the majority of research on general visual perception has concerned the perception of forms and objects (for a review, see Marr, 1982). Accordingly, cues for visual perception are usually described as pictorial/time-independent features. It could be then, that most descriptions of visual speech information have been (tacitly) based on descriptions of general visual and face perception information.

Not surprisingly, there is evidence that static/time-independent features can convey some visual speech information. Campbell and her colleagues (Campbell, 1986; Campbell, Landis & Regard, 1986) have shown that observers can identify some vowels and consonants from photographs of faces posturing articulatory positions. This fact has been used as support that visual speech information is static or pictorial in nature. However, simply because observers can make use of pictorial information in a laboratory setting does not imply that this is the informational form the visual speech system prefers to work with. This point will be echoed later with regard to auditory speech information.

An alternative view of visual speech suggests that time-varying aspects of visible speech can provide robust information for the perceiver. In one of the first studies to examine this issue, Brooke and Summerfield (1983) performed analyses of lip and jaw movement during production of /VCV/ syllables. They found that phonetic differences were observable in the time-varying differences of these movements. They then used the information gained from these analyses to produce computer-generated facial displays. They found that these displays could convey some vowel information to subjects. Brooke and Summerfield concluded that time-varying parameters could be salient features for speechreading.

Before discussing more recent evidence for time-varying visual speech information, we will review the evidence for time-varying information in the areas of auditory speech and visual event perception. Turning to these fields at this point will allow us to borrow conceptual and methodological tools needed to build our argument.

TIME-VARYING AUDITORY SPEECH INFORMATION

Traditionally, auditory speech information has been construed as relatively discrete in nature. While acoustic structure necessarily occurs over time, many traditional speech cues have been thought of as temporally-limited and relatively unchanging. Examples of these cues include steady-state formant properties and onset spectral composition (e.g. noise bursts) (Liberman & Studdert-Kennedy, 1978). However, recent research has revealed that time-varying parameters of the acoustic signal can be salient. For example, there is evidence that signals which do not involve the traditional cues of formants, transitions, and noise bursts can still be understood as speech (Remez et al., 1981). These signals are composed of a set of sine-waves synthesized to track the pitch and amplitudes of the center formant frequencies of an utterance. This 'sine-wave speech' can be understood well enough for listeners to transcribe sentences and can induce perceptual effects (e.g. vowel normalization, consonantal context effects) characteristic of natural speech stimuli (Remez et al., 1987; Williams, Verbrugge & Studdert-Kennedy, 1983).

Although sinewave speech phenomena show that there is salient information in time-varying aspects of signal dimensions, they leave open the question of the relative salience of these versus more static cues. This issue has been addressed more directly in critiques of vowel target theory. Target theory proposes that vowels, as intended, are best described as static, sustained postures of the vocal tract (Joos, 1948; Ladefoged & Broadbent, 1957; Lieberman, Crelin & Klatt, 1972). From this perspective, the acoustic information for vowels is comprised of steady-state formant values associated with static articulator positions. However, Jenkins (1987) and others (House & Fairbanks, 1953; Lindblom, 1963) have pointed out that natural production of vowels are affected by factors such as the rapidity of production, coarticulation, and articulator inertia. These factors cause vowels to rarely achieve target positions and to produce acoustic signals which only briefly (if at all) reach target formant values. Nonetheless, target theory would maintain that since the goal of vowel production is to provide information which is stable and unchanging, then the best information for vowels should be in the least coarticulated, steady-state, parts of the signal.

In fact, evidence suggests that the steady-state vowel portions of the signal are not the most informative. For example, Strange and her colleagues (Strange et al., 1976; Verbrugge et al., 1976) have found that listeners are better at identifying vowels that are produced in a CVC context than those produced in isolation—even though the formants of isolated vowels are necessarily closer to canonical target values. Also, Strange and her colleagues (Strange, Jenkins & Johnson, 1983) have found that up to 60% of a vowel nucleus can be deleted without seriously jeopardizing identification of vowels in a CVC context. Apparently, the most salient vowel information is available in the transitions into and out of the syllable nucleus. In other words, the most useful information seems to be in the most coarticulated portions of the signal. This seems to also be the case for consonants: context-independent spectral information for a stop-release is not as informative as the (vowel) context-dependent transitions (Blumstein, Isaacs & Mertus, 1982; Walley & Carrell, 1983).

Fowler (1987) has speculated on why the most time-varying/coarticulated parts of the signal provide the best information for segments. First, she proposes that segments—as intended, produced, acoustically instantiated, and perceived—should be considered dynamic gestures rather than as the static/abstract segments endemic to most traditional (e.g. target) theories (see also Browman & Goldstein, 1986). Thus, it would not be surprising that the time-varying aspects of the signal would be most informative for dynamic perceptual objects. Second, Fowler proposes that the coarticulated parts of the signal provide information about overlapping consonant and vowel gestures. She suggests that slow global changes in the acoustic signal correspond to the slow global changes of the vocal tract used for vowel production. Superimposed on this are more quickly changing dimensions of the signal that correspond to the quick vocal tract changes used for consonant production. Potentially then, listeners can perceive segments by performing an auditory 'vector analysis' through which they parse the slow and fast changing parts of the signal. Since the fast (consonantal) changes in the signal would be most conspicuous when in the context of the slower (vowel) changes, perceivers would be best off attending to the most coarticulated/time-varying parts of the signal.

Thus, many contemporary speech researchers now consider the primary information for auditory speech to be time-varying. The primacy of time-varying over time-independent information is reflected in the comment of Remez et al. that: "traditional speech cues are themselves approximations of second-order signal properties to which listeners attend when they perceive speech" (1981, p.212). In other words, static cues (e.g. sustained vowel formants) might be informative in some contexts just as a snapshot of an event (e.g. swinging a baseball bat) might be informative about that event to some degree. However, static speech cues, like photographs, are impoverished approximations of the time-varying information and are not what perceptual systems have evolved to recover.

This argument has implications for visual speech perception. Many existing characterizations of visual speech information are analogous to older characterizations of auditory speech features. As stated, information has been described in terms of lip shape, visible tongue height, place of cavity constriction, and visible teeth (Montgomery & Jackson, 1983; Petajan, 1984; Summerfield & McGrath 1984; McGrath, 1985; Massaro & Cohen, 1990; Braida, 1991). These descriptions for static target values are similar to the target values originally believed to underlie auditory speech perception. Target theories in auditory speech perception have been largely rejected by researchers based on two factors:

1. empirical evidence that the time-varying/coarticulated information is the most salient part of the signal
2. the conceptualization of speech events as gestural.

Should these factors influence our conceptualization of visual speech information? We believe that the relative salience of time-varying and time-independent information in visual speech is an empirical question, and will offer some preliminary findings which address this issue. However, with regard to 2., we believe that a conceptualization of speech events as gestural forces a serious consideration of visual information as time-varying. This follows from the fact that gestures are necessarily defined over time, therefore information for gestures which is stripped of that dimension will have to be converted back to a time-dependent representation. If, however, perceptual information for visual speech is defined as time-varying, then the conversion is not necessary.

There is another reason why considering auditory speech information as time-varying begs a similar consideration for visual speech information: audio-visual integration. Summerfield (1987) has suggested that the metric for audio-visual information at the point of integration could take an articulatorily-based, modality-neutral (amodal) form (see also Studdert-Kennedy, 1989). Potentially, this information could include time-varying patterns that are instantiated in both auditory and visual modalities which serve to specify articulatory dynamics (see Fowler and Rosenblum, 1991). Thus, the mechanism ultimately responsible for integration would be sensitive to the same general time-varying patterns in any modality. If the auditory information for integration is time-varying (as the recent evidence shows), and the visual information is similarly construed, then integration could proceed without the extra step of translating the auditory and visual information into an integratable form.

Thus, a survey of the recent auditory speech literature compels a serious consideration of time-varying visual speech information. Next, we will look to the field of visual event perception to further motivate our argument as well as to borrow some methodological techniques.

TIME-VARYING INFORMATION FOR VISUAL EVENT PERCEPTION

The majority of research on visual perception has been concerned with how forms are recovered (for a review, see Marr, 1982). However, there is literature which examines the salience of time-varying information and the primacy of visual *event* perception (Bingham, 1987; Gibson, 1979;

Johansson, 1973). There is evidence that the visual system prefers to work with time-varying stimulation and in fact, breaks down when forced to deal with a frozen image (Pritchard, Heron & Hebb, 1960). Furthermore, there is evidence that pictorial features are not needed for event recognition. Since the mid-1970s, much research has shown that isolated time-varying dimensions can provide rich information for events (Johansson, 1973; Runeson, 1977; Bingham, 1987; Bingham, Rosenblum & Schmidt, 1995). In the classic demonstrations, time-varying properties are isolated by attaching small lights to the major joints of a darkened actor's body (Johansson, 1973). The actor is then videotaped performing various activities in the dark and these videotapes are presented to subjects through a contrast-adjusted video monitor so that only the movement of the lights can be seen. These 'point-light' displays have been shown to convey rich information about the performed action (Johansson, 1973), the gender of the actor (Kozlowski & Cutting, 1977), the amount of lifted weight (Runeson & Frykholm, 1981; Bingham, 1987), as well as various inanimate events (Bingham, Rosenblum & Schmidt, 1995). The point-light technique has also been applied to human faces to show that emotional expressiveness, age-related "person qualities", and face identity can be recovered from these displays (Bassili, 1978; Berry, 1990; Bruce & Valentine, 1988; Yakel & Rosenblum, 1996).

Importantly, point-light stimuli can not be recognized when frozen in time, suggesting that they lack adequate static/pictorial cues. Thus, these phenomena demonstrate that time-varying information—isolated from static pictorial cues—is sufficient to specify events. It has been suggested that observers are able to recover event details from point-light displays through a visual vector analysis (Johansson, 1973; Börjesson & Von Hofsten, 1975). For example, a point-light walker moving forward forms a common motion vector for all the points as well as specific vectors associated with the points on the (swinging) limb joints. By separately detecting the common and joint-specific vectors, the perceiver could recover the general event along with its detail (e.g. walker gender). In fact, it is this sort of vector analysis explanation that Fowler (1987) cites as inspiration for her model of vowel and consonant gesture recovery (outlined earlier).

In summary, much recent research in visual perception has emphasized the primacy of events along with their specifying time-varying information. This fact, along with the previous discussion of auditory speech information, motivates the question of whether time-varying information for an articulating face might be salient for speechreading. As mentioned, there is evidence that the static, time-independent information available in photographs can be used for speechreading (Campbell, 1986). Might isolated time-varying visual speech information also be useful? Next, we will report on a series of experiments that make use of the point-light technique to answer this question.

EXPERIMENTS ON POINT-LIGHT VISUAL SPEECH

Summerfield (1979) used a point-light methodology to test whether visible lip motion could help observers better hear speech against a background of interfering prose. He placed four point-lights on the lips: one each at the center of the upper and lower lip, and one at each lip corner. He found that although observers were able to see moving lips from these displays, the point-lights only marginally improved comprehension. These findings have been interpreted as evidence that lip movements alone do not provide sufficient visual speech information and that some aspect of texture and/or form needs to be seen (Campbell, 1989).

However, we have recently found evidence for successful point-light specification of speech events (Rosenblum & Saldaña, 1996; Rosenblum, Johnson & Saldaña, in press; Rosenblum, Johnson & Mahmood, in preparation). Our point-light displays involve more—and more strategically placed—points than those used by Summerfield (1979). Our selection of point-light positions is based on previous research which used the technique for speech and nonspeech demonstrations (Bassili, 1978; Berry, 1990; Brooke & Summerfield, 1983). In addition, we now know that speechreaders make use of more than lip information (McGrath, 1985; Vatikiotis-Bateson, Eigsti & Yando, 1994). Accordingly, we often place dots on the lips, cheeks, and chin, as well as on the teeth and tongue-tip.

To create our point-light displays, the inside of an actor's mouth is made black with food coloring and theatrical tooth paint. The points are constructed of 3 mm diameter paper dots which are painted with fluorescent yellow paint. The dots are applied to features of the face with medical adhesive (on the face) and dental adhesive (on the teeth and tongue). The actor is then asked to articulate speech material under fluorescent black light illumination. This technique produces video-recorded images in which only the dots and their movements can be seen.

We will next present two experiments which demonstrate the salience of our point-light speech displays. This will be followed by discussions of whether point-light speech recovery occurs through normal perceptual operations, as well as how these stimuli fair relative to static speech stimuli.

Point-light information for enhancing speech in noise and consonant speechreading

As a follow-up to Summerfield's study, we tested whether different point-light configurations could enhance speech in noise (Rosenblum, Johnson & Saldaña, 1996). While Summerfield (1979) only used points on the lips, we tested three different point-light configurations which extended beyond the lips (see Figure 6). We found that each of these point configurations

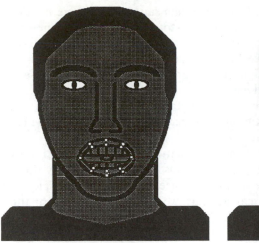

(a)   (b)

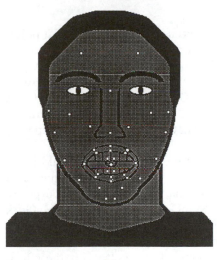

(c)

FIG. 6.   Schematic representation of three
point-light configurations.

significantly helped normal hearing adults recover sentences embedded in white noise. This held true for the lips-only points condition (Figure 6a) suggesting our configuration was more informative than that used by Summerfield (1979). In addition, adding points to the teeth and tongue (Figure 6b) substantially improved performance, whereas adding points to facial features outside the mouth (Figure 6c) did not significantly improve performance over the lips, teeth, and tongue configuration. (For speculation about why the various configurations were differentially effective, see

Rosenblum et al., 1996.) Overall, these results suggest that there is salient information available in point-light displays to enhance speech in noise.

We have conducted other experiments to test whether point-light speech can be used for a straight speechreading task (Rosenblum et al., in preparation). The three point configurations portrayed in Figure 6 were used to test whether consonants could be perceived in CV contexts. Our results show that, much like the speech in noise performance, observers are able to recover segments from these stimuli, with accuracy dependent on the configuration and number of points.

The results of our experiments suggest that there is visual speech information available in point-light stimuli. Because observers typically do not interpret frozen images of these stimuli as a face, there is not static/pictorial information available in these images. Thus, we believe that the information available in our point-light stimuli is time-varying in nature.

Point-light speech information for influencing heard speech

Our speechreading and speech in noise experiments demonstrate that point-light displays can be used for visual speech recovery. However, it could be that these stimuli are recovered through processes which are not truly *perceptual*. Possibly, use of point-light stimuli involves some conscious, attention-demanding, post-perceptual process. Our observers might approach point-light speech recognition as a problem-solving task: an operation which is certainly less perceptual than what is used for normal speech-reading.

To address this issue, we tested whether point-light stimuli could influence perception when observers are not asked to make explicit judgments on the images themselves (Rosenblum & Saldaña, 1996). For these purposes, we used the McGurk effect (McGurk & MacDonald, 1976). In the McGurk effect, visual speech information is found to integrate and even override discrepant auditory speech information (for more thorough descriptions of the effect, see Green & Jordan, this volume). Importantly, for the effect, visual speech influences perception even when observers are asked to base their judgments on the auditory component. The effect is also robust to the extent that it works even if the observer is completely aware of the discrepancy in the stimuli. In this way, the effect is generally considered a true perceptual phenomenon, and not one based on post-perceptual decision processes (Liberman & Mattingly, 1985; McGrath, 1985; Rosenblum & Saldaña, 1992; Summerfield et al., 1989).

For our McGurk point-light test, an audio /ba/ was dubbed with a visual /va/. The point-light stimulus comprised 28 points arranged in a way fairly similar to that portrayed in Figure 6c. Results showed that naïve observers displayed a significant visual influence ("va" responses) 55% of the time. Interestingly, post-experiment interviews revealed that even subjects who never recognized the stimuli as a face still showed a significant visual influence. This suggests that explicit knowledge of the point-light stimuli as a face is not needed for an influence to occur. A follow-up experiment supported this suggestion by showing that subjects who were given explicit information about the visual stimulus (how it was created and where the points were placed) showed the same degree of visual influence as the naïve observers.

Thus, we believe that the information available in point-light displays allows for recovery through visual speech *perception*. As there is insufficient pictorial information in these displays to be recognizable when static, their effectiveness seems based on time-varying information. Possibly, observers perceive speech from these displays by performing a visual vector analysis (Johansson, 1973), whose goal is to recover the types of speech events considered by Fowler (Fowler, 1987).

Relative salience of point-light and static visual speech

While our point-light experiments demonstrate that time-varying visual information can specify speech events, they do not directly address the question of the relative salience of time-varying and time-independent information. However, we believe that considering further details of our results could be illuminating in this regard.

First, it is the case that our point-light stimuli were never as effective as the analogous fully-illuminated moving face stimuli. Thus, none of the point-light configurations were able to enhance speech in noise, specify consonant visemes, and influence heard speech to the same degree as a fully-illuminated moving face. This is an important point which we do not take lightly. After all, it could be that the time-independent static features (e.g. textures of the surfaces of the teeth, tongue, lips, and facial skin) provided in fully-illuminated displays are indispensable. However, this need not be the case. Possibly, our reduced point-light effects are a consequence of point arrangements which are less than optimal for capturing all of the salient time-varying information. It is known that point-light placement is important for accurate portrayal of full-body activities (Runeson, 1993). It could be that another arrangement of points on the face would provide enhancement equivalent to fully-illuminated faces.

It is also possible that the differential effectiveness of fully-illuminated and point-light displays is simply a consequence of experience with the two types of stimuli. Observers have infinitely more experience with fully-illuminated speaking faces. Given that our point-light placement might not be optimal, it could take some time for observers to extract the necessary time-varying information from our displays. In fact, we have found evidence in all of our experiments for learning effects with point-light stimuli—either through simple experience with the stimuli (Rosenblum, Johnson & Saldaña, 1996; Rosenblum et al., in preparation) or through priming with fully-illuminated faces (Rosenblum & Saldaña, 1996). In fact, we found that after three hours of experience, the point configuration portrayed in Figure 6c enhanced speech in noise recovery nearly as much as a fully-illuminated face (after one hour of experience).

There is another reason we believe that the superiority of fully-illuminated faces is not necessarily based on the availability of static/pictorial information. This reason is based on results of two follow-up experiments from the McGurk effect project (Rosenblum & Saldaña, 1996). Recall that the first two experiments showed that point-light displays are treated as real visual speech to the extent that they can influence heard speech. Two follow-up experiments tested whether static (fully-illuminated) speech displays could influence heard speech in the same way. We reasoned that if time-independent speech information is similarly informative, then a visual influence would be observed for these stimuli. The static stimulus we chose was of a /va/ articulation captured at the point just prior to release of the labio-dental constriction. Observers had no problem speechreading this stimulus as a 'va'. However, when it was paired with an audio /ba/ (and observers were clear on the instructions), the influence of the visual stimulus was negligible.

The fact that static visual speech does not integrate with auditory speech suggests that it might not be recovered through normal perceptual processes. This would confirm our (the authors') phenomenological experience that static speech displays are recognized through some type of post-perceptual, problem-solving operation. These results also suggest that the observed point-light effects were not based on a process that made reference to static facial features. We believe that the salient aspect of point-light displays is not that they contain any pictorial aspects of a face, but that they contain relevant time-varying articulatory information.

ADDITIONAL EVIDENCE FOR TIME-VARYING INFORMATION

There is other recent evidence for the primacy of time-varying speech information. Vitkovitch, Barber and their colleagues (Barber et al., 1990; Vitkovitch & Barber, 1994) have tested the effect of presentation frame-rate of visual speech stimuli. These authors found that stimuli presented at faster frame rates (e.g. 16.5; 30Hz) are much better at conveying visual speech than images presented at slower rates (8.3; 12.5Hz). They conclude that specific visual information becomes available with increases in the temporal resolution of the stimulus. It would seem that a likely candidate for this information would be time-varying patterns. Next, work by Goldschen (1993) has tested the relative salience of 35 static and time-varying features of the oral cavity for automatic speechreading. By applying a principle component analysis, he found that the 13 most informative features were time-varying in nature.

There is also evidence that observers are sensitive to coarticulatory properties of visual speech. Benguerel and Pichora-Fuller (1982) found evidence that vowel context significantly affects accuracy for identifying visible consonants. Relatedly, Cathiard and her colleagues (Cathiard & Lallouache, 1992; Cathiard et al., 1995) have shown that there is visual information for vowels available up to 160ms before the (acoustic) voicing onset of that vowel. In fact, these authors claim that in many cases, visual information for a segment is available long before the auditory information for that segment. Regardless, this research shows that visible segmental information can be spread beyond the 'steady-state' portion of that segment.

Recent work using the McGurk effect also demonstrates that observers are sensitive to coarticulatory information when integrating audio-visual speech. Green and Gerdeman (1995) found that when vowels are audio-visually discrepant (e.g. audio /bi/ + visual /ga/), the magnitude of the consonantal McGurk effect (audio /b/ + visual /g/ = perceived /d/) is reduced relative to when the vowels were the same (e.g. audio /ba/ + visual /ga/). These authors conclude that the perceptual system is sensitive to cross-modal discrepancies in coarticulatory information. They state that their results are also consistent with the notion that time-varying (versus static) information, spread over the consonant and vowel, is extracted from both modalities during integration. Green has given a similar interpretation for his finding that manipulation of formant transitions has a substantially greater impact on the McGurk effect than manipulation of aspiration and bursts (Green & Norrix, submitted). By adopting a time-varying perspective on both auditory and visual information, these authors provide a parsimonious interpretation of integration.

RECENT ARGUMENTS AGAINST TIME-VARYING INFORMATION

A number of recent reports have criticized the proposed primacy of time-varying information (Cohen, Walker & Massaro, 1996; Benoît et al., 1995; Campbell, 1996; Campbell et al., submitted). Since most of these papers present preliminary data, we will address them only in so far as they allow us to sketch our anticipated replies. For the most part, the arguments in these papers are based on three general types of results. First, a number of papers report equivalent results for static and (fully-illuminated) moving visual speech displays (Benoit et al., 1995; Campbell, 1996; Cathiard, Tiberghien & Abry, 1992; Cathiard & Tiberghien, 1994). For example, both Cathiard et al. (1992; 1995) and Campbell (1996) have reported significant McGurk effect influences with static (or very low frame rate) displays. These results would seem at odds with our static display McGurk results (Rosenblum & Saldaña, 1996). In fact, we found that if subjects are unclear on the task, results suggesting a static display effect can be obtained (Rosenblum & Saldaña, 1996). If, however, subjects are further informed of the task by first judging the standard moving (fully-illuminated) stimuli, no static stimulus influence occurs. (This manipulation does not degrade the influence of point-light stimuli.) To us, this suggests that static stimuli do not truly integrate with auditory speech in the same way as normal dynamic and point-light stimuli. It is possible that the static display influences reported by Campbell (1996) and Cathiard et al., (1992; 1995) are a result of subjects misunderstanding the task.

The second type of results cited as evidence against the primacy of time-varying information portray poor relative performance with point-light—or other reduced dynamic—displays (Campbell, 1996; Campbell et al., submitted; Cohen et al., 1997). For example, Cohen et al. (1997) found less segmental recovery with synthetic point-light versus full face displays, and conclude that isolated time-varying properties are not sufficiently informative. Similarly, Campbell (1996; Campbell et al., submitted) found that brightness reversed (negative image) dynamic displays could not be speechread and did not influence auditory speech in a McGurk test. She argues that since these displays should maintain the same face-feature landmarks (that could serve as point-trajectories) as those contained in normal displays, these results show that time-varying dimensions are not sufficient.

In responding to this class of arguments, we would like to make an important clarifying point about time-varying information. We would never claim that *any* time-varying facial display would provide salient speech information. Instead, we simply claim that the most salient information available for visible speech takes the form of *some* time-varying dimensions. Thus, although Campbell's brightness reversed (and Cohen et al.'s synthetic point-light) displays do portray some time-varying dimensions, they might not capture the most salient time-varying speech *information*. Certainly, a similar argument would be made for time-varying information outside the realm of visual speech. As stated, point-light specification of full-body actions requires a specific placement of the points. With regard to auditory speech, although the center formant frequency trajectories of sinewave speech can provide sufficient information, it is likely that other isolated time-varying dimensions of the signal would not (e.g. F0; F2 bandwidth).

The third type of results cited as evidence against the primacy of time-varying information is from neuropsychological research. Campbell (1996; Campbell, et al. submitted) has reported on the speechreading abilities of patients with lesions in visual cortex. Some of these patients have damage to areas thought to be responsible for form perception, and although they have intact motion perception, show no speechreading (and audio-visual integration) ability. Other patients are reported to have no motion perception but are able to speechread from still photographs. Campbell (1996) concludes that motion perception may help in speechreading when some form perception is intact, but it is not in itself sufficient when form perception is absent.

We believe that these observations should be interpreted more cautiously. First, we feel that the extreme individual differences existent for speechreading in the normal population (Demorest, Bernstein & DeHaven, submitted) needs to be considered. As we do not know the speechreading ability of these patients before their damage, it is difficult to determine if their current ability is based solely on their lesions. We, therefore, have concerns about drawing conclusions with so few subjects.

We also have concerns about drawing conclusions from the particular patients and evaluative tests Campbell discusses. Although the tests employed (e.g. direction sensitivity from random dot displays) might reveal that a subject has some spared motion perception, it might not be the sort of motion sensitivity used for extracting visual speech. The two patients reported to have intact motion perception, but no speechreading ability, had damage to areas V1 and V2. Although complex motion might be ultimately processed at V5, the extraction of component motion might occur at V1 (Movshon, 1990) and might, therefore, affect the perception of some complex motions. Additionally, damage to these areas is thought to affect stereopsis (Poggio, 1990) which is highly related to the perception of depth. Depth perception is important for identifying relative motion (e.g. between the lips and teeth), which, we have argued (Rosenblum et al., 1996), is a critical component of time-varying information. Thus, while certain tests might indicate that these patients have intact motion perception, their lesions might inhibit extraction of the complex motion information needed for speechreading.

In summary, we believe that neuropsychological research will ultimately be a useful way to test questions about time-varying information. However, we believe that conclusions should be drawn cautiously from the data currently available.

FUTURE RESEARCH AND CONCLUSIONS

Certainly, more research is needed to test the relative salience of time-varying and time-independent information. For this purpose, researchers could borrow from the analogous work conducted on auditory speech information. As mentioned, two general methodologies have been employed to test time-varying auditory information. First, sinewave speech has been used to show that stimuli that do not contain static cues can still convey speech information (Remez et al., 1981). We believe that our point-light displays provide a visual analogue to sinewave speech in extracting out time-independent/pictorial forms. Both types of stimuli demonstrate the salience of isolated time-varying speech information. Point-light displays also afford straightforward kinematic analyses for determining salient segmental information (e.g. Bingham, 1987; Bingham, Rosenblum & Schmidt, 1995). We are currently conducting kinematic analyses on our CV point-light displays (Rosenblum et al., in preparation). Uncovering the salient kinematic information for perceptually-distinct tokens should add support to the time-varying information thesis.

The second methodology used to test time-varying auditory speech information has involved isolating different portions of the signal (e.g. Strange et al., 1983). This technique has shown that the coarticulated portions of the signal are most salient. As to date, we are not aware of analogous research on visual speech. As mentioned, work by Cathiard and her colleagues (Cathiard & Lallouache, 1992; Cathiard et al., 1995) has shown that visual information for vowels can be spread widely throughout an utterance. Still, the question remains of where the most salient visual information lies. According to the time-varying information thesis, the most coarticulated portions of the utterance should be most visually salient. Specific predictions could be made based on the auditory speech findings: for example, dynamic margins around a visible vowel should be more informative than the 'steady-state' portions. Thus, examining the salience of coarticulated portions of visible speech should be a straightforward way to test time-varying information.

In conclusion, we believe that the time-varying dimensions of visible speech should be given serious consideration as the most salient informational form. This is not to say that static, time-independent features are not usable as visual speech information. Instead, we propose that the recent evidence on speechreading, auditory speech and visual event perception— along with a new conception of speech events as gestural—supports time-varying information as primary. We would encourage speech researchers to consider time-varying features as the input to their models of speechreading and audio-visual integration. Future research will reveal exactly what these features are, as well as further examine the relative salience of time-varying and time-independent information.

ACKNOWLEDGEMENTS

Preparation of this chapter was supported by NSF Grant DBS-9212225 awarded to Lawrence D. Rosenblum.

Lawrence D. Rosenblum, Department of Psychology, University of California, Riverside, Riverside, California, 92521. Helena M. Saldaña, House Ear Institute, 2100 West Third Street, Los Angeles, California, 90057.

NOTE

1. We have chosen to use the more general term "time-varying" to describe the informational form sometimes known as dynamic (Benoit et al., 1995; Green & Gerdeman, 1995) or kinematic (Rosenblum and Saldaña, 1996; Rosenblum, Johnson & Saldaña, 1996). Formally, visual (and auditory) information cannot truly be "dynamic" in that it does not contain a relevant mass component (see Runeson & Frykholm, 1981). Although the term "kinematic" is appropriate, it does not seem to be the term of choice for either visual or auditory speech researchers. The term "time-varying" provides a clear description of the changes that occur in information over the course of an utterance/event.

REFERENCES

Barber, P.J., Vitkovitch, M., Wallbott, H., Ellgring, H.E. & Kotthaus, B. (1990). Recommendations for screen display parameter settings for a videolink from a human performance perspective. *European Commission, RACE-Project*, R1086 TELEMED.

Bassili, J.N. (1978). Facial motion in the perception of faces and of emotional expression. *Journal of Experimental Psychology: Human Perception and Performance, 4*, 373–9.

Benguerel, A.P. & Pichora-Fuller, M.K. (1982). Coarticulation effects in lipreading. *Journal of Speech and Hearing Research, 25*, 600–607.

Berry, D.S. (1990). What can a moving face tell us? *Journal of Personality and Social Psychology, 58*, 1004–14.

Benoît, C., Abry, C., Cathiard, M.A., Guiard-Marigny, T. & Lallouache, M.T. (1995). Read my lips: Where? How? When? And so ... What? In B.G. Bardy, R.J. Bootsma & Y.Guiard (Eds), *Studies in Perception and Action III* (pp. 423–6).

Bingham, G.P. (1987). Scaling and kinematic form: Further investigations on the visual perception of lifted weight. *Journal of Experimental Psychology: Human Perception and Performance, 13*, 155–77.

Bingham, G.P., Rosenblum, L.D. & Schmidt, R.C. (1995). Dynamics and the orientation of kinematic forms in visual event recognition. *Journal of Experimental Psychology: Human Perception and Performance, 21(4)*, 1473–93.

Blumstein, S., Isaacs, E. & Mertus, J. (1982). The role of gross spectral shape as a perceptual cue to place of articulation in initial stop consonants. *Journal of the Acoustical Society of America, 72*, 43–50.

Börjesson, E. & Von Hofsten, C. (1975). A vector model for perceived object rotation and translation in space. *Psychology Research, 38*, 209–30.

Braida, L.D. (1991). Crossmodal integration in the identification of consonant segments. *The Quarterly Journal of Experimental Psychology, 43*, 647–77.

Brooke, N.M. & Summerfield, A.Q. (1983). Analysis, synthesis and perception of visible articulatory movements. *Journal of Phonetics, 11*, 63–76.

Browman, C.P. & Goldstein, L. (1986). Toward an articulatory phonology. In C. Ewan & J. Anderson (Eds), *Phonology Yearbook (3*, pp. 219–54). Cambridge: Cambridge University Press.

Bruce, V. (1988). *Recognising faces*. Hove, UK: Lawrence Erlbaum Associates Ltd.

Bruce, V. & Valentine, T. (1988). When a nod's as good as a wink: The role of dynamic information in facial recognition. In M.M. Gruneberg, P.E. Morris & R.N. Sykes (Eds), *Practical Aspects of Memory: Current Research and Issues (1*, pp. 169–74). New York: John Wiley & Sons.

Campbell, R. (1986). The lateralisation of lipread sounds: A first look. *Brain and Cognition, 5*, 1–21.

Campbell, R. (1989). Lipreading. In A.W. Young & H.D. Ellis (Eds), *Handbook of Research on Face Processing*. Elsevier, North-Holland.

Campbell, R. (1992a). The neuropsychology of lipreading. *Philisophical Transcriptions of the Royal Society of London, 335*, 39–45.

Campbell, R. (1992b). The neuropsychology of lipreading. In V. Bruce, A. Cowey, A.W. Ellis, & D.I. Perrett (Eds), *Processing the Facial Image* (pp. 39–45). Oxford, England: Clarendon Press/Oxford University Press.

Campbell, R. (1996). Seeing speech in space and time: Psychological and neurological findings. *Proceedings of the 4th International Conference on Spoken Language Processing, Philadelphia (University of Delaware and AI Dupont)*, 1493–1497.

Campbell, R.T., Landis, T. & Regard, M. (1986). Face recognition and lip-reading: A neurological dissociation. *Brain, 109*, 509–21.

Campbell, R., Zihl, J., Massaro, D.W., Munhall, K.G. & Cohen, M.M. (submitted). Speechreading in a patient with severe impairment in visual motion perception (akinetopsia).

Cathiard, M-A. & Lallouache, M.T. (1992). L'apport de la cinematique dans la perception visuelle de l'anticipation et de la retention labiales. *Actes des 19èmes Journées d'Études sur la Parole*, Bruxelles, 19–22.

Cathiard, M-A. & Tiberghien, G. (1994). Le visage de la parole une coherence bimodale temporalle ou configurationelle? *Psychologique Française, 39*, 357–74.

Cathiard, M-A., Lallouache, M.T., Mohamadi, T. & Abry, C. (1995). Configurational vs. temporal coherence in audio-visual speech perception. *Proceedings of the 13th International Congress of Phonetic Sciences, 3*, 218–21.

Cathiard, M-A., Tiberghien, G. & Abry, C. (1992). Face and profile identification skills for liprounding in normal-hearing French subjects. *Bulletin de la Communication Parleé, 2*, 43–58.

Cohen, M.M., Walker, R.L. & Massaro, D.W. (1997). Perception of synthetic visual speech. In D. Stork (Ed.), *Speechreading by Man and Machine: Models, Systems, and Applications*. NATO ASI workshop, Chateau de Bonas, France: Springer Verlag.

Cooper, F.S., Delattre, P.C., Liberman, A.L. & Gerstman, L.J. (1952). Some experiments on the perception of synthetic speech sounds. *Journal of the Acoustical Society of America, 24*, 597–606.

Delattre, P., Liberman, A.M. & Cooper, F.S. (1955). Acoustic loci and transitional cues for consonants. *Journal of the Acoustical Society of America, 27*, 769–73.

Delattre, P., Liberman, A.M., Cooper, F.S. and Gerstman, L.J. (1952). An experimental study of the acoustic determinants of vowel color: Observations on one- and two-formant vowels synthesized from spectrographic patterns. *Word, 8*, 195–210.

Demorest, M.E., Bernstein, L.E. & DeHaven, G.P. (submitted). Sources of variability in speechreading nonsense syllables, isolated words, and sentences for subjects with normal hearing.

Fowler, C.A. (1987). Perceivers as realists, talkers too: Commentary on papers by Strange, Diehl et al., Rakerd and Verbrugge. *Journal of Memory and Language, 26*, 547–87.

Fowler, C.A. and Rosenblum, L.D. (1991). Perception of the phonetic gesture. In I.G. Mattingly and M. Studdert-Kennedy (Eds), *Modularity and the Motor Theory*. Hillsdale, NJ: Lawrence Erlbaum Associates.

Gibson, J.J. (1979). *The Ecological Approach to Visual Perception*. Boston: Houghton-Mifflin.

Goldschen, A.J. (1993). Continuous Automatic Speech Recognition By Lipreading. Ph.D. Dissertation, September, George Washington University, Washington, DC.

Green, K.P. & Gerdman, A. (1995). Cross-modal discrepancies in coarticulation and the integration of speech information: The McGurk effect with mismatched vowels. *Journal of Experimental Psychology: Human Perception and Performance*, 21, 1409–26.

Green, K.P. & Norrix, L.W. (submitted). Auditory cues to place of articulation and the McGurk effect: The role of burst, aspiration, and formant transitions.

House, A.S. & Fairbanks, G. (1953). The influence of consonant environment upon the secondary acoustical characteristics of vowels. *Journal of the Acoustical Society of America*, 25, 105–13.

Jenkins, J. (1987). A brief history of vowel theories. *Journal of Memory and Language*, 26, 542–9.

Johansson, G. (1973). Visual perception of biological motion and a model for its analysis. *Perception and Psychophysics*, 14, 201–11.

Joos, M. (1948). Acoustic phonetics. *Language Mongraph No. 23*. Linguistics Society of America, Baltimore: Waverly.

Kozlowski, L.T. & Cutting, J.E. (1977). Recognizing the sex of a walker from a dynamic point light display. *Perception and Psychophysics*, 21, 575–80.

Ladefoged, P. & Broadbent, D.E. (1957). Information conveyed by vowels. *Journal of the Acoustical Society of America*, 29, 98–104.

Liberman, A.M. & Studdert-Kennedy, M. (1978). Phonetic Perception. In R. Held, H. Leibowitz & H.L. Teuber (Eds.), *Handbook of Sensory Physiology*, (7). New York: Springer-Verlag.

Liberman, A.M. & Mattingly, I.G. (1985). The motor theory of speech perception revised. *Cognition*, 21, 1–36.

Lieberman, P., Crelin, E.S. & Klatt, D.H. (1972). Phonetic ability and related anatomy of the newborn and adult human. Neanderthal man and the chimpanzee. *American Anthropologist*, 74, 287–307.

Lindblom, B. (1963). Spectrographic study of vowel reduction. *Journal of the Acoustical Society of America*, 35, 1773–81.

McClelland, J.L. & Elman, J.L. (1986). The TRACE model of speech perception. *Cognitive Psychology*, 18, 1–86.

McGrath, M. (1985). An examination of cues for visual and audio-visual speech perception using natural and computer-generated faces. Unpublished doctoral dissertation, University of Nottingham, Nottingham, UK.

McGrath, M. & Summerfield, A.Q. (1985). Intermodal timing relations and audio-visual speech recognition by normal-hearing adults. *Journal of the Acoustical Society of America*, 77, 678–85.

McGurk, H. & MacDonald, J.W. (1976). Hearing lips and seeing voices. *Nature*, 264, 746–8.

MacLeod, A. and Summerfield, Q. (1987). Quantifying the contribution of vision to speech perception in noise. *British Journal of Audiology*, 21, 131–41.

Marr, D. (1982). *Vision*. New York: W.H. Freeman.

Massaro, D.W. (1987). *Speech Perception by Ear and Eye: A Paradigm for Psychological Inquiry*. Hillsdale, New Jersey: Lawrence Erlbaum Associates.

Massaro, D.W. & Cohen, M.M. (1990). Perception of synthesized audible and visible speech. *Psychological Science*, 1, 55–63.

Montgomery, A.A. & Jackson, P.L. (1983). Physical characteristics of the lips underlying vowel lipreading performance. *Journal of the Acoustical Society of America*, 73, 2134–44.

Movshon, A. (1990). Visual processing of moving images. In H. Barlow, C. Blakemore & M. Weston-Smith (Eds), *Images and Understanding: Thoughts About Images; Ideas About Understanding* (pp. 122–37). New York: Cambridge University Press.

Petajan, E.D. (1984). Automatic lipreading to enhance speech recognition. *Proceedings of the IEEE Communications Society*, November 26–29, Atlanta, Georgia.

Poggio, G.F. (1990). Cortical and neural mechanisms of stereopsis studied with dynamic random-dot stereograms. Cold Spring Harbor Symposium. *Quantitative Biology*, *55*, 749–58.

Pritchard, R.M., Heron, W. & Hebb, D.O. (1960). Visual perception approached by the method of stabilized images. *Canadian Journal of Psychology*, *14*, 67–77.

Remez, R.E., Rubin, P.E., Nygaard, L.C. & Howell, W.A. (1987). Perceptual normalization of vowels produced by sinusoidal voices. *Journal of Experimental Psychology: Human Perception and Performance*, *13*, 40–61.

Remez, R.E., Rubin, P.E., Pisoni, D. & Carrell, T. (1981). Speech perception without traditional speech cues. *Science*, *212*, 947–50.

Rosenblum, L.D. & Saldaña, H.M. (1992). Discrimination tests of visually-influenced syllables. *Perception and Psychophysics*, *52*, 461–73.

Rosenblum, L.D. & Saldaña, H.M. (1996). An audio-visual test of kinematic primitives for visual speech perception. *Journal of Experimental Psychology: Human Perception and Performance*, *22(2)*, 318–31.

Rosenblum, L.D., Johnson, J.A. & Mahmood, C. (in preparation). Kinematic features for visual speech perception.

Rosenblum, L.D., Johnson, J.A., & Saldaña, H.M. (1996). Visual kinematic information for embellishing speech in noise. *Journal of Speech and Hearing Research*, *39*, 1159–1170.

Runeson, S. (1977). On the visual perception of dynamic events. *Acta Universitatis Upsaliensis: Studia Psychologica Upsaliensia* (Series No. 9).

Runeson, S. (1993). Personal Communication, November 11.

Runeson, S. & Frykholm, G. (1981). Visual perception of lifted weight. *Journal of Experimental Psychology: Human Perception and Performance*, *7*, 733–40.

Stevens, K.N. & Halle, M. (1964). Remarks on analysis by synthesis and distinctive features. In W. Wathen-Dunn (Ed.), *Proceedings of the AFCRL Symposium on Models for the Perception of Speech and Visual Form*. Cambridge, Mass: MIT Press.

Strange, W., Jenkins, J. & Johnson, T. (1983). Dynamic specification of coarticulated vowels. *Journal of the Acoustical Society of America*, *74*, 694–705.

Strange, W., Verbrugge, R., Shankweiler, D. & Edman, T. (1976). Consonant environment specifies vowel identity. *Journal of the Acoustical Society of America*, *60*, 213–24.

Studdert-Kennedy, M. (1989). Reading gestures by light and sound. In A.W. Young & H.B. Ellis (Eds), *Handbook of Research on Face Processing* (pp. 217–22). Amsterdam: Elsevier-North-Holland.

Sumby, W.H. & Pollack, I. (1954). Visual contribution to speech intelligibility in noise. *Journal of the Acoustical Society of America*, *26*, 212–15.

Summerfield, A.Q. (1979). Use of visual information for phonetic perception. *Phonetica*, *36*, 314–31.

Summerfield, A.Q. (1987). Some preliminaries to a comprehensive account of audio-visual speech perception. In B. Dodd and R. Campbell (Eds), *Hearing by Eye: The Psychology of Lipreading* (pp. 3–51). Hove, UK: Lawrence Erlbaum Associates Ltd.

Summerfield, A.Q. & McGrath, M. (1984). Detection and resolution of audio-visual incompatibility in the perception of vowels. *Quarterly Journal of Experimental Psychology*, *36A*, 51–74.

Summerfield, A.Q., MacLeod, P., McGrath, M. & Brooke, N.M. (1989). Lips, teeth, and the benefits of lipreading. In A.W. Young & H.B. Ellis (Eds), *Handbook of Research on Face Processing* (pp. 223–33) Amsterdam: Elsevier-North-Holland.

Tartter, V.C. & Knowlton, K.C. (1981). Perception of sign language from an array of 27 moving spots. *Nature*, *289*, 676–8.

Vatikiotis-Bateson, E., Eigsti, I.-M. & Yando, S. (1994). Listener eye movement behavior during audio-visual perception. In *Proceedings of the ICSLP-94*, 527–30.

Verbrugge, R.R., Strange, W., Shankweiler, D. & Edman, T. (1976). What information enables a listener to map a talker's vocal tract? *Journal of the Acoustical Society of America, 60*, 198–212.

Vitkovitch, M. & Barber, P.J. (1994). Effect of video frame rate on subjects' ability to shadow one of two competing verbal passages. *Journal of Speech and Hearing Research, 37*, 1204–11.

Walley, A. & Carrell, T. (1983). Onset spectra and formant transitions in the adult's and child's perception of place of articulation in stop consonants. *Journal of the Acoustical Society of America, 73*, 1011–22.

Williams, D.R., Verbrugge, R.R. & Studdert-Kennedy, M. (1983). Judging sinewave stimuli as speech and nonspeech. *Journal of the Acoustical Society of America, 74*, S66.

Yakel, D. & Rosenblum, L.D. (1996). Face identification using visual speech information. Poster presented at the Society for Cognitive Science, July, 12, San Diego, CA.

ENGINEERING MODELS OF VISIBLE AND AUDIO-VISUAL SPEECH

Ten years after Summerfield: a taxonomy of models for audio-visual fusion in speech perception

Jean-Luc Schwartz *Institut de la Communication Parlée, Grenoble, France*

Jordi Robert-Ribes *CSIRO Division of Information Technology, Macquarie University, North Ryde, Australia*

Pierre Escudier *Institut de la Communication Parlée, Grenoble, France*

INTRODUCTION

Since the pioneering work by Petajan (1984; Brooke & Petajan, 1986), researchers in automatic speech recognition have addressed the problem of audio-visual speech in order to increase the robustness of their systems, particularly in noise, where the role of visual speech in improving intelligibility has been repeatedly demonstrated (Sumby & Pollack, 1954; Erber, 1975; Benoît et al., 1996). However, one must acknowledge that almost nothing about human audio-visual speech perception is incorporated in these systems, except the mere fact that speech is audio-visual! On the other hand, a number of cognitive models, both quantitative and qualitative, have been proposed in the past 10 years to account for human perceptual data. Although these models generally focus on fusion architectures, they almost completely neglect the signal processing component, and directly consider arbitrary monomodal (namely auditory-alone or visual-alone) internal representations on which they perform a number of computations in order to predict bimodal performance. Our long-term goal is to attempt to build a bridge to link these two banks of the same river, and to determine what components or constraints need to be incorporated in order to design a system able to process audio-visual speech in a plausible and efficient way. This requires a clear understanding of plausible fusion architectures and the internal structure of auditory and visual stimuli. With this aim in mind, we have completed a set of experiments

85

on the auditory, visual and audio-visual identification of French oral vowels in acoustic noise (Robert-Ribes et al., submitted), showing the "dual-optimality" of audio-visual speech, both at the information (audio-visual complementarity) and the information processing (audio-visual synergy) levels. At the same time, we have submitted various automatic audio-visual speech recognition systems to a series of "benchmark" tests on our corpus of noisy vowels, in order to compare their robustness (Teissier et al., submitted), and have introduced a "timing-target model of audio-visual speech perception" and shown how it can cope with experimental data (Robert-Ribes et al., 1996). Our aim for the future will be to achieve the implementation of this model and test its ability to deal with experimental data on human audio-visual speech perception and to provide a speech recognition system robust in adverse conditions.

The core of an audio-visual speech processing system is the fusion process, namely the device by which auditory and visual inputs merge or are combined in order to access a linguistic code. Summerfield (1987) considered "five metrics for audio-visual integration" related to the possible representations of the auditory and visual streams of information at their conflux, namely:

> (1) phonetic features; (2) the filter function of the vocal tract; (3) vectors representing the magnitudes of independent acoustical and optical parameters; (4) successive static vocal-tract configurations; and (5) time-varying kinematic patterns providing evidence of articulatory dynamics.
>
> (Summerfield, 1987, p. 4)

This proposal could provide a comprehensive account of all current and prospective models for audio-visual fusion in speech identification, and hence a very useful basis for comparing these models. In our laboratory, we have been exploring these five metrics in terms of their relationship with neighbouring fields, namely sensory interactions in cognitive psychology and sensor fusion in signal processing, their adequacy to the main theories of speech perception, their plausibility in relation to experimental data, and their efficacy in automatic recognition of audio-visual speech (Robert-Ribes, Schwartz & Escudier, 1995; Robert-Ribes et al. 1996). It is, therefore, timely to "revisit" Summerfield's proposal.

Throughout this chapter, we shall assume that within the speech processing device—be it the human speech perception system or an algorithm for automatic speech recognition—a sub-system exists in which some auditory and visual inputs are transformed into some linguistic (phonetic) code (see Figure 7), and our discussion will focus on the nature of the black box which effects this transformation. Thus, a number of questions will not be addressed directly in this chapter, such as the precise nature of the

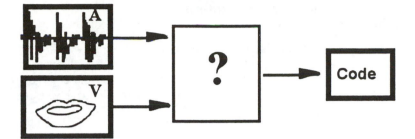

FIG. 7. The core of an audio-visual integration process in speech perception.

auditory and visual parameters that specify the black box inputs, the content of the linguistic representation at the black box output, and the variety of feedbacks or recursions that could enable either the output to modify the input (top-down processes) or one of the inputs to affect the other directly (the possibility of dependence between the inputs).

We will discuss the problem of "architecture", namely the nature of levels (or the format of representations) which play a role in the fusion/identification process. First, we will examine how this problem is addressed generally, and then we will focus on audio-visual speech and come back to Summerfield's five metrics. We will show that these five metrics can in fact be reduced to four basic architecture types organised around three major questions. We will describe the implications of experimental results in relation to these questions, and how the various models proposed in the literature fit into the four categories of architectures. Finally, we will address the question of "process", namely the way fusion is realised and the contextual parameters on which it could depend.

"EXTERNAL" CONSIDERATIONS ON ARCHITECTURES

Audio-visual fusion in speech perception is by no means the only type of sensory interaction in human or animal behaviour. We will take a broader perspective for the moment and consider two points of view which provide natural general frameworks for the study of speech, namely cognitive psychology, in which speech is considered as a major cognitive process in the human brain, and signal processing, in which speech is considered in terms of man-man and man-machine communication. In the next section, we will see that architectures for audio-visual fusion in speech perception and identification can emerge from the crossing of these two perspectives.

Three routes for intermodal interactions in cognitive psychology

The problem of intermodal transfer and integration is well-known and intensively studied in psychology. Among the diversity of experimental configurations, data and models, three kinds of proposals emerge (for a detailed review from which the following discussion is largely drawn see Hatwell, 1993).

Language

First, language may constitute the intersection point between two sensorial routes. For many years, the assumption that intermodal transfers were based on symbolic—mainly linguistic—mediation was supported by the difficulty of observing such transfer in non-verbal subjects (animals) or pre-verbal ones (infants). However, since around 1970, a number of experimental procedures have demonstrated that transfer between audition, vision, touch, proprioception and prehension can occur in animals and infants. For example, in the field of audio-visual pairing, one of the first pieces of evidence for innate audio-visual interaction came from Wertheimer's (1961) report of oculomotor responses toward a sound-emitting toy in a newborn a few minutes old. A review of neurophysiological and behavioural data on audio-visual interactions for localisation in animals can be found in Stein and Meredith (1993) (see also a recent demonstration that dolphins are able to immediately recognise a variety of complex shapes both within the senses of vision and echolocation, and across these two senses: Pack & Herman, 1995). However, linguistic mediation could facilitate these transfers, both for animals (e.g. in linguistically-trained chimpanzees, Savage-Rumbaugh, Sevcik & Hopkins, 1988) and humans (Johnson, Paivio & Clark, 1989). Hence, in general terms, a number of intersensorial transfers in the infant or the animal do not involve language, but verbal communication may enhance them.

Dominant modality

The second possible intersection may be one of the interacting modalities itself. In this schema, one modality is supposed to be "dominant" for a given task, which means that it is more efficient for this task, and the information from the other modality is "recoded" in a format compatible with the representations provided by the dominant one. This has been proposed for spatial localisation, in which vision is supposedly dominant in humans (Welch & Warren, 1986; Radeau, 1994). Auditory information based on such cues as interaural time or intensity differences is binaurally processed and organised in an (egocentric) spatially coherent system (map) within the auditory pathway, at the level of the inferior colliculus (Knudsen & Konishi, 1978a, 1978b). Tactile estimation of spatial localisation is also believed to be recoded in the dominant visual modality (Hatwell, 1986). Finally, the three modalities converge at single sites in the superior colliculus (Stein & Meredith, 1993). In general terms, recoding in the dominant modality (vision) seems to provide the basic scheme for the processing of shape and size (Hatwell, 1993), if not for space (Driver & Grossenbacher, 1996).

Amodal representation

A third possibility for intermodal transfer is that features may themselves not be confined to one sensory modality but may encompass attributes such as intensity or duration that are essentially isomorphic across different modalities. These could be considered to be "transverse" features. For example, audio-visual interactions for the estimation of rhythm are likely to occur at the level of an amodal representation of time. Another possibility is that amodal features are related to physical properties of the source, as suggested by direct-realist theory. This proposes that all sensed information acquires structure from systematic environmental regularities. The environment itself carries the pattern, which is simply picked up by whatever sensory apparatus interacts with it. Such structure can, therefore, be independent of the nature of the sensory input, and so amodal (Gibson, 1966). In general terms, amodal processing is likely to entail the perception of intensity and spatio-temporal patterns across sense modalities.

Three routes for sensor fusion in signal processing

In recent years, the sensor fusion problem has been the object of much attention in the field of pattern recognition and decision theory (Faugeras, Ayache & Faverjon, 1986; Basir & Shen, 1992; Beckerman, 1992; Crowley & Demazeau, 1993). In this framework, sensor fusion is the study of optimal information processing in distributed multisensor environments through intelligent integration of the multisensor data. In a recent review of decision fusion, Dasarathy (1994) proposes a classification of sensor fusion architectures according to the level at which fusion occurs in the identification process. He considers three possible input or output levels, namely data, features and decisions. The status of features is not completely clear in respect to perceptual architectures, hence we shall concentrate on the data level and the decision level. Under this scheme, data are directly measured by the sensors on a given object, while decisions involve a comparison with any kinds of prototypes or rules. There are, therefore, three possible fusion architectures: direct identification of combined data, in a data-to-decision process (Type A), fusion of decisions in a decision-to-decision process (Type B), and data fusion in a data-to-data process (Type C) (see Figure 8).

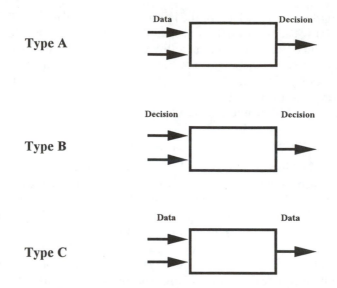

Type A

Type B

Type C

FIG. 8.   Three types of sensor fusion architectures in signal processing (from Dasarathy, 1994).

ARCHITECTURES FOR AUDIO-VISUAL SPEECH PERCEPTION

Four basic models for audio-visual speech perception

From the relationship between both sets of routes proposed in the previous section, a classification naturally emerges and leads to four possible architectures (Figure 9). Let us start from the "signal processing" point of view, with Dasarathy's classification. In Type A, fusion coincides with the identification process, while it follows identification (or part of it) in Type B. In both cases, the individual sensor routes converge at a level where the format of the representation is "decision", hence, in the taxonomy of cognitive psychology, "language". In the first case (Type A), there is "direct identification" of the message from the two sensory inputs, namely sound and image (Figure 9a). In the second case (Type B), there is "separate identification" of the message from each sensory input, and fusion occurs on the separate decisions (Figure 9b). In Type C, fusion occurs before identification, and thus begs the question: What is the format of data at the fusion level? Cognitive psychology proposes two possible answers to this question. The common format may be provided by the dominant modality if there is one (Figure 9c), or it may be amodal, be it "physical", as in the direct realist theory, or otherwise (Figure 9d). Let us examine these four architectures in more detail.

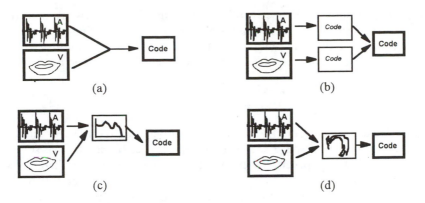

FIG. 9.   The four basic models of audio-visual integration: a – DI, b – SI, c – DR and d – MR.

Direct identification model (DI)

The direct identification of audio-visual configurations model (DI) is inspired by the "lexical access from spectra" model of Klatt (1979), which becomes in this framework a bimodal "lexical access from spectra and face parameters" model. The input signals are transmitted directly to the classifier, which is bimodal. This classifier may employ a look-up table in which it chooses the closest prototype to the inputs.

Separate identification model (SI)

This model supposes two parallel recognition processes: one for each modality. Afterwards, the phonemes or phonemic features obtained from each modality are fused. Fusion can be realised on logical values, like in the VPAM ("vision place audition manner"), where each modality operates for a specific group of phonetic features (McGurk & MacDonald, 1976; Summerfield, 1987). It could also operate on probabilistic (or fuzzy-logical) values (as in the "fuzzy logical model of perception" (FLMP), proposed by Massaro, 1987). In this case, each input is compared to (unimodal) prototypes to obtain two degrees of support for each category. Then, each pair of values is fused by means of probabilistic calculations.

Dominant recoding model (DR)

The dominant recoding model considers the auditory modality as being the dominant modality for speech perception and, thus, more adapted to it. The visual input is recoded into a representation of the dominant modality, for instance, the transfer function of the vocal tract. This transfer fuction is estimated independently from the auditory input (by source-filter deconvolution methods, such as cepstral analysis) and from the visual input (e.g. by association). These two estimations are then fused. The source characteristics (voiced, nasal, etc.) are estimated only from the auditory information. The whole source-filter set estimated in this way is then presented to the phonetic classifier.

Motor recoding model (MR)

In this model, both inputs are projected into an amodal (neither auditory nor visual) common space and fused in that space. In classical versions of amodal fusion for speech, either in the framework of motor theory (Liberman & Mattingly, 1985) or direct realist theory (Fowler, 1986), the amodal space is related to the characteristics of speech gestures (vocal tract configurations or motor programs), hence we call this architecture "motor recoding model" (MR). For instance, a vocal tract configuration can be derived independently for each modality: the resultant configurations are fused and then presented to the phonetic classifier. The fusion process can take into account the fact that some dimensions cannot be seen (e.g. the velum) and weights these accordingly. Additionally or alternatively, the dynamics of the vocal tract based on kinematic data (positions, velocities and accelerations) could be derived separately for vision and for audition which fuse in amodal motor space for classification. In all cases, the sensori-to-motor "mapping" (Abry & Badin, 1996) may be achieved directly, by associations (Robert-Ribes et al., 1996), or by more complex inversion processes (Bailly, 1995; Laboissière & Galvan, 1995).

Three questions for a taxonomy

Our four architectures can be organised around three basic questions forming a decision tree (Figure 10), which will allow us to classify all systems described in the literature, and possibly choose one architecture as the most compatible with experimental data on audio-visual speech.

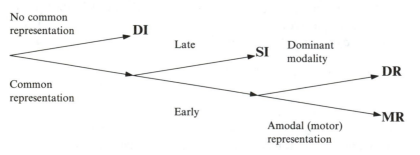

FIG. 10.   Taxonomy of the four basic models.

Existence of an intermediary representation

The major characteristic of model DI is that it is the only architecture in which there is no stage in auditory or visual pathways where the internal representations are expressed in a common format: fusion is simply the juxtaposition of inputs for a global decision. Hence, the first question: Is there a common space where both modalities are projected before the final identification, enabling the comparison of an auditory and a visual stimulus and even an estimate of distances between them? If the answer is "no" then the architecture is in category DI, if the answer is "yes", then the DI model is inadequate as formulated, and the next question should be addressed. Notice that this first question corresponds quite closely to the first general question posed at the *Attention and Performance XVI* symposium (1994): "Are there supramodal representations for integration across modalities, or is integration merely mutual constraint between modality or dimension-specific representation?" (Inui, 1996, p. 9).

Early versus late integration

If there is a common intermediate representation, the next question is: Is the common space derived from any kind of linguistic process? (A straightforward criterion could be: is the common space language-dependent?) If the answer is "yes", then the architecture is in category SI, which is also called a "late integration process", because integration occurs at a later stage than a comparison with prototypes. Otherwise, in the "early integration" case, the next question should be addressed.

Nature of the intermediate representation

If there is a common pre-linguistic representation, it may either be amodal or compatible with one, supposedly dominant, route, hence the last question: Is there a dominant (namely auditory or visual) modality providing the common intermediate representation in an early integration model? If the answer is "yes", then the architecture is in category DR. If the answer is "no", then the architecture is in the category "amodal recoding", for which the only type proposed until now is the MR model.

Relationship with existing models

We argue that any model of audio-visual speech perception or automatic recognition necessarily deals with the sensor fusion problem through one of these four architectures or possibly a mixture of them. We will now relate a number of systems described in the literature to our basic categories.

DI model

This architecture corresponds to Summerfield's third metric (Summerfield, 1987, pp. 31–7), namely "acoustic spectra and visible patterns". The key characteristic, namely the absence of intermediary representation, is related to the principle of "delayed commitment" ("no level of representation between the acoustic spectrum and the word", p. 33). In the field of speech recognition, there have been some implementations of DI architectures (e.g. Braida et al., 1986; Adjoudani & Benoît, 1996; Cosi & Magno-Caldognetto, 1996; Dalton et al., 1996; Movellan & Chadderdon, 1996; Silsbee & Su, 1996). In the field of psychophysical models, the so-called "pre-labelling model" proposed by Braida (1991) is also a DI architecture, as is the implementation of the TRACE model (McClelland & Elman, 1986) for audio-visual speech, which Campbell (1988) suggested could be extended to accommodate visual (face action) features.

SI model

This architecture corresponds to Summerfield's "first metric" (Summerfield, 1987, pp. 7–16), namely "phonetic features". In the field of speech recognition, the first system, created by Petajan (1984; Brooke & Petajan, 1986), relied upon a code-book of images to determine the template which best matched the spoken utterance, and used the visual recognition device to select one of the two first candidates chosen by the acoustic recogniser, hence it was an implementation of architecture SI. Since then, most implementations for speech recognition have used architectures SI (see Stork, Wolff & Levine, 1992; Bregler et al., 1993; Duchnowski, Meier & Waibel, 1994; Adjoudani & Benoît, 1996; Goldschen, Garcia & Petajan, 1996). In the field of psychophysical models, Massaro's FLMP (Massaro, 1987, 1989) is the most well-known example of SI architecture, and the so-called "post-labelling model" proposed by Braida (1991) is also a SI architecture.

DR model

This architecture corresponds to Summerfield's second metric (Summerfield, 1987, pp. 17–23), namely "the filter function of the vocal tract". Implementations of this architecture in the field of speech recognition are few (Yuhas, Goldstein & Sejnowski, 1989; Yuhas et al., 1990; Watanabe & Kohda, 1990; Robert-Ribes et al., 1996; see also an application of the DR architecture for noisy speech enhancement, Girin et al., 1996), and it has never been applied to psychophysical modelling.

MR model

This architecture could correspond both to Summerfield's fourth metric (Summerfield, 1987, pp. 38–9), namely "vocal-tract configurations" and to the "fifth metric" (Summerfield, 1987, pp. 40–5), namely "articulatory dynamics".

Indeed, "articulatory configurations" and "articulatory dynamics" (or "gestures") are both compatible with the motor theory (as is the shift from configurations to gestures in Liberman & Mattingly, 1985). In the framework of the direct realist theory, we can say that the structure of speech signals is due both to the "shape" of the instrument—the vocal tract—and to the intrinsic dynamics of speech gestures. Regarding Summerfield's fourth metric, one could ask if we can "hear the shape of a drum", that is recover shape from sound, following the question asked by the mathematician Mark Kac in 1966 (see a discussion in Cipra, 1992). Concerning Summerfield's fifth metric, one could ask whether the knowledge that a speaker has about the general laws of biological movements may constrain his or her perception of someone else's movements (as it seems to be the case in the visual perception of a traced object, see Viviani & Stucchi, 1992).

Therefore, the distinction between Summerfield's fourth and fifth metrics seems to be a matter of the content of the articulatory representation rather than a true matter of architecture. Similarly, within architectures DI, SI or DR, a distinction may be drawn between the representation of shapes and the representation of movement (for a demonstration that both shape and movement are processed in lipreading, see Campbell, 1996; for the distinction between perceptual processing of movement and sensori-motor interactions in perceptual representations, see Abry & Badin, 1996). These considerations of the *characteristics of the representational code* are orthogonal to the questions of model architecture and hence the five metrics proposed by Summerfield may be reduced to our four basic architectures.

To our knowledge, the only implementation of an MR architecture is the one we have proposed (Robert-Ribes, Schwartz & Escudier, 1995; Robert-Ribes et al., 1996).

Compatibility with experimental data

Data from the literature on audio-visual speech perception suggest some possible answers to the three questions of Figure 10. These answers are based on an important a priori, which can obviously be contested, but which seems secure from a methodological point of view. We first look for the simplest model, so discarding "hybrids" (i.e. mixtures of basic categories), unless it is shown that no "pure" model category can explain all the data at the same time.

The need for a common representation

Several studies using conflicting auditory and visual stimuli show that subjects can detect audio-visual incompatibility and quantitatively estimate a perceptual distance between auditory and visual stimuli, while still being able to fuse both inputs (Summerfield & McGrath, 1984; Sekiyama 1994). Even four-month-old babies are sensitive to the correspondence between auditory and visual information of a speaking face (Kuhl & Meltzoff, 1982; see Burnham, this volume). Therefore, the need for a common representation of auditory and visual stimuli (where both modalities can be compared) seems uncontroversial. Taken at face value, this is incompatible with architecture DI.

Early versus late integration

The visual component of an audio-visual stimulus does not affect auditory adaptation (Roberts & Summerfield, 1981). This has been used as an argument against early integration (Vroomen, 1992). However, the difference between auditory and visual adaptors could be due to low-level auditory mechanisms (e.g. adaptation in the auditory nerve: Delgutte & Kiang, 1984; see Robert-Ribes, Schwartz & Escudier, 1995). This is not, therefore, clear-cut evidence against early integration. By contrast, the findings that seen speech rate affects the classification of a heard token (Green & Miller, 1985) and that there are systematic effects of visual coarticulation on auditory classification (Green, this volume) are not compatible with late integration. The characteristics of speeded or coarticulated speech are not represented in the (phonetic) prototype. Furthermore, the data using lip movements combined with sounds, delivered by auditory pulse tones and generated by vocal fold activity (Rosen, Fourcin & Moore, 1981; Grant et al., 1985; Breeuwer & Plomp, 1986) indicate that subjects are identifying the voicing feature audio-visually, despite identification failure with the ear or the eye alone. This may be because they are able to extract temporal co-ordination of the auditory and visual signal (audio-visual voice onset time: see Green & Kuhl, 1989; Green, this volume). These findings are incompatible with a late-integration model, in which neither the auditory nor the visual phonetic decoding modules would provide any cue to enable a decision to be taken with respect to the voicing feature. These are strong grounds to propose that fusion must be realised at an early stage of processing, which is incompatible with late integration (SI model).

Dominance and complementarity

Several data suggest that audition may not be completely dominant for speech perception, since vision may be crucial for the identification of some place contrasts, particularly in noise (Summerfield, 1987; Robert-Ribes et al.,

1996). This makes the DR rather unlikely. Let us mention a more technical argument.The DR model predicts that a given visual input can modify an auditory percept only if the visual input is conflicting or if the auditory input is noisy. Indeed, if the auditory stimulus is clean and compatible with the visual stimulus, the visual input is transformed into an "equivalent" auditory pattern which should be close to the true audio pattern, hence auditory and audio-visual percepts should be more or less the same. However, Lisker and Rossi (1992) report data showing that a visual input can bias the perception of an auditory stimulus which is neither conflicting nor noisy. Their subjects (French-speaking speech researchers) had to judge the rounding category of a vowel. Let us concentrate on the case of [ɯ]. This vowel when presented visually was considered a rounded vowel in 1% of the responses, whereas when presented auditorily, it was considered rounded (60% of rounded responses). Finally, when presented audio-visually the percentage of rounding responses dropped to 25% (versus 75% unrounded). That is, some subjects perceived the vowel [ɯ] as rounded when presented auditorily, but they judged it unrounded when presented visually or audio-visually. In summary, vision seems able to "dominate" audition for at least some contrasts, rendering a general DR model less feasible.

From MR to hybrids

Our reasoning leads to the proposal that the MR architecture is the only one compatible with all experimental data considered together. We show elsewhere (Robert-Ribes, Schwartz & Escudier, 1995; Robert-Ribes et al., 1996) how this architecture could deal with a number of experimental results on audio-visual speech perception. However, there is an alternative, which is to propose a hybrid model. This is particularly clear in a recent paper by Massaro and Cohen:

> The degrees of support provided by . . . one modality for a given alternative are not modified by the information presented along other modalities. At the same time, the temporal relationship between modalities might be used as an additional source of information.
>
> (Massaro & Cohen, 1995, p. 109)

This corresponds in our taxonomy to a hybrid DI + SI model, including three phonetic classifiers, an auditory, a visual and an audio-visual one (the DI component), the three decisions being fused by a SI fusion process. Obviously, such a model can cope with the common representation point thanks to its SI component, and with the audio-visual co-ordination point thanks to its DI component. The only counterclaim is Occam's razor: as long as a simple model such as MR can cope with experimental data, it is to be preferred to a hybrid model.

TUNING THE FUSION PROCESS

Whatever the choice of the architecture between the four basic categories we have introduced, a crucial characteristic of the fusion model is the nature of the fusion process. We will first describe the categories of fusion processes as they appear in signal processing. Then we will focus on the tuning problem, namely the way one should control the respective importance of the auditory and visual inputs in the fusion. We will examine which experimental parameters could play a role in tuning, and how a controllable tuning process can be implemented within each of the four architectures.

Classification of fusion operators

In her comparative review of data fusion operators, Bloch (1994) defines various possible behaviours for a fusion operator. Her taxonomy relies first on a separation between context-independent operators, which are computed without any external or contextual input, and context-dependent operators, where various sources of contextual information are provided to the fusion process, such as the detection of a conflict between sources or the estimation of the reliability of a given source of information. Within this framework, we may distinguish stimulus-independent and stimulus-dependent contextual factors affecting audio-visual fusion.

Stimulus-independent factors in integration tuning

Individual differences in lipreading

While much research has indicated individual differences in speechreading skill, these do not appear to correlate reliably with psychometric or psychophysiological measures, except possibly the speed of visual neural processing (see the controversy between Shepherd et al., 1977, and Rönnberg et al., 1989). A detailed analysis of the auditory, visual and audio-visual perception of opening and rounding gestures in French vowels by Cathiard (1994) shows a remarkably small interindividual variability for visual identification, but a large interindividual variability for audio-visual identification of conflicting stimuli, though some visual-to-audio-visual correlations can be demonstrated. To some degree, then, the tuning of audio-visual interaction functions may be subject-dependent.

Linguistic specificity

Sekiyama and Tohkura (1991) showed that McGurk fusion illusions were reduced in Japanese compared with English participants. Since then, several studies have investigated comparative language effects for audio-visual speech integration: English versus Japanese (Sekiyama & Tohkura, 1993;

Kuhl et al., 1994), English versus Japanese versus Spanish (Massaro et al., 1993), Spanish versus German (Fuster-Duran, 1995) or German versus Hungarian (Grassegger, 1995). A number of differences have been reported. Some of them come from the nature of the stimuli, differing from language to language. However, the remaining differences between linguistic groups perceiving the same stimuli, either compatible with their language or not, may be attributed to two different origins. Sekiyama and Tohkura (1993) claim that they reflect variations in the weight that different linguistic communities would attribute to the visual input in the integration process. They suggest that the Japanese community could make less use of the visual input because of a cultural difference, namely that "it may be regarded as impolite in Japan to look at someone's face" (pp. 442). On the other hand (Massaro et al., 1993; Kuhl et al., 1994) these differences may arise from variations in the inventory of linguistic prototypes rather than from social or cultural variations in the tuning of the audio-visual process, hence this question remains open (see Burnham, this volume).

Attentional factors

We have seen that audio-visual speech integration is mandatory. However, intersensory interaction can depend on the observer's distribution of attention to each modality (Welch & Warren, 1986). Some data suggest that the weight of the visual input could be moderated by attentional factors (Massaro & Warner, 1977; Summerfield & McGrath, 1984; see also a comment by Welch, 1989), hence the repartition of attention between the auditory and the visual inputs could be part of the contextual influences on audio-visual fusion.

Recent work by Driver and his colleagues suggest that attention could also intervene in sensorial interactions in a more complex way. It appears that the sensorial input in one modality can focus the attention of another modality on a specific part of its input. This has been demonstrated by Driver and Grossenbacher (1996) for visual–proprioceptive–tactile interactions and by Driver (1996) for audio-visual interactions. In this last case, Driver presents strong evidence that one of the functions of temporally integrated heard and seen speech is to partition effective speech processing by enabling spatial distinctions to be made concerning the perceived origins of heard speech. He showed that a speaking face corresponding to one of two monaurally recorded messages emanating from a single loudspeaker not only enhanced report of that message, but enhanced comprehension of the "unseen" message when the perceiver was under the illusion that the aural message was spatially separated into two locations. Such data are very important in respect to the "dependence versus independence" question: Does the "information value of one source remain independent of the information value of the other" (Massaro, 1989, p. 749)? They show that audio-visual interactions could comprise a module enabling not only to perform spatial localisation (Radeau, 1994), but in more general terms what we propose to call "audio-visual scene analysis", in reference to the domain of "auditory scene analysis" (Bregman, 1990) which focuses a great deal of interest in the field of audition. Whatever the content of the blackbox displayed in Figure 7 and the relations of the "audio-visual scene analysis" module with the speech perception module (Fisher, 1991; Bertelson et al., 1994), Driver's data raise a severe doubt on the assumption that audition and vision are evaluated independently at the input of the audio-visual speech identification process.

Stimulus-dependent factors in integration tuning

Integration disrupted by large audio-visual discrepancies

Audio-visual integration appears to be quite a robust mechanism, able to resist a number of incompatibilities between sound and image: discrepancies in the place of articulation, as in the McGurk effect for consonants or in the case of vowels in Summerfield and McGrath (1984) (e.g. audio /i/ fused with video /a/; e.g. Cathiard, 1994); discrepancies in the manner of articulation (Manuel et al., 1983); discrepancies in the voice/face gender (Green et al., 1991); temporal discrepancies (Campbell & Dodd, 1980; McGrath & Summerfield, 1985; Smeele & Sittig, 1991; Massaro & Cohen, 1993); or spatial localisation discrepancies (Fisher, 1991; Bertelson et al., 1994). However, a mechanism of disruption of integration might exist in the case of extremely large discrepancies. The question has been explicitly raised by Manuel et al. (1983) in relation to the well-known resistance of the acoustic syllable /da/ to optic influences in bimodal perceptual experiments. They wondered if it could be linked to the fact that subjects appear to be more aware of acoustic-optic conflicts with this acoustic token rather than others in their perceptual rating data. For incongruent audio-visual vowel stimuli, Summerfield and McGrath (1984) suggested the opposite: "There is some evidence that the effect of vision increases with the degree of incompatibility between the visual and acoustical components of the stimuli" (Summerfield & McGrath, 1984, p. 62). However, Robert-Ribes (1995) remarked that the effect of vision should be measured in terms of *relative* displacement in a perceptual space, instead of absolute shift as suggested by Summerfield and McGrath (see also Welch, 1994), and he showed that in this case there is some trend that the effect of vision decreases for large conflicts, especially for a video /a/ paired with an acoustic /i/–/a/ continuum. This seems to be confirmed and refined by Sekiyama (1994), who shows the existence of an inverse correlation between the detection of audio-visual conflict and the influence of the visual input on the audio-visual decision, particularly for noisy acoustic stimuli. Notice, however, that these two factors could also have a common cause: the more "ambiguous" the auditory input (because of noise, for example), the more difficult the conflict detection, and the more important the role of the visual input.

Reliability of each modality in the fusion process

It is "a strongly held belief in the area of intersensory bias that the weighting of a sensory cue is positively correlated with its *precision*" (Welch, 1989, p. 777). So does the precision with which the ear and the eye are able to estimate the various phonetic dimensions of speech signals play a part in the fusion process? To our knowledge, no perceptual experiment directly addresses this question. However, a number of audio-visual fusion models in speech recognition control the weight of the auditory input in relation to the level of acoustic noise (Yuhas, Goldstein & Sejnowski, 1989; Robert-Ribes et al., 1996; Teissier et al., submitted), with the implicit assumption that in a large level of noise, audition is less reliable and, hence, it should play a smaller role in the decision process.

The same kind of argument has been used by Massaro to defend the multiplicative integration process of fuzzy-logical values delivered by separate modalities in his fuzzy logical model of perception (see also Campbell, 1974). Indeed, considering that multiplicative fusion corresponds to an "optimal integration rule" in a Bayesian framework, he notices that "optimal integration requires that more ambiguous sources be given less a say in the decision" (Massaro, 1989, p. 749). However, there could be a confusion between two different things, namely the *precision* or *reliability* of the perceptual measure which provides the input to the "feature evaluation" process and the *ambiguity* or *degree of confidence* in an assumption at the output of this process. As a matter of fact, a crucial characteristic of the FLMP is that if a modality attributes a completely ambiguous score to a given modality at the output of the evaluation process, it does not play any part in the final result of the fusion process. This is not bound to be the case. For example, there are some cases in Lisker and Rossi's data on the audio-visual identification of vowel rounding where the auditory modality provides quite ambiguous responses, namely rounding scores around 50%, but influences the audio-visual decision process by strongly increasing the "rounded" score, though the visual score is close to 0% (see Figures 6 and 8 in Lisker & Rossi, 1992, pp. 405–8). This is quite contradictory with FLMP predictions. For example, if we come back to their scores for /ɯ/ given previously, a 1% visual score for rounding combined with a 60% auditory score leads to the prediction of a 1.5% audio-visual score, while the true audio-visual score was about 25%. By contrast, Robert-Ribes (1995) shows that in noisy conditions, subjects may happen to take a systematic (hence *unambiguous*) decision in the auditory modality (e.g. classify all vowels as an

/i/ in a very large amount of noise), but they do not pay much attention to this decision for audio-visual judgements (see subject MV, p. 246), probably since they know it is *unreliable*. Therefore precision rather than ambiguity should be the correct criterion. We have suggested elsewhere (Robert-Ribes et al., 1995) that the precision of a given modality could be defined by the inverse of the *variance* of the estimates provided by this modality in a given task.

Implementation of contextual factors in the fusion process

The previous sections showed that the audio-visual fusion process in speech perception is likely to be context-dependent. We have indicated three stimulus-independent factors, namely a "subject-specific" component, a "language-specific" component and an "attentional" component, and two stimulus-dependent factors, namely estimation of the audio-visual incompatibility and estimation of the reliability of each modality for a given task. This raises two problems: how to estimate all these factors and how to tune the fusion process.

Estimating the context factors

Our current knowledge of stimulus-independent factors is quite poor and not much can be said on their estimation. In respect to stimulus-dependent factors, conflict detection is a necessary part of an audio-visual speech perception model, even if it does not play a part in fusion itself. As we have seen, this shows that, at some level, there must exist a common representation of the two modalities, be it "linguistic" (in model SI), "auditory" (in model DR) or "motor" (in model MR).

The reliability of a given modality may itself comprise two components: one really stimulus-dependent, incorporating a signal-to-noise ratio estimation, and the other stimulus-independent, specifying the precision of each modality for the estimation of each component of the common representation. This last point constitutes the main drawback of the DR model, since the association of a visual input to an auditory input results in inextricably mixing in the "guessed" spectrum (the transfer function of the vocal tract) what is easy to see (e.g. lip rounding) with what is hard to see (e.g. tongue opening) or impossible to see (e.g. front-back gestures). This is the reason why the DR model is rather inefficient as an automatic speech recognition architecture (Robert-Ribes et al., 1996).

Controlling the fusion process

The SI, DR and MR models share the common assumption that there exists a common representation space in which auditory and visual speech inputs are separately projected before integration and final decision. The integration process generates a common fused representation from the two separate projections, hence the context sources may globally control the *weight* of each projection in the computation of the integrated representation (Robert-Ribes et al., 1996).

The case of model DI is more complex. However, in the context of a Gaussian classifier applied to audio-visual inputs, it can be solved either by selectively weighting specific components of the audio-visual covariance matrices or by weighting both inputs and class means for a given modality, without modifying the matrices (Teissier, 1995).

All these methods result in potentially increasing the robustness of an automatic audio-visual speech recognition device in acoustic noise, if the acoustic signal-to-noise ratio is provided to the fusion process and increases the weight of the visual input for large levels of noise.

CONCLUSION

The aim of this chapter was to define the basic ingredients of an audio-visual fusion model for speech perception. This has resulted in specifying a number of choices, clearly explicated and organised in relation to each other, rather than in definitive answers concerning the correct architecture for understanding human audio-visual speech. However, 10 years after Summerfield's contribution, his statement that "any comprehensive account of how speech is perceived should encompass audio-visual speech perception" (Summerfield, 1987, p. 47) seems uncontroversial. It is our deep belief that progress in this field will need a good co-ordination between the cognitive psychology approach and the signal processing approach, in order to realise models that are both plausible and efficient.

ACKNOWLEDGEMENTS

This work has been supported by ESPRIT-BR funding (Speech-MAPS). It has benefited from many useful discussions with C. Abry, M.A. Cathiard, M. Piquemal and P. Teissier. Thanks also to A. Guérin-Dugué who allowed us to discover the "signal processing" contributions by Dasarathy and Bloch.

REFERENCES

Abry, C. & Badin, P. (1996). Speech mapping as a framework for an integrated approach to the sensori-motor foundations of language. *4th Production Seminar, 1st ETRW on Speech Production Modeling: From Control Stategies to Acoustics* (pp. 175–84). Autrans, France.
Adjoudani, A. & Benoît, C. (1996). On the integration of auditory and visual parameters in an HMM-based ASR. In D.G. Stork & M.E. Hennecke (Eds), *Speechreading by Humans and Machines: Models, Systems and Applications* (pp. 461–72). NATO ASI Series, Berlin: Springer.

Bailly, G. (1995). Recovering place of articulation for occlusives in VCV's. *Proceedings of the XIIIth International Congress of Phonetic Sciences, 2,* 230–33.

Basir, O.A. & Shen, H.C. (1992). Sensory data integration: A team consensus approach. *Proceedings the 1992 IEEE International Conference on Robotics and Automation* (pp. 1683–8). Nice, France.

Beckerman, M. (1992). A Bayes-maximum entropy method for multi-sensor data fusion. *Proceedings the 1992 IEEE International Conference on Robotics and Automation* (pp. 1668–74). Nice, France.

Benoît, C., Guiard-Marigny, T., Le Goff, B. & Adjoudani, A. (1996). Which components of the face do humans and machines best speechread? In D.G. Stork & M.E. Hennecke (Eds), *Speechreading by Humans and Machines: Models, Systems and Applications* (pp. 315–28). NATO ASI Series, Berlin: Springer.

Bertelson, P., Vroomen, J., Wiegeraad, G. & de Gelder, B. (1994). Exploring the relation between McGurk interference and ventriloquism. *Proceedings International Conference on Spoken Language Processing* (pp. 559–62). Yokohama, Japan.

Bloch, I. (1994). *Information Combination Operators for Data Fusion: A Comparative Review with Classification.* Internal report, Telecom Paris, 94 D 013.

Braida, L.D. (1991). Crossmodal integration in the identification of consonant segments. *Quarterly Journal Experimental Psychology, 43,* 647–77.

Braida, L.D., Picheny, M.A., Cohen, J.R., Rabinowitz, W.M. & Perkell, J.S. (1986). Use of articulatory signals in automatic speech recognition. *Journal of the Acoustical Society of America, 80,* S18.

Breeuwer, M. & Plomp, R. (1986). Speechreading supplemented with auditorily presented speech parameters. *Journal of the Acoustical Society of America, 79,* 481–99

Bregler, C., Hild, H., Manke, S. & Waibel, A. (1993). Improving connected letter recognition by lipreading. *International Joint Conference of Speech and Signal Processing* (pp. 557–60). Minneapolis.

Bregman, A.S. (1990). *Auditory Scene Analysis: The Perceptual Organization of Sound.* Cambridge, Mass: Bradford Books, MIT Press.

Brooke, M. & Petajan, E.D. (1986). Seeing speech: investigations into the synthesis and recognition of visible speech movements using automatic image processing and computer graphics. *International Conference on Speech Input/Output, Techniques and Applications* (pp. 104–109). London.

Campbell, H.W. (1974). *Phoneme recognition by ear and by eye: a distinctive feature analysis.* Doctoral dissertation, Katholieke Universiteit te Nijmegen.

Campbell, R. (1988). Tracing lip movements: making speech visible. *Visible Language, 22,* 33–57.

Campbell, R. (1996). Seing brains reading speech: a review and speculations. In D.G. Stork & M.E. Hennecke (Eds), *Speechreading by Humans and Machines: Models, Systems and Applications* (pp. 115–34). NATO ASI Series, Berlin: Springer.

Campbell, R. & Dodd, B. (1980). Hearing by eye. *Quarterly Journal of Experimental Psychology, 32,* 85–9.

Cathiard, M.A. (1994). *La perception visuelle de l'anticipation des gestes vocaliques: cohérence des événements audibles et visibles dans le flux de la parole.* Thèse de Doctorat en Psychologie Cognitive. Université Pierre Mendès, Grenoble, France.

Cipra, B. (1992). You can't hear the shape of a drum. *Science, 225,* 1642–3.

Cosi, P. & Magno-Caldognetto, E. (1996). Lips and jaw movements for vowels and consonants: spatio-temporal characteristics and bimodal recognition applications. In D.G. Stork & M.E. Hennecke (Eds.), *Speechreading by Humans and Machines: Models, Systems and Applications* (pp. 291–314). NATO ASI Series, Berlin: Springer.

Crowley, J.L. & Demazeau, Y. (1993). Principles and techniques for sensor data fusion. *Signal Processing, 32,* 5–27.

Dalton, B., Kaucic, R. & Blake, A. (1996). Automatic speechreading using dynamic contours. In D.G. Stork & M.E. Hennecke (Eds), *Speechreading by Humans and Machines: Models, Systems and Applications* (pp. 373–82). NATO ASI Series, Berlin: Springer.

Dasarathy, B.V. (1994). *Decision Fusion*. Los Alamitos, California: IEEE Computer Society Press.

Delgutte, B. & Kiang, N.Y.S. (1984). Speech coding in the auditory nerve: IV. Sounds with consonant-like dynamic characteristics. *Journal of the Acoustical Society of America, 75*, 897–907.

Driver, J. (1996). Enhancement of selective listening by illusory mislocation of speech sounds due to lip-reading. *Nature, 381*, 66–8.

Driver, J. & Grossenbacher, P.G. (1996). Multimodal spatial constraints on tactile selective attention. In T. Inui & J.L. McClelland (Eds.), *Attention and Performance XVI: Information Integration in Perception and Communication* (pp. 209–36). Cambridge, Mass: Bradford Books, MIT Press.

Duchnowski, P., Meier, U. & Waibel, A. (1994). See me, hear me: integrating automatic speech recognition and lip-reading. *International Conference on Spoken Language Processing* (pp. 547–50). Yokohama, Japan.

Erber, N.P. (1975). Auditory-visual perception of speech. *Journal of Speech and Hearing Disorders, 40*, 481–92.

Faugeras, O., Ayache, N. & Faverjon, B. (1986). Building visual maps by combining noisy stereo measurements. *IEEE International Conference on Robotics and Automation*. San Francisco, CA.

Fisher, B.D. (1991). Integration of visual and auditory information in perception of speech events. Unpublished Doctoral Dissertation, University of California, Santa Cruz, CA.

Fowler, C.A. (1986). An event approach to the study of speech perception from a direct-realist perspective. *Journal of Phonetics, 14*, 3–28.

Fuster-Duran, A. (1995). McGurk effect in Spanish and German listeners. Influences of visual cues in the perception of Spanish and German conflicting audio-visual stimuli. *Proceedings of Eurospeech, 95*, 295–8.

Gibson, J.J. (1966). *The Senses Considered as Perceptual Systems*. Boston: Houghton Mifflin Company.

Girin, L., Feng, G. & Schwartz, J.L. (1996). Débruitage de parole par un filtrage utilisant l'image du locuteur: une étude de faisabilité. *Traitement du Signal, 13*, 319–34.

Goldschen, A.J., Garcia, O.N. & Petajan, E.D. (1996). Rationale for phoneme-viseme mapping and feature selection in visual speech recognition. In D.G. Stork & M.E. Hennecke (Eds), *Speechreading by Humans and Machines: Models, Systems and Applications* (pp. 505–18). NATO ASI Series, Berlin: Springer.

Grant, K.W., Ardell, L.H., Kuhl, P.K. & Sparks, D.W. (1985). The contribution of fundamental frequency, amplitude envelope, and voicing duration cues to speechreading in normal-hearing subjects. *Journal of the Acoustical Society of America, 77*, 671–7.

Grassegger, H. (1995). McGurk effect in German and Hungarian listeners. *Proceedings of the XIIIth International Congress of Phonetic Sciences, 3*, 210–13.

Green, K.P. & Kuhl, P.K. (1989). The role of visual information in the processing of place and manner features in speech perception. *Perception and Psychophysics, 45*, 34–42.

Green, K.P. & Miller, J.L. (1985). On the role of visual rate information in phonetic perception. *Perception and Psychophysics, 38*, 269–76.

Green, K.P., Kuhl, P.K., Meltzoff, A.N. & Stevens, K.N. (1991). Integrating speech information across talkers, gender, and sensory modality: Female faces and male voices in the McGurk effect. *Perception and Psychophysics, 50*, 524–36.

Hatwell, Y. (1986). *Toucher l'espace. La main et la perception tactile de l'espace*. Lille: Presses Universitaires de Lille.

Hatwell, Y. (1993). Transferts intermodaux et intégration intermodale. In M. Richelle, J. Reguin & M. Robert (Eds), *Traité de Psychologie Expérimentale* (pp. 543–84). Paris: Presses Universitaires de France.

Inui, T. (1996). Mechanisms of information integration in the brain. In T. Inui & J.L. McClelland (Eds), *Attention and Performance XVI: Information Integration in Perception and Communication* (pp. 3–12). Cambridge, Mass: Bradford Books, MIT Press.

Johnson, C.J., Paivio, A.V. & Clark, J.M. (1989). Spatial and verbal abilities in children's crossmodal recognition: a dual coding approach. *Canadian Journal of Psychology, 43*, 397–412.

Kac, M. (1966). Can one hear the shape of a drum? *Ann. Math. Monthly, 73*, 1–23.

Klatt, D.H. (1979). Speech perception: A model of acoustic-phonetic analysis and lexical access. *Journal of Phonetics, 7*, 279–312.

Knudsen, E.I. & Konishi, M. (1978a). Space and frequency are represented separately in auditory midbrain of the owl. *Journal of Neurophysiology, 41*, 870–84.

Knudsen, E.I. & Konishi, M. (1978b). A neural map of auditory space in the owl. *Science, 200*, 795–7.

Kuhl, P.K. & Meltzoff, A.N. (1982). The bimodal perception of speech in infancy. *Science, 218*, 1138–41.

Kuhl, P.K., Tsuzaki, M., Tohkura, Y. & Meltzoff, A.N. (1994). Human processing of auditory-visual information in speech perception: Potential for multimodal human-machine interfaces. *International Conference on Spoken Language Processing* (pp. 539–42). Yokohama, Japan.

Laboissière, R. & Galvan, A. (1995). Inferring the commands of an articulatory model from acoustical specifications of stop-vowel sequences. *Proceedings of the XIIIth International Congress of Phonetic Sciences, 1*, 358–61.

Liberman, A., & Mattingly, I. (1985). The motor theory of speech perception revised. *Cognition, 21*, 1–36.

Lisker, L. & Rossi, M. (1992). Auditory and visual cueing of the [±rounded] feature of vowels. *Language and Speech, 35*, 391–417.

McClelland, J.L. & Elman, J.L. (1986). The TRACE model of speech perception. *Cognitive Psychology, 18*, 1–86.

McGrath, M. & Summerfield, A.Q. (1985). Intermodal timing relations and audio-visual speech recognition by normal-hearing adults. *Journal of the Acoustical Society of America, 77*, 678–85.

McGurk, H. & MacDonald, J. (1976). Hearing lips and seeing voices. *Nature, 264*, 746–8.

Manuel, S.Y., Repp, B.H., Studdert-Kennedy, M. & Liberman, A.M. (1983). Exploring the "McGurk effect". *Journal of the Acoustical Society of America, 74*, S1, S66.

Massaro, D.W (1987). *Speech Perception by Ear and Eye: A Paradigm for Psychological Inquiry*. Hillsdale, NJ: Lawrence Erlbaum Associates Inc.

Massaro, D.W. (1989). Multiple book review of speech perception by ear and eye: A paradigm for psychological inquiry. *Behavioral and Brain Sciences, 12*, 741–94.

Massaro, D.W. & Cohen, M.M. (1993). Perceiving asynchronous bimodal speech in consonant-vowel and vowel syllables. *Speech Communication, 13*, 127–34.

Massaro, D.W. & Cohen, M.M. (1995). Modeling the perception of bimodal speech. *Proceedings of the XIIIth International Congress of Phonetic Sciences, 3*, 106–13.

Massaro, D.W. & Warner, D.S. (1977). Dividing attention between auditory and visual perception. *Perception and Psychophysics, 21*, 569–74.

Massaro, D.W., Cohen, M.M., Gesi, A., Heredia, R. & Tsuzaki, M. (1993). Bimodal speech perception: An examination across languages. *Journal of Phonetics, 21*, 445–78.

Movellan, J.R. & Chadderdon, G. (1996). Channel separability in the audio-visual integration of speech: a Bayesian approach. In D.G. Stork & M.E. Hennecke (Eds), *Speechreading by Humans and Machines: Models, Systems and Applications* (pp. 473–88). NATO ASI Series, Berlin: Springer.

Pack, A.A. & Herman, L.M. (1995). Sensory integration in the bottlenosed dolphin: immediate recognition of complex shapes across the senses of echolocation and vision. *Journal of the Acoustical Society of America*, 98, 722–33.

Petajan, E.D. (1984). *Automatic lipreading to enhance speech recognition*. Doctoral Thesis, University of Illinois.

Radeau, M. (1994). Auditory-visual spatial interaction and modularity. *Cahiers de Psychologie Cognitive*, 13, 3–51.

Robert-Ribes, J. (1995). *Modèles d'intégration audiovisuelle de signaux linguistiques: de la perception humaine à la reconnaissance automatique des voyelles*. Thèse de Docteur de l'INPG, Signal-Image-Parole.

Robert-Ribes, J., Piquemal, M., Schwartz, J.L. & Escudier, P. (1996). Exploiting sensor fusion architectures and stimuli complementarity in AV speech recognition. In D.G. Stork & M.E. Hennecke (Eds), *Speechreading by Humans and Machines: Models, Systems and Applications* (pp. 193–210). NATO ASI Series, Berlin: Springer.

Robert-Ribes, J., Schwartz, J.L. & Escudier, P. (1995). A comparison of models for fusion of the auditory and visual sensors in speech perception. *Artificial Intelligence Review Journal*, 9, 323–46.

Robert-Ribes, J., Schwartz, J.L., Lallouache, T. & Escudier, P. (submitted). Complementarity and synergy in bimodal speech: auditory, visual and audio-visual identification of French oral vowels in noise.

Roberts, M. & Summerfield, A.Q. (1981). Audio-visual presentation demonstrates that selective adaptation in speech perception is purely auditory. *Perception and Psychophysics*, 30, 309–14.

Rönnberg, J., Arlinger, S., Lyxell, B. & Kinnefords, C. (1989). Visual evoked potentials: relation to adult speechreading and cognitive function. *Journal of Speech and Hearing Research*, 32, 725–35.

Rosen, S., Fourcin, A.J. & Moore, B. (1981). Voice pitch as an aid to lipreading. *Nature*, 291, 150–52.

Savage-Rumbaugh, S., Sevcik, R.A. & Hopkins, W.D. (1988). Symbiolic cross-modal transfer in two species of chimpanzees. *Child Development*, 59, 617–25.

Sekiyama, K. (1994). Differences in auditory-visual speech perception between Japanese and Americans: McGurk effect as a function of incompatibility. *Journal of the Acoustical Society of Japan (E)*, 15, 143–58.

Sekiyama, K. & Tohkura, Y. (1991). McGurk effect in non-English listeners: Few visual effects for Japanese subjects hearing Japanese syllables of high auditory intelligibility. *Journal of the Acoustical Society of America*, 90, 1797–825.

Sekiyama, K. & Tohkura, Y. (1993). Inter-language differences in the influence of visual cues in speech perception. *Journal of Phonetics*, 21, 427–44.

Shepherd, D.C., DeLavergne, R.W., Frueh, F.X. & Clobridge, C. (1977). Visual-neural correlate of speechreading ability in normal-hearing adults. *Journal of Speech and Hearing Research*, 20, 752–65.

Silsbee, P.L. & Su, Q. (1996). Audio-visual sensory integration using Hidden Markov Models. In D.G. Stork & M.E. Hennecke (Eds), *Speechreading by Humans and Machines: Models, Systems and Applications* (pp. 489–96). NATO ASI Series, Berlin: Springer.

Smeele, P.M.T. & Sittig, A.C. (1991). The contribution of vision to speech perception. *Proceedings of the 2nd European Conference on Speech Communication and Technology* (pp. 1495–7). Genova, Italy.

Stein, E.B. & Meredith, M.A. (1993). *The Merging of Senses*. Cambridge, London: The MIT Press.

Stork, D.G., Wolff, G. & Levine, E. (1992). Neural network lipreading system for improved speech recognition. *IJCNN-92*, Baltimore MD, 2, 285–95.

Sumby, W.H. & Pollack, I. (1954). Visual contribution to speech intelligibility in noise. *Journal of the Acoustical Society of America*, 26, 212–15.

Summerfield, A.Q. (1987). Some preliminaries to a comprehensive account of audio-visual speech perception. In B. Dodd and R. Campbell (Eds), *Hearing by Eye: The Psychology of Lipreading* (pp. 3–51). Hove, UK: Lawrence Erlbaum Associates Ltd.

Summerfield, A.Q. & McGrath, M. (1984). Detection and resolution of audio-visual incompatibility in the perception of vowels. *Quarterly Journal of Experimental Psychology: Human Experimental Psychology, 36*, 51–74.

Teissier, P. (1995). *Fusion audiovisuelle avec prise en compte de l'environnement*. DEA Signal-Image-Parole, INPG.

Teissier, P., Robert-Ribes, J., Schwartz, J.L. & Guérin-Dugué, A. (submitted). Comparing models for audio-visual fusion in a noisy-vowel recognition task. Submitted to *IEEE Transactions on Speech and Audio Processing*.

Viviani, P. & Stucchi, N. (1992). Biological movements look uniform: evidence of motor-perceptual interactions. *Journal of Experimental Psychology: Human Perception and Performance, 18*, 603–23.

Vroomen, J.H.M. (1992). Hearing voices and seeing lips: Investigations in the psychology of lipreading. Doctoral Dissertation, Katolieke Univ. Brabant, 18 September.

Watanabe, T. and Kohda, M. (1990). Lip-reading of Japanese vowels using neural networks. *Proceedings of the International Conference Spoken Language Processing, 90*, Kobe, Japan, 1373–6.

Welch, R.B. (1989). A comparison of speech perception and spatial localization. *Behavioral and Brain Sciences, 12*, 776–7.

Welch, R.B. (1994). The dissection of intersensory bias: Weighting for Radeau. *Current Psychology of Cognition, 13*, 117–23.

Welch, R.B. & Warren, D.H. (1986). Intersensory interactions. In K.R. Boff, L. Kaufman and J.P. Thomas (Eds), *Handbook of Perception and Human Performance, Volume I: Sensory Processes and Perception* (pp. 25-1–25-36). New-York: Wiley.

Wertheimer, M. (1961). Psychomotor coordination of auditory-visual space at birth. *Science, 134*, 1692.

Yuhas, B.P., Goldstein, M.H. & Sejnowski, T.J. (1989). Integration of acoustic and visual speech signals using neural networks. *IEEE Communications Magazine*, November, 65–71.

Yuhas, B.P., Goldstein, M.H., Sejnowski, T.J. & Jenkins, R.E. (1990). Neural network models of sensory integration for improved vowel recognition. *Proceedings IEEE, 78*, 1658–68.

CHAPTER FIVE

Computational aspects of visual speech: machines that can speechread and simulate talking faces

N. Michael Brooke   *Media Technology Research Centre,*
Department of Mathematical Sciences, University of Bath, UK

INTRODUCTION

Technology is now able to support a wide range of powerful techniques for processing acoustic speech signals. Their success has led to the deployment of automatic systems for many applications involving human interaction with machines. As the use of automatic speech processing spreads, the requirements become more demanding and the search for additional sources of knowledge grows more intense. In particular, there is now a requirement for automatic speech recognition systems that can operate in significant levels of ambient noise and, conversely, for systems that can augment the limited auditory input where background noise or hearing impairment degrades speech intelligibility by a listener. Here, the inherent limitations of processing only the acoustic component of the speech signal become critical.

The visible aspects of speech production have long been recognised as a valuable source of information, especially by the hearing-impaired. Even for those who hear normally, seeing the face of a speaker can significantly increase speech intelligibility in a noisy environment (MacLeod & Summerfield, 1987). There are good reasons for this and they have been set out in more detail elsewhere (Summerfield, 1987). In simple terms, the visible articulatory movements of a speaker's face can often convey cues to the place of articulation which are acoustically less robust and easily masked by noise. Cues to the manner of articulation, on the other hand, are generally acoustically robust though visual cues may be weak or absent; for example, voiced and voiceless sounds are distinguished by the behaviour of the vocal cords, which are not visible. Although the visible aspects of the speech signal include linguistically informative movements of visible facial features such as the eyes and eyebrows, as well as of the whole head and body (Ekman, 1979), most work on visible speech signals concentrates on the movements of the lower face which convey most of the primary, articulatory cues to speech events. The complementary nature of the visual and acoustic cues suggests that augmentation of conventional speech processing systems by the use of visual signals should enhance their performance, as it does that of human beings. Possible applications for speech systems embodying a visual component have been suggested elsewhere (Hennecke, Stork & Prasad, 1996; Brooke & Scott, 1994a).

The same increase in computer-processing power that has contributed to advances in acoustic speech technology also offers the potential for handling visual signals. Even so, the machine processing of the visible speech signals in the form of facial image sequences can impose very large computational loads and some form of visual data compression is still required if processing is to be possible within reasonable timescales. A second major area for current research, especially in automatic speech recognition, is how to integrate the acoustic and the visual data so that the two modalities can be used together to the best effect (and see Schwartz et al., this volume). Although not attempting a complete review of the field, which has been done elsewhere (Stork & Hennecke, 1996), this chapter will set out some of the major issues in the two problem areas just mentioned to show how they are guiding current progress in both automatic speech recognition and in "video speech synthesis", that is, the development of computer graphics packages that can generate animated displays of facial images which simulate the movements of speech production.

COMPRESSING IMAGE DATA

The most direct method for reducing the volume of image data is to identify the visual cues that are relevant to the intelligibility of speech and then to extract, analyse and classify the facial features which embody these cues. This task is complicated by the superimposed movements of the head and body that speakers make, so that features have first to be located and the measurements made after eliminating the effects of the global movements. Consequently, attempts to measure visible speech movements often either fix the head position, which imposes unnatural constraints on a speaker, or locate skeletally-rigid points on the head whose movements allow variations in head position and orientation to be separated from the purely articulatory movements (Brooke & Summerfield, 1983; Petajan, 1984). The earliest methods were semi-manual and often relied upon the tracking of marked points on the face of a speaker from frame to frame of films or video recordings. Despite attempts to create one (Finn, 1986), no generally accepted or complete catalogue of relevant visual cues has yet been constructed.

The development of image-processing permitted the measurement process to be automated. For example, Petajan was able to capture oral images in real-time and code them so that the oral cavity appeared black and the teeth and tongue were white (Petajan, 1984). Features such as the oral cavity area and perimeter, cavity width and cavity height could then be extracted and plotted as time-varying templates representing specific speech utterances. Another successful technique extracts images of the lip area from colour video-recorded images in which the lips are painted cyan blue so that their chroma is unique (Benoit et al., 1992). Specific measurements can then be readily extracted from the reduced images. Some systems have also extracted differences between successive images as a means for capturing the time-variations of visible speech articulations (Nishida, 1986; Movellan, 1995). More recently, sophisticated active contour-tracking methods have been applied to automate the measurement of complete lip outlines (e.g. Bregler & Omohundro, 1994; Blake & Isard, 1994).

Data-driven image compression

The processing power now available permits images to be processed without the prior need to extract features. Consequently, a data-driven approach can be taken in which the images themselves act as a source of data whose statistical properties can be explored. Little or no pre-processing of the images is necessary (e.g. Brooke & Templeton, 1990).

Artificial neural networks

Data-driven processing was given a considerable boost by the development of artificial neural networks (ANNs). These consist of highly connected arrays of rather simple elements which can operate collectively and in parallel, for example, to learn mappings between sets of inputs and outputs. A priori knowledge of the nature and structure of the input is not essential. Trained networks can be used, for example, to classify speech patterns into phoneme categories. Multilayer perceptrons (MLPs) form one class of ANN whose basic structure is shown in Figure 11.

Each element has inputs and an output. The elements are usually arranged in two, three or four layers and each element is connected in parallel to every element in the layer above (the input units are the bottom layer). Each element may have a bias and the connections between elements are individually weighted; these comprise the parameters of the system. The output of each element is computed from the bias and the weighted input

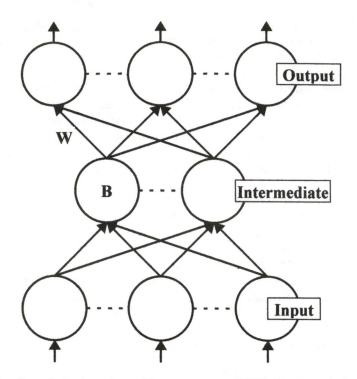

FIG. 11. General structure of a multilayer perceptron (MLP). The network elements are arranged in layers. There may be one or two intermediate layers and any number of elements may be present in each layer. Each element may have a bias (B) and each connection has a weight (W). These form the parameters of the system and can be computed from training data using well-defined algorithms.

values, typically using a non-linear function. By repeatedly applying items from a set of training patterns to the input layer of the network and comparing the outputs with the desired outputs of the system (with which the training patterns are labelled), it is possible to adjust and refine the parameters at every network element until the system has learned the mapping function (Elman & Zipser, 1986). The learned knowledge is distributed throughout the network and MLPs can generalise, that is, classify test patterns similar to, but not identical with, patterns seen during training.

MLPs were used in several early visual vowel identification studies. The intensities of the pixels making up the images were supplied at the input elements, one pixel per element. One output element per vowel class was allocated to categorise the input token. In one early visual experiment (Peeling, Moore & Tomlinson, 1986), the vowels /a/, /i/ and /u/ were identified from static, monochrome, images of the oral region comprising 16

× 16 pixels. This required three layers of elements, the central layer con-
taining two units. In a later experiment, test tokens of the 11 British-English
vowels in a /bVb/ context were identified, using monochrome images of the
oral region of a single speaker, with a spatial resolution of 16 × 12 pixels
(Brooke & Templeton, 1990). Single images from the vowel nuclei were used
and average identification rates of 91% (84% in the worst case) were
attained using a 3-layer MLP with just 6 elements in the central layer. In
both of the experiments, the central layer represents an internal representation of the inputs that will map the input patterns to the outputs with
maximum discriminability. The ability of images with spatial resolution of
around 16 × 16 pixels essentially to retain useful visual cues was supported
by a perceptual experiment in which recorded images of a speaker enunciating the five long vowels of British English in a /hVd/ context were
digitally processed so that they could be replayed to subjects as randomised
dynamic displays at different spatial resolutions. However, the chief contribution of the MLP experiments was to show that a form of data encoder
was possible which could compress low-resolution image data still further.

Principal component analysis

MLPs can be difficult to train and may offer no advantages over principal component analysis (PCA). PCA is a statistical technique that
attempts to transform a pattern space into a new space in which as much of
the data variance as possible is accounted for by the minimum number of
transformed axes, or principal components (see Chatfield & Collins, 1980).
An n-pixel image can be represented as one point in an n-dimensional
pattern space in which each dimension represents the intensity of a single
pixel. It is this space that is transformed by PCA. Since facial images are
highly structured, PCA should offer a significant degree of data compression (e.g. Turk & Pentland, 1991). That is, if most of the variance can be
accounted for by a small number of principal components, these can be used
to encode the images. Furthermore, if the PCA encoder is based on the
analysis of a sufficiently representative set of oral images, it should be
possible to use the components derived from this "training" process to
encode unseen images. An experiment with a training set comprising about
17,000 monochrome 32 × 24-pixel images of the oral region of a single
speaker enunciating utterances of digit triples like "three seven six" showed
that about 82% of the data variance could be accounted for by just 15
principal components (Brooke & Scott, 1994b). The quality of the images
reconstructed from a 15-component encoding compared with the original
images is illustrated in Figure 12.

The adequacy of a 15-component encoding scheme was confirmed by
encoding images of digit triples both within and outside the training set

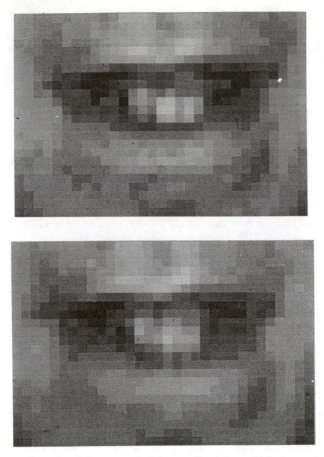

FIG. 12.   Monochrome oral images and their encoding using principal component analysis (PCA). An illustrative facial image of 32 × 24 pixels resolution is shown (top) in its original form. A reconstruction of the same image from a 15-component encoding is also shown (bottom).

and performing visual digit identification experiments using both original images and images reconstructed from the PCA encodings. Single digit identification rates changed little from 70% for the original images down to 64–66% for 15-component encodings. There was no significant difference between reconstructions of test and training images. Also, PCA encoding is stable; the time-varying behaviour of the component values in image sequences is smooth and continuous as Figure 15 shows. Additionally, changes in magnitude of the code values reflect the magnitude of changes in the images.

AUDITORY-VISUAL RECOGNITION: INTEGRATING ACOUSTIC AND VISUAL SPEECH DATA

Early speech processing of both acoustic and, later, of visual speech signals, typically used relatively simple template matching methods based on time-varying feature measurements. However, conventional, acoustic speech recognition using data-driven techniques has achieved considerable success by developing models that can reflect the variability and phonetic context sensitivity of real speech. The use of ANNs to classify input patterns with, for example, phonetic class labels, has achieved some success. ANNs are not, however, ideally suited for adaptation so that they can account for the time variations in speech patterns, though these can be handled by a variant known as a time-delay neural network (TDNN). This class of ANN accepts a set of input patterns from within a window of finite duration, which moves through the time domain. They have been used for auditory-visual speech recognition, though usually taking measured features as their inputs, rather than raw images (e.g. Stork, Wolff & Levine, 1992; Lavagetto & Lavagetto, 1996).

Hidden Markov models

An alternative, stochastic approach to automatic speech processing is currently dominant and naturally embodies the time-variation (and variability) of speech signals. Hidden Markov models (HMMs) are finite-state machines that model speech production via a series of states between which transitions can take place. State transition probabilities govern the likelihood of any specific transition taking place. Each state conceptually generates an output pattern. The output that each state generates is not fixed; it can be any one of the full range of allowed outputs, but is probabilistically governed by a state-dependent probability density function (PDF). The PDF gives the probability of occurrence of each possible output in that state. The general structure of a HMM is shown in Figure 13. HMMs operate synchronously.

To perform speech recognition, separate HMMs are built for each of a set of vocabulary items—typically words, phones or even sub-phone units. The models are trained by initially estimating the values of the parameters (PDFs and state transition probabilities) and then using real examples of the appropriate speech unit to re-estimate and refine the parameters. In recognition, the HMM, or sequence of HMMs, that would have the highest probability of generating any observed set of input patterns is computed. There are well-defined algorithms for training and recognition using HMMs (Rabiner, 1989). To deal with phonetic context sensitivity, so-called "tri-phone" models are often employed, in which each phone is modelled in every possible preceding and succeeding phone context.

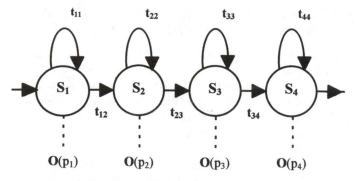

FIG. 13.   General structure of a hidden Markov model (HMM). This shows a "conventional", left-to-right architecture. HMMs are probabilistic finite-state machine models of speech production. Transitions between states i and j are governed by state transition probabilities, t(ij), and each state, k, can generate an output, O, that is determined by a state-dependent probability density function, p(k). These parameters are derived from examples of real speech using well-established algorithms.

Architectures for integrating auditory and visual data

The outputs of the states are simply pattern vectors. In acoustic speech recognition, for example, the vector may be a set of mel frequency-scaled cepstral coefficients (e.g. Simons & Cox, 1990). The visual part of a speech signal could be added by using, for example, the PCA encoding of a facial image. If visual and acoustic data are both to be processed, they need to be integrated so that the best use can be made of them together. Recent work on human speech processing has suggested at least four architectural possibilities (Robert-Ribes et al., 1996; Schwartz et al., this volume). In "direct identification" (DI), acoustic and visual data are combined and transmitted to a single, bimodal classifier. In "separate identification" (SI), two, parallel, unimodal classifiers are used and the results are fed forward to a final decision-making stage. Auditory processing takes precedence in "dominant recoding" (DR) and the visible signals are recoded into the dominant modality. Each modality therefore generates a representation appropriate to the dominant modality and it is these that feed forward to the final classification process. Finally, in "motor-space recoding" (MR), both inputs are recoded into an amodal common space and these representations are fed forward for fusion and final classification. There is no general acceptance of any one of these models, though evidence suggests that fusion takes place in human speech processing somewhere above the peripheral input level, but below the categorical level (Summerfield, 1991; Massaro, 1996).

A wide range of bimodal, auditory-visual speech recognition systems using both ANNs and HMMs has now been investigated and many of these have been reviewed (Stork & Hennecke, 1996). No work has yet been reported that employs a system with the MR architecture, though an early recogniser used ANNs to implement a DR model in which facial images were recoded into acoustic spectral envelopes (Sejnowski et al., 1990). The SI architecture was well exemplified by Petajan's early work (Petajan, 1984). Time-varying templates of features were used to classify speech events visually. This classification was then heuristically combined with the output of a separate, acoustic speech recogniser and subjected to a final decision-making stage. It is possible to use separate HMM recognisers in the same way, and they lie at one end of a continuum of architectures. At the opposite end are the DI architectures, that is, HMMs in which acoustic and visual data is input as a single, combined pattern vector and processed as a composite pattern throughout. An architecture of this kind was used to examine the benefits of using the visible speech signal for processing speech in noise (Brooke, Tomlinson & Moore, 1994). Speaker-dependent digit triple utterances formed the vocabulary. A 26-channel filterbank output was used to encode the acoustic signal and a 10-channel PCA encoder was used to represent 10×6-pixel images of the oral region of the speaker's face. These were concatenated to form 36-element composite pattern vectors. Three-state triphone HMMs were trained using 200 digit triples from a standard list and tested on 100 digit triples. Simulated, spectrally-flat noise was added to the acoustic channels of the test tokens at different levels. The results showed that useful gains in recognition under noisy conditions were possible by adding the visual component, but grand variance HMMs with silence tracking and noise-masking were needed to prevent acoustic noise swamping the effects of the visual component. The gains were typical of those obtained with other HMM recognisers lying in the SI to DI continuum of architectures, but none has produced a bimodal performance that is uniformly better at all acoustic noise levels, which is characteristic of human performance (see Adjoudani & Benoit, 1996).

Typical DI-type architectures, however, assume strict time-locking of auditory and visual events, which may be unduly restrictive. A variant HMM-based architecture has therefore been investigated, which, in addition to processing acoustic and visual data together, like the DI architectures, also allows limited asynchrony between the acoustic and visual components of the input (Tomlinson, Russell & Brooke, 1996). Triphone units are modelled and at present synchrony is re-asserted at the phone boundaries. The architecture is illustrated in Figure 14.

Table 5 illustrates the performance of this so-called "cross-product" HMM architecture compared with that of the left-to-right HMMs described earlier. A significant result is that the cross-product architecture shows improvements extending across all acoustic noise levels. Furthermore, the performance is better than that of either acoustic-only or visual-only

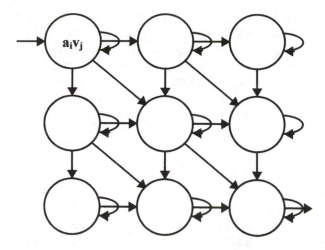

FIG. 14. A cross-product HMM architecture. Acoustic and visible signals are decomposed into a two-dimensional array of states. Row i corresponds to state i of an acoustic model and column j to state j of a visual model. Entry is via the top, left state and exit via the bottom, right state and modal asynchrony results in a non-diagonal path through the state array. The system parameters are computed from separate acoustic and visual models.

TABLE 5
Percentage word error rates for audio-only and audio-visual, grand variance HMM recognisers. The error rates are shown as a function of the level of simulated noise added to the acoustic signal. Visual-only recognition of an uncontaminated input signal has a 23% error rate

Acoustic SNR (dB)	Audio-alone	Audio-visual, standard model	Audio-visual, cross-product model
23	15.3	1.7	1.3
14	14.0	3.7	4.3
5	16.0	10.7	10.7
−4	67.7	22.3	19.0
−13	100.0	25.7	20.3
−22	100.0	25.7	20.3

recognisers. Development of this type of recognition model is continuing and asynchronies that extend beyond phone boundaries are also being examined.

COMPUTER GRAPHICS OF TALKING FACES AND THE DATA-DRIVEN APPROACH

The development of video speech synthesisers has been reviewed elsewhere (Brooke, 1992a; Brooke, 1992b; Brooke, 1996). Many packages employ a three-dimensional framework description of a head. By moving the points of the framework from frame to frame and then displaying frames at 25–50 per second, movement can be simulated. The surface of the framework can be shaded and textured to look like the face of a human (Parke, 1975). The main difficulty of this type of model is the derivation of the movement data. The principal methods can be summarised as follows. First, the framework model can be configured for each of a series of idealised, target gestures corresponding to specific speech sounds. By concatenating and interpolating between these target configurations, continuous speech can be synthesised, for example, from a phonetic description of an utterance. Most models that do this successfully require hand tuning and must embody explicit techniques for modelling coarticulatory variations (Cohen & Massaro, 1993). A second way to derive driving data is to attempt to model the musculature of the head and face and to specify the actions of muscle-based parameters (e.g. Terzopoulos & Waters, 1990). There is, however, no complete description of the mapping between a phonetic description of speech and the muscle actions that produce the articulations. It is also difficult to observe and measure muscle activity.

Data-driven methods can overcome many of these limitations. In particular, HMMs can be invoked in sequence to generate output patterns. An early video synthesiser of this kind was driven by an acoustic speech input and used a fully-connected HMM with 16 states, each corresponding to a vector-quantised lip-shape. The teeth and tongue were inserted randomly and the generated images were rendered at a later stage (Simons & Cox, 1990). This idea has been extended, using triphone HMMs whose outputs were 15-component PCA encodings of 32×24-pixel monochrome oral images (Brooke & Scott, 1994a). The synthesiser was tested on continuously spoken digit strings generated from orthographic specifications via a phonetic transcription. The HMMs had between 3 and 9 states and assumed a single, multivariate Gaussian distribution of the 15 PCA code values in each state. Their parameters were computed using a Baum-Welch algorithm, with 200 digit triples as training examples. The coded outputs were constrained to generate the smoothly changing behaviour imposed by the anatomical constraints of the human speech production system and images were reconstructed from the encodings. The time-varying tracks of the code values of a real and synthesised digit utterance are compared in Figure 15.

To test the quality of the syntheses, subjects were presented with a series of visual displays of the oral area and asked to identify the spoken digit triples. Both syntheses and original images were presented, in random order. Recognition rates for single digits were approximately 69% correct for the original images and only slightly lower for the syntheses at 64%, even though this included both PCA encoding and HMM synthesis errors.

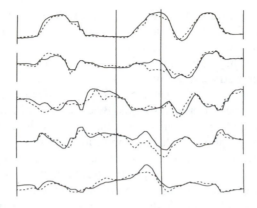

FIG. 15.   The time-varying behaviour of PCA components derived from oral images. The tracks of channels 3 (top) to 7 (bottom) of a PCA encoder are illustrated for the utterance "seven four six" with time increasing from left to right. Vertical bars show the word boundaries. The time-aligned tracks for the original image sequence (solid line) and the output of a HMM-based synthesiser (dotted line) are compared.

SUMMARY AND CONCLUSIONS

Both automatic speech recognition and synthesis can potentially benefit from the addition of visible speech signals to the conventional acoustic signals. However, there is still insufficient knowledge to specify completely the relevant image features and, thus, effectively to compress the visible signal data so that it can be processed in reasonable timescales. It is, therefore, attractive to use data-driven methods for image analysis and synthesis. Data-driven techniques require no knowledge about the structure or meaning of the data they are analysing and can find highly compressed internal representations of the attributes of the visual input data that can, for example, categorise speech events. In particular, no model of the structure and anatomy of the human head is involved. Because images of real speech productions are used as input to these systems, all the naturally visible features can be directly incorporated. These include skin shadowing and texturing as well as articulators like the teeth and tongue, whose observation is difficult as the articulators are only partially or intermittently visible. Furthermore, the natural variability of real speakers and at least some of the effects of coarticulation can be accounted for. Data-driven methods like PCA have not yet been investigated fully under varying lighting levels, head position and speaker identity. Nonetheless, data-driven methods have successfully demonstrated the benefits of using the visible speech signals for speech recognition in noise and have permitted investigation of a number of different architectures for integrating auditory and visual data to make the best use of the modalities together. The ability to synthesise plausibly realistic talking faces using computer graphics, at timescales only slightly above real time has also been successfully demonstrated. The syntheses are speech-readable. As a result, it is possible to envisage using them in interactive environments, for example, by offering hearing-impaired subjects adaptable stimuli to assess and improve their speechreading skills. At present, most methods rely upon pre-prepared material.

REFERENCES

Adjoudani, A. & Benoît, C. (1996). On the integration of auditory and visual parameters in an HMM-based ASR. In D.G. Stork & M.E. Hennecke (Eds), *Speechreading by Humans and Machines*. Berlin: Springer, 461–72.

Benoît, C., Lallouache, T., Mohamadi, T., & Abry, C. (1992). A set of French visemes for speech synthesis. In G. Bailly, C. Benoit, & T.R. Sawallis (Eds.), *Talking machines: Theories, models and designs* (pp. 485–504). Amsterdam: Elsevier.

Blake, A. & Isard, M. (1994). 3D position, attitude and shape input using video tracking of hands and lips. *Computer Graphics Proceedings, Annual Conference Series (ACM)*, 185–92.

Bregler, C. & Omohundro, S. (1994). Surface learning with applications to lip reading. *International Computer Science Institute Report TR-94-001*. Berkeley, California.

Brooke, N.M. (1992a). Computer graphics animations of speech production. *Advances in Language, Speech and Hearing, Volume 2*. London: JAI Press, 87–134.

Brooke, N.M. (1992b). Computer graphics synthesis of talking faces. In Bailly, G., Benoit, C. & Sawallis, T.R. (Eds), *Talking Machines: Theories, Models and Designs*. Amsterdam: Elsevier, 504–22.

Brooke, N.M. (1996). Talking heads and speech recognisers that can see: the computer processing of visual speech signals. In D.G. Stork & M.E. Hennecke (Eds), *Speechreading by Humans and Machines*. Berlin: Springer, 351–73

Brooke, N.M. & Scott, S.D. (1994a). Animated computer graphics of talking faces based on stochastic models. *Proceedings of the International Symposium on Speech, Image-processing and Neural Networks, Hong Kong (IEEE)*, 73–6.

Brooke, N.M. & Scott, S.D. (1994b). PCA image coding schemes and visual speech intelligibility. *Proceedings of the Institute of Acoustics (Autumn Meeting, Windermere)*, *16(5)*, 123–9.

Brooke, N.M. & Summerfield, A.Q. (1983). Analysis, synthesis and perception of visible articulatory movements. *Journal of Phonetics*, *11*, 63–76.

Brooke, N.M. & Templeton, P.D. (1990). Visual speech intelligibility of digitally processed facial images. *Proceedings of the Institute of Acoustics (Autumn Meeting, Windermere)*, *12(10)*, 483–90.

Brooke, N.M., Tomlinson, M.J. & Moore, R.K. (1994). Automatic speech recognition that includes visual speech cues. *Proceedings of the Institute of Acoustics (Autumn Meeting, Windermere)*, *16(5)*, 15–22.

Chatfield, C. & Collins, A.J. (1980). *Introduction to Multivariate Analysis*. London: Chapman & Hall.

Cohen, M.M. & Massaro, D.W. (1993). Modeling coarticulation in synthetic visual speech. In Thalmann, N.M. & Thalmann, D. (Eds), *Computer Animation*, *93*, Tokyo: Springer-Verlag, Berlin, 139–56.

Ekman, P. (1979). About brows: emotional and conversational signals. In von Cranach, M., Foppa, K., Lepenies, W. & Ploog, D. (Eds), *Human Ethology*. Cambridge: Cambridge University Press, 169–202.

Elman, J.L. & Zipser, D. (1986). Learning the hidden structure of speech. *Journal of the Acoustical Society of America*, *83*, 1615–26.

Finn, K.I. (1986). An investigation of visible lip information to be used in automatic speech recognition. *PhD. Thesis*. Washington D.C.: Georgetown University.

Hennecke, M.E., Stork, D.G. & Prasad, K.V. (1996). Visionary Speech: looking ahead to practical speechreading systems. In D.G. Stork & M.E. Hennecke (Eds), *Speechreading by Humans and Machines*. Berlin: Springer, 331–50.

Lavagetto, F. & Lavagetto, P. (1996). Time delay neural networks for articulatory estimation from speech: suitable subjective evaluation protocols. In D.G. Stork & M.E. Hennecke (Eds), *Speechreading by Humans and Machines*. Berlin: Springer, 437–44.

MacLeod, A. & Summerfield, A.Q. (1987). Quantifying the contribution of vision to speech perception in noise. *British Journal of Audiology*, *21*, 131–41.

Massaro, D.W. (1996). Bimodal speech perception: a progress report. In D.G. Stork & M.E. Hennecke (Eds), *Speechreading by Humans and Machines*. Berlin: Springer, 79–102.

Movellan, J.R. (1995). Visual speech recognition with stochastic networks. In Tesauro, G., Touretzky, D. & Leen, T. (Eds), *Advances in neural information processing systems, (7)*. Cambridge, Mass.: MIT Press, 851–8.

Nishida, S. (1986). Speech recognition enhancement by lip information. *Proceedings of CHI 86 (ACM)*, 198–204.

Parke, F.I. (1975). Parametrized models for facial animation. *IEEE Computer Graphics and Applications*, *2*, 61–8.

Peeling, S.M., Moore R.K. & Tomlinson, M.J. (1986). The multilayer perceptron as a tool for speech pattern processing research. *Proceedings of the Institute of Acoustics (Autumn Meeting, Windermere)*, *8(7)*, 307–14.

Petajan, E.D. (1984). Automatic lipreading to enhance speech recognition. *Proceedings of the Global Telecommunications Conference, Atlanta, Georgia (IEEE Communication Society)*, 265–72

Rabiner, L.R. (1989). A tutorial on hidden Markov models and selected applications in speech recognition. *Proceedings of the IEEE*, *77*, 257–86.

Robert-Ribes, J., Piquemal, M., Schwartz, J-L. & Escudier, P. (1996). Exploiting sensor fusion architectures and stimuli complementarity in AV speech recognition. In D.G. Stork & M.E. Hennecke (Eds), *Speechreading by Humans and Machines*. Berlin: Springer, 193–210.

Sejnowski, T.J., Yuhas, B.P., Goldstein, M.H. & Jenkins, R.E. (1990). Combining visual and acoustic speech signals with a neural network improves intelligibility. In Touretzky, D.S. (Ed.), *Advances in Neural Information Processing Systems (2)*. San Mateo, California: Morgan-Kaufman Publishers.

Simons, A.D. & Cox, S.J. (1990). Generation of mouthshapes for a synthetic talking head. *Proceedings of the Institute of Acoustics (Autumn Meeting, Windermere)*, *12(10)*, 475–82.

Stork, D.G. & Hennecke, M.E. (Eds) (1996). *Speechreading by Humans and Machines*. Berlin: Springer, .

Stork, D.G., Wolff, G. & Levine, E. (1992). Neural network lipreading system for improved speech recognition. *Proceedings of the International Joint Conference on Neural Networks, Baltimore (IEEE)*, *2*, 285–95.

Summerfield, A.Q. (1987). Some preliminaries to a comprehensive account of audio-visual speech perception. In Campbell, R. & Dodd, B. (Eds), *Hearing by Eye: The Psychology of Lipreading*. Hove, UK: Lawrence Erlbaum Associates Ltd.

Summerfield, A.Q. (1991). Visual perception of phonetic gestures. In Mattingley, I.G. & Studdert-Kennedy, M. (Eds), *Modularity and the Motor Theory of Speech Perception*. Hillsdale, NJ: Lawrence Erlbaum Associates, 117–38.

Terzopoulos, D. & Waters, K. (1990). Physically-based facial modelling, analysis and animation. *Journal of Visualisation and Computer Animation*, *1*, 73–80.

Tomlinson, M.J., Russell, M.J. & Brooke, N.M. (1996). Integrating audio and visual information to provide highly robust speech recognition. *Proceedings of ICASSP, Atlanta, Georgia (IEEE)*, 821–4.

Turk, M. & Pentland, A. (1991). Eigenfaces for recognition. *Journal of Cognitive Neuroscience*, *3*, 71–86.

CHAPTER SIX

The moving face during speech communication

Kevin G. Munhall *Department of Psychology, Queen's University, Kingston, Ontario, Canada*

Eric Vatikiotis-Bateson *Human Information Processing Research Laboratories, ATR Laboratories, Kyoto, Japan*

OVERVIEW

It has been recognised for many years that viewing the face during auditory speech perception can influence phonetic categorisation. For example, under noisy conditions the face supplements the auditory signal and perceptual accuracy is increased (e.g. Sumby & Pollack, 1954). Even with clearly audible signals, viewing the face can modify the perceived place of articulation (McGurk & MacDonald, 1976) and perceived voicing categories of consonants (Green & Miller, 1985). Although static or configurational information (Fromkin, 1964; Abry & Boë, 1986; Badin et al., 1994) contributes to this cross-modal effect, in this paper we focus on the dynamic characteristics of the moving face during speech (e.g. Rosenblum, 1994). In doing so, we try to establish what dynamic visual information is available and try to uncover its possible usefulness to the perceiver.

Characterising the parameters of the moving face is important for a number of theoretical and practical reasons. Foremost among the practical reasons is the need to explicitly describe the visual stimuli used in audio-visual perception experiments. Individual speakers differ in the extent and clarity of the phonetic information that their faces provide (Demorest & Bernstein, 1992; Gagné et al., 1995) and different speaking styles can influence the visual contribution to phonetic judgements (Munhall et al., 1996; Gagné et al., 1995). However, little is known about the motion parameters of the face that produce these intraspeaker and interspeaker effects. Indeed, it is common in audio-visual speech research to report experimental findings with no details about the parameters of the visual stimuli beyond the gender of the speaker. We believe that until the facial motion parameters can be characterised a significant proportion of the variance in such experiments will necessarily remain uncontrolled and unaccounted for.

A second reason for putting emphasis on the characterisation of facial movement parameters is our belief that speech perception and production share the same cognitive primitives and, therefore, should be modelled together. We know that much of the phonetically relevant visual information used by perceivers is the direct by-product of the production of the speech acoustics and thus can be modelled from the same neuromotor control source (Vatikiotis-Bateson et al., 1996; Vatikiotis-Bateson & Yehia, 1996). By detailing the movements of the face, we hope to simultaneously provide parameters for this modelling effort and for audio-visual speech perception.

As the motion of the face provides a number of challenges for measurement and presumably for the perceptual system as well, we begin by reviewing what is known about the kinematics of face and head motion from the speech production literature. Next, we summarise some of our work on tracking motion of the full face and describe how phonetic information is distributed across the facial surface. Finally, we describe work that reveals how well this distributed information predicts phonetic structure.

KINEMATICS OF THE HEAD AND FACE

Before describing the face and head kinematics, two features of orofacial motion must be noted. First, the motion of the head and face during speech is a combination of rigid and nonrigid motion. In rigid motion, the object maintains its three-dimensional form and the observed motion is only the result of position and orientation changes. In nonrigid motion, the object can change its shape as well as its position and orientation. Thus, nonrigid motion presents a more complex problem for visual motion decomposition than does rigid motion (Black & Yacoob, 1995).

Second, the motion of the speech articulators is relative motion. That is, the speech articulators are attached to, or supported by, other moving bodies. For example, jaw and lip motions are superimposed onto larger and slower head motions or full-body motions. The combined motion of the head/body and speech articulators creates displacements and movement velocities much larger than the movements that are directly responsible for phonetic information. In measuring facial motion then, the data must be referenced to head co-ordinates to allow measurement of the *relative* motion of the lips and jaw (i.e. with head motion removed). Some perceptual process presumably must perform equivalent co-ordinate transformations to register the facial motion for visual phonetic perception. In the data reviewed in the following pages, we will be discussing the relative motion of each articulator, not the absolute motion of the articulators that would be observed by perceivers in natural communication settings.

The head moves as a rigid body during conversation providing conventional gestures such as nods and less conventional, rhythmic movements associated with the prosody of the utterance (McNeill, 1992). In head-turning experiments, self-generated head movements can reach velocities as high as 800 degrees/s (Pulaski, Zee & Robinson, 1981; Segal & Katsarkas, 1988). Head displacement and velocities in absolute terms and also displacements and velocities referenced to the torso can be even higher in activities such as walking, running and jumping (Pozzo, Berthoz & Lefort, 1989). Most head movements in speech, however, are much lower in velocity and smaller in movement range.

The jaw, like the head, also moves as a rigid body in three dimensions (Vatikiotis-Bateson & Ostry, 1995). While most of the motion in speech lies in translations and rotations within the mid-sagittal plane, smaller motions outside of this plane are also observed. Some of these motions are due to structural asymmetries in the mandible (Ferrario et al., 1994) but behavioural asymmetries in oral activity have also been noted (Campbell, 1982; Wolf & Goodale, 1987). The amplitudes of non mid-sagittal movements during speech usually do not exceed 1–2 mm for translation and 2–3 degrees for rotation (Vatikiotis-Bateson & Ostry, 1995). The motions in the mid-sagittal plane are considerably larger than this and vary in size and speed depending on the vowel, consonant and prosodic context (Vatikiotis-Bateson & Ostry, 1995; Ostry & Munhall, 1994). The motions of the mandible in this plane can be as large as 10 mm of translation and 10–15 degrees of rotation.

The primary sources of visible phonetic information are the nonrigid motions of the facial surface and oral aperture. These movements are produced largely by the action of a complex network of facial and perioral muscles, but movements of the mandible and intra-oral air pressures influence the visible morphology of the face as well. In fact, speechreading guides frequently cite changes in the facial morphology due to air pressure as a cue to distinguish voicing categories (Jeffers & Barley, 1971).

Most production research on the face during speech has dealt only with the motion of mid-sagittal points on the upper and lower lips. The kinematics of these points are used to estimate the change in the oral aperture and can do so with reasonable accuracy (Ramsay et al., 1996). Studies of the principal components of variation of static lip shape (Linker, 1982) and the kinematics of lip movement (Ramsay et al., 1996) have revealed a small number of modes of variation. In Linker's data, the vowels of English can be distinguished on the basis of a single measure, horizontal opening, while the vowels of Cantonese required two factors and Finnish, Swedish and French three factors. Ramsay et al. (1996) calculated the principal components of lip motion in English for the three-dimensional motion of eight markers positioned around the oral aperture. The motion along a single dominant trajectory accounted for much of the variance in the data and the motion of any single position marker on the lip was strongly one-dimensional. The proportion of variance accounted for by the first principal component was on average greater than 80%.

The motions of the lips themselves vary for different phonetic contexts but on average are relatively small with the upper lip typically moving much less than the lower lip (for a review of speech articulation, see Smith, 1992). Sussman, MacNeilage & Hanson (1973), for example, report average vertical movements of approximately 6 mm for upper lip movements with lower lip movements almost twice this value on average. These data were the average of movements for /p/, /b/, and /m/ in three different front vowel contexts. Gracco (1988) reports the same range of displacements for upper and lower lip closing movements for the first /p/ in "sapapple". Rounding or protrusion movements for both lips are similarly small with maximum rounding frequently below 5 mm (Daniloff & Moll, 1968; Lubker & Gay, 1982; Perkell, 1986; Boyce, 1988). The size and velocity of the lip movements vary with lexical stress, speaking rate, speaking volume, clarity of speech and the vowel environment (Vatikiotis-Bateson & Kelso, 1993). The relationship between the peak instantaneous velocity and the displacement is largely linear (e.g. Vatikiotis-Bateson & Kelso, 1993; Ostry & Munhall, 1985) as both velocity and displacement increase with slower rates, greater stress, greater speaking volume and more open vowels.

The timing of the movements of the facial articulators is not synchronous. The upper lip, lower lip and jaw exhibit consistent but phase-shifted timing patterns (Gracco, 1988, 1994; Gracco & Abbs, 1986, 1988). For example, Gracco (1988) reported that during the production of the word "sapapple" subjects consistently initiated movement toward the closure for the first /p/ in the order upper lip first, lower lip second and, finally, jaw (c.f. McClean, Kroll & Loftus, 1990; DeNil & Abbs, 1991). The onsets of movements also are not synchronous with acoustic events. For example, oral closure in bilabials occurs around peak closing velocity and the lips continue to move together during the closure interval (Fujimura, 1961; Löfqvist & Gracco, 1996). This means that the observable end of the closing movement occurs after the acoustic closure interval begins.

The fundamental frequency of facial movement is generally low. In a study of jaw motion during oral reading, Ohala (1975) found that the primary spectral peak of the movements was around 4 Hz. Muller and MacLeod (1982) report a similar range for lip-movement frequencies

($<10\,Hz$). (See later.) While the modal syllable rate in speech is low, movements of the lips have higher frequency components for some sounds. The opening movements for /p/, for example, can be quite rapid due to the combined aerodynamic and muscular forces at oral release (Fujimura, 1961). Even in oral closing movements, the motions of the lips contain higher frequency components than the syllable rate. Indeed, the syllable rate and speed of articulator movements are to some extent independent. For example, deaf speakers tend to produce syllable durations which are much longer than those of hearing speakers, but their articulator transitions into and out of bilabial closure (/p, b, m/) are no different from those of normal speakers (McGarr, Löfqvist & Seider-Story, 1987). Rather, differences in lip-motion speed are primarily phonetic, indicative of segment level factors such as aerodynamics. For example, the velocity of syllable final /p/ can be higher than that of final /b/ (e.g. Folkins & Canty, 1986; Gracco, 1994; Smith & McLean-Muse, 1987).

By examining the spectra of the motions of the face for a phonetically balanced passage such as the Rainbow Passage (Fairbanks, 1960), we can provide a more exact estimate of the frequency range over which the facial information is conveyed. Further, we can examine the spatial range across the face over which this information is spread.

The facial movements of two subjects were recorded while they read the Rainbow Passage. Movements were transduced in three dimensions using OPTOTRAK and subsequently the long-term average spectra were calculated for each spatial dimension for each marker. Subjects wore a head-jig to transduce head motion and seven markers were placed on the face: two on the mid-sagittal vermilion borders of the upper and lower lips, one on the chin, one on the lip corner and three on the face at a distance from the oral aperture (see Figure 16; the IRED locations marked with black circles (1, 2, 3, 5, 7, 9 and 11) were used in this analysis). Using the position data from the head-jig, the facial movements were transformed into head co-ordinates for all subsequent analyses.

Figure 17 shows the long-term average spectra for the vertical motion of the seven of the IREDs (1, 2, 3, 5, 7, 9 and 11). Three observations are noteworthy in these data. First, the frequency of the movements is limited to a narrow bandwidth. As can be seen in Figure 17, most of the power in the signals lies below 10 Hz. Second, the rank ordering of the spectra relates to the location of the IRED and the amount of motion at this position on the face. The top two spectra in Figure 17 represent the data for the IREDs on the centre of the lower lip and the chin. The bottom two spectra represent the data for the smaller movements of markers farther away from the mouth (IREDS 9 and 11). Finally, the spectra are very similar in shape across the different facial recording sites. While the overall power in the spectra varies at different positions on the face, this analysis suggests that similar infor-

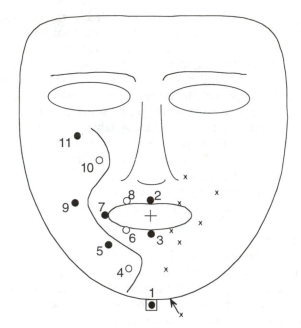

FIG. 16. Schematic facing showing positions of 11 IRED markers and EMG insertion sites for 8 muscles (the wavy line separates "inner" from "outer" marker groups and the cross denotes the co-ordinate origin).

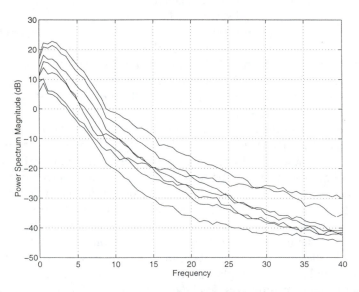

FIG. 17. Long-term average power spectra of vertical motion of seven IREDs (IRED 2, 3, 5, 7, 9 and 11) for one subject's reading of the Rainbow Passage.

128

mation is available at many different facial locations. In the following section we will explore this issue directly.

THE DISTRIBUTION OF MOTION ACROSS THE FACE

In order to study the relation between the movement of the face and the accompanying acoustics, we collected OPTOTRAK data from 11 IRED positions and also recorded electromyographic (EMG) signals using hooked wire electrodes from 8 muscles. In addition, acoustic recordings were made simultaneously. Subjects produced a variety of utterance types ranging from spontaneously generated sentences to repetitive sequences of nonsense vowel-consonant-vowel strings (VCVs; e.g. /æpæ/). The position of the infrared markers and the EMG electrodes are shown in Figure 16. The positions of markers on the head were also recorded and used to correct the facial markers for head motion. The data for the 11 facial IREDs were referenced to head co-ordinates with the origins of the co-ordinates at the maxillary incisors.

In the first analysis, we examined whether the motions of the perioral markers (those immediately surrounding the lips; IREDs 2, 3, 6, 7, 8) are predictable from the motions of the more peripheral markers. Figure 18 shows the three-dimensional motion of the perioral IREDs for the utterance: "When the sunlight strikes raindrops in the air, they act like a prism and form a rainbow" plotted against a linear combination of the peripheral five IREDs for the vertical, lateral and protrusion dimensions of the lip motion. We used an MMSE (minimum mean square error) procedure to produce the linear combination used to approximate the perioral markers. As can be seen in the figure, the shape and motion of the lip motion can be recovered at better than 95% by using the motion of more remote regions. The R^2 values are shown in the lower right-hand corner of each panel. Somewhat lower R^2 values are observed for the lateral motion of the upper-lip markers. Since there is little movement in this direction, these smaller R^2 values can be accounted for by the small range of the oral aperture data.

In order to examine the relationship between the facial motion across the different facial regions and the segmental structure of the speech stimuli, we tested whether we could estimate the RMS amplitude of the acoustics with combinations of the IRED motion data. Figure 19 shows the estimated and recorded RMS amplitude of the speech signal for all the markers (top panel) and selected groupings of the markers. The more peripheral markers are shown in the second panel from the bottom and the perioral markers are shown in the bottom panel. The R^2 values for the peripheral and perioral IREDs are quite high, which suggests that they both contain substantial information about the acoustic structure. However, the increase in R^2 for

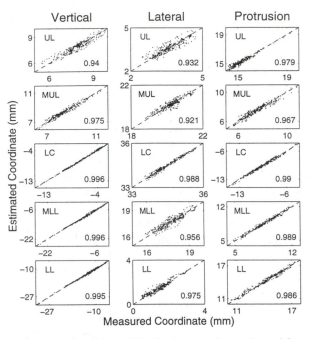

FIG. 18.   Three-dimensional positions of the five inner markers estimated from the motion of the five outer markers (axes are scaled in mm and R^2 values are given at the lower right of each panel; UL – IRED #2; MUL – IRED #8; LC – IRED #7; MLL – IRED #6; LL – IRED #3.

the use of all the IREDs indicates that the motion of more peripheral points on the face and the motion of the points on the lips contain independent variance components and thus provide potentially independent information for the perceiver. Recent visual perception studies have supported this finding. Smeele et al. (1995) found that the McGurk effect was stronger when parts of the face in addition to the lips were shown. Guiard-Marigny, Ostry & Benoît (1995) reported similar findings in a lipreading task. Performance was enhanced when the motion of the jaw was visible as well as the lips.

The strong correlation between facial motion and acoustic rms amplitude suggests that the face indexes the basic spatio-temporal behaviour of the vocal tract, namely, the time course and amplitude of vocal tract opening and closing. By extension, the facial motion may be correlated with the time-varying spectral acoustics that are generated by the moving vocal tract. To test this, linear predictive coding analysis was used to estimate the time-varying reflectance coefficients (PARCOR; Markel & Gray, 1976) at positions about 1.5 cm apart along the vocal tract for a training set of 14 sentences (5 repetitions each of two sentences and 4 repetitions of a third

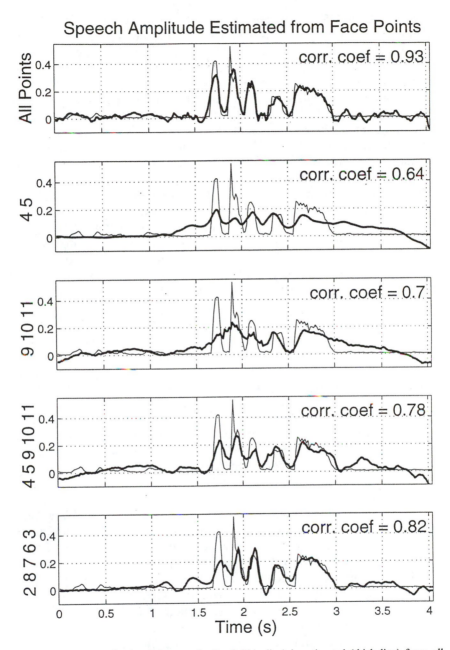

FIG. 19. RMS amplitude of the speech signal (thin line) is estimated (thick line) from all markers (top panel) and from selected combinations of IREDs (IREDs 4 and 5 – 2nd panel; IREDs 9, 10, 11 – 3rd panel; IREDs 4, 5, 9, 10, 11 – 4th panel; IREDs 2, 8, 7, 6, 3 – bottom panel).

sentence). An MMSE technique was used to correlate the estimated coefficients with the three-dimensional motions of the facial markers. The resulting correlations were then used to predict the reflectance coefficients for a sentence repetition not included in the training set (for details, see Vatikiotis-Bateson & Yehia, 1996). Time series for the first five predicted and observed coefficients, corresponding to the anterior portion of the vocal tract, are plotted in Figure 20. The panels on the right correspond to estimations based on markers around the lips while the panels on the left correspond to estimations based on all of the facial markers with the chin excluded. Not surprisingly, estimation was best at the lips (r1), but in general the values were high all along the front (oral) cavity.

The estimated spectra and rms amplitudes were then combined with the original noise source (amplitude normalised) to generate an audible acoustic signal. Listeners judged the signal to be moderately intelligible. Although we do not believe that perceivers transform orofacial motion into formant acoustics, the high overall correlation between facial motion and the vocal tract events associated with generating the speech acoustics provides strong circumstantial support for the proposal that both behaviours stem from a common control source.

We examined this idea more directly by determining how well lip and more remote facial motions could be estimated from the activity of eight perioral muscles. Although the relation between muscle force and articulator motions is inherently non-linear and the relationship between EMG activity and muscle force is unclear, the preceding analyses have shown that orofacial motion is highly linearised. Therefore, as a first approximation, we used a linear second-order model (Figure 21) to estimate the relation between muscle EMG activity and the position of the markers on the lips and face approximately 20 ms later. The results were about the same as our earlier effort using non-linear estimates of muscle force to estimate oral aperture (Hirayama et al., 1994), and were achieved at a much lower computational cost.

Two aspects of the results are particularly interesting and are being examined further using linear and non-linear techniques. First, motions of markers on the cheeks and lower face were recovered just as well as those placed on the lips (i.e. 40–96% of the variance). This result provides direct physiological support for the claim that the system controlling lip and jaw motion dynamically affects the entire facial structure below the eyes. That is, linguistically relevant audio-visual information can be modelled from a single motor control source.

Second, there are a number of indications that the acoustics of nonsense and real speech are not the same (Remez, Lipton & Fellowes, 1996). Comparison of the nonsense and sentence utterances within the corpus of this study reveals at least one aspect of this difference at the level of speech

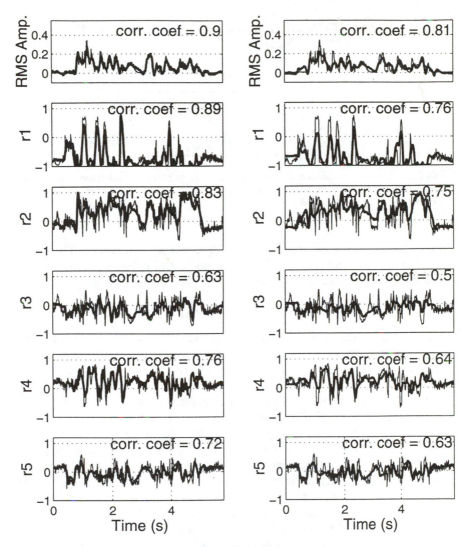

FIG. 20.   RMS amplitude and PARCOR coefficients (thin lines) for a test sentence and estimated RMS amplitude and PARCOR coefficients (thick lines) based on the motion of the lip markers (right panels) and all of the facial markers (left panels).

motor control. Specifically, when the relation between EMG activity and motion was estimated for repetitive nonsense utterances (e.g., /æpæ/) lip recovery was slightly better (5–10%) than for the spontaneous sentences and for the recited text, but recovery of the remote facial locations was much worse. For example, recovery of the cheek motion dropped from about 80%

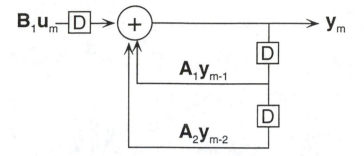

FIG. 21.   Schematic of the second order AR model used to estimate marker motion (y_m) from the EMG activity of the previous sample (B_1u_{m-1}), conditioned by the marker position of the previous two samples (y_{m-1} and y_{m-2}).

for spontaneous speech to 40% for the nonsense utterances. These two results are consistent with the loss of prosodic and other expressive details that occurs when speech material is too simple and repetitive.

THE MOVING FACE AS VISUAL INFORMATION

It is clear from the review just given that the face is a rich source of information about the speech signal. How the listener in face-to-face communication extracts the relevant information is not clear. In this section we consider some evidence about listener perceptual behaviour and also consider the perceptual problem that speechreading presents.

In recent work at ATR Research Laboratories, we have examined the eye movement behaviour of subjects watching video images of a talker (Vatikiotis-Bateson, Eigsti & Yano, 1994; Vatikiotis-Bateson et al., in press; Eigsti et al., 1995). The rationale for the research was to identify the regions of the face that attracted the most visual attention and, thus, to identify the regions of the face that were the most informative. Japanese- and English-speaking subjects viewed recorded monologues that were projected at various sizes onto a large screen. The acoustic portion of the monologues was played simultaneously at a number of signal-to-noise ratios. Overall, subjects fixated on the eyes for a large proportion of the trials. The fixation pattern was not influenced by the size of the projected facial image but was influenced by the listening conditions (see Figure 22). The amount of time spent fixating on the mouth ranged from approximately 35% in the no-noise condition to approximately 55% in the high noise condition. Thus, eye fixations decreased and mouth fixations increased as the signal became more difficult to hear.

Initially, we were surprised that the eyes were such a potent visual target but a number of possible explanations have emerged. It may be that

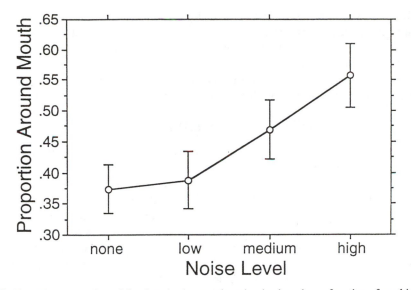

FIG. 22.   The proportion of fixations in the mouth region is plotted as a function of masking noise level.

foveating on the eyes is required for non-phonetic reasons (e.g. socio-linguistic) and that this is done in a trade-off with phonetic perception. The more interesting possibility is that fixating on the eyes produces no per-ceptual deficit. This could occur for two reasons. The visual system is known to show different sensitivities across the visual field. The foveal region dis-plays higher acuity and colour vision while the peripheral visual field shows greater sensitivity to motion. If major phonetic cues are dynamic (e.g. Rosenblum, 1994), then the listener may be aided by viewing the oral region with the peripheral visual field. A related explanation derives from our work on the distribution of facial motion. It is clear from the work reviewed earlier that the movements of regions of the face away from the immediate oral region are highly correlated with the movements of the oral aperture. Thus, it may be that the lips themselves need not be fixated on to visually perceive speech.

    Finally, the fixation on the eyes may serve a purpose in the perceptual processing of the phonetic facial motion. In face-to-face communication the decoding of the stream of visual speech is complicated by the fact that the head is not stationary during articulation. The head and body move simultaneous with the speech-relevant lip and face movements. If the head is nodding without the individual speaking, the lips move in the visual field as a result of the head motion. However, the motions that are important to speech perception are relative motions, the lip motions relative to the head.

Thus, in lipreading you have to be able to parse the full motion of the lips into the contributions made by the head and the phonetically relevant contributions made by the lips and vocal tract. This is not a trivial task for computer recognition of facial motions (Horn, 1987) or for the human perceptual system. One possibility is that the listener uses eye fixations to register the head position and, thus, to determine the relative facial motions.

MODELLING THE FACE IN SPEECH

Recently, we have begun work on a physiological model of the full face (Vatikiotis-Bateson et al., 1996). This work is an extension of the muscle-based animation of Terzopoulos and his colleagues (Terzopoulos & Waters, 1990; Lee, Terzopoulos & Waters, 1995). In this approach, called "physical modelling", the dynamic form of the animation is determined by the biophysical characteristics of the animated object. In the case of facial animation, different layers of facial tissue are represented by a multi-layered deformable mesh of nodes and springs. The spring constants in the mesh reproduce the stress/strain characteristics of the different layers of the facial tissue. The mesh is deformed by forces generated by the set of modelled muscles. Input to the model is in the form of stylised EMG that activates the muscles and produces muscle contraction.

There are a number of general advantages to this modelling approach, including greater computational efficiency and a high level of realism. From our perspective, however, the most important outcome of the synthesis of moving faces from neuromotor and biophysical parameters is that a more rational approach to speech research is brought about by pursuing production and perception work together rather than separately. Through realistic animation, in which we use known physiological parameters to control the visual stimuli for perception experiments, we can search for a set of neuromotor primitives that simultaneously accounts for oral motor control as well as perceptual structure.

ACKNOWLEDGEMENTS

This work was supported by grants from NIH (DC-00594 from the National Institute of Deafness and other Communication Disorders) and NSERC. Monique Charest and Pam Thompson made helpful comments on earlier versions of the manuscript.

REFERENCES

Abry, C. & Boë, L.J. (1986). Laws for lips. *Speech Communication*, 5, 97–104.
Badin, P., Motoki, K., Miki, N., Ritterhaus, D. & Lallouache, M.T. (1994). Some geometric and acoustic properties of the lip horn. *Journal of the Acoustical Society of Japan (E)*, 15, 243–53.

Black, M. & Yacoob, Y. (1995). Tracking and recognising rigid and non-rigid facial motions using local parametric models of image motion. *Proceedings of the Fifth International Conference on Computer Vision (ICCV'95)*. Boston.

Boyce, S.E. (1988). *The influence of phonological structure on articulatory organization in Turkish and in English: Vowel harmony and coarticulation*. Unpublished doctoral dissertation. Yale University.

Campbell, R. (1982). Asymmetries in moving faces. *British Journal of Psychology, 73*, 95–103.

Daniloff, R.G. & Moll, K.L. (1968). Coarticulation of lip rounding. *Journal of Speech and Hearing Research, 11*, 707–21.

Demorest, M.E. & Bernstein, L.E. (1992). Sources of variability in speechreading sentences: A generalizability analysis. *Journal of Speech and Hearing Research, 35*, 876–91.

DeNil, L. & Abbs, J.H. (1991). Influence of speaking rate on the upper lip, lower lip, and jaw peak velocity sequencing during bilabial closing movements. *Journal of the Acoustical Society of America, 89*, 845–9.

Eigsti, I.-M., Munhall, K.G., Yano, S. & Vatikiotis-Bateson, E. (1995). Effects of listener expectation on eye movement behavior during audio-visual perception. *Journal of the Acoustical Society of America, 97*, 3287.

Fairbanks, G. (1960). *Voice and Articulation Drillbook*. New York: Harper and Row.

Ferrario, V., Chiarella, S., Poggio, C. & Tartaglia, G. (1994). Distance form symmetry: A three-dimensional evaluation of facial asymmetry. *Journal of Oral Maxillofacial Surgery, 52*, 1126–32.

Folkins, J.W. & Canty, J. (1986). Movements of the upper and lower lips during speech: Interactions between lips with the jaw fixed at different position. *Journal of Speech and Hearing Research, 29*, 348–56.

Fromkin, V.A. (1964). Lip positions in American English vowels. *Language and Speech, 7*, 215–25

Fujimura, O. (1961). Bilabial stop and nasal consonants: A motion picture study and its acoustical implications. *Journal of Speech and Hearing Research, 4*, 233–47.

Gagné, J.-P., Querengesser, C., Folkeard, P., Munhall, K.G. & Masterson, V. (1995). Auditory, visual and audiovisual speech intelligibility for sentence-length stimuli: An investigation of conversational and clear speech. *The Volta Review, 95(1)*, 33–51.

Gracco, V.L. (1988). Timing factors in the coordination of speech movements. *Journal of Neuroscience, 8*, 4628–34.

Gracco, V.L. (1994). Some organizational characteristics of speech movement control. *Journal of Speech and Hearing Research, 37*, 4–27.

Gracco, V.L. & Abbs, J.H. (1986). Variant and invariant characteristics of speech movements. *Experimental Brain Research, 65*, 156–66.

Gracco, V.L. & Abbs, J.H. (1988). Central patterning of speech movements. *Experimental Brain Research, 71*, 515–26.

Green, K.P. & Miller, J.L. (1985). On the role of visual rate information in phonetic perception. *Perception and Psychophysics, 38(3)*, 269–76.

Guiard-Marigny, T., Ostry, D.J. & Benoît, C. (1995). Speech intelligibility of synthetic lips and jaw. *Proceedings of the 13th International Congress of Phonetic Sciences* (3) (pp. 222–5). Stockholm, Sweden.

Hirayama, M., Vatikiotis-Bateson, E., Gracco, V.L. & Kawato, M. (1994). Neural network prediction of lip shape from EMG in Japanese speech. *Proceedings of the International Conference on Spoken Language Processing (ICSLP-94)* (2) (pp. 587–90). Yokahama, Japan.

Horn, B.K.P. (1987). Closed-form solution of absolute orientation using unit quaternions. *Journal of the Optical Society of America, 4*, 629–42.

Jeffers, J. & Barley, M. (1971). *Speechreading (lipreading)*. Springfield, IL: Charles C. Thomas Publisher.

Lee, Y.V., Terzopoulos, D. & Waters, K. (1995). Realistic modeling for facial animation. In R. Cook (Ed.), *Proceedings of SIGGRAPH '95* (pp. 55–62). Los Angeles: ACM SIGGRAPH.

Linker, W. (1982). Articulatory and acoustic correlates of labial activity in vowels: A cross-linguistic study. *UCLA Working Papers in Phonetics, 56*, 1–154

Löfqvist, A. & Gracco, V. (1996). Labial kinematics in stop consonant production. *Journal of the Acoustical Society America, 99*, 2472 (A).

Lubker, J.F. & Gay, T.J. (1982). Anticipatory labial coarticulation: Experimental, biological and linguistic variables. *Journal of the Acoustical Society of America, 71*, 437–48.

Markel, J. & Gray, A. (1976). *Linear Prediction of Speech.* Springer-Verlag: New York.

McClean, M.D., Kroll, R.M. & Loftus, N.S. (1990). Kinematic analysis of lip closure in stutterers' fluent speech. *Journal of Speech and Hearing Research, 33*, 755–60.

McGarr, N.S., Löfqvist, A. & Seider-Story, R. (1987). Jaw kinematics in hearing-impaired speakers. *Proceedings of the 11th International Congress of Phonetic Sciences* (4) (pp. 173–6). Tallinn: Academy of Sciences of the ESSR.

McGurk, H. & MacDonald, J. (1976). Hearing lips and seeing voices. *Nature, 264*, 746–8.

McNeill, D. (1992). *Hand and mind.* Chicago: University of Chicago Press.

Muller, E.M. & MacLeod, G. (1982). *Perioral biomechanics and its relation to labial motor control.* Paper presented at the meeting of the Acoustical Society of America, Chicago.

Munhall, K.G., Gribble, P., Sacco, L. & Ward, M. (1996). Temporal constraints on the McGurk effect. *Perception and Psychophysics, 58*, 351–62.

Ohala, J.J. (1975). The temporal regulation of speech. In G. Fant & M.A.A. Tatham (Eds), *Auditory Analysis and Perception of Speech.* London: Academic Press.

Ostry, D.J. & Munhall, K.G. (1985). Control of rate and duration of speech movements. *Journal of the Acoustical Society of America, 77*, 640–48.

Ostry, D.J. & Munhall, K.G. (1994). Control of jaw orientation and position in mastication and speech. *Journal of Neurophysiology, 71*, 1515–32.

Perkell, J.S. (1986). Coarticulation strategies: Preliminary implications of a detailed analysis of lower lip protrusion movements. *Speech Communication, 5*, 47–68.

Pozzo, T., Berthoz, A. & Lefort, L. (1989). Head kinematic during various motor tasks in humans. *Progress in Brain Research, 50*, 377–83.

Pulaski, P., Zee, D. & Robinson, D. (1981). The behavior of the vestibulo-ocular reflex at high velocities of head rotation. *Brain Research, 222*, 159–65.

Ramsay, J.O., Munhall, K.G., Gracco, V.L. & Ostry, D.J. (1996). Functional data analyses of lip motion. *Journal of the Acoustical Society of America, 99*, 3718–27.

Remez, R., Lipton, J. & Fellowes, J. (1996). Perceiving the difference between spontaneous and read speech: The role of physical duration. *Journal of the Acoustical Society of America, 99*, 2493.

Rosenblum, L.D. (1994). How special is audiovisual speech integration? *Current Psychology of Cognition, 13*, 110–16.

Segal, B. & Katsarkas, A. (1988). Long-term deficits of goal-directed vestibulo-ocular function following total unilateral loss of peripheral vestibular function. *Acta Otolaryngol (Stockholm), 106*, 102–10.

Smeele, P., Hahnlen, L., Stevens, E., Kuhl, P. & Meltzoff, A.N. (1995). Investigating the role of specific facial information in audiovisual speech perception (abstract). *Journal of the Acoustical Society of America, 98*, 5aSC7.

Smith, A. (1992). The control of orofacial movements in speech. *Critical Reviews in Oral Biology and Medicine, 3*, 233–67.

Smith, B.L. & McLean-Muse, A. (1987). Kinematic characteristics of postvocalic labial stop consonants produced by children and adults. *Phonetica, 44*, 227–37.

Sumby, W. H. & Pollack, I. (1954). Visual contribution to speech intelligibility in noise. *Journal of the Acoustical Society of America, 26*, 212–15.

Sussman, H.M., MacNeilage, P.F. & Hanson, R.J. (1973). Labial and mandibular dynamics during the production of bilabial consonants: Preliminary observations. *Journal of Speech and Hearing Research*, *16*, 397–420.

Terzopoulos, D. & Waters, K. (1990). Physically-based facial modeling, analysis, and animation. *Visualization and Computer Animation*, *1*, 73–80.

Vatikiotis-Bateson, E. & Kelso, J.A.S. (1993). Rhythm type and articulatory dynamics in English, French and Japanese. *Journal of Phonetics*, *21*, 231–65.

Vatikiotis-Bateson, E. & Ostry, D.J. (1995). An analysis of the dimensionality of jaw motion in speech. *Journal of Phonetics*, *23*, 101–17.

Vatikiotis-Bateson, E. & Yehia, H. (1996). Physiological modeling of facial motion during speech. *Transactions of the Technical Committee on Psychological and Physiological Acoustics, H-96-65*, 1–8.

Vatikiotis-Bateson, E., Eigsti, I.-M. & Yano, S. (1994). Listener eye movement behavior during audiovisual perception. *Proceedings of the International Conference on spoken Language Processing-94*, 527–30.

Vatikiotis-Bateson, E., Eigsti, I.-M., Yano, S. & Munhall, K.G. (in press). Listener eye movement behavior during audiovisual perception. *Perception and Psychophysics*.

Vatikiotis-Bateson, E., Munhall, K.G., Hirayama, M., Lee, Y.V. & Terzopolous, D. (1996). Dynamics of facial motion in speech: Kinematic and electromyographic studies of orofacial structures. In D.G. Stork & M. Hennecke (Eds), *Speechreading by Humans and Machines*. *NATO-ASI Series F* (150) (pp. 221–32). Berlin: Springer-Verlag.

Wolf, M.E. & Goodale, M.A. (1987). Oral asymmetries during verbal and nonverbal movements of the mouth. *Neuropsychologia*, *25*, 375–96.

PSYCHOLOGICAL AND NEUROPSYCHOLOGICAL FACTORS IN SPEECHREADING

CHAPTER SEVEN

Conceptual constraints in sentence-based lipreading in the hearing-impaired

Jerker Rönnberg, Stefan Samuelsson and Björn Lyxell
Department of Education and Psychology, Linköping University, Sweden

INTRODUCTION

From a perceptual and a cognitive point of view, processing of information in normal listening conditions represents a quite effortless task for the normal hearing individual in a situation without noise. This is one important factor in most models of auditory speech perception. However, for the hearing impaired, the communicative task forces the individual to rely on other forms of communication to understand spoken information. All alternative speech-based communicative forms (e.g. lipreading or lipreading with devices such as hearing-aids, tactile aids or cochlear implants) require that the information is processed in a different and more cognitively demanding way than for normal hearers in normal listening conditions.

If it is true that speech-based (not sign) alternatives to listening represent different speech processing modes, then such communication might be better described by models other than those based simply on auditory speech perception. A further implication, as a consequence of more effortful cognitive processing of the spoken signal, is that individual differences in cognitive capacity could play a more important role in explaining performance.

The suggestion that there are conceptual constraints in lipreading is that the visual signal is insufficiently specific for the ready extraction of spoken language information, and that conceptual factors therefore come into play to increase intelligibility of the poor or distorted speech signal. Understanding how people lipread may, therefore, rely on assumptions specific to this process, rather than assumptions (e.g. of serial bottom-up, on-line analysis of the speech signal) from the auditory speech perception perspective.

Let us first examine a few empirical observations that relate to the proposal of conceptual constraints in lipreading.

SPECIFICATION OF STIMULUS

Is the visual signal really as poor as, for example, general estimates of phoneme visibility demonstrate (i.e. ranging from 10% to 25%, Lyxell, 1989; Woodward & Barber, 1960)? The answer seems to be "yes". Without contextual constraints, and supposedly lacking the activation of relevant conceptual information prior to or during lipreading, lipreading isolated sentences is extremely hard to accomplish (approximately 5% of correctly identified words in sentences; Samuelsson & Rönnberg, 1991, 1993). It should be noted that eliminating lipreading, while maintaining context, i.e. having the subjects guess from the context only, resulted in similar very low levels of performance. In other words, lipreading of isolated sentences and pure guessing converge on the same accuracy levels (5%; Samuelsson & Rönnberg, 1991). Thus, it is the joint contribution of lip movement information and context that contribute to performance levels that vary from 5% to 45%, depending on the conditions for interaction between sensory and contextual information (Samuelsson & Rönnberg, 1993). However, it should be noted that the visibility of the signal can be improved by certain speaker characteristics and by how clearly speech is articulated (Gagné & Rochette, 1996), but such effects do not compensate for a lack of appropriate context.

Another aspect of facial movement in relation to the production of the speech signal is the emotional expression conveyed. Our data suggest that emotionally charged sentences (i.e. sentences with happy content spoken with a smiling face) are relatively easier to lipread, taken across a variety of stereotyped contextual settings (i.e. scripted, situation-based knowledge). However, the effect is subordinated to the interaction with context, that is, the fit between emotional content of the contextual script and type of emotion (Johansson & Rönnberg, 1995, 1996). Thus, again, contextual/ conceptual constraints *are* decisive for understanding natural lipspoken utterances.

SPECIFICATION OF SKILL

We have found no systematic evidence of spontaneous compensation in moderately hearing-impaired or profoundly deaf individuals (with acquired deafness) in the development of lipreading skills, i.e. performance is no better in hearing impaired groups compared to matched controls, whatever materials, tests and communicative forms, or period of handicap we tested, (Lyxell & Rönnberg, 1989; Rönnberg, 1990; Rönnberg, Öhngren & Nilsson, 1982, 1983; Hygge et al., 1992). However, early onset of hearing loss seems to contribute to superior lipreading skills, at least when the impairment is relatively severe (Tillberg et al., 1996). Case studies in our laboratory further support this proposal: expert lipreaders tend to have early onset hearing loss (Rönnberg, 1995). This general result is also in agreement with studies from other laboratories (Bernstein et al., this volume; Cowie & Douglas-Cowie, 1992; Mogford, 1987), as well as with results pertaining to cortical reorganisation (Wolff & Thatcher, 1990).

Despite the potential predictive power of onset age, what accounts more for variations in lipreading skill is the cognitive architecture underlying the skill. A summary of our main findings in the hard-of-hearing and deaf in this respect demonstrates the following.

1. Decoding skill constitutes an important *direct* predictor of sentence-based lipreading when the decoding task triggers lexical activation, as opposed to the mere visual discrimination of lip movements (Lyxell & Rönnberg, 1991).

2. Information-processing speed is especially important when text-based reaction-time tasks emphasise lexical and semantic access speed, as opposed to physical and name-matching speed (Lyxell, 1989; Rönnberg, 1990).

3. When verbal inference-making is tested by a sentence completion test rather than a word completion test, it is associated with successful sentence-based lipreading (Lyxell & Rönnberg, 1989).

Important *indirect* predictors of sentence-based lipreading include:

1. VN 130/P200 peak-to-peak amplitude measure in the visual evoked potential (Rönnberg et al., 1989).

2. Working memory capacity, measured by the reading-span task (Lyxell & Rönnberg, 1989).

3. Verbal ability (Lyxell & Rönnberg, 1992).

From three case studies, we have found that best lipreading skill is characterised by normal speed and decoding functions, but typically by very high levels of working-memory capacity and verbal inference-making skill (Lyxell, 1994; Rönnberg, 1993, 1995).

Thus far, we have learned that it takes contextual/conceptual constraints to make the lipreading task manageable and it requires a particular cognitive architecture to be able to handle these constraints fully.

MODEL SPECIFICATION OF CONCEPTUAL
CONSTRAINTS IN LIPREADING

In order to understand the nature of the interaction between sensory and contextual information in a lipreading task, Samuelsson and Rönnberg (1991, 1993) proposed a model based on a series of experiments on script use in lipreading. The main results of the experiments suggest that sentences typical of a particular script (such as the restaurant script, see Abbot, Black & Smith, 1985) always were better lipread than atypical sentences. Typical statements in a particular script represent higher levels of base-line activation of stored knowledge than atypical statements. Typicality may in turn be governed by a frequency-of-exposure principle (e.g. Galambos, 1983). The typicality effect is modified by the degree of contextual specificity provided immediately prior to the task. A highly specific context improves lipreading for both typical and atypical sentences, whereas general context (less specific) *only* improves lipreading of the typical sentence, with no effect on the atypical one.

An additional important prerequisite is that the context actually should be provided prior to, as opposed to immediately after, the presentation of the stimulus sentence. Thus, the effects are predictive rather than retrieval-based.

Figure 23 (from Samuelsson and Rönnberg, 1993) indicates how these three factors may be conceptualised in modelling lipreading in different contexts and different individuals. The general principle that can be derived from these studies is that, once the level of prediction/guessing of the message is induced by the particular conceptual context, lipreading is facilitated for *all* types of materials, at or above the level provided by guessing.

SPECIFICATION OF IMPLICIT ACTIVATIONS

Some dimensions that characterise a script are assumed to be activated in an implicit manner, whereas others have to be elaborated more explicitly. Samuelsson and Rönnberg (1993) suggested that typical representations are activated implicitly, but are late (as opposed to early) in the script. One reason we suggested this is that when individuals were informed about the sentence to be lipread, they were misled in half of the cases to believe that, for example, a typical sentence was atypical, that an early sentence was late in the script, etc. The logic behind this manipulation was that those scripted activations amenable to explicit control and manipulation should be specifically sensitive to this false information. Recognizing that one is misled implies a mismatch between predictions/expectations and actual script activation, hence signalling that something is wrong. In order to deal with

A Script Model of Lipreading

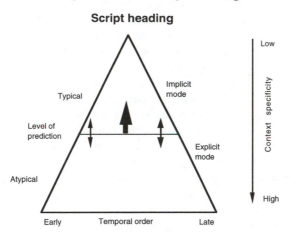

FIG. 23. A model of the interaction between contextual specificity and type of stimulus sentences. The bold arrow indicates the direction of activation, given a certain level of prediction. The level of prediction for a given script (e.g. Restaurant) is set by the contextual specificity (e.g. low specificity: ordering; high specificity: "You think something is incorrectly prepared"), combined with either a typical (e.g. "Would you like to recommend something from the menu?") or an atypical sentence (e.g. "The sauce with the boiled salmon was too thick").

this mismatch, explicit working-memory-based processing resources are assumed to be taken into account. If, on the other hand, the processing of the sentence primarily is carried out implicitly (that is, it is automatic), then no disturbances due to false dimensional cueing are predicted.

The data are clear on this point: typicality represents the implicit dimension (i.e. subjects do not suffer from false cueing), whereas the temporal dimension of a scripted package of knowledge suffers from this manipulation (i.e. is explicit; see Figure 23).

WORKING MEMORY

Capacity

The conception of a working-memory-based speechreading system is partly based on results from three case studies of extreme speechreading skill (Lyxell, 1994; Rönnberg, 1993; Rönnberg et al., 1996a). Although all three are extremely skilled speechreaders, they have different communicative strategies (Rönnberg, 1995). However, all of them have superior higher-order working-memory functions measured by the reading-span task (Daneman & Carpenter, 1980; Pichora-Fuller, Schneider & Daneman, 1995), whereas for simpler forms of short-term memory (e.g. digit span and indices of speeded word recognition), performance was on par with matched controls. In Daneman and Carpenter's (1980) task, subjects must understand a spoken or written story and also remember (probed) words in sentences. Thus, there seems to be a threshold function which defines the limits for lexical access speed and accuracy from speech gestures per se. Decoding and speed (i.e. lower-order functions) are important when the population as a whole is studied (Rönnberg, 1990), but do not capture the variation of *extreme* skill in the individual case. To surpass the threshold (at some hypothetical point) with respect to its contribution to lipreading of sentences and discourse, extremely skilled individuals need to have (or develop) a highly capacious, higher-order, working memory (see Figure 24).

A capacious working memory of the sort measured by the Daneman and Carpenter task works proactively and retroactively by releasing spare capacity for predicting what is to come in a conversation, and by having a larger capacity for maintaining previously encountered stimuli/contextual information in an active state, and hence being able to retrospectively dis- ambiguate speech information in the light of new information.

Phonological processing

As in reading print, reading of lips relies and capitalises on phonological processing (Conrad, 1979). Phonological processing during lipreading can be more analytically construed and includes a recoding or translation pro- cess of visual input, a mapping of the recoded percept to intact or impaired phonological representations (Lyxell, Rönnberg, & Samuelsson, 1994), and phonological activation of the lexicon. This can be amply demonstrated by experiments from a variety of paradigms.

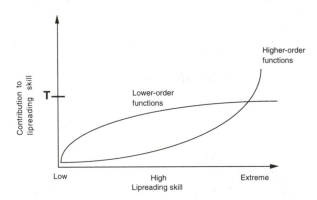

FIG. 24.   The threshold hypothesis: the relative contribution of higher and lower-order cog- nitive functions to lipreading skill.

Suffix-effects in short-term memory can be obtained with both mouthed and silently lipread stimuli in normal listeners (Campbell & Dodd, 1980; Greene & Crowder, 1984); concurrent articulation does not selectively affect recall of heard and lipread lists (Campbell & Dodd, 1984), and digit-span performance is also similar comparing the two presentation modes (Campbell, 1990).

From the perspective of a working-memory-based model of lipreading, it seems reasonable to assume that the phonological processing just listed takes processing resources into account. The individual's capacity to deal with this processing load in working memory may be one important determinant of lipreading skill. This processing load may be hard to reduce through practice.

One of the reasons is that there is no simple means of conceptualizing an efficient and automatised pattern recognition system based on dynamic variations of lip movements (within and across talkers) which at the kinematic level can specify speech sounds uniquely (for a discussion, see Summerfield, 1987). For print, a visual input lexicon can be constructed (Ellis & Young, 1986), where the letter-to-sound correspondence is higher than between lip movements and sound. Also, the lack of practice effects, at least when it comes to spontaneous improvements in lipreading skill in the hearing impaired, indirectly supports the notion that phonological processing remains one of the bottlenecks in working memory (Öhngren, 1992).

Research focused on the phonological aspect of working memory in lipreading in the hearing impaired (Lyxell, Rönnberg & Andersson, 1995) suggests that accuracy of written rhyme judgements is significantly correlated with both visual decoding of words and sentence-based lipreading among deafened adults. Therefore, we would suggest that accurate phonological representations constitute an important prerequisite for lipreading ability in the hearing impaired.

Our hypothesis is that phonological processing is a mandatory and unreflective modus operandi in lipreading. The reason why some people become more visual in their processing may have to do more with distorted phonological representations (i.e. due to acquired deafness; Lyxell, Rönnberg & Andersson, 1995) or with a relatively early onset of hearing-impairment (Tillberg et al., 1996) than with any conscious evaluation of audio-visual benefits.

A PROPOSED WORKING-MEMORY MODEL FOR LIPREADING

Here, we focus on the phonological processing aspect of a working-memory system for lipreading. Except for the more obvious role of phonology in recoding and lexically accessing what is seen (Rönnberg, 1995), we assume that phonological patterning of the speech signal also serves the overall purpose of accessing global, implicit knowledge of the communicative situation. The implication is that phonological patterning directs accessing of information to larger, supralexical units of information.

Working memory is assumed to operate most efficiently with implicit knowledge structures, which seems to be a straightforward assumption based on the script-model data (Samuelsson & Rönnberg, 1993). The reason is that implicit information (i.e. typical and highly script-frequent knowledge structures) is more predictable and, therefore, demands less maintenance or recycling of information in working memory. Finally, the accessing of implicit knowledge is assumed to depend on the individual's phonological representations, in the sense that a better individual ability to pattern the visual spoken signal will also allow for most efficient access to typical-script features. This represents an interaction where redundant information (typical-script information) can be processed with the help of an incompletely specified spoken signal.

TESTS OF ASSUMPTIONS

We have derived three critical assumptions to be tested in the evaluation of the present working memory notion:

1. Global, prosodic patterning of visual speech plays an important role when it comes to accessing contextual, and hence scripted, knowledge.
2. Implicit as opposed to explicit knowledge will contribute to lipreading and characterise lipreading skill.
3. Comparing lipreadability of typical and atypical sentences, typical sentences should either be relatively enhanced when prosodic support is added in some physical form or decreased when the prosodic aspect of phonology is disrupted.

Rönnberg et al. (1996b) have conducted an experiment to determine the relative contribution of the relevant variables, as well as their potential interactions: presentation mode, i.e. presence or absence of a low-frequency (F_0) supplement to lipreading (Breeuwer & Plomp, 1986), high versus low contextual specificity (defined by the levels manipulated in the script model) and typicality (i.e. high versus low typicality sentences). The auditory low-frequency supplement was used to present some of the relevant information in global, phonological patterning of the visual signal.

We predicted an interaction between typicality and presentation mode (see third assumption). The interaction between typicality and supplemented auditory low-frequency information should give greater facilitation for audio-visual perception of typical information than for atypical information. The alternative prediction states that adding sound to lip-reading (i.e. low-frequency information) should be additive with the effect of typicality.

The results were straighforward. All three manipulated variables generated three main effects. No interactions were statistically reliable. That is, global prosodic patterning per se is facilitative of lipreading performance. Furthermore, the typicality manipulation was comparably much stronger in its effect on lipreadability than either the auditory F_0 supplement or contextual specificity. This in itself is an important demonstration as it again testifies to the power of cognitive representations relative to sensory input. Typicality was also the only variable that interacted with overall lipreading skill, implying that efficient processing of implicit materials in working memory may be what characterises the skilled lipreader, offering support to the second assumption (Samuelsson & Rönnberg, 1991).

Contrary to the expectation, however, the results did not confirm the prediction of an interaction between low-frequency supplements to lip-reading and typicality, hence not supporting the third assumption that global prosodic patterning would ameliorate lipreading especially for typical, implicit materials.

In a recent unpublished study (Rönnberg, Samuelsson & Andersson, 1996), we wanted to test these assumptions using a different methodology. Concurrent distracting speech should interfere with phonological recoding and rehearsal—as long as the speech used has similar phonemes to those in the message. In order to disrupt the phonological loop during lipreading, a distracting voice read Swedish nonwords during the actual TV-presentation of the sentences to be lipread (typical and atypical). The data once again seem very clear: two main effects and no interaction. Typical sentences were much easier to lipread and the phonological, nonword-level type of distraction was highly effective, but the two variables did not interact significantly. In a second experiment we replicated this pattern for a foreign (distracting) phonology which is dissimilar to Swedish and totally incomprehensible to our subjects (i.e. Mandarin Chinese), suggesting that the distracting effect is not occurring because of phonological confusions between target and distractor messages.

GENERAL CONCLUSION

The proposed working-memory model for lipreading has gained support in two respects, but not with respect to the third assumption, namely that typicality and phonological recoding effects may be interactive in the lip-reading of sentences. This assumption may simply be wrong. In any case, further experiments will clarify the precise relationship between input variables on the one hand, and cognitive ones on the other.

REFERENCES

Abbot, V., Black, J.B. & Smith, E.E. (1985). The representation of scripts in memory. *Journal of Memory and Language*, 24, 179–99.

Breeuwer, M. & Plomp, R. (1986). Speechreading supplemented with auditorily presented speech parameters. *Journal of Acoustical Society of America*, 79, 481–99.

Campbell, R. (1990). Lipreading, neuropsychology, and immediate memory. In G. Vallar and T. Shallice (Eds), *Neuropsychological Impairments of Short-term Memory* (pp. 268–86). Cambridge: Cambridge University Press.

Campbell, R. & Dodd, B. (1980). Hearing by eye. *Quarterly Journal of Experimental Psychology, Human Learning and Memory*, 32, 85–100.

Campbell, R. & Dodd, B. (1984). Aspects of hearing by eye. In H. Bouma and D.G. Bouwhuis (Eds), *Attention and Performance X* (pp. 300–11). Hove, UK: Lawrence Erlbaum Associates Ltd.

Conrad, R. (1979). *The deaf schoolchild.* Harper and Row: London.

Cowie, R. & Douglas-Cowie, E. (1992). *Postlingually Acquired Deafness: Speech Deterioration and the Wider Consequences.* New York: Mouton de Gruyter.

Daneman, M. & Carpenter, P. (1980). Individual differences in working memory and reading. *Journal of Verbal Learning and Verbal Behavior*, 19, 450–66.

Ellis, A.W. & Young, A.W. (1986). *Human Cognitive Neuropsychology.* Hove, UK: Lawrence Erlbaum Associates Ltd.

Gagné, J.P. & Rochette, A.-L. (1996). Auditory, audiovisual, and visual clear speech effects. Paper presented in the lipreading session at the *XXVI Congress of Psychology*, Montreal, August.

Galambos, J.A. (1983). Normative studies of six characteristics of our knowledge of common activities. *Behavior Research Methods and Instrumentation*, 15, 327–40.

Greene, R.L. & Crowder, R.G. (1984). Modality and suffix effects in the absence of auditory stimulation. *Journal of Verbal Learning and Verbal Behavior*, 23, 371–82.

Hygge, S., Rönnberg, J., Larsby, B. & Arlinger, S. (1992). Normal and hearing-impaired subjects' ability to just follow conversation in competing speech, reversed speech, and noise backgrounds. *Journal of Speech and Hearing Research*, 35, 208–15.

Johansson, J. & Rönnberg, J. (1995). The role of emotionality and typicality in speechreading. *Scandinavian Journal of Psychology*, 36, 189–200.

Johansson, K. & Rönnberg, J. (1996). Speech gestures and facial expression in speechreading. *Scandinavian Journal of Psychology*, 37, 132–9.

Lyxell, B. (1989). Beyond lips: Components of speechreading skill. Ph D thesis, Department of Psychology, University of Umeå, Sweden.

Lyxell, B. (1994). Skilled speechreading: a single case study. *Scandinavian Journal of Psychology*, 35, 212–19.

Lyxell, B. & Rönnberg, J. (1989). Information processing skills and speechreading. *British Journal of Audiology*, 23, 339–47.

Lyxell, B. & Rönnberg, J. (1991). Visual speech processing: Word decoding and word discrimination related to sentence-based speechreading and hearing-impairment. *Scandinavian Journal of Psychology*, 32, 9–17.

Lyxell, B. & Rönnberg, J. (1992). Verbal ability and speechreading. *Scandinavian Audiology*, 21, 67–72.

Lyxell, B., Rönnberg, J. & Andersson, J. (1995). *Phonological deterioration and speechreading ability in the severely hearing impaired.* Manuscript submitted, Department of Education and Psychology, Linköping University, Sweden.

Lyxell, B., Rönnberg, J. & Samuelsson, S. (1994). Internal speech functioning and speechreading in deafened and normal hearing adults. *Scandinavian Audiology*, 23, 181–5.

Mogford, K. (1987). Lipreading in the prelingually deaf. In B. Dodd & R. Campbell (Eds), *Hearing by Eye: The Psychology of Lipreading* (pp. 191–212). Hove, UK: Lawrence Erlbaum Associates Ltd.

Öhngren, G. (1992). Touching voices: Components of direct tactually supported speechreading. Ph D thesis, Department of Psychology, Uppsala University, Sweden.

Pichora-Fuller, M.K., Schneider, B.A. & Daneman, M. (1995). How young and old adults listen to and remember speech in noise. *Journal of Acoustical Society of America, 97*, 593–608.

Rönnberg, J. (1990). Cognitive and communicative function: The effects of chronological age and "handicap age". *European Journal of Cognitive Psychology, 2*, 253–73 .

Rönnberg, J. (1993). Cognitive characteristics of skilled tactiling: The case of GS. *European Journal of Cognitive Psychology, 5*, 19–33.

Rönnberg, J. (1995). What makes a skilled speechreader? In G. Plant & K. Spens (Eds), *Profound Deafness and Speech Communication* (pp. 393–416). London: Whurr Publications.

Rönnberg, J., Andersson, J., Samuelsson, S., Lyxell, B., Söderfeldt, B. & Risberg, J. (1996a). The sign-speech bilingual enrichment hypothesis: The case of MJ. Manuscript submitted, Department of Education and Psychology, Linköping University, Sweden.

Rönnberg, J., Arlinger, S., Lyxell, B. & Kinnefords, C. (1989). Visual evoked potentials: Relation to adult speechreading and cognitive function. *Journal of Speech and Hearing Research, 32*, 725–35.

Rönnberg, J., Öhngren, G. & Nilsson, L.-G. (1982). Hearing deficiency, speechreading and memory functions. *Scandinavian Audiology, 11*, 261–8.

Rönnberg, J., Öhngren, G. & Nilsson, L.-G. (1983). Speechreading performance evaluated by means of TV and real-life presentation: A comparison between a normally hearing, moderately impaired and profoundly hearing-impaired group. *Scandinavian Audiology, 12*, 71–7.

Rönnberg, J., Samuelsson, S. & Andersson, J. (1996). *Phonological properties of a working memory in lipreading*. Manuscript submitted.

Rönnberg, J., Samuelsson, S., Lyxell, B. & Arlinger, S. (1996b). Lipreading supplemented by auditory low-frequency information: Contextual constraints. *Scandinavian Audiology, 25*, 127–32.

Samuelsson, S. & Rönnberg, J. (1991). Script activation in lipreading. *Scandinavian Journal of Psychology, 32*,124–43.

Samuelsson, S., & Rönnberg, J. (1993). Implicit and explicit use of scripted constraints in lipreading. *European Journal of Cognitive Psychology, 5*, 201–33.

Summerfield, A.Q. (1987). Some preliminaries to a comprehensive account of audiovisual speech perception. In B. Dodd & R. Campbell (Eds), *Hearing by Eye: The Psychology of Lipreading* (pp. 3–51). Hove, UK: Lawrence Erlbaum Associates Ltd.

Tillberg, I., Rönnberg, J., Svärd, I. & Ahlner, B. (1996). Audio-visual tests in a group of hearing-aid users: The effects of onset age, handicap age, and degree of hearing loss. *Scandinavian Audiology, 25*, 267–272.

Wolff, A.B. & Thatcher, R.W. (1990). Cortical reorganization in deaf children. *Journal of Clinical and Experimental Neuropsychology, 12*, 209–21.

Woodward, M.F. & Barber, C.G. (1960). Phoneme perception in lipreading. *Journal of Speech and Hearing Research, 3*, 212–22.

CHAPTER EIGHT

Effects of facial image size on visual and audio-visual speech recognition

Timothy R. Jordan and Paul C. Sergeant University of St Andrews, Scotland, UK

INTRODUCTION

Although a great deal of knowledge has been accumulated about auditory speech information, relatively little is known about visual speech information and the conditions under which it is accurately encoded (for a review, see Summerfield et al., 1989). One outstanding goal is to determine the extent to which perception of visual speech is affected by "everyday" variations in the visual appearance of a talker's face. In particular, shifts in a talker's posture and position relative to an observer can substantially alter the visibility of facial information which, in turn, may affect perception of visual speech and its influence on auditory speech recognition. Indeed, Jordan and Bevan (1997) recently reported that a wide range of changes to the orientation of a talker's face can affect perception of visual speech per se and the influence of visual speech on recognition of auditory speech sylla-bles (see also Green, 1994; Bertelson et al., 1994; Massaro & Cohen, 1996). However, while Jordan and Bevan's findings indicate that visual speech perception is susceptible to everyday variations in the appearance of a talker's face, the effects of other everyday variations have yet to be fully explored. One such variation is the size of the image produced by the talker's face on the retinae of the observer.

Changes in facial image size can occur in a number of ways. For example, the physical proportions of faces often differ between one talker and the next, and sometimes, as in the case of differences between adults and young children, these physical proportions can differ considerably. The effects of this variation are compounded by the fact that changes in the size of the facial image can also be produced by changes in viewing distance, where even modest changes in distance between an observer and a talker can produce considerable changes in image size. For example, at a speaker–observer distance of two metres, a decrease of one metre doubles the size of the facial image experienced by the observer. In addition, it is now common to encounter talking faces presented in a wide range of media, including cinema, television and computer displays, and on a range of different screen sizes which can also determine the size of the talking face we see. Indeed, the trend to technological miniaturisation, the increasing role of dynamic facial images in communications, and the role of bandwidth constraints in image transmission mean that current technology is probably producing the smallest talking faces ever experienced by human observers. However, whereas encountering talking facial images of different sizes is a common part of everyday experience, little is known about the impact of facial image size on perception of visual speech per se and on the effects exerted by visual speech on auditory speech recognition.

Changes in the size of a talking facial image may affect perception of visual speech if a shift in the size of the image creates a concomitant shift in the quantity and/or quality of information encoded from visible articulators. However, the dearth of research in this area makes it difficult to predict precisely which aspect of visual speech information is likely to be susceptible to changes in image size. For example, the human eye is usually considered to be able to resolve a static visual angle of 30 seconds of arc, based on the distribution and size of cones in the fovea (for an overview, see Wandell, 1995). This corresponds to an image height of 0.147 mm at a viewing distance of 1 metre. Now consider a lip separation of 5 mm in a full-size talking face viewed at 1 metre. If this facial image were reduced to 2.5% of full size, the corresponding lip separation would be reduced to just 0.125 mm, which is beyond the theoretical resolving power of the eye. However, the limits of visual acuity and, therefore, the potential of the visual signal to affect speech recognition, cannot be assessed entirely in terms of the resolving power of the eye. In fact, the relative positions of visual stimuli can be judged with much greater precision than that defined by the size and distribution of foveal cones (McKee, 1991). These fine spatial judgements, or hyperacuities, are often measured in terms of Vernier offset, orientation, curvature or spatial interval, and are inspired by inference and influenced by aspects such as contrast, colour and texture. Similarly, the detection of motion is also a hyperacuity. For example, Burr (1991) states that the minimum displacement necessary for perception of motion is about 10 seconds of arc which is one-third of minimum static resolution. Therefore, depending on the precise nature of the facial information involved in visual speech perception, visual speech may be encoded from a dynamic talking facial image even when the size of the image is so reduced that individual static features are invisible.

These variations in visual acuity are particularly relevant to the study of visual speech, where perception of detailed pictorial information about the appearance of the face (i.e. the sort of information that may be present in a static facial image) *and* perception of facial movements (i.e. the sort of information that is conveyed by changes in the facial image over time) may both be involved in visual and audio-visual speech recognition (for further discussion of these two aspects of visual speech information, see Rosenblum & Saldaña, 1996). For example, consider the appearance of the articulation for the spoken English syllable /ba/ which begins with bilabial closure followed by a predominantly vertical movement which separates the lips (Conrad, 1979; Utley, 1946). In a larger facial image (produced by, say, a full-sized adult face viewed at 1 metre), detailed pictorial information may help demarcate facial features by providing information about texture and colour which help distinguish, for example, the skin of the lips from the surfaces of the tongue, teeth and cheeks. With this level of detail, information about the amount and shape of mouth opening, teeth visibility and position of the tongue (all of which could be critical features for visual speech perception; see Massaro & Cohen, 1990; Montgomery & Jackson, 1983; Petajan, 1984; Summerfield, 1987, 1992; Summerfield & McGrath, 1984) may be accurately encoded. However, perception of this fine-grained information may be highly susceptible to restrictions imposed by the acuity of human vision when the image produced by the face of the talker is reduced in size.

The amount of pictorial detail available for encoding may not be the only way in which facial image size influences visual speech perception. Rosenblum and Saldaña (1996; see also Johnson, Rosenblum & Saldaña, 1994; Rosenblum, Johnson & Saldaña, 1995; Saldaña, Rosenblum & Osinger, 1992) investigated the influence of visual speech on auditory speech recognition when the visibility of a talker's face was reduced using a point-light technique in which reflective dots were placed on various parts of the talker's face, including lips, teeth, tongue and jaw. The talker was then videotaped in virtual darkness, and the resultant displays were seen merely as bright moving dots against a black background. Under these conditions, participants were unable to identify a frozen frame of these stimuli as a face. Nevertheless, dynamic presentations of these point-light stimuli resulted in significant influences on identification of heard speech syllables. As Rosenblum and Saldaña (1996) point out, these findings suggest that important information about changes in the facial image over time (the "kinematic properties" of visual speech), involving displacement, velocity and acceleration, can be conveyed in the absence of pictorial information. This may mean that loss of pictorial detail with smaller facial images has little impact on perception of the kinematic properties of visual speech, and, therefore, that perception of facial movement is relatively resistant to reductions in image size. However, it is well known that perception of motion can be impaired when the retinal distance travelled by an object is reduced (Aubert, 1886; Vandegrind, Koenderink & Vandoorn, 1992) and kinematic properties of visual speech are likely to become more difficult to encode as facial images become smaller. In sum, if access to mental representations for visual speech is facilitated by the pictorial and/or kinematic information available in larger facial images, access to these representations may be more difficult when visual speech is encountered in smaller facial images. On balance, perception of kinematic information may be more resistant to reductions in image size and this may bolster the perception of visual speech as image size decreases. However, the extent to which visual speech perception can tolerate reductions in facial image size remains something of a mystery.

The possibility that perception of visual speech changes with image size has important implications for theories of visual and audio-visual speech recognition. In particular, it is generally (and reasonably) assumed that basic visual cues must be encoded for visual speech to be recognised and to affect auditory speech recognition in face-to-face interactions (Massaro & Cohen, 1990; Montgomery & Jackson, 1983; Petajan, 1984; Summerfield, 1987, 1992; Summerfield & McGrath, 1984). However, attempts to identify the nature of such cues make the implicit assumption that observers potentially have access to all the information provided by the unoccluded components of a talking face that may conceivably underlie visual speech perception. So, for example, most analyses of visual speech address the role of such detailed information as lip shape (open, rounded, closed or even protruding), tongue position and shape, and teeth visibility. In contrast, consideration of the potential variations that can occur in the size of facial images introduces the possibility that the availability of visual speech information may alter dramatically with image size, and so the perception of visual speech and its effect on auditory speech recognition may depend critically on the size of the facial image encountered. Thus, whereas information about lip shape, tongue position, tongue shape and teeth visibility *may* be encoded from larger facial images, such cues may be lost when smaller facial images are encountered. However, other cues, like the simple presence or absence of mouth opening, may be more robust and continue to exert an effect even when encountered in facial images too small to provide greater detail. Consequently, if facial image size influences visual speech perception and the effects of visual speech on auditory speech recognition, it will no longer be sufficient to argue simply that certain visual cues are important for visual and audio-visual speech recognition. Rather, the more complete picture must involve the delineation of basic visual cues that are important within the constraints imposed by the size of the talking facial image encountered by an observer. Thus, by determining the extent to which perception of visual and audio-visual speech resists reductions in facial image size, the validity and generality of theories of visual and audio-visual speech recognition can be assessed.

The purpose of our study was to investigate the influence of reducing the size of a talking face on visual and audio-visual speech recognition. Previous studies of effects of facial image size on speech recognition are rare. However, the findings of a number of investigations into effects of distance are at least consistent with the notion that perception of visual speech becomes impaired as image size decreases. In a study by Erber (1971), a talker presented common nouns to profoundly deaf children who observed the talker from distances of 5, 10, 20, 40, 70 and 100 feet. Speechreading performance decreased substantially from almost 80% correct at 5 feet to 20% correct at 100 feet. In a similar study, also involving profoundly deaf children, Erber (1974) found that speechreading declined by about 20% as talker–observer distance increased from 6 feet to 24 feet. Finally, Neely (1956) examined the contribution of visual speech to auditory speech recognition by normal-hearing adults. Observers were seated at distances of 3, 6 and 9 feet from the talker and auditory signals were provided at each viewing position via headphones. Neely found a slight decrease in performance as distance increased to 9 feet, although this was not significant.

These findings offer support for the notion that smaller facial images impair visual and audio-visual speech recognition but the picture they present is far from clear. The majority of the experiments were driven by the worthy goal of improving communication with deaf children in the classroom. However, these findings may tell us little about the effects of image size on visual and audio-visual speech recognition in normal-hearing individuals for whom vision in spoken communication is just one of two available modalities (i.e. visual *and* auditory). Moreover, while Neely (1956) did use normal-hearing participants, the use of headphones violated the spatial relationship that normally exists between auditory and visual speech, making it difficult to determine just how reductions in image size influence perception of audio-visual information encoded from a normal talking facial stimulus. In addition, although the findings of Neely provide some indication that congruent audio-visual speech recognition becomes impaired as image size decreases, it remains to be seen whether performance with incongruent (McGurk) audio-visual stimuli is affected in the same way. In particular, Jordan and Bevan (1997) point out that a visual speech signal may need to be particularly strong in order to impair identification of incongruent auditory speech, while a weaker visual speech signal is sufficient to improve identification of congruent auditory speech. This view gains support from Jordan and Bevan's finding that whereas the beneficial effects of visual speech on performance with congruent auditory stimuli were largely unaffected by shifts in facial orientation, the disruptive effects of visual speech on performance with incongruent auditory stimuli were substantially reduced when faces were presented away from the vertical. Further support is provided by the study of Rosenblum and Saldaña (1996) in which effects of visual speech information provided by full face and point-light face stimuli were compared. Incongruent auditory speech report was disrupted much less by point-light stimuli than by full face stimuli whereas both types of visual speech produced near-perfect levels of congruent auditory speech report. Consequently, the use of congruent and incongruent audio-visual stimuli promises to provide a more complete picture of the effects on audio-visual speech recognition produced by manipulating the quality of visual speech by changing facial image size.

The two experiments reported in this chapter investigated the effects of facial image size on perception of visual speech per se and on the influence exerted by visual speech on auditory speech recognition using a talking face presented to normal-hearing adults. Our goal was to examine the limits imposed on visual and audio-visual speech perception as facial images were reduced from full size. Consequently, five sizes of talking face were used: 100% (full size), and the following proportions of the full-size image: 20%, 10%, 5%, and 2.5%. All faces were viewed at a constant distance of one metre. Auditory signals were presented by a loudspeaker adjacent to the facial images. Effects on auditory speech perception were examined using congruent audio-visual stimuli in which visual speech matched the auditory signal (as in normal audio-visual speech recognition) and incongruent (McGurk) audio-visual stimuli in which visual speech was dubbed onto an incongruent auditory signal. In order to emphasise the role played by visual speech in these effects and to de-emphasize effects of redundancy provided by scriptual, expressive or contextual constraints (see, e.g., Gailey, 1987; Rönnberg, 1993; Samuelsson & Rönnberg, 1993; Sudman & Berger, 1971), stimuli were individual syllables (/ba/, /bi/, /ga/, and /gi/) articulated by a face showing a neutral expression.

EXPERIMENT 1

Method

Participants

Twenty adult native speakers of British English each took part in a single one-hour session. All participants had normal or corrected to normal vision and good hearing.

Stimuli

The stimuli were created by videotaping the face and voice of a 42-year-old male onto S-VHS tape while he fixated the video camera. Recordings were made of the talker saying each of the four consonant-vowel syllables /ba/, /bi/, /ga/ and /gi/ a number of times in British English. Recordings were also made of the face making no movements (with mouth closed). Each syllable was articulated naturally with no artificial emphasis on articulation. From these recordings, one example of each of the four audio-visual syllables and one example of the static face (for the auditory speech condition) were selected. Examples were chosen for clarity and were matched for duration.

Each voice–face combination was presented at five different sizes; with head heights at the screen of 210 mm (full size), 42 mm, 21 mm, 10.5 mm and 5.25 mm, corresponding to 100%, 20%, 10%, 5% and 2.5%, respectively, of the full-size image. Each facial image was then dubbed to give the following 14 stimulus types.

    a. Auditory speech: auditory /ba/, /bi/, /ga/ and /gi/, all presented with the static face.
    b. Visual speech: visual /ba/, /bi/, /ga/ and /gi/, all with no auditory signal.
    c. Congruent audio-visual speech: auditory-visual /ba/, /bi/, /ga/ and /gi/.
    d. Incongruent audio-visual speech: auditory /ba/ paired with visual /ga/, auditory /bi/ paired with visual /gi/.

These combinations are known to produce powerful McGurk effects (Green, Kuhl & Meltzoff, 1988; Green et al., 1991).

Visual signals were presented on a high-resolution colour monitor; auditory signals were presented via an adjacent loudspeaker at a sound level of approximately 55 dB recorded at the position of each participant. Each facial image was shown centred on a black screen for 4 seconds, after which the screen remained black except for 10 response buttons displayed in the lower part of the screen. Response buttons were labelled with the syllables "ba", "ga", "da", "tha", "bga", "bi", "gi", "di", "thi", "bgi". Pre-testing had established that these 10 responses constituted greater than 97% of participants' perceptions of the stimuli used in the experiment (see also Jordan & Bevan, 1997). When questioned at the end of the experiment, no participant indicated that they had been restricted by these alternatives. Each facial image remained motionless (with mouth closed) for 1 second at the start of each trial. For auditory speech stimuli, the facial image remained motionless, with mouth closed, throughout each trial. Stimuli were shown in five blocks, corresponding to the five image sizes. The order of presenting each size was re-randomised for each participant. Within each block, all 14 speech stimuli were shown in a different random order.

Procedure

Each participant was seated at a table in front of the screen with his or her head level with the screen and resting on a chin rest. The distance between the centre of the screen and each participant's forehead was exactly 1 metre. Participants were instructed to watch and listen to each trial and to enter their response by using a mouse pointer and clicking on the appropriate on-screen response button which corresponded to the syllable they *heard* (the emphasis in the instructions being on *heard*). Participants were asked to choose the syllable they thought was being articulated when presented with visual speech trials.

Results

Auditory Speech Stimuli

Mean per cent correct responses to /ba/, /bi/, /ga/ and /gi/ auditory speech stimuli are shown in Figure 25. Auditory stimuli were identified with 95% accuracy or more at each size. A two-way analysis of variance (ANOVA) conducted on accuracy scores, with factors stimulus type (/ba/, /bi/, /ga/, /gi/) and image size (100%, 20%, 10%, 5%, 2.5%) revealed no main effect or interaction.[1] Thus, all auditory stimuli were essentially unambiguous.

Visual Speech Stimuli

Mean per cent correct responses to /ba/, /bi/, /ga/ and /gi/ visual speech stimuli are shown in Figure 26. An ANOVA with factors stimulus type and image size revealed a main effect of stimulus type, $F (3, 57) = 21.58$, $p < .0001$, image size, $F (4, 76) = 48.86$, $p < .0001$, and an interaction between these two factors, $F (12, 228) = 7.06$, $p < .0001$. Newman Keuls tests showed that overall performance with /b_/ tokens was more accurate

Auditory Stimuli

■ /ba/ □ /bi/ ■ /ga/ □ /gi/

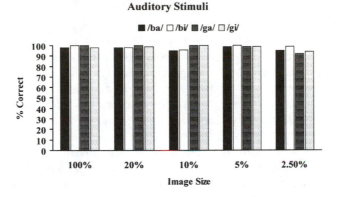

FIG. 25.   Mean percentage of auditory speech stimuli correctly identified in Experiment 1 for each image size.

Visual Stimuli

■ /ba/ □ /bi/ ■ /ga/ □ /gi/

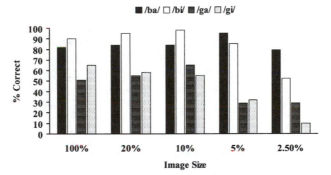

FIG. 26.   Mean percentage of visual speech stimuli correctly identified in Experiment 1 for each image size.

than with /g_/ tokens in both vowel contexts ($ps < .01$). Moreover, performance with full-size /ba/ stimuli was unaffected by any image size reduction, and performance with full-size /bi/ stimuli was affected only when image size was reduced to just 2.5% ($p < .01$ for comparisons with all larger image sizes). However, for /ga/ and /gi/, while performance with 100%, 20% and 10% images remained about equal, performance with each of these three sizes dropped significantly when image size was reduced to 5% (all $ps < .01$) and to 2.5% (all $ps < .01$). A drop in performance was also observed for /gi/ as image size was reduced from 5% to 2.5% ($p < .01$). Thus, perception of /g_/ tokens was more sensitive to reduction in the size of the facial image.

Congruent audio-visual speech stimuli

Mean per cent correct responses to the auditory signal of congruent audio-visual stimuli are shown in Figure 27. Overall response accuracy was high across all image sizes (mean = 98%), although accuracy with /ga/ and /gi/ stimuli dropped slightly (non-significantly) when presented at the smallest image size. An ANOVA revealed no main effects or interactions, indicating the effect of congruent visual speech on auditory speech perception was unaffected by changes in image size. However, overall performance was near perfect, and this may have prevented effects of image size from showing through in the data. Indeed, a comparison between performances in the congruent audio-visual and auditory speech conditions, with factors of presentation condition (congruent audio-visual, auditory), auditory stimulus type (/ba/, /bi/, /ga/, /gi/) and image size revealed no significant improvement in performance for auditory stimuli presented in the congruent condition at any image size, indicating that the clarity of the auditory signal may have suppressed effects of image size on congruent audio-visual speech recognition.

Incongruent audio-visual speech stimuli

Mean per cent correct responses to the auditory signal of incongruent audio-visual stimuli (auditory /ba/—visual /ga/, auditory /bi/—visual /gi/) are shown in Figure 28. An ANOVA with factors stimulus type (auditory /ba/—visual /ga/, auditory /bi/—visual /gi/) and image size revealed a main effect of image size ($F (4, 76) = 8.30, p < .001$). The other main effect and

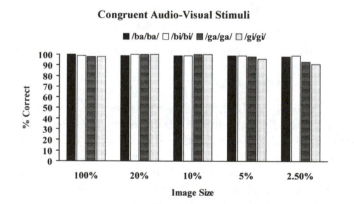

Congruent Audio-Visual Stimuli

■ /ba/ba/ □ /bi/bi/ ■ /ga/ga/ □ /gi/gi/

FIG. 27.   Mean percentage of correct responses to the auditory signal of congruent audio-visual stimuli for each image size in Experiment 1 (/ba/ba/ = auditory /ba/ with visual /ba/; /bi/bi/ = auditory /bi/ with visual /bi/, /ga/ga/ = auditory /ga/ with visual /ga/; /gi/gi/ = auditory /gi/ with visual /gi/).

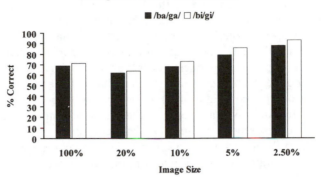

Incongruent Audio-Visual Stimuli

■ /ba/ga/ □ /bi/gi/

FIG. 28.   Mean percentage of correct responses to the auditory signal of incongruent audio-visual stimuli for each image size in Experiment 1 (/ba/ga/ = auditory /ba/ with visual /ga/; /bi/gi/ = auditory /bi/ with visual /gi/).

the interaction were not significant. Newman Keuls tests revealed that no significant changes occurred across the three largest image sizes but, relative to these three sizes, significantly fewer McGurk effects (i.e. more correct responses to the auditory signal) were produced as image size was reduced to 5% (all $ps < .01$) and to 2.5% (all $ps < .01$).

A comparison between these data and those obtained with /ba/ and /bi/ stimuli in the auditory speech condition with factors presentation condition (incongruent audio-visual, auditory), auditory stimulus type (/ba/ or /bi/) and image size revealed a main effect of presentation condition ($F(1, 19) = 13.17$, $p < .002$), image size ($F(4, 76) = 6.35$, $p < .001$), and a significant interaction between these two factors ($F(4, 76) = 7.53$, $p < .0001$). Newman-Keuls comparisons revealed fewer correct responses in the incongruent audio-visual condition at all image sizes ($ps < .01$) except 2.5%, indicating that the disruptive influence of incongruent visual speech on auditory speech recognition was present for all but the smallest image size used.

Discussion

The findings of Experiment 1 indicate that whereas the size of a talking facial image exerted considerable effects on performance with visual and audio-visual speech stimuli, these effects occurred only when image size was reduced to 5% or less of the full-size image. This resistance to reductions in the size of the facial image suggests that the visual information underlying visual and audio-visual speech recognition in a full-size facial image can still be encoded even when facial images are subjectively very small (just 10% of full-size). However, effects of image size on congruent audio-visual speech recognition remain unclear due to the high overall levels of performance observed in this condition. In particular, because the levels of performance in the auditory speech condition were near perfect, it has yet to be seen just how effective small facial images are in enhancing performance with congruent auditory signals. This question, in particular, has important implications for understanding the influence of reduced facial image sizes (e.g. actual, televisual or computational) in everyday face-to-face situations where congruent audio-visual speech is the mode of communication. One way to examine this issue is to use a less distinct auditory signal in order to lower overall levels of performance sufficiently to reveal size effects, should they exist, with congruent audio-visual stimuli. This procedure was adopted in Experiment 2.

EXPERIMENT 2

Method

Participants

Twenty new participants from the same population as Experiment 1 took part in Experiment 2.

Stimuli

The auditory, visual, congruent audio-visual and incongruent audio-visual speech stimuli used in Experiment 1 were used in Experiment 2, at the same (55 dB) intensity level. However, these stimuli were now presented in a background of continuous white noise at a sound level of 70 dB. Pre-testing had established that a signal-to-noise ratio of −15 dB produced approximately 50% correct responses to auditory stimuli, thereby allowing room for influences of congruent and incongruent visual speech. All remaining aspects of this experiment were the same as in Experiment 1.

Results

Auditory speech stimuli

Mean per cent correct responses to /ba/, /bi/, /ga/ and /gi/ auditory speech stimuli are shown in Figure 29. Overall identification accuracy for auditory speech stimuli was 49%, with means of 62% (/ba/), 46% (/bi/), 63% (/ga/) and 25% (/gi/) for each image size. An ANOVA revealed a main effect of stimulus type (F (3,57) = 14.79, $p < .0001$). Newman Keuls tests revealed greater report accuracy for /ba/ and /ga/ than for /bi/ and /gi/ ($ps < .01$), and greater report accuracy for /bi/ than /gi/ ($p < .01$).

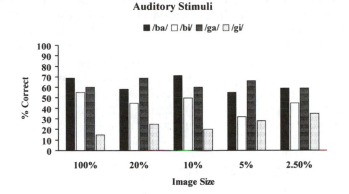

FIG. 29.   Mean percentage of auditory speech stimuli correctly identified in Experiment 2 for each image size.

Visual speech stimuli

Mean per cent correct responses to visual /ba/, /bi/, /ga/ and /gi/ are shown in Figure 30. The findings essentially replicated those of Experiment 1. Main effects of stimulus type ($F(3,57) = 45.88, p < .0001$)) and image size ($F(4,76) = 22.52, p < .0001$)) were found, together with an interaction between these two factors ($F(12,228) = 5.91, p < .0001$)). As in Experiment 1, Newman Keuls tests showed that overall performance with /b_/ tokens was more accurate than with /g_/ tokens in both vowel contexts ($ps < .01$). Moreover, performance with full-size /ba/ stimuli again showed no effect of

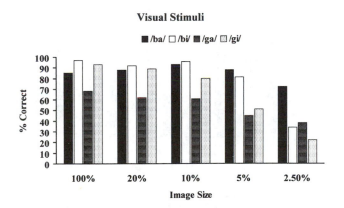

FIG. 30.   Mean percentage of visual speech stimuli correctly identified in Experiment 2 for each image size.

reduced image size, and performance with full-size /bi/ stimuli became significantly poorer only when image size was reduced to just 2.5% ($p < .01$ for comparisons with all larger image sizes). However, for /ga/ and /gi/, although performance with 100%, 20% and 10% images remained about equal, performance with each of these three sizes dropped significantly when image size was reduced to 5% (all $ps < .01$) and to 2.5% (all $ps < .01$). A drop in performance for /gi/ was also observed as image size was reduced from 5% to 2.5% ($p < .01$). Thus, as in Experiment 1, perception of /g_/ tokens was more sensitive than /b_/ tokens to reduction in the size of the facial image.

Congruent audio-visual speech stimuli

Mean per cent correct responses to the auditory signal of congruent audio-visual speech stimuli are shown in Figure 31. Main effects of stimulus type ($F(3,57) = 39.07$, $p < .0001$)), image size ($F(4,76) = 10.96$, $p < .0001$)), and an interaction between these factors ($F(12,228) = 2.66$, $p < .0001$)) were found. Newman Keuls tests showed that accuracy of report for /ba/ and /ga/ was unaffected by reductions in image size. However, for /bi/ and /gi/, although performance with 100%, 20%, 10%, and 5% images remained about equal, performance with each of these four sizes dropped significantly when image size was reduced to 2.5% (all $ps < .01$).

A comparison between these data and those obtained in the auditory speech condition revealed a three-way interaction between presentation condition, stimulus type and image size ($F(12,228) = 4.34$, $p < .0001$). Newman Keuls tests showed that congruent visual speech improved accu-

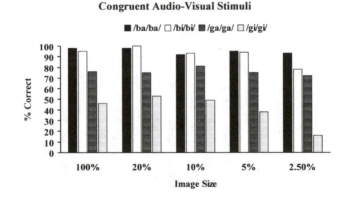

FIG. 31. Mean percentage of correct responses to the auditory signal of congruent audio-visual stimuli for each image size in Experiment 2 (/ba/ba/ = auditory /ba/ with visual /ba/; /bi/bi/ = auditory /bi/ with visual /bi/; /ga/ga/ = auditory /ga/ with visual /ga/; /gi/gi/ = auditory /gi/ with visual /gi/).

racy of auditory speech report at each image size for all stimulus types (all $ps < .01$) with one notable exception: accuracy of report for /gi/ auditory speech was actually worse when presented with a congruent facial image reduced to 2.5% of full size ($p < .01$).

Incongruent audio-visual speech stimuli

Mean per cent correct responses to the auditory signal of auditory /ba/ with visual /ga/ and auditory /bi/ with visual /gi/ are shown in Figure 32. Only the main effect of image size was significant (F (4,76) = 22.13, $p < .0001$). Newman Keuls tests revealed a similar pattern of effects to those of Experiment 1; namely, no significant changes occurred across the three largest image sizes, but fewer McGurk effects (i.e. more correct responses to the auditory signal) were produced as image size was reduced to 5% ($p < .01$ for comparisons with all three larger sizes) and to 2.5% ($p < .01$ for comparisons with all four larger sizes). A comparison between these data and those obtained with /ba/ and /bi/ stimuli in the auditory speech condition revealed a significant interaction between presentation condition and image size (F (4,76) = 16.57, $p < .0001$). As in Experiment 1, Newman-Keuls comparisons revealed fewer correct responses in the incongruent audio-visual condition at all image sizes ($ps < .01$) except 2.5%, indicating that the disruptive influence of incongruent visual speech on auditory speech recognition was present in all but the smallest facial image used.

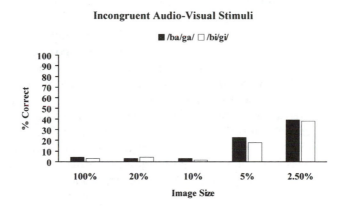

FIG. 32.   Mean percentage of correct responses to the auditory signal of incongruent audio-visual stimuli for each image size in Experiment 2 (/ba/ga/ = auditory /ba/ with visual /ga/; /bi/gi/ = auditory /bi/ with visual /gi/).

Discussion

The results of Experiment 2 essentially duplicate those of Experiment 1 and consolidate the finding that no significant effects of image size were observed even when images were reduced to just 10% of full size. However, the size of a talking facial image exerted considerable effects on performance with visual and audio-visual speech stimuli when image size was reduced to 5% or less. Indeed, while the data obtained with congruent audio-visual stimuli in Experiment 2 indicate that even very small facial images (as little as 5% of full size) can improve congruent auditory speech recognition in noise, the *impairment* observed for congruent /gi/ stimuli when images were just 2.5% of full size provides a particularly powerful indication of how image size may alter the effects of visual speech on auditory speech recognition.

GENERAL DISCUSSION

The major point to emerge from these findings is that performance with visual and audio-visual speech stimuli showed considerable resistance to changes in the size of a talking facial image such that performance with visual speech, and congruent and incongruent audio-visual speech was unaffected by a 90% reduction in image size. One immediate interpretation of this finding is that the visual speech encoded from full-size images can be equally well encoded even when images are reduced in size by 90%. Consequently, from the evidence provided by the two experiments reported here, theories of visual and audio-visual speech recognition based on performance with full-size or near full-size facial images may be generalised more confidently to a substantial proportion of facial image sizes encountered in everyday face-to-face spoken communication.

Determining the precise nature of the visual information underlying this resistance to changes in facial image size is the next goal of this line of research. However, the experiments reported here provide a number of clues. In particular, the considerable resistance to reductions in image size suggest that the visual cues underlying visual speech perception with full-size faces are relatively coarse, such that even when viewed in a facial image just 10% of full-size, the perceptibility of these cues remains unimpaired. Studies of viseme confusibility lend further support to the importance of relatively coarse visual cues in visual speech perception and provide an indication of the nature of these cues (e.g. Binnie, Montgomery & Jackson, 1974; Walden et al., 1977; Woodward & Barber, 1960). In particular, Walden et al. (1977) found that participants' perceptions of visible articulations clustered into a relatively small number of viseme groups. For example, participants were often unable to distinguish between the syllables /pa/, /ba/ and /ma/, and between the syllables /ga/, /ka/, /na/, /ta/, /da/ and /ya/, but could readily distinguish between syllables drawn from each of these two groups. Moreover, confusions occurred despite highlighting the physical differences among consonant articulations using lighting which illuminated the lips and the anterior portion of the tongue, suggesting that the information which bounded consonants within the same viseme category and divided consonants between viseme categories did not incorporate all available visual information. One persuasive interpretation of these viseme groupings is that they reflect the importance of robust visual cues to places of articulation that are often difficult to determine from auditory information alone (Summerfield, 1987). For example, articulation of /pa/, /ba/ and /ma/ involves a bilabial closure followed by an open mouth, both of which are directly visible. In addition, articulation of /ga/, /ka/, /na/, /ta/, /da/ and /ya/ involves an open mouth throughout each articulation, indicating articulatory manoeuvres within the vocal tract (e.g. velar, alveolar), although the actual constrictions used to distinguish these manoeuvres are not directly visible. If participants in our experiments were using similar basic visual cues to places of articulation, the apparent distinctiveness of these cues and their powerful influence on visual speech perception may have helped inspire the general resistance to facial image size we observed.

The different patterns of performance produced by different syllables add support to the notion that the resistance to reductions in image size reflected the use of relatively coarse visual cues to place of articulation. The articulation of /ba/ and /bi/ syllables in a full-size image began with a bilabial closure followed by a vertical mouth opening of 3.50 cm (for both /ba/ and /bi/), which involved considerable movement of the talker's lower lip and jaw and little movement of the talker's upper lip. In contrast, the articulation of /ga/ and /gi/ involved a change in mouth opening of just 0.50 cm, from a vertical lip separation of 1.50 cm at the beginning of each utterance to a vertical lip separation of 2.00 cm at the end of each utterance. Thus, as image size was reduced, the bilabial articulation of /b_/ tokens is likely to have remained relatively distinct. This would explain why identification of visual speech per se was more resistant to reductions in image size for /b_/ tokens than for /g_/ tokens in both experiments.

It remains to be seen whether the basic visual cues which survive reductions in facial image size reflect the use of pictorial or kinematic cues, because both may have become impaired in our experiments. From the work of Rosenblum and colleagues, one way of teasing apart the effects of these two types of visual speech would be to contrast the effects of reduced image size on performance with normal and point-light facial stimuli. The findings of Rosenblum and Saldaña (1996; see also Johnson, Rosenblum & Saldaña, 1994; Rosenblum, Johnson & Saldaña, 1995; Saldaña, Rosenblum & Osinger, 1992) described previously suggest that both types of stimuli should influence the identification of auditory speech with larger facial images. However, contrasting the decline in visual influence exerted by these two types of facial stimuli as image size decreases would throw important light on the relative roles of these two types of visual speech information as facial images alter in size.

Despite the considerable resistance shown to reductions in facial image size, it is clear that reducing facial image size to less than 10% creates substantial impairments in identification of unimodal visual speech. Difficulty with encoding visual speech from the two smallest image sizes is also reflected in the pattern of performance observed with incongruent audiovisual speech. However, performances with congruent audio-visual speech in Experiment 2 (where the absence of ceiling effects allows more meaningful interpretation) showed little deterioration as image size decreased to 5% and even 2.5%. Indeed, while performance with /bi/–/bi/ audio-visual speech deteriorated at only the smallest image size, performances with /ba/–/ba/ and /ga/–/ga/ stimuli showed no deterioration across the entire range of image sizes. This difference between the sensitivity of congruent and incongruent audio-visual speech recognition to reductions in the size of the facial image adds support to the view that a visual speech signal needs to be stronger to impair identification of incongruent auditory speech, whereas a weaker visual speech signal is sufficient to improve identification of congruent auditory speech. Repeated experience with congruent audio-visual stimuli in everyday life may lead to the development of interactive links between representations for the auditory and visual forms of the same speech sound. Thus, when presented with congruent audio-visual stimuli, the activation created by one signal (e.g. auditory) may initially augment the activation created by the other (i.e. visual speech). Moreover, as the activation produced by the visual signal increases, this may then feedback to the activation created by the auditory signal in true interactive-activation fashion (McClelland & Rumelhart, 1981, 1988; Rumelhart & McClelland, 1982), leading to improvement in the perception of a congruent auditory signal even when information in the visual modality is impaired. Similar links are unlikely to exist for incongruent auditory and visual speech. For example, when the auditory syllable /ba/ is presented with the visual syllable /ga/, the auditory signal may generate considerable activation in representations responsible for perceiving /ba/ visual speech, but no activation in the representations responsible for perceiving other visual speech, including the /ga/ visual speech presented in the stimulus. Indeed, illusory auditory percepts may occur only when sufficient visual speech information can be encoded to:

1. Inhibit the activation generated by the auditory signal in auditory and visual representations which are inconsistent with the visual speech information encoded.

2. Generate fresh activation in auditory and visual representations which are consistent both with the visual speech information encoded and with the activation created by the auditory signal.

Thus, when presented with auditory /ba/ accompanied by visual /ga/, a considerable amount of information about the visual speech actually presented may be required in order to inhibit the activation generated by the auditory signal and replace it with activation consistent with a different, illusory percept (i.e. /da/ or /tha/). This would explain why incongruent audio-visual stimuli showed a sharper decline in their effect than congruent audio-visual stimuli as facial image size was reduced.

However, it is clear from the findings obtained with /gi/ stimuli that not all congruent audio-visual speech stimuli are insensitive to reducing a facial image to just 2.5% of full size. In particular, auditory speech recognition was actually impaired when congruent visual speech was presented at this size, suggesting that reductions in facial image size may not simply diminish the chances of encoding visual speech information per se but actually alter the type of visual speech information perceived. But how might this have happened with /gi/ stimuli? One possibility is that, when image size was reduced to 2.5%, participants were unable to discriminate the slight lip separation that actually existed at the start of each /gi/ articulation and, instead, perceived a closed mouth. Thus, when lip separation increased as /gi/ was articulated, the subjective impression with these small facial images may have been of a bilabial closure followed by a slight vertical mouth opening. This possibility is supported by an analysis of the errors made for /gi/ stimuli in Experiment 2. Of the errors made to unimodal /gi/ visual speech, 41% were bilabial (/ba/ or /bi/). Moreover, 40% of errors made to congruent audio-visual /gi/ stimuli were /bi/, indicating that a misperceived bilabial closure accompanied by an auditory /gi/ signal was sufficient to produce a visually dominated illusory percept of the type often reported with *incongruent* audio-visual speech stimuli (Diesch, 1995; Liberman & Mattingly, 1985; MacDonald & McGurk, 1978; McGurk & MacDonald, 1976; Rosenblum & Saldaña, 1992).

Clearly, reductions in the size of a talking facial image can actually distort the perception of visual speech rather than merely removing its influence. Indeed, the finding that auditory speech recognition was actually impaired when congruent visual speech was presented places an important caveat on the use of small talking faces for communication purposes, including television images and video-conferencing. In particular, while considerations of bandwidth, storage and processing times play an important part in determining the size of a talking image presented in a medium, there may be occasions when image size is so reduced that using no talking image produces greater recognition accuracy for auditory speech. Nevertheless, the finding that facial images reduced by as much as 90% from full-size produce the same levels of visual and auditory speech recognition as a full-size face provides an important indication that talking faces can effectively contribute to spoken communication even when images are substantially less than full size. Indeed, we found these effects using just syllables and are now investigating whether higher order influences such as lexical, syntactic and semantic constraints can extend even further the resistance to facial image size reduction we observed.

NOTE

1. An alternative way of analysing the data in these experiments would have been to use a three-way ANOVA with factors of image size, consonant (b, g) and vowel (a, i). At first sight, such an analysis may appear to offer insight into how consonant and vowel contexts interact in visual and audio-visual speech recognition. However, such an analysis would be valid only if each consonant and vowel remained physically identical across stimuli; for example, if the phoneme /a/ remained constant in ba and in ga, such that the only difference between the physical composition (auditory *and* visual) of these two syllables was due to the articulation of their consonant. As in normal speech, this was not the case in our experiments due to effects of co-articulation which alter the physical nature of phonemes and visemes. Consequently, while the three-way analysis would be appropriate for an experiment incorporating syllables formed by splicing, for example, different consonants onto physically identical vowels, the most appropriate way to analyse the data in Experiment 1 was to treat each syllable as a physically distinct stimulus.

Correspondence concerning this work should be addressed to Timothy R. Jordan, School of Psychology, University of St Andrews, St Andrews, Fife, Scotland, KY16 9JU. Electronic mail may be sent to trj@st-andrews.ac.uk.

REFERENCES

Aubert, H. (1886). Die Bewegungsempfindung. *Archiv für die Gesamte Psychologie, 39*, 347–70.

Bertelson, P., Vroomen, J., Wiegeraad, G. & de Gelder, B. (1994). *Exploring the relation between McGurk interference and ventriloquism.* Paper presented at the International Conference on Spoken Language Processing, September. Yokohama, Japan.

Binnie, C.A., Montgomery, A.A. & Jackson, P.L. (1974). Auditory and visual contributions to the perception of selected English consonants for normally hearing and hearing-impaired listeners. In H. Birk Nielsen & E. Kampp (Eds), *Visual and Audio-visual Perception of Speech* (Scandinavian Supplementum 4, pp. 181–209). Stockholm: Almquist & Wiksell.

Burr, D.C. (1991). Human sensitivity to flicker and motion. In J.J. Kulikowski, V.Walsh and I.J. Murray (Eds), *Vision and Visual Dysfunction* (5) (pp. 147–59). London: Macmillan.

Conrad, R. (1979). *The Deaf Schoolchild.* London: Harper & Row.

Diesch, E. (1995). Left and right hemifield advantages of fusions and combinations in audiovisual speech perception. *Quarterly Journal of Experimental Psychology, 48A*, 320–33.

Erber, N.P. (1971). Effects of distance on the visual reception of speech. *Journal of Speech and Hearing Research, 14*, 848–57.

Erber, N.P. (1974). Effects of angle, distance and illumination on visual reception of speech by profoundly deaf children. *Journal of Speech and Hearing Research, 17*, 99–112.

Gailey, L. (1987). Psychological parameters of lip-reading skill. In B. Dodd & R. Campbell (Eds), *Hearing by Eye: The Psychology of Lipreading* (pp. 115–41). Hove, UK: Lawrence Erlbaum Associates Ltd.

Green, K.P. (1994). *The influence of an inverted face on the McGurk effect*. Poster presented at the spring meeting of the Acoustical Society of America. Cambridge, Massachusetts. *Journal of the Acoustical Society of America, 95*, 3014 (Abstract).

Green, K.P., Kuhl, P.K. & Meltzoff, A.N. (1988). Factors affecting the integration of auditory and visual information in speech: The effect of vowel environment. *Journal of the Acoustical Society of America, 84*, 155.

Green, K.P., Kuhl, P.K., Meltzoff, A.N. & Stevens, E.B. (1991). Integrating speech information across talkers, gender and sensory modality: Female faces and male voices in the McGurk effect. *Perception and Psychophysics, 50*, 524–36.

Johnson, J.A., Rosenblum, L.D. & Saldaña, H.M. (1994). The contribution of a reduced visual image to speech perception in noise. Poster presented at the spring meeting of the Acoustical Society of America. Cambridge, Massachusetts. *Journal of the Acoustical Society of America, 95*, 3009 (Abstract).

Jordan, T.R. & Bevan, K.M. (1997). Seeing and hearing rotated faces: Influences of facial orientation on visual and audio-visual speech recognition. *Journal of Experimental Psychology: Human Perception and Performance, 23*, 388–403.

Liberman, A.M. & Mattingly, I.G. (1985). The motor theory of speech perception revised. *Cognition, 21*, 1–36.

McClelland, J.L. & Rumelhart, D.E. (1981). An interactive activation model of context effects in letter perception: Part 1. An account of basic findings. *Psychological Review, 88*, 375–407.

McClelland, J.L. & Rumelhart, D.E. (1988). *Explorations in Parallel Distributed Processing*. Cambridge, Massachusetts: MIT Press.

MacDonald, J. & McGurk, H. (1978). Visual influences on speech perception processes. *Perception and Psychophysics, 24*, 253–7.

McGurk, H. & MacDonald, J. (1976). Hearing lips and seeing voices. *Nature, 264*, 746–8.

McKee, S.P. (1991). The physical constraints on visual hyperacuity. In J.J. Kulikowski, V. Walsh and I.J. Murray (Eds), *Vision and Visual Dysfunction* (5) (pp. 221–33). London: Macmillan.

Massaro, D.W. & Cohen, M.M. (1990). Perception of synthesized audible and visible speech. *Psychological Science, 1*, 55–63.

Massaro, D.W. & Cohen, M.M. (1996). Perceiving speech from inverted faces. *Perception and Psychophysics, 58*, 1047–65.

Montgomery, A.A., & Jackson, P.L. (1983). Physical characteristics of the lips underlying vowel lipreading performance. *Journal of the Acoustical Society of America, 73*, 2134–2144.

Neely, K.K. (1956). Effect of visual factors on the intelligibility of speech. *Journal of the Acoustical Society of America, 28*, 1275–1277.

Petajan, E.D. (1984). Automatic lipreading to enhance speech recognition. Proceedings of the IEEE Communications Society, 265–72.

Rönnberg, J. (1993). Cognitive characteristics of skilled tactiling: The case of GS. *European Journal of Cognitive Psychology, 5*, 19–33.

Rosenblum, L.D. & Saldaña, H.M. (1992). Discrimination tests of visually influenced syllables. *Perception and Psychophysics, 52*, 461–73.

Rosenblum, L.D. & Saldaña, H.M. (1996). An audiovisual test of kinematic primitives for visual speech perception. *Journal of Experimental Psychology: Human Perception and Performance, 22*, 318–31.

Rosenblum, L.D., Johnson, J.A. & Saldaña, H.M. (1995). Determining the kinematic features for visual speech perception. Unpublished manuscript.

Rumelhart, D.E. & McClelland, J.L. (1982). An interactive activation model of context effects in letter perception: Part 2. The contextual enhancement effect and some tests and extensions of the model. *Psychological Review, 89,* 60–94.

Saldaña, H.M., Rosenblum, L.D. & Osinger, T. (1992). Visual influence on heard speech syllables with a reduced visual image. *Journal of the Acoustical Society of America, 92,* 2340 (Abstract).

Samuelsson, S. & Rönnberg, J. (1993). Implicit and explicit use of scripted constraints in lipreading. *European Journal of Cognitive Psychology, 5,* 201–33.

Sudman, J.A. & Berger, K.W. (1971). Two-dimension vs. three-dimension viewing in speechreading. *Journal of Communication Disorders, 4,* 195–8.

Summerfield, A.Q. (1987). Some preliminaries to a comprehensive account of audio-visual speech perception. In B. Dodd & R. Campbell (Eds), *Hearing by Eye: The Psychology of Lipreading* (pp. 3–51). Hove, UK: Lawrence Erlbaum Associates Ltd.

Summerfield, A.Q. (1992). Lipreading and audio-visual speech perception. In V. Bruce, A. Cowey, A.W. Ellis & D.I. Perrett (Eds), *Processing the Facial Image* (pp. 71–8). Oxford: Oxford University Press.

Summerfield, A.Q. & McGrath, M. (1984). Detection and resolution of audio-visual incompatibility in the perception of vowels. *Quarterly Journal of Experimental Psychology, 36A,* 51–74.

Summerfield, A.Q., MacLeod, P., McGrath, M. & Brooke, N.M. (1989). Lips, teeth, and the benefits of lipreading. In A.W. Young and H.B. Ellis (Eds), *Handbook of Research on Face Processing* (pp. 223–33). Amsterdam: North-Holland.

Utley, J. (1946). A test of lip-reading ability. *Journal of Speech Disorders, 11,* 109–16.

Vandegrind, W.A., Koenderink, J.J. & Vandoorn, A.J. (1992). Viewing distance invariance of movement detection. *Experimental Brain Research, 91,* 135–50.

Walden, B.E., Prosek, R.A., Montgomery, A.A., Scherr, C.K. & Jones, C.J. (1977). Effects of training on the visual recognition of consonants. *Journal of Speech and Hearing Research, 20,* 130–45.

Wandell, B.A. (1995). *Foundations of Vision.* Sunderland, Mass: Sinauer Associates.

Woodward, M.F. & Barber, C.G. (1960). Phoneme perception in lipreading. *Journal of Speech and Hearing Research, 3,* 212–22.

CHAPTER NINE

How brains see speech: the cortical localisation of speechreading in hearing people

Ruth Campbell *Department of Human Communication Science, University College, London, UK*

INTRODUCTION

This chapter reviews studies of the localisation of seen speech. From an ambiguous starting point, which first seemed to show that seen speech was preferentially localised to the right and then that the left cerebral hemisphere was critical, it has become clear that speechreading makes use of structures on either side of the brain and of systems that rely differentially on right-sided and on left-sided structures.

Functional neuroimaging suggests that speechreading is a unique visual-language ability, reflecting its special status as a task requiring the analysis of faces-in-action with direct associations with heard speech. Silent speechreading can activate primary auditory cortex (lateral temporal sites) as well as specific parts of visual cortex (occipital and occipito-temporal sites)—bilaterally. It also generates large-scale activation in auditory association cortex. Audio-visual speech makes more limited use of these association areas, since identification of the speech event is more constrained when one can hear as well as see the speaker. The patterns of speechreading impairment in patients with localised lesions and speechreading-related performance asymmetries in normal people are discussed in relation to these neurophysiological findings.

LIPREADING GOES RIGHT ... NO, LEFT

In the first edition of *Hearing by Eye* (Campbell, 1987) I reported two studies on the cortical localisation of speechreading which came to diametrically opposed conclusions concerning the preferred cortical hemisphere that hearing people use in seeing speech. One experiment (Campbell, 1986) investigated right-handed hearing students who matched an image of a face speaking; a mouthshape of, for example, "ee" or "ff" to an after-coming heard speech sound by key pressing for a "same" or a "different" match. Matching was faster and more accurate when the image was displayed in the left visual field (LVF), projecting to the right hemisphere. While heard speech localises to the left hemisphere, right hemisphere superiority was not unexpected for this task. It had already been established that this was the superior hemisphere at a number of other aspects of face-processing (Ellis, 1983).

Meanwhile, a natural experiment had been prepared by Landis and Regard at the University Hospital of Zürich. They had recently examined two patients who were similar in age, background and type and extent of acquired brain lesion. Both had suffered strokes due to blockage of the middle cerebral artery. In one patient (Mrs T), this affected only the left hemisphere, in the other patient (Mrs D) only the right. Both patients recovered from the initial effects of the stroke and were left with residual visual-cognitive deficits, with no other behavioural impairment. Mrs T could no longer read: she was alexic. She had not lost her knowledge of letters or words, for she could describe letter forms and write to dictation, and she could spell words aloud. Moreover, her spoken language was completely intact both in production and perception. However, she could no longer recognise words by sight. By contrast, she was able to recognise all manner of objects other than written words by sight—flags of different countries, symbols. She could discriminate real letters from made-up ones. She could identify pictures, line drawings and photographs, making no errors even when the material was visually confuseable (e.g. different types of citrus fruit). She was excellent at recognising faces and facial expressions.

Mrs D, on the other hand, had no reading problem and no problem in performing high-level visual tasks such as recognising local patterns in global forms or, conversely, global forms described by local features. However, she did have some difficulties in recognising objects—in particular in identifying objects and places as familiar or not. So, for instance, she felt that her own apartment was "unfamiliar" and had some difficulty remembering routes because she was unable to gauge their familiarity. Above all, however, she was impaired at recognising faces. This is not to say that she failed to recognise people: she always addressed me correctly—even after a three year gap between visits! But it was quickly clear that she made these discriminations on the basis of multimodal information and did not rely, as most of us do, on the face. When the three clinicians changed their labcoats and sat in front of her, silently and with a neutral fixed expression, she was quite unable to distinguish them—even though one was male and balding, another a silver-haired woman with spectacles and the third a dark-haired woman. Mrs D was also impaired at recognising pictures of facial expressions from photographs or from (posed) live facial actions.

On the basis of the laterality study with normal subjects, I had anticipated that Mrs T would be able to speechread but that Mrs D would not. Mrs D had damage to the right cerebral hemisphere and, moreover, this clearly affected her ability to "read faces" in other tasks. But in fact the pattern was quite the opposite. While Mrs D was unable to match pictures of different views of one person or to match pictures for facial expression, she was completely unimpaired at matching face pictures on the basis of the speechsound they were making. So, for instance, she was able to match two different faces showing the liprounding for an "oo" sound—and could do this across a three-quarter face and a full-face without any difficulty. The clinching aspect of her unimpaired speechreading skill was that she was susceptible to visual influences in reporting dubbed audio-visual speech, where some of the tokens were designed to elicit fusion responses (McGurk & MacDonald, 1976).

Mrs T, however, despite completely unimpaired face processing in all other domains, was a poor speechreader. She could not always distinguish speaking-face pictures from those of a face making a nonsense expression such as puffing out the cheeks or sticking out the tongue ("gurning face"), and then was not able to classify speaking-face photographs on the basis of their mouthshape. Her most profound deficit was in audio-visual speech perception; she showed no effect of vision on audition with the McGurk stimuli (Campbell, Landis & Regard, 1986). Although she looked intently at the screen during the sessions and was able to identify other face actions (e.g. expressions) and the identity of the speaker, she responded to audio-visual stimuli as if her eyes had been closed throughout—she just reported the heard speech sound. No other control subject did this.

Thus, while experiments with normal subjects suggest speechreading is better when it is done in the right hemisphere, the dissociated patterns of face processing and speechreading in Mrs D and Mrs T told a different story. Mrs T's deficit suggested that the left hemisphere is needed for speechreading. Moreover, her speechreading and her reading deficit suggest that the same—or overlapping—sites have a crucial role to play in both these ways of achieving speech from vision. Over the past 10 years a number of findings have helped to suggest how these paradoxical findings have come about and how they may be interpreted.

LEFT, RIGHT OR BOTH? SPEECHREADING IN SPLIT-BRAIN PATIENTS

One potentially useful source of information could be the speechreading of patients whose cerebral commissures—the fibre bundles connecting the two cortical hemispheres—had been surgically separated. If speechreading required a function exclusively located in one cortical hemisphere, then these patients might make this clear, since it is well established that their cortical hemispheres function separately and distinctively for speech (left hemisphere) and for visuospatial tasks, including face analysis (right hemisphere).

NG was one such patient, investigated with D. and E. Zaidel (see Campbell, 1992). She could recognise number forms equally well with either hemisphere as long as she was not required to name the number aloud (this was only possible with her left hemisphere). NG was shown mouthed numbers to speechread in central vision, that is both hemispheres had access to this information. A number was then displayed right or left of a central fixation screen, which she was required to match to the lipspeech number by a handpress response. This lateralised task meant that the written number information went separately to each cortical hemisphere. Under these conditions, NG was equally good with either (disconnected) hemisphere. This suggests there can be similar potential in either hemisphere for the analysis of lipspoken numbers, at least.

RELATIVE NOT ABSOLUTE DIFFERENCES?

Since NG can match numbers to seen-speech using either disconnected hemisphere, it suggests that there may be similar potential for speechreading in either hemisphere. For *hearing* speech, this is much less likely.[1] This makes Mrs T's problem even more puzzling. Why couldn't she use her undamaged right hemisphere for speechreading? An answer to this will be attempted at the end of this chapter. If speechreading might be more bilateral than either hearing speech or viewing faces, we can at least ask which side is better—and for what aspect of the task? A somewhat different question is: To what extent are patterns of localisation specific to silent speechreading, rather than to the analysis of other facial actions? Some recent studies with normal subjects start to offer some answers to these questions. Smeele and her colleagues (see Smeele, 1996) explored lateralisation of computer-animated faces using a central dot-counting task to maintain central fixation and varying retinal eccentricities of the animated stimulus face, which could be saying /ba/, /va/, /da/ or /θa/. She found a slight RVF (right visual field, that is left hemisphere) advantage in accuracy of report for relatively fast rates of speech and for some more eccentric (peripheral) locations and no advantage at all for smaller visual angles and for slower rates of speech. The RVF advantage persisted for one other face action, too: that of tongue protrusion. So this finding contrasts with Campbell's (1986) finding of a LVF advantage in matching still images to heard speech sounds. Is image animation the critical factor in switching hemisphere localisation? In a further study (Campbell, de Gelder & de Haan, 1996), hearing participants were required to match a face photograph appearing on a computer monitor to one seen a second or so previously from a different viewpoint (three-quarter to full face or vice versa). The photographs were of different people or the same person. When the match was on the basis of lipshape ("Is he saying 'oo' or 'ee'?") there was a clear advantage to the RVF (left hemisphere) in right handers, which was absent in left handers. When the match was on the basis of identity ("Same person or different people?") the RVF advantage disappeared. Since both Smeele's and our (1996) task produced a RVF processing advantage it would appear that time-varying image characteristics, per se, were not the reason for the left hemisphere advantage. Nor can the asymmetrical advantage in this latest study be ascribed to verbal report, for the task only required a visual match. The analysis of silent seen-speech forms can show an advantage to the left hemisphere. It can be found for the identification both of still and moving lipshape images.

WHAT EXACTLY IS THE ROLE OF THE RIGHT HEMISPHERE IN SPEECHREADING?

The earlier finding of a right hemisphere advantage (Campbell, 1986) for a lipshape matching task should not, however, be discounted. It may have reflected the specific visual demands of that task (that study used low illumination, fast tachistoscopic exposure of low-contrast half-tone pictures—all of which are generally conducive to a right hemisphere advantage in visual image processing). Some right hemisphere abilities are likely to be useful in speechreading, in particular when the image quality is poor and/or the image is transient.

The developmental prosopagnosic AB (Campbell et al., 1990; Campbell, 1992) could also be brought in to support this idea. AB has always been poor at recognising faces and shows some other visual object recognition difficulties (de Haan & Campbell, 1991). We believe that her right hemisphere visual skills may have developed anomalously. At all events, she is poor at a range of live speechreading tasks, although she can classify still images of mouthshapes well.

LATERALISATION OF AUDIO-VISUAL SPEECH

In speechreading a silent face, a target speech pattern must be sought, constructed or held for matching to the image. By contrast, for audio-visual speech, and for influences of vision on audition more generally, the requirement is not to identify the seen image in terms of speech sound but for sound and vision to be processed in a unitary manner for an identification response. Is this best done by one or other hemisphere, or by both? Our studies with NG, the commissurotomised (split-brain) patient showed she was susceptible to the McGurk fusion illusion under free viewing/

listening conditions. That is, the illusion does not require comissural transfer. Baynes et al. (1994) tested normal subjects and a split-brain patient more systematically. They used auditory-visual stimuli comprising both congruent and incongruent stimuli. Incongruent pairs comprised synchronised heard and seen words such as (heard) "bat" + (seen) "vet", which gave rise to the illusion that "vat" has been spoken. Subjects were instructed to fixate left or right of videoclips showing these stimuli and matched what they believed they had heard to an aftercoming written word. Written word pairs appeared left or right of centre screen for 180 ms after the videoclip. Under these conditions, more visually influenced reports occurred when the written words appeared in the right visual field, but also when the videoclip had projected to the left visual field. These effects were not very strong, reaching only the 5% level of significance. Nevertheless, they appear to be valid, for they were absent in a group of tested left handers: left handers are more likely to have anomalous patterns of cortical lateralisation for speech. They suggest that seen speech is most efficiently processed when the face projects to the right hemisphere (LVF) and the response choice of printed words is available from the left hemisphere (RVF). JW, the split-brain patient, showed fewer audio-visual fusion responses than other neurological controls on their task, confirming this interpretation.

Diesch (1995) presented subjects with pairs of faces, seen left and right of fixation, one of which was speaking a monosyllable such as "ga" or "ba". Corresponding auditory speech tokens were located in central space. Under these conditions, there was a tendency for fusion responses to be reported more frequently from the LVF than the RVF. Combination responses (e.g. "bga" for seen "ba" and heard "ga") lateralised the opposite way. This pattern conforms reasonably well with Baynes et al.'s findings. Under audio-visual presentation conditions, visually influenced responses are slightly more likely when the face projects to the right rather than the left hemisphere and when the fusion percept is phonotactically acceptable. We might add that the phonological requirements for reporting the combination responses, being phonotactically unusual, may make special demands on left-hemisphere systems.

To summarise, recent studies suggest that the left hemisphere may have the advantage in analysing face images for speech when the task is vowel image matching ("oo or ee?") from face photographs or when precise place of consonant articulation ("ba, va, da or tha?"—also tongue movement) has to be identified from a lateralised animated image at high levels of eccentricity. Audio-visual fusions tend to be stronger when the image projects to the right hemisphere, except when the speech target is a "blend" such as "bga" or "bda", where the pattern can reverse. AB, whose right hemisphere performance was anomalous in several ways, was poor at live speechreading and failed to show McGurk effects, that is, her speechreading debilities fit this general picture of lateralisation. Patients with surgically separated cortices show that such lateralised differences may be relative, not absolute: silent speechreading (for appropriate material) can occur intrahemispherically, although Baynes'' study suggests that optimal audio-visual speech integration may be bi-hemispheric.

SOME INTERPRETATIONS

There are a number of reasons why a mild right-hemisphere advantage for processing visual inputs might interact with a left-hemisphere advantage in audible speech processing to generate higher levels of fusion response with LVF visual presentations. The visual capacities of the right hemisphere—especially in the processing of form-from-motion and in its (assumed) enhanced abilities in processing lower spatial frequencies—could preferentially deliver visual coarticulation information to left cortical sites for integration with auditory processing. The synchronisation of seen and heard events may be more accurately managed under right hemisphere-vision and left hemisphere-hearing conditions—at least for phonotactically regular speech events ("da" or "va" but not "bga" or "vtha").

It is also possible that audio-visual inputs may reorganise cortical processing directly. That is, different processing channels may be selected for unimodal than bimodal inputs. Under bimodal conditions, audition may be left hemisphere-prioritised and viewing right-prioritised. This is one explanation for the discrepant findings of Campbell (1986) and Campbell, de Gelder and de Haan (1996). The earlier study required matching of a seen-speech image to a heard but non-coincident speech sound; the later study was entirely silent, requiring only matching to an internally generated speech sound template ("Are the faces saying 'oo' or 'ee'?"). Further shifting of functional localised expertise may occur when the heard-and-seen speech material stresses the system by speedier rates of presentation and/or further degradation of the input. Under these conditions, the left hemisphere may dominate for audio-visual speech input because of its more general flexibility in speech processing and its presumed superiority in fine temporal discrimination (Hellige, 1993).

CORTICAL IMAGING

We have recently been able to explore some of these inferences directly by cortical imaging. This project was initiated by G. Calvert (Oxford University, with S.D. Iversen) and a team of psychiatrists and cortical image analysts at the Institute of Psychiatry, London (A.S. David, E. Bullmore, M. Brammer, P. Woodruff, S. Williams & P. McGuire), using functional magnetic resonance imaging (fMRI). This technique makes use of the interactions between a strong magnetic field (1.5 tesla) and the small electro-magnetic field established by localised brain activity. As in other cortical imaging methodologies, the favoured experimental paradigm is subtractive: that is, as far as possible, an experimental and a baseline condition are contrasted in one experiment. The pattern of imaged brain activity then reflects the *differential* activation of the experimental over the control condition. Spatial resolution using this completely noninvasive imaging method is currently around 3 mm. This is at the cost of temporal resolution: currently images showing summed activation over 15 seconds on task are the best that can be achieved. In the studies reported here, images showing summed activity over 30 seconds on-task were analysed over a small group of right-handed subjects, using appropriate statistical techniques (Bullmore et al., 1996).

In the studies reported here (and see Calvert et al., 1996) four conditions—each comprising an experimental (ON) and control (OFF) condition—were compared for five right-handed volunteer subjects. The first condition contrasted hearing spoken numbers by a single female speaker with hearing nothing at all. Each condition alternated, lasting for 30 seconds over 5 minutes or so. The subject's task was simply to rehearse the heard numbers silently to himself or herself and, for the silent condition, to mentally rehearse the series "one-one-one". This condition would generate the appropriate auditory speech processing baseline for comparison to other conditions (i.e. activation pattern for the OFF condition of no auditory speech was subtracted from the activation pattern for the ON condition— auditory speech input). This should show, for each subject, where the primary auditory cortex is located.

The second condition explored *audio-visual* processing. A videotape showing the female speaker saying numbers was presented in the ON condition. The OFF condition was the same person's face seen at rest, but accompanied by heard numbers. The contrast here (congruent audio-visual display minus auditory display with still-face picture) should show activity related to the addition of congruent seen speech to hearing. The third condition contrasted silent speechreading of numbers (ON) with an audiovisual baseline (OFF) and, finally, silent speechreading (ON) was contrasted with a still face (OFF). In this condition, as in condition 1, subjects were required to say "one ... one ..." continually to themselves during the OFF condition. In the other two conditions, they mentally rehearsed the speechread, heard or audio-visually spoken numbers.

Heard speech (condition 1: listening to spoken numbers between 1 and 10) activated classical auditory reception areas, including primary auditory cortex (Brodmann's area 41) bilaterally. In some subjects, left-dominance was more marked than in others.

In condition 2, audio-visual speech (seen-and-spoken numbers: ON) was compared with viewing a still face accompanying the spoken number soundtrack (hearing-only: OFF). There was no (differential) activation in the primary auditory areas or in auditory association areas under these conditions. This suggests that both the ON and the OFF conditions activated these speech areas identically. Those parts of visual cortex that analyse visual movement (MT, also called V5) were reliably differentially active in all subjects—bilaterally. These parts of visual cortex are very close to the fusiform and lingual gyri which have been implicated in face processing in other imaging studies (Sergent, MacDonald & Zuck, 1995),[2] and in this case they indicate that the seen-speaking face activated specific areas of extrastriate visual cortex.

In condition 3, when subjects were speechreading silently spoken numbers (ON) in contrast to seeing and hearing the speaker (OFF), the areas of activation common to all five subjects were quite small: they included primary visual areas (V1 and V2) and some slightly posterior association (temporal) cortex. The relative lack of differential activation in this condition, in conjunction with the patterns of conditions 1 and 2 suggested to us that both silent speechreading and audio-visual speech activate the same substrate comprising the auditory speech reception areas (Wernicke's area) including Brodmann's area 41 in the left hemisphere, but that there is a slight, yet significant, additional contribution for seen speech from primary visual areas and from some superior temporal sites, bilaterally.[3]

From these findings, we thought that silent speechreading (condition 4: silent speechreading ON; still face, no speech OFF) might show just two areas of specific activity: classical speech reception sites around Wernicke's area in the region of the left superior temporal gyrus and also some visual area activation, especially visual movement analysis (V5). Indeed, we did find activation in just these sites. It is noteworthy that Brodmann's area 41 (classical primary auditory cortex) was activated by this condition. We believe this is the first time that a visual display has been shown to activate auditory cortex directly in hearing people. Primary auditory cortex is not activated by silent reading of written words or syllables. But more extensive areas of activation were recorded for silent speechreading in addition to this. Large regions of lateral superior temporal cortex (Brodmann's area 22) were indicated in all scans. This activation was noteworthy for its robustness and reliability: it was the area of strongest activation in all subjects, and was bilateral. It was also somewhat more extensive in the right than the left hemisphere of most of these right-handed subjects.[4] These findings are summarised in Figure 33.

So, silent speechreading activates auditory receptive cortex. In addition, superior temporal regions are active when viewing a moving (speaking) face. It is well established that different sites (right parahippocampal gyrus and the right fusiform gyrus) are active when people view pictures of faces for identity or for facial expression judgements (Sergent, MacDonald & Zuck, 1995; Haxby et al., 1995). Different areas again (primarily left infero-temporal) are

experimental (ON)	control (OFF)	main areas of differential activation (ON minus OFF) across all subjects. Since these were similar for each hemisphere, only the LH is shown.
1 hearing spoken numbers (no vision)	nothing (silence, no vision)	
2 audio-visual spoken numbers	unmoving face: heard speech	
3 silent speechreading of numbers	audio-visual spoken numbers	
4 silent speechreading of numbers	still face: no heard speech	

in this condition only more activation observed in some RH than LH areas

FIG. 33.   A schematic outline of fMRI tasks and major areas of activation.

active in reading (Price et al., 1994). That is, this pattern of activation does seem to be "special for speechreading". How specific is it? Can it be produced by watching any face actions? In a second study, Calvert and colleagues showed that facial gurning—movements of the lower face with the mouth closed—did not activate this area specifically, but that watching open mouth movements did. These actions were performed at a natural speechrate and "looked like speech", although no words could be identified. This display was "pseudospeech": the mouth and face actions seemed to viewers to be those of someone "speaking a foreign language". Thus, a viewing condition which contrasted silent speechreading for "real numbers" being spoken (ON) and for pseudospeech (OFF) showed no differential pattern of activation in these language areas (Calvert et al., 1997).

INTERPRETING SUPERIOR TEMPORAL ACTIVATION BY SILENT SPEECH AND BY SILENT "PSEUDOSPEECH"

The activation of these areas—a broad (8 cm) swathe running approximately from the top of one ear to the top of the other ear—is intriguing. These areas are classically, but loosely, defined as association cortex. That is, they are not as intimately tied to modality of input or action as many other cortical sites. However, the associations which are made here are not so general as to suggest that all or any new multimodal task may produce such activation. Gurning did not activate superior temporal regions. Face actions that could be construed as speech were critical. It is likely that these large areas are recruited when the sensory input is partial and the identification of the speech event requires access to prior knowledge, such as context. Indeed similar widespread temporal activation, although not in precisely the same areas, has been reported when written nonsense words like FLIM or SPREN are shown (Price, Wise & Frackowiak, 1996), and many computational models of word recognition explicitly build in a processing stage wherein any single word (or speech event) may activate a range of potential targets that share some of its features. Identification under these schemes is then a competitive process, whereby the match of the stimulus to the stored representation evolves through iterative procedures that home in on the best-fitting target (Rumelhart & McClelland, 1981). Thus, such observed widespread temporal activation may signal the operation of "top-down" processing as the recruitment of a large number of lexical candidates for matching to the speechread stimulus is engaged.

Audio-visual speech, by contrast, delivers more distinctive sensory information, because of the additional, informative acoustic channel. Speech delivered "by ear" could be readily reported in these imaging experiments, despite the noisy conditions induced by the scanner. There is less need to recruit top-down information in the hearing or audio-visual conditions. This functional difference between audio-visual and silent speechreading tasks may drive the differing configurations—including patterns of localisation—of the cortical structures involved.

INTERPRETING CORTICAL IMAGING: CONSIDERING SPACE AND TIME

The cortical imaging studies clarify several points. First, silent speechreading is special in its ability to activate the primary auditory cortex directly. Second, both this activation site and the others that have been described appear, at this stage of exploration, to be essentially bilateral. How can these findings be accommodated to clinical and experimental results which show a mixture of patterns of lateralisation: right-hemisphere localisation inferred for "low level" image processing, left-hemisphere localisation for identifying seen-speech patterns, especially when they are phonotactically plausible, and left localisation, also, for matching faces for mouthshape and for discriminating small image differences as in "ba-va-tha-da" discrimination?

One probable answer lies in the temporal characteristics of cortical recruitment. fMRI cannot show when specific areas become active, only where they are. Reaction-time studies, on the other hand, show which hemisphere is faster off the mark. This may reflect a number of further possibilities. The first area to be activated may "gate" consequent activity in other areas or it may represent a "first pass" analysis occurring in parallel with slower processing in another site. It is very probable that in audio-visual speechreading right-hemisphere processes are recruited first and allow a first pass at interpreting the facial image while the specialised auditory processing sites for speech in the left hemisphere are also activated early.

Multichannel EEG (electroencephalograph) recordings of evoked cortical potentials can capture some of these temporal characteristics. Neuromagnetic (MEG) recordings are a further development. They now allow patterns of temporal and spatial cortical activity from the outer surface of the brain to be reliably recorded from the scalp in alert subjects. Equivalent current dipole measures (ECDs) can be deduced from the magnetic fields induced by such neural activity. Sams et al. (1991) reported that audio-visual speech (McGurk "da", given heard "ba" and seen "ga") first generated a specific temporal pattern of excitation (mismatch negativity), indicating that these stimuli were perceived differently ("da") than the heard stimulus ("ba"). Second, he showed that such audio-visual material activated an area slightly posterior to primary auditory cortex. Spatial resolution with MEG is still not good enough to be able to make firmer localisation conclusions. More recent studies (Sams, 1996) confirm these earlier observations and extend them to bihemispheric measurements. To date, these studies suggest bilateral patterns of activation, rather than anything else.

VISUAL SPEECHBLINDNESS: A CRITICAL LOCUS IN SPEECHREADING

This review has emphasised that speechreading is not exclusively localised to one or other hemisphere. Why then should we should find patients like Mrs T or even AB who cannot read speech from faces?[5] In both cases, we have suggested that their dysfunction is quite discretely localised, so why can't the other parts of the brain take over? For Mrs T, whose lesion caused damage to medial parts of the temporal lobe on the left, the failure to speechread may appear puzzling for another reason. We have shown not only that there is equipotentiality but also that it is lateral temporal cortex (e.g. Brodmann areas 41 and 22) not the medial parts, that are implicated.

First, it is important to know just what Mrs T could and could not do with seen-speaking faces. She was not too bad at sorting face pictures into piles representing speech sounds and nonspeech sounds, but she did classify one or two obviously gurning faces as speaking faces. She also was not too bad at then sorting these speech faces into speech classes ("oo", "ee", "f", "sh", etc.), but she made around 10% errors (all control subjects were perfect at this). Her main difficulty was with audio-visual speech. For dubbed material which generated McGurk effects in elderly controls, she simply repeated what was heard, not the fusion, despite looking hard at the screen. AB showed a similar dense "blindness" to visual inputs under audio-visual testing conditions (Campbell et al. 1990) and a relative sparing of identification of photo-images of seen speech.

In both individuals, then, the pattern suggests that identifying lipshapes may be relatively intact, but that the influence of vision on audition is lost or reduced. The classical explanation for Mrs T's other deficit, pure alexia, is that the lesion disconnects visual processing from access to specific word recognition sites in the left hemisphere (Wernicke's area generally and the supramarginal gyrus). Because the lesion is medially placed, it can block inputs from the right hemisphere which access the left hemisphere by posterior commissural fibres. For alexia, it is also necessary to posit that left-hemisphere visual analysis, too, blocks access to language representation sites. However, for audio-visual speechreading it may just be sufficient that right-hemisphere analysis fails to access the left-hemisphere-based representation sites in temporal register with the analysis of the heard speech event. This may explain why people with very different lesion locations, including a left hemisphere medial posterior temporal lesion (Mrs T), commissural lesions (JW) and a possible general right hemisphere visual deficit (AB), all show "McGurk failure" despite reasonable visual analytic skills in identifying mouthshapes. It is this fast analysis of seen-speech forms while concurrently listening to speech that requires intact posterior right-hemisphere analysis of the visual form and effective access to left-hemisphere speech sites.

This may not be the only critical deficit. It should be clear that any number of visual analytic abilities (the perception of movement, faces and small feature differences) and of speech processing skills (identification and maintenance of a phonological or lexical record) may be implicated in speechreading. These are localised in different ways, but the model sketched above may well be *specific* to audio-visual speech. Moreover, it should be noted that whatever it is that the right hemisphere does better in spee-chreading may dissociate from other facereading tasks. Mrs D's ability to speechread, although she was unable to perform other face processing tasks, may rely not only on intact left-hemisphere analysis but on a finer functional dissociation: her damaged right hemisphere could support the analysis of facial images for speech which could access the language sites in the left hemisphere in a sufficiently temporally integrated way for her to be misled by audio-visual illusions.

CONCLUSIONS

Speechreading in hearing individuals is an intriguing function from the perspective of neurofunctional localisation because it might indicate the line between language processing on the one hand, and the processing of faces—the most naturally complex visual forms in terms of their social and emotional salience—on the other. In the most general terms, language and non-linguistic facial processing can be managed separately by the left and the right hemisphere respectively. In the last 10 years, great advances have been made in direct and relatively noninvasive methods for measuring the localisation of brain function. There are two distinct strands to these investigations which were, themselves, prefigured by arguments in the 1980s concerning modularity of function (Fodor, 1983). On the one hand, there has been a successful and ongoing exploration for more distinctive modular systems of process and representation. These studies indeed reflect a new phrenology. They can show us, for example, that very circumscribed areas of the brain are critical for lexical representations for inanimate objects such as tools, while different loci are implicated for representing objects such as animals (Damasio et al., 1996). On the other hand, there have been studies which explore process and representation more dynamically and which suggest variable and relative contributions of different processing areas to a specific task. Moreover, the temporal patterning and recruitment of these is critical and can involve various forms of feedback ("re-entry").

I do not believe that there is a specific area of the brain devoted to speechreading; that is, there is unlikely to be a speechreading module. However, there are certainly cortical areas that specialise in processing and representing the different requisites of speechreading. In this chapter, I have concentrated on some vision-related ones. One task for the future is to explore some of these even more carefully. For example, what is the relative contribution of the perception of movement and of static form to speech-reading (see Rosenblum, this volume)? Another is to explore the relation between speaking and seeing speech in more detail (speech planning and representation). Calvert et al.'s (1997) cortical imaging study has started to explore the most devious and frustrating aspect of speechreading: if you can hear, you can usually *almost* lipread (as when viewing "pseudospeech"). Looking at a speaker whom one cannot hear provides an impoverished sensory input for a highly detailed and complex process and requires a great deal of contextual filling in to work properly (see Rönnberg et al., this volume; Pichora-Fuller, 1996).

The precise calibration of cortical processes underpinning multimodal processing have not even begun to be explored in ways that can offer insights into the perception of real events in the world. Eventually these will offer not only an intriguing perspective on brain function, but hope for those who rely on speechreading because of encroaching deafness or who, having been born deaf, use speech to communicate with the hearing world.

NOTES

1. Although the relevant hearing-to-written number matching tasks have not been reported, as far as I know.
2. We would not expect activation of these "face-specific" areas because both the control condition and the experimental condition showed a facial display, so this would subtract out.
3. Calvert and colleagues are currently exploring the pattern of audio-visual activation in much more detail, both within subjects and in terms of activation patterns in common across subjects: the summary results given reflect a first-pass at the data, delineating only the major differences between conditions, applicable to all subjects.
4. The significance of this right-hemisphere lateralised pattern is obscure: while it was very marked for five/five subjects reported in the main experiment, it was less so for the second set of five subjects who viewed gurning and pseudo-speaking faces in addition to silent spee-chreading. The task environment may set the pattern of lateralisation in modifiable ways and/or the statistical power of the effect may be small.
5. Failure to speechread is not construed here as poor speechreading, rather a failure to identify a face action when a great deal of context is given ("Did I say 'foot' or 'teeth'?") and where control subjects reach ceiling levels. For audio-visual speech, it is a failure to show an effect of vision on audition: a pattern of response that is equivalent to unimodal heard speech responses for that individual and where control subjects do show a consistent influence of vision on audition.

REFERENCES

Baynes, K., Funnell, M.G. & Fowler, C.A. (1994). Hemispheric contributions to the integration of visual and auditory information in speech perception. *Perception and Psychophysics*, *55*, 633–41.

Bullmore, E.T., Brammer, M.J., Williams, S.C.R., Rabe-Hesketh, S., Janot, N., David, A.S., Mellers, J.D.C., Howard, R.J. & Sham, P. (1996). Statistical methods of estimation and inference for function MR image analysis. *Magnetic Resonance in Medicine*, *35*, 261–77.

Calvert, G., Campbell, R., Bullmore, E., Brammer, M., Woodruff, P., Williams, S., McGuire, P. & David, A.S. (1996). *FMRI studies of speechreading: abstract*. International Congress of Psychophysiology. Tampere, Finland.

Calvert, G., Bullmore, E., Brammer, M., Campbell, R., Woodruff, P., McGuire, P., Williams, S., Iversen, S.D. & David, A.S. (1997). Activation of auditory cortex during silent speechreading. *Science*, *276*, 593–596.

Campbell, R. (1986). The lateralization of lipreading: A first look. *Brain and Cognition*, *5*, 1–21.

Campbell, R. (1987). The cerebral lateralisation of lipreading. In B. Dodd & R. Campbell (Eds), *Hearing by Eye: The Psychology of Lipreading*. Hove, UK: Lawrence Erlbaum Associates Ltd.

Campbell, R. (1990). Lipreading, neuropsychology and immediate memory. In G. Vallar & T. Shallice (Eds), *Neuropsychological Impairments of Short-term Memory* (pp. 268–86). Cambridge, UK: Cambridge University Press.

Campbell, R. (1992). The neuropsychology of lipreading. *Philosophical Transactions of the Royal Society of London, B*, *335*, 39–45.

Campbell, R., de Gelder, B. & de Haan, E.H.F. (1996). The lateralisation of lipreading: A second look. *Neuropsychologia*, *34(12)*, 1235–40.

Campbell, R., Garwood, J., Franklin, S., Howard, D., Landis, T. & Regard, M. (1990). Neuropsychological studies of the auditory-visual fusion illusion. *Neuropsychologia*, *28*, 787–802.

Campbell, R., Landis, T. & Regard, M. (1986). Face recognition and lipreading: A neurological dissociation. *Brain*, *109*, 509–21.

Damasio, H., Grabowski, T.J., Tranel, D., Hichwa, R.D. & Damasio, A.R. (1996). Neural bases for lexical retrieval. *Nature*, *380*, 499–504.

de Haan, E.H.F. & Campbell, R. (1991). A fifteen year follow-up of a case of developmental prosopagnosia. *Cortex*, *27*, 489–509.

Diesch, E. (1995). Left and right hemifield advantages of fusions and combinations in audiovisual speech perception. *Quarterly Journal of Experimental Psychology*, *48A*, 320–33.

Ellis, H.D. (1983). The role of the right hemisphere in face perception. In: A. Young (Ed.), *Functions of the Right Hemisphere* (pp. 33–64). London: Academic Press.

Fodor, J. (1983). *The Modularity of Mind*. Cambridge, Mass: MIT Press.

Haxby, J.V., Ungerleider, L.G., Horwitz, B., Rapoport, S.I. & Grady, C.L. (1995). Hemispheric differences in neural systems for face working memory: A PET rCBF study. *Human Brain Mapping*, *3*, 68–82.

Hellige, J. (1993). *Hemispheric Asymmetry: What is Left and What is Right?* Cambridge: Harvard.

McGurk, H. & MacDonald, J. (1976). Hearing lips and seeing voices. *Nature*, *264*, 746–8.

Pichora-Fuller, M.K. (1996). Working memory and speechreading. In D.G. Stork & M.E. Hennecke (Eds), *Speechreading by Humans and Machines: Models, Systems and Applications* (pp. 259–74). Berlin: Springer.

Price, C.J., Wise, R., Frackowiak, R.S.J. (1996). Demonstrating the implicit processing of visually presented words and pseudowords. *Cerebral Cortex*, *6*, 62–70.

Price, C.J., Wise, R.J.S., Watson, J.D.G., Patterson, K., Howard, D. & Frackowiak, R.S.J. (1994). Brain activity during reading. *Brain*, *117*, 1255–69.

Rumelhart, D. & McClelland, J.L. (1981). Interactive processing through spreading activation. In A.M. Lesgold & C. Perfetti (Eds), *Interactive processes in Reading*, Hillsdale, NJ: Lawrence Erlbaum Associates.

Sams, M. (1996). *MEG activation for audiovisual speech*. Paper to the International Congress of Psychophysiology. Tampere, Finland, June.

Sams, M., Aulanko, R., Hämäläinen, M., Hari, R., Lounasmaa, O.V., Lu, S.-T. & Simola, J. (1991). Seeing speech: visual information from lipmovements modifies activity in the human auditory cortex. *Neuroscience Letters*, *127*, 141–5.

Sergent, J., MacDonald, B. & Zuck, E. (1995). Structural and functional organization of knowledge about faces and proper names: A PET study. In M. Moscovitch & C. Umilta (Eds), *Conscious and Nonconscious Information Processing: Attention and Performance Volume X* (pp. 204–28). Cambridge, Mass: MIT Press.

Smeele, P.M.T. (1996). Psychology of human speechreading. In D.G. Stork & M.E. Hennecke (Eds), *Speechreading by Humans and Machines: Models, Systems and Applications* (pp. 3–16). Berlin: Springer.

CHAPTER TEN

Impaired speechreading and audio-visual speech integration in prosopagnosia

Beatrice de Gelder, Jean Vroomen and
Anne-Catherine Bachoud-Levi *Department of Psychology,*
Tilburg University, Tilburg, The Netherlands

INTRODUCTION

Visual agnosia is the condition following cortical insult that results in an inability to recognise visually presented objects. In severe cases all classes of visual object recognition may be impaired. There is debate concerning the loss of face processing ability in this context (Farah, 1991), but the general pattern is for face recognition skills to be very impaired (prosopagnosia) in most cases of visual object agnosia. Despite such profound loss, copying and imagery skills may be relatively normal, indicating a breakdown in the recognition mechanism that can dissociate from spared visual processing and spared visual knowledge. Speech is not usually construed as a "visual object" in the sense that an orange or an automobile—or even a facial identity or expression—may be. So might speechreading be spared in patients with visual agnosia?

In this chapter we report a case of dense visual agnosia affecting the processing of all visual material, including faces and written words, who could nevertheless perform some speechreading tasks. We speculate on the implications of this for modelling speechreading in neurophysiological systems.

SPEECHREADING IN VISUAL AGNOSIA: PREVIOUS CASES

Several cases have been reported that have a bearing on this question. One study which suggested that speechreading was a different sort of visual object than most others was the report of patient Mrs D (Campbell et al.,

195

1986). She was densely agnosic with profound prosopagnosia, yet could sort pictures of faces according to speechsound and was sensitive to the effects of seeing the speaker in reporting heard speech (McGurk effects). She could speechread silent spoken numbers and could discriminate lipspoken vowels and consonants.

By contrast, patient Mrs T was unable to perform such tasks, although she had no difficulty recognising faces or facial expressions or other visual objects. Mrs T was also unable to read any word presented to her although she could spell words perfectly, a letter at a time, when she heard the word (pure alexia). Mrs T's lesion was unilateral and affected the left hemisphere, Mrs D's only affected the right. Patient HJA (Campbell, 1992) had bilateral lesions of occipito-temporal areas. He was unable to recognise faces or words presented to him and could not classify photographs of speaking faces. However, he was completely normal in speechreading moving faces and in showing McGurk effects for incongruent auditory-visual speech stimuli. This suggests that HJA's impairment was at a lower functional level than that of Mrs T: under certain visual conditions (moving stimuli) he could speechread, while Mrs T was unable to speechread even moving faces.

HJA's visual impairment affects all stationary objects—letters, faces, common objects, drawings—but spares moving ones, when tested (see also Humphreys et al., 1993). The critical importance of visual movement pathways to speechreading is illustrated by case LM (Campbell, 1996; Campbell et al., submitted). LM's lesion affects only the cortical visual movement areas, including area V5, and sparing areas V1–V4 which are all damaged in HJA. LM can only speechread in the sense of being able to classify still photographs of seen speech. She does not show McGurk effects and cannot read silently spoken speech.

Thus, studies reported to date suggest that visual speech may be construed as a visual object—but as a rather special one. First, some aspects of its recognition and classification call on specific language processing sites, probably in the left hemisphere (Mrs T). Second, speech may be more dependent than other visual objects on the integrity of visual movement processing: dynamic aspects of speechreading may be among its defining aspects (Rosenblum & Saldaña, this volume).

THE PRESENT STUDY

In this chapter we present data on speechreading from a visual agnosic patient, BC, who was densely prosopagnosic and alexic, but with normal auditory language skills, good drawing, copying and visual imagery abilities. We tested her ability to classify speech from still and moving faces and to integrate seen and heard speech. We finally tested her ability to remember seen speech.

CASE REPORT

BC suffered in May 1995 from a haematoma located across the left tem-poro-occipital sulcus, involving the middle occipital gyrus and the inferior temporal gyrus (Brodmann areas 18, 19, and 37). She presented with a right homonymous hemianopsia and showed a mild anomia, without any com-prehension or repetition deficit, that subsided after some weeks. No other linguistic deficits were present, apart from a pure alexia. After some weeks, Goldmann perimetry showed a residual right para-central scotoma, which disappeared with IV/4 test. In December 1995 she suffered from a second, right-sided haematoma, almost symmetrical to the first. The lesion was centred on the middle occipital gyrus, just posteriorly to the temporo-occipital sulcus, involving area 19 and the white matter underlying area 18. After the occurrence of the second stroke, BC found herself unable to recognise familiar faces and common objects by sight, and complained of seeing the world in shades of grey. Goldmann perimetry showed a central scotoma with II/4 test. Visual evoked responses with black and white pat-tern were normal for latency and amplitude. She named about half of a set of black and white realistic drawings without any systematicity in subsets (Snodgrass & Vanderwart, 1980). When asked to name real objects pre-sented by the examiner, she was 13/35 correct on visual presentation, claiming that she was unable to recognise the other items. Tactile naming of the same objects was flawless.

Since her injury, BC has suffered from visual agnosia, prosopagnosia, alexia, and achromatopsia. We have also reported some aspects of her object and face recognition impairments (de Gelder et al., 1996). Notwith-standing all these perceptual impairments, mental imagery was intact in all these domains (Bartolomeo et al., in press).

Early visual processing (i.e. from the retina to V1) is unimpaired when assessed by MRI, by normal visual evoked potentials and by her good performance on copying drawings and line orientation judgment. Her per-fect performance on imagery tasks and tactile naming indicates that her knowledge of objects, letters, colours, and faces is preserved.

FACE PROCESSING

A number of aspects of face processing have been examined which we briefly review before presenting the evidence on speechreading.

Examination of face processing in BC started in March 1996 (three months after the second CVA) with subtests from the face recognition battery (Bruyer & Schweich, 1991). Structural encoding, as examined by the facial decision subtest, was clearly impaired. Her face/nonface deci-sions were based on recognition of individual features and noticing their incorrect location in the face. Gender and age decisions were at chance levels. Direction of gaze, examined with still pictures, was well below normal.

There was no indication of preserved face recognition in overt or covert tasks (de Gelder et al., in preparation). In contrast, facial imagery was preserved equally well for overall configurational properties of familiar faces and for specific facial features. BC could produce clearly recognisable drawings of faces as well as of parts of faces.

Expression recognition was severely impaired when tested with static pictures but was near normal when tested with short video clips showing the full transition from a neutral resting state to a full display of the emotion achieved after 5sec. Neither the initial states nor the end states presented in isolation could however be recognised. Categorisation of facial expressions was clearly impaired even for a continuum of face images from happy to sad. There was no indication of any language-related impairment except for reading.

SPEECHREADING

Speechreading from still photographs, in normal facial context, and in isolation

Testing started by administering the subtest "facial speech" from the prosopagnosia test battery (Bruyer & Schweich, 1991). Performance was within chance levels. Given this poor performance, we re-examined her with new materials. These consisted of 16 black and white photographs (4 actors, 4 mouth positions, i.e. saying /a/, /i/, /o/, or making a face). BC was given the pictures one by one and asked to put each one on the table under one of the three written labels for the vowel (which were repeatedly pronounced by the experimenter) or put it aside as a grimace. Her total score was 6/16 correct (chance is 4/16, þ2(1) = 1.33 p > .10). None of the subcategories was dealt with better than any other (6 photographs were assigned to "grimace" with 3/6 correct; 3 to /o/ with 1/3 correct; 5 to /i/ with 1/5 correct; 2 to /a/ with 1/2 correct).

Since BC had difficulties with facial decision and part/whole recognition tasks, there was reason to suspect that the full facial context might have a detrimental effect on the recognition of the lip shapes. We therefore administered the same task in a later session, this time presenting each of the photographs with a white mask over the face and a window made into it that left only the lip shapes and the area immediately around it visible. However, this appeared to make the task even more difficult. We must conclude that speechreading from still pictures is entirely inaccessible to BC. Her face recognition impairment seems to be so dense that mouth shapes cannot be identified. Even simple forced choice among limited alternatives fails to benefit her. But BC shows some preserved visual form abilities with face-like material. In the face decision task, non-face stimuli consisting of a facial contour with jumbled facial parts inside it were often correctly rejected on the basis of comments about the location of the mouth (e.g. when the mouth was drawn on the forehead). One possibility might be that it is difficult for BC to focus on the mouth region alone. This suggestion receives some support from the comments she gave when isolated mouth parts were shown for speech classification. BC indicated that she saw nothing in such displays, while with full faces at least some effort was made to decode the form of the lips. In general terms, BC resembles HJA who could not speechread from still faces. HJA did reasonably well with dynamic stimuli; would this be true for BC?

Speechreading from movement

BC shows greatly impaired perception of visual forms in relation to faces with very few spared discrimination abilities. However, some speechreading skill might still be present in BC because there was no indication that area V5 was damaged by her strokes and there was no clinical indication of movement perception disorder. For this purpose a videotape was made showing a female speaker (BdG) pronouncing a lists of vowel-varied or consonant-varied items. For the consonant-varied list, five visually distinct consonants embedded in VCV cluster were used: /apa, ata, aka, afa, awa/. Each of them was repeated six times in random order. The vowel-varied list required speechreading of vowels embedded in a CV syllable: /bi, ba, bu/. Each CV sequence was repeated six times in random order. The videotape was presented (no sound) for repetition by BC. Her result on the consonant-varied list was above chance level. The overall score was 14 out of 30 correct (chance level is 6 out of 30, þ2(1) = 13.33, p < .001). Most mistakes were made on speechreading /apa/(perceived as /awa/), and /aka/ (also perceived as /awa/). In speechreading /bi, ba, or bu/, 14 out of 18 trials were correct (chance level is 6 out of 18, þ2(1) = 16.00, p < .001). The errors were evenly distributed across the response categories: visual /bi/ was perceived once as /bu/, visual /ba/ was perceived once as /bu/, and there were two misses in speechreading /bu/. Compared to the recognition of static lip shapes, the dynamic speechreading task yields reasonable scores. Dynamic facial actions carry useable speech information, partly available to BC.

Audio-visual speech

In the following tasks, speechreading skill is examined in the context of auditory input. It remains to be seen then if the performance with unimodal dynamic stimuli can be maintained in bimodal conditions. The following reported tasks were given to BC a few weeks later. We administered three tasks designed to appreciate the separate processing of auditory and visual input as well as their combination, the conflicts, and the audio-visual conflicts.

Visual bias in audio-visual token identification

Massaro and Cohen (see Massaro & Cohen, 1983, experiment 2) have developed a videotape of dubbed, synchronised speech that measures the influence of vision on auditory categorisation. The auditory stimuli were a nine-step /ba/ to /da/ continuum. These nine auditory tokens were facto-rially combined with two possible visual articulations, /ba/ or /da/. These 18 trials represent the bimodal condition. There was also an auditory-only and a visual-only condition. In the auditory-only condition, one of the nine auditory stimuli was presented, but the speaker did not move his mouth. In the visual-only condition, the speaker articulated either /ba/ or /da/, but no auditory speech was presented. In this case, the subject had to rely entirely on lip-reading. In every block of 54 trials, there were 18 bimodal conditions, 18 auditory-only conditions, and 18 visual-only conditions, in random order. The experiment consisted of 5½ blocks of trials preceded by 10 practice trials, producing a total of 307 trials. Participants report whether the speaker said /ba/ or /da/. Previous studies have shown that visual information systematically affects the categorisation of the speech sound. Seeing "ba" moves the categorical boundary for the auditory series towards the "ba" end of the continuum, seeing "da" towards the "da" end. Unim-odal presentations (i.e. auditory token with a still face and visual token without sound) are judged in their own right and offer a second metric for assessing the influence of the mixed modality. In control subjects, visual unimodal inputs tend to be correctly reported, while the auditory-only input constitutes a baseline for establishing the effect of the mixed-mode condition.

BC showed an unusual pattern. In speechreading visual-only /ba/ or /da/, she reported almost exclusively /ba/ (visual /ba/ was 96% of the time cor-rectly perceived as /ba/, but visual /da/ was 86% of the time perceived as incorrect /ba/). So the total percentage of correct responses on the visual-only part of the test was only 55% ($\beta2(1) = 1.02$, p > .10). A similar strange pattern was observed with the auditory-only and the audio-visual trials. On the auditory-only (with still silent face) trials, she reported on 93% of the trials /da/, independent of which stimulus from the auditory /ba/ to /da/ continuum was presented. On the audio-visual trials, she reported /ba/, 88% of the time, independent of what was heard or seen. It thus appeared that her response strategy was based on whether or not the lips moved. If the lips moved, as in the visual-only and audio-visual trials, then /ba/ was given as response. This response was given independent of whether /ba/ or /da/ was said by the speaker. If the lips did not move, as in the auditory-only trails, she responded /da/, independent of whether /ba/ or /da/ was said. There was no indication that this behaviour was in relation to a perse-veration strategy.

In order to confirm this surprising behaviour, BC was tested two weeks later with the same videotape. Her response pattern on this occasion was exactly the same, except that the response labels were switched: in the visual-only and audio-visual trials she reported hearing /da/ (78% for visual-only, and 86% for the audio-visual trials), and in the auditory-only trials she reported hearing /ba/ on 90% of the trials. Both kinds of unimodal stimuli were judged very poorly. For the visual-only stimuli her responses appear not to be related to the phonemic information but to whether or not a cue to movement was present. More surprisingly even, a similar overall strategy seems to have generated the auditory responses (unimodal auditory tokens were dubbed to a still face). Findings from other testing sessions may throw some light on this particular result. First, there is no reason to suspect a deficit in auditory processing (timed semantic decisions on auditory stimuli were 100% correct and RTs well within the normal range). Second, in a task examining categorical perception of expressions presented bimodally, performance was less erratic but the categorisation of unimodal stimuli presented in the experiment was, as here, different from those obtained in a testing session where only visual stimuli were presented. The interesting finding is that where performance is tested on two modalities, one of which is impaired, there is interference with processing in the *good* modality. We keep this point in mind while testing it in a somewhat different way.

Audio-visual speech with an artificial synthesized face

The next task was administered a few weeks later and consisted of a videotape showing an artificially created synthesized face (Massaro & Cohen, 1990). One possibility in "visual bias in audio-visual token identification" is that BC was, for some reason, particularly affected by some idiosyncrasy of the speaker's face. Another, of course, is that the still face interfered with her auditory processing in an abnormal way. The material used in the present test first established how general these effects might be across different speaking faces. Because the audio-only token occurs without a visual display in this videotape, her auditory report may be less affected than in the previous test.

The synthetic face is controlled by 11 display parameters which determine jaw rotation, lip protrusion, upper lip raise, etc. By varying these parameters, a mobile image of a face is created that articulates "ba", "da" or any intermediate position between these two syllables. In the test, five levels of audible speech varying between "ba" and "da" were crossed with five levels of visible speech varying between "ba" and "da". These 25 stimuli comprise the audio-visual condition. The auditory and visual stimuli were also presented alone, so that there was a total of 25 + 5 + 5 = 35 independent stimulus events. The whole test consisted of 6 sets of these 35 trials in which the order of items was randomised.

The performance of BC was compared with four French-speaking control subjects of the same age. They were instructed to listen and to watch the videotape and to identify each token as "ba", "da", "bda", "dba", "va", "tha", "ga", or "other". There were thus 8 response possibilities × 35 trial types = 280 categories. In order to decrease this number, we scored the number of "ba"—and "bda"—responses as one category, and "da"—and "tha"—responses as another category, because these categories are visually very similar and they accounted for more than 91% of BC's judgments. We then computed four different performance measures: the visual and auditory influence in the bimodal condition, and the percentage correct in visual-only and auditory-only trials.

BC's visual influence in bimodal trials was very small: it was only 4% vs 26% (range 8%–43%) for control subjects. Her auditory influence in bimodal trials was large: 75% for BC vs 26% (range 8%–43%) for control subjects. Surprisingly, in the visual-only trials BC performed extremely well: 88% correct for BC vs 55% (range 46%–67%) for the controls, but in the auditory-only trials, BC performed poorly (29% correct for BC vs 64% correct for control). BC thus can discriminate visual-only "ba" from "da", but nevertheless, her visual influence in bimodal trials is almost non-existent.

This performance suggests that BC's anomalous results with auditory-plus-still-face displays may not have accounted fully for her impaired auditory performance in the previous tests. Even when, as in this study, auditory tokens were not accompanied by a visual display, she was poor at identifying them. In most people this would be a good indication for reliance on visual input for audio-visual displays—but for BC this was not the case. As in the previous test, BC, while able to identify silent speech tokens accurately, failed to integrate them in her reports of audio-visual events.

Audio-visual conflict

The previous tests used material originally designed for testing American speakers. It would be more appropriate to test BC with material for French speakers, while further probing this surprising and hitherto unreported failure to integrate seen and heard speech. For instance, audio-visual speechreading is to some extent sensitive to phonetic constraints of the listener's native language as shown in de Gelder et al. (1995; see also Burnham, this volume). Unimodal visual classification of, for example, "ba" and "da" might make use of language-general mechanisms that are less sensitive. On this sort of explanation, BC's integration difficulties could reflect an impairment in the processing of visual speech that may be language-specific. In this test a videotape was made of a female speaker pronouncing a series of VCV sequences. Each sequence consisted of one of the four plosive stops /p, b, t, d/ or a nasal /m, n/ in between the vowel /a/ (e.g. /aba/ or /ana/). There were three presentation conditions: an audio-visual, an auditory-only, and a visual-only presentation. In the audio-visual presentation, dubbing operations were performed on the recordings so as to produce a new videotape comprising six different auditory-visual combinations: auditory /p, b, t, d, m, n/ were combined with visual /t, d, p, b, n, m/, respectively. The visual place of articulation feature thus never matched the auditory place feature. Appropriate dubbing ensured that there was auditory-visual coincidence of the release of the consonant in each utterance. In addition, unimodal presentation conditions were produced. For the auditory-only condition, the original auditory signal was dubbed onto the speaker's non-moving image. For the visual-only condition, the auditory channel was deleted from the recording, so the subject had to rely entirely on speechreading. Each presentation condition comprised three replications of the six possible stimuli. BC was instructed to watch the speaker and repeat what she said. In the audio-visual conflict condition, there were only 3 fusions out of 18 trials (16%) while normal performance is about 50% (see de Gelder, Vroomen & van der Heide, 1991). The fusion response occurred when auditory /ana/ was combined with visual /ama/, whereupon BC reported hearing /ama/. In all other trials she reported the audio-part of the audio-visual stimulus. Auditory-only reports were accurate, except that auditory /ana/ was perceived as /ama/ in two out of three cases. This qualifies her fusion responses in the audio-visual case, because it might well be that her /ama/ responses in the auditory /ana/–visual /ama/ trials were exclusively based on the auditory part of the stimulus that was misperceived as /ama/.

Performance on the 18 visual-only trials was quite good. For the visual-only trials, two response categories were made, based on two broad viseme classes: lingual (d, t, n) or bi-labial (b, p, m). She never confused a lingual (d, t, n) with a bi-labial (b, p, m), and she confused a bi-labial with a lingual just once. Six out of nine linguals were perceived as lingual, there was one non-response, and /awa/ was reported twice. On the nine bi-labial trials, she reported six times a bi-labial, once an /ata/ and twice /awa/. So 12 out 17 trials (excluding the non-response) fell within the same viseme class and there was only one confusion between the visually distinct viseme classes.

On this test BC, once more, showed good unimodal visual discrimination, adequate unimodal auditory discrimination, but a lack of normal auditory-visual integration, despite attending fully to all stimuli and despite the fusion stimuli being phonotactically acceptable in French. BC's performance on previous bimodal tasks (in "Visual bias in audio-visual token identification" and "Audio-visual speech with an artificial synthesized face") was not due to unfamiliarity (different language) of the stimulus materials.

Short-term memory for heard and speechread digits

One possible reason for BC's failure to show normal integration is that while viseme discrimination is adequate, driven by knowledge of facial speech (top-down information), nevertheless the achieved representations from the stimulus display (bottom-up information) are insufficiently specified *phonetically* to integrate with heard speech elements (see Green, this volume). It has been well established that in normal speaker-hearers, silently speechread material is remembered as if it has been heard rather than if it has been read (e.g. de Gelder & Vroomen, 1992, 1994). If BC remembers silently lipread material well then we should search for another explanation of her "failure to integrate".

Materials were constructed along the general lines of previous studies where three presentation conditions were contrasted (de Gelder & Vroomen, 1992, 1994). Memory lists contained five French digits (pseudo-randomly selected from the digits 2, 4, 5, 6, 8) spoken by a female speaker and recorded on videotape. The items were presented in three different formats: hearing-plus-speechreading, hearing-only, speechreading-only.

Each condition consisted of 10 experimental trials. The presentation was blocked, and each block was preceded by one warming-up trial. The test started with a practice session of six trials, two of each type. An item was scored correct only if recalled in the correct serial position. BC's overall score for the heard-plus-speechread, heard-only, and speechread-only conditions was .76, .77, and .07, respectively. Her memory for speechread items was thus impaired, but in the heard-plus-speechread and heard-only condition BC had a normal primacy and recency effect. BC has normal verbal memory function when tested with auditory or auditory-visual material.

Recognition of silently spoken digits

One possibility is that speechreading the digits is more effortful for BC than for normals, and that during her effortful speechreading fewer mental resources are allocated for storage and rehearsal. To test this hypothesis BC was presented some weeks later with a new test—this time not involving memory but simple recognition of the same mouthed digits. When tested on speechreading single digits (same digits spoken by the same speaker) only, she scored 17 out of 30 correct ($\flat2(1) = 25.2$, p < .001). This is well above chance. BC can recognise and report single speechread items but cannot retain these phonetic forms for rehearsal and recall. Speechread representations can be generated but not sustained.

Together, these findings suggest that BC has *some* capacity to achieve a phonetic representation of seen lexical items by speechreading alone, but that this is weak and, either for structural or for strategic reasons, is insufficient to support verbal memory processes.

GENERAL DISCUSSION

Can seen speech be perceived by a visual agnosic patient with no observable auditory language difficulties and with very dense face-perception impairments but good face knowledge? BC, like HJA (another dense visual agnosic), but unlike the pure prosopagnosic Mrs D (see Campbell, 1992), was impaired at *some* speechreading tasks. Like HJA, her speechreading was much better when the stimulus was a moving face, rather than a still one, and this is in line with her demonstrated lesion sites (bilateral medial occipito-temporal areas, including areas V1 to V4, but sparing V5). However, unlike HJA, and unlike other cases reported to date, facial movement did not afford *full* speechreading capabilities in BC.

BC was able to discriminate silent seen speech quite well and even to identify speechread segments when required, but this ability did not support the integration of seen and heard speech under audio-visual presentation conditions and failed to support immediate memory for seen speech. This pattern of performance has not been reported in patients or in other speechreaders before: auditory-visual fusion effects appear to be mandatory under the sort of presentation conditions used here and are predicted by visual and by auditory identification skills (Massaro & Cohen, 1983). Moreover, auditory-visual fusions have often been considered an index of "implicit" effects of vision on audition: people are usually sensitive to the effects of vision on audition even when they are unwilling to report the classification of the visual stimulus alone (i.e. explicit processing of seen speech alone (e.g. Jordan & Bevan, 1996) Silent speech, moreover, is consistently remembered well by hearing viewers (de Gelder & Vroomen, 1992, 1994).

It would appear from these findings that there is a route to identifying and classifying seen speech that BC can use, but which does not mesh with auditory speech effectively at the phonetic level required to support audio-visual integration and immediate memory for speech that is seen but not heard (Campbell, 1990). There are at least three ways to conceive of this difficulty:

1. The representation derived from silent seen speech is simply too poor or too transient to integrate effectively with heard speech.

2. The temporal processing characteristics of silent seen speech have become desynchronised from those for heard speech in processing, thus losing the temporal-binding feature necessary to effective integration.

3. The way that BC speechreads is qualitatively very different from the way that other people speechread because of over-reliance on a dynamic processing route.

This third possibility is unlikely given the finding that purely dynamic (point-light) displays can generate McGurk effects (Rosenblum & Saldaña, this volume)—at least at first sight. It is possible, however, that point-light displays may access speech-form representations indirectly, and that this is denied to BC. The second possibility, that of some phenomenological desynchronisation of seen and heard speech may be worth further investigation: it could help explain why, under some circumstances (see "Audio-visual speech"), BC is actually *worse* at reporting the auditory component of an audio-visual display than at auditory-only report. This phenomenon is harder to explain on the intuitively appealing idea that BC lacks a robust, stable representation of seen speech because of her brain damage.

Whatever the ultimate explanation of BC's speechreading difficulties, this detailed case study shows there is more to "hearing by eye" than might be predicted from previous case studies, and suggests that the nature and processes of auditory-visual integration in patients with circumscribed visual processing disorders will be worth examining in more depth.

REFERENCES

Bartolomeo, P., Bachoud-Levi, A.-C., & Denes, G. (in press). Preserved imagery for colours in a patient with cerebral achromatopsia. *Cortex.*

Bruyer, R., & Schweich, M. (1991). A clinical test battery of face processing. *International Journal of Neuroscience, 61,* 19–30.

Campbell, R. (1990). Lipreading, Neuropsychology and Immediate Memory. In G. Vallar & T. Shallice (Eds), *Neuropsychological Impairments of Short-term Memory.* Cambridge, UK: Cambridge University Press.

Campbell, R. (1992). The Neuropsychology of Lipreading. *Phil Trans Roy Soc London, B, 335,* 39–45.

Campbell, R. (1996). Seeing Speech in Space and Time. *Proceedings of the 4th International Conference on Spoken Language Processing.* Philadelphia, October.

Campbell, R., de Gelder, B. & de Haan, E. (1996). Lateralization of lipreading: A second look. *Neuropsychologia, 34,* 1235–40.

Campbell, R., Garwood, J., Franklin, S., Howard, D., Landis, T., & Regard, M. (1990). Neuropsychological studies of auditory-visual fusion illusions: Four case studies and their implications. *Neuropsychologia, 28,* 787–802.

Campbell, R., Landis, T. & Regard, M. (1986). Face recognition and lipreading: A neurological dissociation. *Brain, 109,* 509–521.

Campbell, R., Zihl, J., Massaro, D., Munhall, K. & Cohen, M.M. (submitted). *Speechreading in a patient with severe impairment in visual motion perception (akinetopsia).*

de Gelder, B. & Vroomen, J. (1992). Abstract versus modality-specific memory representations. *Memory and Cognition, 20,* 533–538.

de Gelder, B. & Vroomen, J. (1994). Memory for consonants versus vowels in heard and lipread speech. *Journal of Memory and Language, 31,* 737–756.

de Gelder, B., Bertelson, P., Vroomen, J., & Chen, H.C. (1995). Inter-language differences in the McGurk effect for Dutch and Cantonese listeners. *Proceedings of the Fourth European Conference on Speech Communication and Technology* (pp. 1699–1702). Madrid.

de Gelder, B., Vroomen, J. & Van der Heide, L. (1991). Face recognition and lip-reading in autism. *European Journal of Cognitive Psychology, 3,* 69–86.

Farah, M.J. (1991). Patterns of co-occurrence among the associative agnosias: implications for visual object representation. *Cognitive Neuropsychology, 8*, 1–19.

Humphreys, G.W., Donnelly, N. & Riddoch, J. (1993). Expression is computed separately from facial identity and it is computed separately for moving and static faces. *Neuropsychologia, 31*, 173–181.

Jordan, T.R. & Bevan, K.M. (1996). Seeing and hearing rotated faces: influences of facial orientation on visual and audio-visual speech recognition. *Journal of Experimental Psychology: Human Perception and Performance.*

Massaro, D.W. & Cohen, M.M. (1983). Evaluation and integration of visual and auditory information in speech perception. *Journal of Experimental Psychology: Human Perception and Performance, 9*, 753–751.

Massaro, D.W. & Cohen, M.M. (1990). Perception of synthesized audible and visible speech. *Psychological Science, 1*, 1–9.

Milner, A.D., Perrett, D.I., Johnston, R.S., Benson, P.J., Jordan, T.R., Heeley, D.W., Bettucci, D., Mortara, F., Mutani, R., Terazzi, E. & Davidson, D.L.W. (1991). Perception and action in visual form agnosia. *Brain, 114*, 405–408.

Snodgrass, J.G. & Vanderwart, M. (1980). A standardized set of picture norms. *Journal of Experimental Psychology, Human Learning and Memory, 6*, 174–215.

DEAFNESS, LANGUAGE AND SPEECHREADING: SPEECH-BASED APPROACHES

CHAPTER ELEVEN

What makes a good speechreader? First you have to find one

Lynne E. Bernstein   *Spoken Language Processes Laboratory, House Ear Institute, Los Angeles, California, USA*

Marilyn E. Demorest   *Department of Psychology, University of Maryland Baltimore County, Baltimore, Maryland, USA*

Paula E. Tucker   *Spoken Language Processes Laboratory, House Ear Institute, Los Angeles, California, USA*

INTRODUCTION

Throughout the twentieth century, the question, "What makes a good speechreader?"[1] has motivated researchers whose mission was to improve the lives of and to educate deaf[2] children and adults (see Jeffers & Barley, 1971; and O'Neill & Oyer, 1961 for comprehensive reviews of earlier studies). In the absence of direct methods to determine the causes of good speechreading, numerous correlational studies were conducted (particularly during the early and middle part of the century) for which measures were obtained on psychological, demographic, intellectual, academic, and audiological attributes thought to be possibly indicative of potential for proficient speechreading. A reasonable rationale for this method is that if measures other than speechreading can predict acquisition of speechreading proficiency, the teacher or clinician can predict the future outcome of training or development. Unfortunately, overall, measures that correlate best with speechreading tend to be other measures of speechreading (Jeffers & Barley, 1971; Summerfield, 1991), a result not helpful to managing the education of young deaf children who have not yet acquired, or have only rudimentary speechreading proficiency and oral language.

Visual speech perception (mostly by hearing people) has gained attention recently from scientists who have recognized its potential to reveal facts about the fundamental nature of speech perception (Bernstein & Benoît, 1996). However, the questions and results that have received the most attention have

211

concerned how visible speech is integrated with acoustic speech, not how speech is perceived by vision alone (e.g. Braida, 1991; Green & Miller, 1985; Kuhl & Meltzoff, 1982; Massaro, 1987; Summerfield, 1987, 1991).

Given that visual speech perception is characterized in the scientific literature as highly inaccurate, we need hardly be surprised that the question "What makes a good speechreader?" has not been a prominent one in the context of research on speech perception. Estimates of average speech-reading accuracy for hearing adults are low. Studies of phoneme identification have estimated accuracy to be in the range of approximately 40–60% phonemes correct in nonsense syllables (see, e.g. Montgomery & Jackson, 1983; Montgomery et al., 1987). Breeuwer and Plomp (1986) measured visual speech perception with connected speech in a group of Dutch adults with normal hearing. Stimuli were short meaningful sentences. The percentage of correct syllables was 10.6% on the first presentation and 16.7% on the second. Demorest and Bernstein (1992) reported on 104 college students with normal hearing who attempted to identify words in sentences. Overall, the students correctly identified 20.8% of the words. What averages fail to convey, however, is that some speechreaders with normal hearing are moderately accurate. For example, in Demorest and Bernstein (1992), the highest observed score was 54% words correct in sentences.

Individuals with congenital or prelingual profound hearing losses are frequently said to be less proficient speechreaders—or at least not better—than individuals with normal hearing (Conrad, 1977; Massaro, 1987; Mogford, 1987; Summerfield, 1991). Mogford (1987) states, "That auditory experience of speech enhances visual speech recognition is shown by the fact that the hearing are more competent at lip-reading [sic] than the deaf" (p. 191).

Our experience led us to doubt, however, that the best speechreaders are hearing people. In formal (Bernstein et al., 1991, 1993) and informal observations of young adults with profound hearing losses, particularly at Gallaudet University,[3] we obtained evidence that the most accurate speechreaders are deaf people. In studies undertaken as part of a program to develop vibrotactile speech aids (Bernstein et al., 1991, 1993), individuals were observed whose speechreading accuracy far exceeded that which we had observed in hearing adults (Demorest & Bernstein, 1992). Our casual conversations with students and others at Gallaudet University further supported impressions that speechreading in some deaf people is exceedingly accurate.

With the purpose of obtaining normative data on the range of speech-reading proficiency in adults, we conducted a systematic, relatively large-scale study of speechreading in adults with normal hearing (N = 96) and with severe to profound hearing losses (N = 72) (Bernstein et al., 1996). Study participants identified phonemes in consonant-vowel nonsense syllables and words in isolation and in sentences. The results were unqualified support for superior speechreading in the group of deaf participants, such that for most measures, the entire upper quartile of scores of deaf participants exceeded the maximum scores of hearing participants. For example, the range of *fourth quartile* scores obtained from deaf subjects who speechread B-E Sentences (Bernstein et al., 1996) with a male talker was 61–80% words correct, and the range obtained from the hearing subjects was 36–57% words correct. These results convincingly supported the assertion that the best speechreaders are deaf people.

However, as is typically the case, a wide range of speechreading proficiency was observed in Bernstein et al. (1996), such that the least proficient deaf speechreaders in the study identified few words correctly in isolation or in sentences. Thus, even for this deaf population engaged in undergraduate education it was reasonable to ask what characteristics were associated with the better speechreaders. The results of examining those characteristics are described below and are discussed in relation to other results in the literature (Geers & Moog, 1989; Moores & Sweet, 1991).

STUDY OF SPEECHREADING IN DEAF UNDERGRADUATES

Participants in the study

Participants were all enrolled as undergraduates at Gallaudet University. A complete description of the screening criteria is given in Bernstein et al. (1996). The 72 participants were between 18 and 41 years of age. They all had sensorineural hearing losses greater than 65 dB HL pure-tone average in the better ear across the frequencies 500, 1000, and 2000 Hz. Fifty-one subjects (71%) had profound hearing losses (90 dB HL or greater three-frequency pure-tone average, bilaterally). Forty-two of the participants (66%) reported congenital hearing loss. Seventeen participants (23%) reported onsets of hearing loss between 2 and 36 months. Thus the majority experienced hearing loss either prior to or during the period of normal language acquisition. The causes of hearing loss were distributed as follows:

- unknown—30
- meningitis—11
- maternal rubella—11
- other—6
- genetic—5
- premature birth—4
- high fever—3
- scarlet fever—1
- diabetic pregnancy—1.

None of the participants reported disabilities other than hearing loss and no disabilities were revealed by University records obtained for the study. Participants reported that English was their family's primary language and their own native language. Participants had all attended a mainstream and/ or oral educational program for eight or more years during primary and secondary school. All had 20/30 (normal or corrected) vision in each eye.

These criteria were designed to select participants for whom speech-reading is a socially important and well-practiced skill, and for whom American Sign Language was not a first language. In order to assure that participants had not experienced American Sign Language as the primary language in school, deaf students who reported that they had been educated primarily in residential schools (in which spoken English is frequently not the language of instruction) were excluded. Students who reported that they used any form of manually coded English[4] were included in the study, if they satisfied all the other criteria. Estimates of English reading and writing abilities were obtained from the Gallaudet University English Department in the form of scores on the Gallaudet University English Placement Test (EPT). This test was selected despite the lack of normative statistics, because it was the only one with which every student had been tested.

Stimuli, procedures, and measures used to assess speechreading

A detailed description of the speechreading experimental procedures and results is in Bernstein et al. (1996). Here we are concerned with the relationship between the performance measures reported there and the additional data obtained for each of the deaf participants.

The speechreading procedures comprised identification of phonemes in nonsense syllables and identification of words in isolation and in sentences. All of the stimulus materials were pre-recorded on laser videodisc (Bernstein & Eberhardt, 1986a, 1986b) and were presented under computer control. The stimuli employed for phoneme identification were spoken by both a male and a female talker. Stimuli were composed of 22 initial consonants followed by the vowel /ɑ/, plus two tokens of the vowel /ɑ/ alone. The consonants were: /p b m f v ʃ tʃ w r t θ ð d s z k g n l h dʒ ʒ/

The words selected for presentation in isolation were spoken by the male talker only and were from the clinical version (Kreul et al., 1968) of the Modified Rhyme Test (MRT) (House et al., 1965). The MRT comprises 50 6-word ensembles. Two words were selected from each of the ensembles so as to yield 100 different words.

Fifty sentences from the Bernstein and Eberhardt (1986a) recordings of the lists of CID Everyday Sentences (Davis & Silverman, 1970) were presented, 25 spoken by each of the talkers. An additional 25 sentences for each talker were presented from Corpus III and Corpus IV of Bernstein and Eberhardt (1986b) and are referred to here as "B-E Sentences".

Identification of phonemes in nonsense syllables required participants to select their responses from a set of appropriately labelled keys on the computer keyboard. Identification of words in isolation and in sentences required them to type an open-set response at the terminal.

For this chapter, a subset of the speechreading measures was examined in relation to subject data described below. The measures were:

1. Phonemes correct in CV syllables, which was the proportion of correct responses across the entire stimulus set for each of the talkers.
2. Proportion MRT words correct, which was the total number of words correct divided by the total number of words presented.
3. Mean proportion words correct in sentences, which was the mean of the proportion words correct per sentence across the sentence set.

Additional participant data

Audiological records were obtained from the Gallaudet University Department of Audiology and Speech-Language Pathology. The English Department at the University provided the reading and writing scores for the English Placement Test (EPT) administered to each undergraduate student. On the reading comprehension portion, students answer multiple-choice questions after reading short passages. The writing test is an essay. Because students frequently must attempt the test more than once prior to attaining a passing score, the most recent scores were used in the following analyses. Participants also filled in an extensive questionnaire that concerned their educational history, their parents' educational history, the occurrence of hearing loss in their family, their language experience, their preferred modes of communication, and their self-assessed proficiency at oral communication.

Relationships between speechreading measures and personal data

Correlations between speechreading measures and personal data were obtained as the first step in characterizing the proficient speechreaders. The correlations are given in Table 6. Across all the measures reported in Table 6, correlations were generally lower when they involved phoneme identification with nonsense syllables. Bernstein et al. (1996) report that associations between phoneme identification and other speechreading measures are also weaker than associations between measures involving words (in isolation and in sentences). It is also the case that variability in speechreading performance is smaller with phoneme identification. Table 6 reports the

TABLE 6
Correlation coefficients for CID and B-E sentence, MRT word, and CV nonsense syllable
speech perception measures and selected personal variables

Personal variables	Speech perception measures			
	CID	B-E	MRT	CV
Audiological variables				
Age in months hearing loss occurred	−.183	−.240	−.209	−.028
Age in months hearing loss discovered	−.118	−.182	−.163	.024
Medical or surgical treatment for hearing loss	−.093	−.036	−.111	−.189
Age at first hearing aid	−.230	−.259*	−.227	−.102
Presently own hearing aid[a]	−.003	−.043	−.112	.172
Years since last used hearing aid	−.269*	−.324*	−.297*	−.119
Frequency of hearing aid use[b]	.350**	.384**	.358**	−.287*
Anacusic	−.133	−.118	−.128	−.048
Better pure-tone average	−.216	−.228	−.179	.035
Parents' education				
Highest grade mother completed	.097	.143	.013	−.214
Highest grade father completed	.047	.044	−.071	−.022
Home communication practices				
Communicates with speech[c]	−.598**	−.611**	−.584**	−.406**
Communicates with writing[a]	.226	.232	.275	.201
Communicates with signs and speech[a]	.214	.223	.154	−.022
Communicates with fingerspelling[a]	.190	.184	.195	.100
Communicates with American Sign Language[a]	.223	.203	.195	.121
Communicates with gestures or homemade signs[c]	.432**	.433**	.449**	.308**
Public communication practices				
Communicates with speech[c]	−.301*	−.284*	−.256*	−.275*
Communicates with writing[a]	.259*	.242*	.296*	.131
Communicates with signs and speech[c]	.090	.177	.097	−.000
Communicates with fingerspelling[a]	.025	.115	.130	−.024
Communicates with American Sign Language[c]	.088	.032	.085	−.053
Communicates with gestures or homemade signs[c]	.318**	.257*	.335**	.287*
Self-assessed ability to understand via speech				
Hearing friends or relatives[d]	−.397**	−.341**	−.300*	−.239*
Speech of the general public[d]	−.434**	−.424**	−.402**	−.214
Self-assessed ability to be understood via speech by				
Hearing friends or relatives[d]	−.438**	−.398**	−.395**	−.264*
The general public[d]	−.464**	−.441**	−.486**	−.261*
English Placement Test (EPT) scores				
Writing subtest	.282*	.294*	.210	.231
Reading subtest	.379**	.399**	.335**	.257*

[a] These questions were coded: 1 = *yes*, 2 = *no*.

[b] This question was coded 1 = *every waking hour*, 2 = *5 to 8 hours daily*, 3 = *1 to 4 hours daily*, 4 = *1 to 2 occasions per week*, and 5 = *less than the above*.

[c] These questions were coded 1 = *yes*, 2 = *no*, 3 = *accommodates audience*.

[d] These questions were coded from 1 = *very well* to 5 = *not at all*.

* $p < .05$

** $p < .001$

correlations involving nonsense syllables for completeness, but these results are not discussed further, because they do not appear very useful in predicting speechreading proficiency.

Audiological variables

What is most striking about the correlations between speechreading and the various audiological variables is how many correlations show no degree of statistical significance. When the hearing loss occurred, when it was discovered, and whether any medical or surgical treatment was administered were unrelated to speech perception performance. Only one of four speech perception measures resulted in a significant association with the age at which the first hearing aid was used. Hearing levels similarly resulted in no association with speechreading measures.

The most interesting and consistent results involving audiological variables were related to hearing aid use. The significant negative correlations associated with "years since last used hearing aid" suggest that the more time that had elapsed since participants stopped using their hearing aids, the lower were their speechreading scores. The correlations for frequency of hearing aid use in relation to speechreading showed that more frequent use was associated with better speechreading performance.

Interpretation of these correlations is not straightforward. Because sign language is more highly valued than speech communication by many members of the Gallaudet University community, the decision to use a hearing aid may represent for the individual a choice involving group affiliation. Those who chose to discontinue hearing aid use for affiliative reasons would likely also have immersed themselves in sign language use, resulting possibly in poorer speech perception over time. Alternatively, those who used their hearing aids less frequently or had stopped using them earlier might be individuals who simply derived less benefit from their aids. Screening procedures did not exclude participants who, during college, abandoned speech communication in favor of sign. The question of how audiological variables are related to speechreading is discussed further below.

Parents' education

Participants' speechreading proficiency was found to have no association with either parent's highest completed grade in school.

Communication practices

Several items on the questionnaire concerned how the participants communicated at home and with the general public. Participants' responses showed that at-home use of writing, signs in combination with speech, and

American Sign Language were unrelated to speechreading performance. Among the strongest correlations in Table 6 (correlations of $-.584$ to $-.611$ for measures involving words) were those obtained with answers to the question of whether the participant communicates at home with speech. Thirty-six percent of the variance in the speechreading scores involving words was accounted for in terms of responses to this question. Somewhat smaller correlations were obtained for answers to the question of whether gestures or homemade signs were used at home, which suggests that better speechreaders do not use gestures or homemade signs.

The correlations involving public communication practices were not as large as the ones involving home communication, but they followed the same pattern. Use of speech in public was associated with higher speechreading scores, whereas use of gestures or homemade signs was associated with lower speechreading scores. Lower correlations than those involving home communication may reflect the participants' abilities to produce intelligible speech (a factor that was not evaluated within this study), which would likely have a greater effect on public than home communication.

Self-assessed abilities

There were moderate associations between participants' speechreading proficiency and their self-assessed ability to understand or be understood (without the use of sign language) by hearing friends or relatives, and the general public. Nineteen to twenty-four percent of the variance in speechreading scores on sentence or word stimuli was accounted for in terms of the participants' self-assessed spoken language proficiency in communications with the general public (correlations between $-.395$ and $-.438$ for measures involving words).

EPT scores

The two scores on English proficiency, one for writing and the other for reading comprehension, were not equally associated with the speech perception measures. Reading was more highly and more consistently related to speechreading performance. These relationships accounted for between 11% and 16% of the variance.

Regression Analyses

Multiple regression analyses were used to obtain prediction equations for each of the speechreading measures. The personal variables entered into regression equations were selected from those that had resulted in large and/ or significant correlations:

1. Self-assessed ability to be understood by the public.
2. Self-assessed ability to understand the public.
3. Self-assessed ability to be understood by hearing friends and relatives.
4. Self-assessed ability to understand hearing friends and relatives.
5. Use of homemade signs or gestures at home.
6. Use of homemade signs or gestures in public.
7. Communication in public with speech.
8. Communication at home with speech.
9. Communication in public with writing.
10. Frequency of hearing aid use.
11. Years since last used a hearing aid.
12. Better ear pure-tone average threshold.
13. Average pure-tone threshold.
14. Whether the participant was anacusic or not.
15. EPT reading score.
16. EPT writing score.

Exclusion of factors whose coefficients failed to reach significance resulted in equations with coefficients for only three factors:

1. Self-assessed ability to understand the general public.
2. Communication at home with speech.
3. EPT reading score.

The beta weight, multiple R, and R^2 values for each of the regression equations are given in Table 7. As might be anticipated from the results in Table 6, the multiple R for the prediction of phoneme identification in nonsense syllables was small compared with multiple R values for speech-

TABLE 7
Regression analyses

	Nonsense syllables	Words correct		
	Phonemes correct	Words	CID sentences	B-E sentences
Beta$_{EPTR}$	.264	.339	.346	.382
Beta$_{GP}$	−.211	−.373	−.390	−.391
Beta$_{HS}$	−.252	−.412	−.418	−.423
R	.472	.730	.747	.774
R^2	.223	.533	.558	.598

Note: EPTR = EPT reading score; GP = self-assessed ability to understand the general public; HS = use of speech at home.

reading involving words in isolation or in sentences. Substantial multiple R values were obtained for the other regression equations (ranging between .730 and .774). The corresponding R^2 (ranging between .533 and .598) can be interpreted as estimates of proportion variance accounted for in the respective speechreading score. That the beta coefficients (standardized regression coefficients) are all of comparable magnitude suggests that each of the factors entered into determining the coefficients contributed equally to the predicted scores. The beta coefficients are comparable because differences in units of measure are eliminated via transformation to Z-score form. Thus, self-assessed ability to understand the general public contributed equally to the equation as did EPT scores and the report of how the participant communicates at home. Proficient deaf speechreaders from this population are generally people who understand the speech of the public, use speech at home, and are the more proficient readers.

DISCUSSION

Given that the aforementioned results were from a study for which participants were pre-screened on a number of factors, arguments could be made that the results should be interpreted narrowly. Two additional sets of results from the literature are introduced here to argue for generalizability. These two sets were obtained by investigators at the Central Institute for the Deaf (Geers & Moog, 1989) and Gallaudet University (Moores & Sweet, 1991) under a contract with the National Institutes of Health, which sought to discover factors that predict the development of reading and writing skills in 16- and 17-year-olds with profound, congenital hearing losses. Table 8 represents a subset of the results reported by the researchers.

Three types of study participants were explicitly identified:

1. Those with hearing parents enrolled in oral communication programs throughout preschool and elementary school (N = 100) (Geers & Moog, 1989).

2. Deaf children of deaf parents enrolled in residential schools for the deaf (N = 65) (Moores & Sweet, 1991), who presumably learned American Sign Language as their first language.

3. Children who had been enrolled in total communication (instruction in sign and speech) programs from at least the age of four (N = 65) (Moores & Sweet, 1991).

The criteria for inclusion in the groups resulted in comparability of degree of hearing loss (greater than 85 dB pure-tone average bilaterally) and nonverbal intelligence (see Table 8). Most of the obtained measures were of reading and writing. However, speechreading was measured with the

Minimal Auditory Capabilities (MAC) Battery (Owens et al., 1985). The MAC Battery employs sets of CID Everyday Sentences (Davis & Silverman, 1970) under conditions of speechreading without audition and speechreading with hearing aids.

Audiological factors related to speechreading

The results reported in Table 6 showed that hearing levels accounted for only a small proportion of the variance in speechreading measures. The regression analyses in Table 7 showed that none of the audiological variables made a statistically significant contribution to predicting speechreading performance. Table 8 provides converging information for interpreting the role of audiological variables in speechreading proficiency. Across the three groups of deaf teenagers, speechreading proficiency varied, but hearing levels were comparable.

This result appears to contradict Mogford's (1987) assertion that speechreading proficiency is related to auditory perception. However, the results of the Monosyllable, Trochee, Spondee (MTS) test (Erber & Alencewicz, 1976) in Table 8 can be seen as support for Mogford's position. The MTS test is a closed-set listening test that is scored in terms of the number of words correctly recognized and the number of words for which responses correspond accurately to the words' metrical type. Table 8 shows that the oral teenagers scored highest on both the MAC test of lipreading (with and without hearing aids) and the MTS test of auditory perception, holding hearing levels roughly constant. This pattern supports the hypothesis that auditory threshold is not the critical variable in accounting for proficient speechreading. Rather, it appears that use of oral language from early childhood leads to better speechreading *and* is associated with better use of residual hearing.

Communication practices

Mogford (1987) cites several studies in support of the assertion that "there appears to be no evidence to support the claim that learning any manual form of communication interferes with lip-reading [sic] skill" (p. 197). Results presented earlier and in Table 8 suggest that use of manual communication is associated with less proficient speechreading. MAC test scores in Table 8 are higher for the oral deaf teenagers than either group that used manual communication. However, results in Table 6 can be interpreted as partial support for Mogford's assertion. Use of speech at home was correlated with more proficient speechreading, but use of sign at home was unrelated. The use of homemade signs and gestures was, however, related to less proficient speechreading. Parasnis (1983; also cited by Mogford, 1987) studied deaf college students and found that those who were exposed later to

TABLE 8

Measures adapted from Geers and Moog (1989) and Moores and Sweet (1991) for comparable groups of deaf young adults

	Group								
	Oral/Mainstream N = 100			*Deaf of deaf* N = 65			*Total communication* N = 65		
Measure	*Mean*	*SD*	*Range*	*Mean*	*SD*	*Range*	*Mean*	*SD*	*Range*
Age									
Years:Months	16:8	NA	15:10–18:2	16:7	NA	16:0–17:0	17:0	NA	16:0–17:11
Speechreading									
MAC (%)									
Speechreading	57	12	26–90	28	19	0–72	31	18	0–96
Speechreading + Hearing	74	18	26–100	33	23	0–100	37	19	2–100
Auditory perception									
MTS (%)									
Recognition	59	28	3–100	24	27	0–100	20	24	0–100
Categorization	91	14	33–100	68	19	33–100	62	23	0–100
Hearing thresholds									
dB Pure-Tone									
Average									
Better average	100	8	85–128	NA	NA	NA	NA	NA	NA
Right ear	NA	NA	NA	105	NA	NA	106	NA	NA
Left ear	NA	NA	NA	104	NA	NA	104	NA	NA

(Continued)

TABLE 8
(Continued)

Measure	Group								
	Oral/Mainstream N = 100			Deaf of deaf N = 65			Total communication N = 65		
	Mean	SD	Range	Mean	SD	Range	Mean	SD	Range
Reading									
SAT (grade equivalent)									
Comprehension	8.0	3.3	2.3–12.9	7.2[a]	NA	NA	5.8[a]	NA	NA
CAT (grade equivalent)									
Vocabulary	7.6	3.1	3.0–12.9	6.3	2.6	2.2–12.9	5.2	2.5	2.2–12.9
Intelligence									
WAIS (I.Q.)									
Verbal	89	12	62–125	88	11	62–124	83	11	64–116
Performance	111	13	85–149	113	15	84–149	112	15	83–143

Note: NA = not available. Results in this table were adapted from the tables and text in Geers and Moog (1989) (Column 1 in the table) and Moores and Sweet (1991) (Columns 2 and 3 in the table). Some figures were rounded to normalize the level of numerical resolution across reports. Rounding did not affect the relative values of results within types of measures.

[a] These scores were estimated based on the scaled scores reported in Moores and Sweet (1991).

manual communication were the more proficient speechreaders. Taken together, the evidence suggests that the more accurate deaf adult speechreaders have had little exposure to manual communication either at home or at school during early childhood.

Reading results

The EPT reading scores were highly associated with speechreading proficiency in the current study. Geers and Moog (1989) and Moores and Sweet (1991) obtained reading scores with the California Achievement Test (CAT) (1977) vocabulary subtest, and the Stanford Achievement Test (SAT) (Gardner et al., 1982) involving reading of connected texts, among several other tests. Across the three subject groups in Table 8, it can be seen that reading scores were highest among the oral deaf teenagers.

The underlying processes that link reading and speechreading are not understood presently. The literature suggests that reading relies on a phonological code in long-term memory, established through the use of spoken language (Stanovich, 1985; Wagner & Torgesen, 1987). However, once acquired, reading contributes to vocabulary growth, which in turn is likely to enhance speechreading proficiency in deaf individuals. In recent research on word knowledge, we have obtained evidence suggesting that the more proficient speechreaders acquired more words through speech than through reading during middle childhood (Auer et al., 1996).

Conclusions

The most proficient adult speechreaders have the following characteristics in common:

- They are deaf (Bernstein et al., 1996).
- They have extensive oral language experience gained in their homes and schools.
- They are, as a group, the more successful prelingually deaf readers (Geers & Moog, 1989).
- They report that they understand the general public quite well, and that they communicate using speech.

What accounts for the view in the literature that hearing people are the more proficient speechreaders? One answer may be that research with the adult deaf population requires a considerable expenditure in effort to recruit participants, unless the investigator is located in one of the relatively few geographical locations in which many deaf people live and/or attend school.[5] Even then, obstacles remain. Communication with potential study participants requires use of a TTD (telecommunication device for the deaf) , e-mail, and/or relay services during the recruiting process, and participant selection requires knowledge of hearing loss, educational practices, and language (particularly, issues concerning the use of sign language). Given that speechreading is not as effective a means of communication as auditory speech perception, an experimenter proficient in manual communication and certainly one experienced in communicating with deaf people may be required to explain procedures and smooth out difficulties that arise.[6] But setting aside all these and other practical considerations, the reason why little is known about proficient adult deaf speechreaders may be that statements in the literature have seemed to preclude the need to single out these individuals for research on speechreading.

Understanding of what makes a good speechreader requires the participation of deaf individuals who perceive speech primarily through their eyes at levels of accuracy that exceed the average for both hearing people and other deaf people. Having identified who the good speechreaders are, research can focus on discovering those perceptual and cognitive processes that make them good.

NOTES

1. The term "speechreading" in the context of speech perception by individuals with severe to profound hearing losses frequently refers to the combination of visual and auditory speech perception. The term acknowledges that for these individuals, speech perception is primarily visual, but acoustic speech information may also be processed at some minimal level. In this chapter, "speechreading" refers to speech perception by vision alone.
2. Throughout this paper, the term "deaf" is applied to individuals with severe to profound hearing losses who rely primarily on vision for speech perception. These individuals may use hearing aids and gain benefit from residual hearing, but we are concerned with their ability to perceive speech on the basis of vision alone.
3. Gallaudet University was established to provide a liberal arts education to individuals with hearing losses. Many of the faculty and staff also have severe to profound hearing losses.
4. American Sign Language is a gestural language with vocabulary and syntax distinct from English. The term "manually coded English" refers to sign systems that employ English syntax and borrow much of their vocabulary from American Sign Language.
5. We have been fortunate in having access to two pools of deaf college students, first at Gallaudet University and now at California State University, Northridge.
6. The third author, who is a certified sign language interpreter, interacted with the deaf participants throughout the experiment.

ACKNOWLEDGEMENTS

The authors wish to acknowledge the assistance of the English Department at Gallaudet University in providing the English Placement Test scores. The authors also wish to acknowledge the assistance of the Hearing and Speech Clinic in obtaining audiological records for the participants. The research presented here was supported by a grant from the National Institute on Deafness and Other Communication Disorders (DC 02107).

REFERENCES

Auer, E.T., Jr., Waldstein, R.S., Tucker, P.E. & Bernstein, L.E. (1996). Relationships between word knowledge and visual speech perception I: Subjective estimates of word age-of-acquisition. *Journal of the Acoustical Society of America, 100.*

Bernstein, L.E. & Benoît, C. (1996). For speech perception by humans or machines, three senses are better than one. *Proceedings of the Fourth International Conference on Spoken Language Processing.* 3–6 October, Philadelphia, PA.

Bernstein, L.E., Coulter, D.C., O'Connell, M.P., Eberhardt, S.P. & Demorest, M.E. (1993). Vibrotactile and haptic speech codes. In A. Risberg, S. Felicetti, G. Plant, & K.-E. Spens (Eds), *Proceedings of the Second International Conference on Tactile Aids, Hearing Aids, and Cochlear Implants.* 7–11 June 1992, Stockholm (ISSN 0280-9850).

Bernstein, L.E., Demorest, M.E., Coulter, D.C., & O'Connell, M.P. (1991). Lipreading sentences with vibrotactile vocoders: Performance of normal-hearing and hearing-impaired subjects. *Journal of the Acoustical Society of America, 90,* 2971–84.

Bernstein, L.E., Demorest, M.E. & Tucker, P.E. (1996). *Speech perception without hearing.* Manuscript submitted for publication.

Bernstein, L.E. & Eberhardt, S.P. (1986a). *Johns Hopkins Lipreading Corpus I-II: Disc 1.* Baltimore, MD: Johns Hopkins University.

Bernstein, L.E. & Eberhardt, S.P. (1986b). *Johns Hopkins Lipreading Corpus III-IV: Disc 2.* Baltimore, MD: Johns Hopkins University.

Braida, L.D. (1991). Cross-modal integration in the identification of consonant segments. *The Quarterly Journal of Experimental Psychology, 43,* 647–77.

Breeuwer, M. & Plomp, R. (1986). Speechreading supplemented with auditorily presented speech parameters. *Journal of the Acoustical Society of America, 79,* 481–99.

California Achievement Test (1977). Monterey, CA: CTB/McGraw-Hill.

Conrad, R. (1977). Lipreading by deaf and hearing children. *British Journal of Educational Psychology, 47,* 60–65.

Davis, H. & Silverman, S.R. (Eds). (1970). *Hearing and deafness* (3rd Ed.). New York: Holt, Rinehart, Winston.

Demorest, M.E. & Bernstein, L.E. (1992). Sources of variability in speechreading sentences: A generalizability analysis. *Journal of Speech and Hearing Research, 35,* 876–91.

Erber, N.P. & Alencewicz, C. (1976). Audiological evaluation of deaf children. *Journal of Speech and Hearing Disorders, 41,* 256–7.

Gardner, E.F., Rudman, H.C., Karlsen, G. & Merwin, J.C. (1982). *Stanford Achievement Test* (17th Ed.). Cleveland, OH: Psychological Corp.

Geers, A. & Moog, J. (1989). Factors predictive of the development of literacy in profoundly hearing-impaired adolescents. *Volta Review, 91,* 69–86.

Green, K.P. & Miller, J.L. (1985). On the role of visual rate information in phonetic perception. *Perception & Psychophysics, 38,* 269–76.

House, A.S., Williams, C.E., Hecker, M.H.L. & Kryter, K.D. (1965). Articulation-testing methods: Consonantal differentiation with a closed-response set. *Journal of the Acoustical Society of America, 37,* 158–66.

Jeffers, J. & Barley, M. (1971). *Lipreading (Speechreading).* Springfield, IL: Charles C. Thomas.

Kreul, E.J., Nixon, J.C., Kryter, K.D., Bell, D.W. & Lamb, J.S. (1968). A proposed clinical test of speech discrimination. *Journal of Speech and Hearing Research, 11,* 536–52.

Kuhl, P.K. & Meltzoff, A.N. (1982). The bimodal development of speech in infancy. *Science, 218,* 361–81.

Massaro, D.W. (1987). *Speech perception by ear and eye: A paradigm for psychological inquiry.* Hillsdale, NJ: Erlbaum.

Mogford, K. (1987). Lip-reading in the prelingually deaf. In B. Dodd & R. Campbell (Eds), *Hearing by eye: The psychology of lip-reading.* (pp. 191–211). Hove, UK: Lawrence Erlbaum Associates Ltd.

Montgomery, A.A. & Jackson, P.L. (1983). Physical characteristics of the lips underlying vowel lipreading performance. *Journal of the Acoustical Society of America, 73,* 2134–44.

Montgomery, A.A., Walden, B.E. & Prosek, R.A. (1987). Effects of consonantal context on vowel lipreading. *Journal of Speech and Hearing Research, 30,* 50–59.

Moores, D.F. & Sweet, C. (1991). Factors predictive of school achievement. In D.F. Moores & K.P. Meadow-Orlans (Eds), *Educational and developmental aspects of deafness.* Washington, D.C.: Gallaudet University Press.

O'Neill, J.J. & Oyer, H.J. (1961). *Visual communication for the hard of hearing: History, research and methods.* Englewood Cliffs, NJ: Prentice-Hall.

Owens, E., Kessler, D.K., Telleen, C.C., & Schubert, E.D. (1985). *Minimal Auditory Capabilities Battery* (Rev. Ed.). St. Louis, MO: Auditec.

Parasnis, I. (1983). Effects of parental deafness and early exposure to manual communication on cognitive skills and field independence of young deaf adults. *Journal of Speech and Hearing Research, 26,* 588–94.

Stanovich, K.E. (1985). Explaining the variance in reading ability in terms of psychological processes: What have we learned? *Annals of Dyslexia, 35,* 67–96.

Summerfield, A.Q. (1987). Some preliminaries to a comprehensive account of audio-visual speech perception. In B. Dodd & R. Campbell (Eds), *Hearing by eye: The psychology of lip-reading* (pp. 3–51). Hove, UK: Lawrence Erlbaum Associates Ltd.

Summerfield, A.Q. (1991). Visual perception of phonetic gestures. In I.G. Mattingly & M. Studdert-Kennedy (Eds), *Modularity and the motor theory of speech perception* (pp. 117–38). Hillsdale, NJ: Erlbaum.

Wagner, R.K. & Torgesen, J.K. (1987). The nature of phonological processing and its causal role in the acquisition of reading skills. *Psychological Bulletin, 101,* 192–212.

CHAPTER TWELVE

Early lipreading ability and speech and language development of hearing-impaired pre-schoolers

Barbara Dodd   *Department of Speech, University of Newcastle upon Tyne, UK*

Beth McIntosh and Lynn Woodhouse   *Department of Speech Pathology and Audiology, School of Health and Rehabilitation Sciences, The University of Queensland, Brisbane, Australia*

INTRODUCTION

Very strong opinions are held about how children born with severely or profoundly impaired hearing should be taught to communicate. For many years, signing was prohibited in schools in the United Kingdom and elsewhere. More recently, Sacks (1989) has advocated that the sign language of the deaf community is the natural language of deaf people. A compromise adopted by many schools educating children with impaired hearing is "total" or "simultaneous" communication—the use of simultaneously signed and spoken English, where the message is identical in both modes including morpheme markers. By exposing children to precise signed English, it was intended that grammatically well-structured language would be acquired, allowing children to develop the mental schema necessary for comprehending the world and to lay a basis for spoken language and literacy.

Unfortunately, the outcome has not been quite what was expected. In practice, many children educated using "simultaneous" communication seem to have very poor language skills in both spoken and signed English. For example, one study reported no differences between the expressive syntactic abilities of children exposed to both signed and spoken English and those exposed only to spoken English (Geers, Moog & Schick, 1984). Another study found that 8- to 12-year-old deaf children, who were exposed to signed and spoken English, performed below the 4-year-old level on a test of comprehension of grammar (Bishop, 1983). Further, Berent (1996) notes that deaf college students have persistent difficulties with spoken and written English that hinder their educational attainment. Even deaf children with hearing parents may choose to communicate using the sign language of the deaf community (as opposed to signed English), learned from children of deaf families for whom sign is a first language (Dodd & Murphy, 1992).

Nevertheless, there have been some spectacular success stories of children with prelingual, profound hearing impairment who acquire excellent spoken and written language and achieve academic success in the mainstream educational context (for anecdotal evidence, see Sacks, 1989). For example, Dodd and Murphy (1992) reported on two 14-year-old girls with profound hearing impairment who were matched for cause of hearing loss (maternal rubella), non-verbal intelligence, family situation, remedial services and educational placement where they were exposed to simultaneously signed and spoken English. One of these girls had acquired age-appropriate spoken and written language, had excellent lipreading skills and intelligible speech. She subsequently attended university. In contrast, the girl who relied on Auslan (Australian sign language) to communicate had poor spoken and written language.

So, while children born with profoundly impaired hearing *can* develop excellent spoken and written language, most do not. Why do so many deaf children who are exposed to "simultaneous" communication from an early age fail to acquire adequate signed, spoken and written English? This question prompted a longitudinal study of a group of 16 children with severe and profound hearing impairment.

There are a number of explanations that might possibly account for so many children with profound hearing impairment not developing appropriate language skills despite exposure to signed English. Perhaps children's language learning environments are less than ideal in terms of exposure to signed English (Wood & Wood, 1992). Alternatively, Sack's (1989) argument, that signed English is "unnatural" might hold. Another possible explanation relies on the crucial role of phonology in the acquisition of language.

Although it is generally acknowledged that the development of all aspects of language—syntax, semantics and phonology—are interdependent (Panagos & Prelock, 1982), researchers often investigate each separately. Consequently, comparison of the interrelationships between language skills tends to be overlooked. Children with profoundly impaired hearing who are exposed to simultaneously signed and spoken language provide an opportunity to investigate language acquisition in an environment where syntactic and semantic information is fully specified through signs, but where information about phonology must be gleaned from lipreading and residual

hearing. This study focuses on the relationship between the early development of lipreading ability and the subsequent development of phonological
and language skills.

METHOD

Subjects

Sixteen children with impaired hearing were selected for longitudinal testing
over a period of three years at about eight-monthly intervals using obser-
vational and formal testing procedures. In total there were five assessment
sessions. Informed parental consent was sought and obtained for all participants in the study. Students were selected from three special education
units in Queensland, Australia. Table 9 shows the subjects' age at first
assessment, gender, and information on their hearing impairment. Phonological data were available for only 11 of these children (marked by asterisks
in Table 9). Two subjects moved away and three produced too little spoken
language to make phonological analyses possible.

TABLE 9
Subject information

No.	Age in months	Sex	Unaided hearing loss		Aided hearing loss (dB)	Ætiology
			Right	Left		
1	49	M	Profound	Severe	72	Unknown
2*	48	F	Severe–Profound	Moderate–Severe	60	Unknown
3	51	M	Profound	Profound	58	Unknown
4*	57	F	Profound	Profound	49	Unknown
5*	42	F	Severe	Severe	52	Unknown
6*	53	M	Severe	Severe	51	Congenital
7*	47	F	Severe–Profound	Severe–Profound	64	Unknown
8*	50	F	Severe	Severe	31	Rh
9	38	F	Profound	Profound	95	Congenital
10*	46	F	Severe	Severe	61	Rubella
11	49	M	Severe	Severe	51	Unknown
12*	47	F	Profound	Profound	64	Unknown
13	51	M	Severe	Severe	61	Unknown
14*	34	F	Profound	Profound	49	Unknown
15*	54	M	Severe–Profound	Severe–Profound	60	Unknown
16*	30	F	Severe–Profound	Severe–Profound	60	Unknown

Moderate: 56–70 dB
Severe: 71–90 dB
Profound: > 90 dB

Information concerning each child's suitability for inclusion in the study was obtained from existing files, from a case history interview and from a parent questionnaire that focused on audiological, educational, intervention and communication issues. All children who met the following criteria were included in the study:

1. Bilateral severe to profound sensorineural hearing loss: > 60 dB loss in the better ear across four frequencies of the speech range (500, 1000, 2000 and 4000 Hz).
2. No other significant handicaps.
3. No history of chronic middle ear infection.
4. Hearing loss onset prior to 18 months of age.
5. Participated in an early intervention program using the total communication approach, i.e. simultaneously signed and spoken English.
6. Consistently using some form of amplification.
7. Normal oro-motor function.

Procedure

The 16 children were assessed in a quiet room at their schools, with parents present at the first testing session. Parents were not required to attend the four subsequent assessment sessions, although some chose to do so. Standardised tests were given strictly according to the procedures outlined in the testing manuals. The order in which tests were given was the same for all children. Some children were seen more than once to collect the data, because testing sessions were kept to a maximum of 30 minutes to avoid fatigue.

Simultaneous spoken and signed language was used by the investigators when they were assessing the children. All spoken and/or signed utterances used by the children were included in the analyses. The assessment protocol included a mixture of standardised and non-standardised tests, and systematic analyses of spontaneous language samples. As the children became older, additional tests were included to describe their development. A 30-minute spontaneous language sample was recorded on videotape at each testing session. Where possible, this included morning or afternoon tea periods, formal language times in the classroom, play time and part of the actual testing period. The child's regular classroom teacher was often the significant other person in the videos. These videos provided the raw data for the language analyses.

The following assessment procedures were used to examine aspects of cognitive and linguistic development, including both signed and spoken language.

1. Non-linguistic skills
    (i)   Developmental Test of Visual Motor Integration (Beery, 1989),
          a standardised test of non-verbal intelligence appropriate for
          young children.
    (ii) Auditory Sequential Memory Sub-test: Illinois Test of Psy-
          cholinguistic Abilities (Kirk, McCarthy & Kirk, 1968), a stan-
          dardised test of short-term memory.
2. Language comprehension
    (i)   The Reynell Developmental Receptive Language Scale,
          Revised (RDLS; Reynell, 1977), a standardised measure of
          receptive language.
    (ii) Test of Auditory Comprehension of Language, Revised
          (TACL-R; Carrow-Woolfolk, 1985).
    (iii) The Peabody Picture Vocabulary Test, Revised (PPVT; Dunn
          & Dunn, 1981), a receptive vocabulary measure.
3. Expressive language
    (i)   Mean Length of Utterance (Miller, 1981), a commonly used
          measure of expressive language development in the pre-school
          years.
    (ii) The Type Token Ratio (TTR; Templin, 1957), an expressive
          measure of the number of different words used as a ratio of the
          total number of words spoken.
    (iii) The Expressive One-word Picture Vocabulary Test (EPV;
          Gardner, 1979), an expressive vocabulary measure.
4. Phonology
    (i)   Phoneme repertoire: speech sounds used appropriately at least
          twice.
    (ii) Percent consonants correct.
    (iii) Phonological processes: speech error patterns used consistently
          that reflect hearing children's normal developmental errors; or
          atypical (i.e. non-developmental) patterns.
5. Pragmatics
    Dore's (1978) Conversational Act Categories, an elaborate coding
    system based on grammatical form, illocutionary function and con-
    versational contingency. The examiners used a modified version of this
    procedure.
6. Lipreading skills
    Lipreading Assessment for Children with Hearing Impairment
    (LACHI; Dodd, McIntosh & Woodhouse, in preparation. See
    Appendix A). There are no appropriate standardised tests of lip-
    reading available for pre-school children.

Note that all tests, except the speechreading test, were given using simultaneously signed and spoken English.

RESULTS

Non-linguistic skills

Figure 34 presents the results from Visual Motor Integration Test, which measures non-verbal cognitive development in children. It shows that the age-equivalent scores from the VMI mirror the mean chronological age of the children at each testing session. Examination of the range of scores for each testing session, indicate that the poorest performing child was not significantly below his or her chronological age. Thus, the children were functioning at an age-appropriate level on this non-linguistic task, indicating that their poor linguistic skills cannot be explained in terms of intellectual impairment.

Language comprehension

Figure 35 shows two receptive measures in terms of age-equivalent scores: the Reynell Developmental Receptive Language Scales and the Peabody

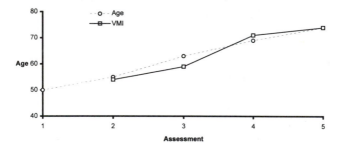

FIG. 34.   Visuo-motor integration: AE score.

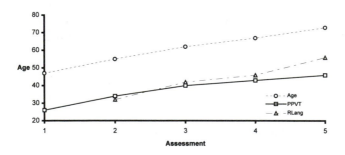

FIG. 35.   Receptive language.

Picture Vocabulary Test. As can be clearly seen, the two sets of scores are similar. The group mean delay (in months) for both tests of language comprehension was 22–24 months below what would be expected for the children's chronological age.

Expressive language

Figure 36 shows the mean comparison between chronological age and the age-equivalent scores taken from the Mean Length of Utterance, a measure of expressive language. It is evident that the MLU age-equivalent scores are markedly lower than the CA and appear to diverge. That is, the older the children become, the more delayed their expressive language skills in terms of MLU. Their expressive vocabulary scores (which measure the ability to label objects and events) are much better than their MLU measure (a measure of their ability to generate sentences).

Phonology

Table 10 shows the mean number of phonemes missing and the percent consonants correct. Given the severity of their hearing loss and their chronological age, the group data are predictable. However, there were large individual differences. Qualitative analyses of the type of errors made revealed that, for the group as a whole, developmental errors constituted over 60% of total errors (see Table 10). The most common developmental error patterns were cluster reduction ([noʊ] for snow), stopping ([tɪp] for ship), final consonant deletion ([mæ] for mat), weak syllable deletion ([nanə] for banana) and gliding ([wʌn] for run). The most common non-developmental phonological error patterns were backing (e.g. [koʊ] for toe), initial consonant deletion ([oʊ] for toe), and affrication ([tʃoʊ] for toe).

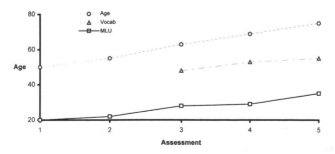

FIG. 36.   Expressive language: AE scores.

TABLE 10
Phonological measures, mean (SD) and range

Measure	Session 3	Session 4	Session 5
Number of phonemes	18.2	16.1	12.0
Missing from consonant	(3.9)	(4.7)	(4.7)
Repertoire (out of 26)	12–23	9–23	6–21
Percent consonants correct	32.8	38.9	42.8
	(13.7)	(20.7)	(19.0)
	17–56	9–71	6–71
Percent deviant errors	25.9	31.0	39.2
	(22.2)	(24.3)	(19.2)
	0–60	0–60	11–75

Lipreading skills

Figure 37 shows the performance of the group on the LACHI test over the three-year period of the longitudinal study. Improvement in lipreading skills was not consistent with the increase in chronological age; speechreading skills seemed to plateau at sessions 4 and 5 (CA 69 months and 74 months). At session 5, 3 children scored 100%; 6 children scored 50–100%; 3 scored below 50% (indicating that they could only cope with the single-word section).

Relationship between early lipreading ability and language development

In a previous paper (Dodd, McIntosh & Woodhouse, 1997), we reported positive correlations between the children's lipreading scores and other non-phonological language measures within and across assessment sessions. To explore the relationship between lipreading ability and the phonological

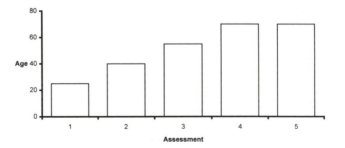

FIG. 37.   Speechreading.

measures, and to further establish the link between lipreading ability and some nonphonological language measures, the children were split into two groups. Group 1 consisted of 4 children (Subjects 2, 4, 6, 8) whose mean performance on the lipreading measure in sessions 1 and 2 was greater than 45% (see Table 11). Group 2 consisted of 7 children (Subjects 5, 7, 10, 12, 14, 15, 16) whose mean performance on the lipreading measure in sessions 1 and 2 was less than 40% (see Table 11). Comparison of these two groups (group 1: early good lipreaders and group 2: poorer lipreaders) allows examination of the hypothesis that the early development of good lipreading skills is a positive prognostic indicator for later language development (phonology, syntax and vocabulary).

The subjects' scores are shown in Table 11. Mann-Whitney U tests revealed that the groups were, in fact, discriminated in terms of their performance on the lipreading measures in sessions 1 and 2 ($p = .006$). Further Mann-Whitney U testing revealed that the poor lipreaders had more phonemes missing from their phonemic repertoires in subsequent assessment sessions than the good lipreaders ($p = .012$). Similarly, the poor lipreaders produced fewer consonants correctly ($p = .012$) and made significantly more non-developmental speech errors ($p = .024$).

Table 12 shows the two groups' nonphonological language measures at the fifth assessment session in the longitudinal study. The scores used are the number of months' delay between the subjects' chronological age at the time of testing and their age-equivalent score on the standard assessments. The

TABLE 11
Mean phonological performance measures for groups 1 and 2

	Lipreading score (%)	Number of phonemes missing	Consonants correct (%)	Deviant errors (%)
Sessions	1 and 2	3, 4 and 5	3, 4 and 5	3, 4 and 5
Group 1: good lipreaders				
2	88	10.6	46.6	7
4	58	9.6	51.3	11
6	66	13.3	71	33
8	46	10.3	71	18.5
Group 2: poor lipreaders				
5	12	18	41.5	19
7	8	18.3	37	32.6
10	8	17	16.3	36.6
12	0	12	42.3	47.3
14	4	22.3	11.3	38
15	28	16.5	21.0	65
16	38	15	48.6	42.6

TABLE 12
Session 5 language performance measures for groups 1 and 2

	Aided hearing loss (dB)	EPV (expressive vocabulary)	PPVT (receptive vocabulary)	Language comprehension	Dores Conversational Acts
Group 1: good lipreaders					
2	Severe	0	22	2	12
4	Profound	13	32	10	10
6	Severe	14	35	15	14
8	Severe	18	32	26	13
Group 2: poor lipreaders					
5	Severe	31	39	15	4
7	Profound	25	36	32	6
10	Severe	12	23	26	11
12	Profound	14	26	30	10
14	Profound	7	20	20	6
15	Profound	22	39	36	3
16	Profound	7	12	43	7

language assessments analysed were: expressive vocabulary (EPV); receptive vocabulary (PPVT); language comprehension (TACL-R) and the number of different conversational acts used throughout the assessment session (Dore's Conversational Acts, e.g. requests for information; responses to requests, descriptions, statements, acknowledgements).

The good lipreaders and the poor lipreaders did not differ in terms of the extent of their delay on the two vocabulary measures (EPV: $p = .527$; PPVT: $p = 1.000$); but the good lipreaders were less delayed that the poor lipreaders on the assessment of their language comprehension ($p = .042$). The good lipreaders also used a significantly greater variety of conversational acts compared to the poor lipreaders ($p = .012$).

In order to ensure that it was lipreading skill rather than degree of hearing impairment that accounted for the differences found, all analyses were redone, but using degree of hearing loss as the grouping factor, rather than lipreading skill. Table 12 shows that 6 of the 11 children were profoundly hearing impaired (in terms of their unaided hearing threshold across both ears), one of whom was in group 1. None of the Mann-Whitney U tests were significant: lipreading performance ($p = .178$); number of phonemes missing from repertoires ($p = .662$); percent consonants correct ($p = .429$); percent of deviant errors ($p = .126$); EPV ($p = .931$); PPVT ($p = .793$); TACL-R ($p = .126$); Dores Conversational Acts ($p = .082$).

DISCUSSION

Children's early lipreading skills are a good prognostic indicator of their developing spoken and signed language skills. That is, not only phonological development but also comprehension of syntax and children's use of language are, at least initially, dependent on lipreading ability. This is despite information about the latter two aspects of language being available through signed English. One reason for this may be that signed English is based on spoken language. When people speak, they do not always sign, or the signed message may not be as extensive as, or different from, the spoken message (Wood & Wood, 1992). There is evidence that hearing parents do not always gain the visual attention of their deaf children before signing, limiting the amount of exposure to signed as well as lipread language (Swisher, 1991). It is also possible that children may learn that what they are not supposed to "hear" is spoken, not signed. That makes spoken stimuli more interesting and may lead to more incidental learning.

However, it seems that the deaf children's poor syntactic and semantic performance cannot be simply attributed to a poor presentation of the signed and spoken message. In a series of studies done in Brisbane (where the data in this chapter were collected), Hyde and Power (1991, 1992) calculated that the 4 teachers-of-the-deaf they recorded had an accurate match between signed and spoken English for between 89.1% and 93.5% of utterances. In another study of 245 teachers, they found that 65% of utterances were both signed and spoken, only 16% were only spoken and only 4% were signed incorrectly.

Indeed, the results provide evidence that children were acquiring a signed vocabulary. The children's expressive vocabulary scores were less delayed than the other measure of their expressive language (see Figure 36), reflecting their tendency to label objects rather than generate sentences. Further, in contrast to the other measures, expressive and receptive vocabulary do not seem to be predicted by early lipreading skills. The children's exposure to signed English allows them to learn signs for objects and actions. It appears to be the syntax of English that limited their receptive and expressive language and consequently the use they could make of their language.

The notion underlying "simultaneous" communication is that children can acquire language as opposed to speech and, thus, develop the concepts and mental schema for organising information about the world. Hyde and Power's studies suggest that children receive adequate exposure, yet our data suggest impoverished use of signed English up to the age of seven. Further, a range of language abilities are predicted by early lipreading skills.

Perhaps spoken language is perceived as the dominant language mode even though deaf children find it hard to decipher.

The results also suggest that lipreading ability is a good predictor of later phonological development. Pre-school hearing-impaired children's access to phonological information is restricted to residual hearing and lipreading. It is hardly surprising, then, that lipreading ability influences the number of phonemes acquired and the number of speech errors made. Another speech measure that was predicted by early lipreading ability was the percent of phonological errors that were atypical of normal development.

Phonology is the linguistic system of contrasts that governs how speech sounds may be combined to convey meaning in a particular language. It consists not only of the phonemic repertoire (allowable consonant and vowel sounds that provide the minimal contrastive units between word pairs, e.g. "pin" and "bin", "hit" and "hat"), but also the constraints governing how speech sounds may be combined (e.g. the velar nasal /ŋ/ cannot occur word initially in English, although it does in Cantonese). Phonological development in hearing children is characterised by the consistent use of particular error patterns (Grunwell, 1981) that may reflect their understanding of the constraints of the phonological system being learned (Dodd, 1995). Although most error patterns evident in the speech of children with profound hearing impairment are similar to those of hearing children, some atypical error patterns are also often consistently used (Dodd, 1976; Abraham, 1989; Stoel-Gamon, 1982; Dodd & So, 1994).

The same atypical error patterns (e.g. backing, initial consonant deletion) in hearing children are indicative of a cognitive-linguistic deficit in abstracting the constraints that govern phonological structure (Dodd, 1995). One plausible explanation that might account for deaf children's use of these error patterns is that lipreading provides incomplete information about the phonological structure of words and, hence, a poor database for the abstraction of the principles that govern the language's phonology. The finding that there is a strong relationship between deaf children's early lipreading ability and the percentage of non-developmental phonological errors provides support for this hypothesis.

However, as with all their other communication skills, the children's phonological skills varied enormously. These huge individual differences need to be explained. They might arise from differences in the quality of the language learning environment, particularly the amount and type of support caregivers are able to provide. Unfortunately, such support is very difficult to measure objectively, as are factors such as motivation and quality of intervention. Other factors that might account for variability are measurable (age, IQ, memory, amount and type of intervention). There would seem to be, however, no single factor that accounts for children's rate of development, since all the factors interact. Nevertheless, lipreading ability seems worth following up in more detail. The variability in lipreading ability was enormous and it would be interesting to know why children differ so. Another question worth asking is: If lipreading could be better taught, what influence would it have on speech and language development?

APPENDIX A: STRUCTURE OF LIPREADING ASSESSMENT FOR CHILDREN WITH HEARING IMPAIRMENT

Section one: Point to (7) miniature objects (e.g. cow, brush, sheep, bed, baby).
Section two: Do what I say (e.g. push car, horse jump, brush hair).
Section three: Say these words after me (e.g. cat, shoe, flower, beautiful).
Section four: Point to the picture (e.g. blue, hat, four, nose, green).
Section five: Point to six objects (chosen randomly from around the room, e.g. light, door).
Section six: Repeat these sentences (e.g. I saw a blue car, John didn't ask her name).
Section seven: Tell me (e.g. What's your name? How old are you? Are you a girl?).
Section eight: Conversational skills (the conversation should evolve around a particular picture or relevant event). Rating: Good/Fair/Poor/Non-existent.

REFERENCES

Abraham S. (1989). Using a phonological framework to describe speech errors of orally trained hearing impaired school-agers. *Journal of Speech and Hearing Disorders*, 54, 600–9.

Beery, K. (1989). *Developmental Test of Visual-motor Integration (3rd Revision)*. Cleveland: Modern Curriculum Press.

Berent, G.P. (1996). Learnability constraints on deaf learners acquisition of *wh*-questions. *Journal of Speech and Hearing Research*, 39, 625–42.

Bishop, D.V. (1983). Comprehension of English syntax by profoundly deaf children. *Journal of Child Psychology and Psychiatry and Allied Disciplines*, 24, 8–12.

Carrow-Woolfolk, E. (1985) *Test for Auditory Comprehension of Language (Revised)*. Texas: DLM Teaching Resources.

Dodd B. (1976). The phonological systems of deaf children. *Journal of Speech and Hearing Disorders*, 41, 185–98.

Dodd, B. (1995). *Differential Diagnosis and Treatment of Speech Disordered Children*. London: Whurr.

Dodd B. & Murphy J. (1992). Visual thinking. In R. Campbell (Ed.), *Mental Lives. Case Studies in Cognition* (pp. 47–60). Oxford: Blackwell.

Dodd, B. & So, L. (1994). The phonological abilities of Cantonese-speaking children who are hearing impaired. *Journal of Speech and Hearing Research*, 37, 671–9.

Dodd, B., McIntosh, B. & Woodhouse, L. (1997). Children with hearing loss: Speechreading skills. In D. Stork & M. Hennecke (Eds.), *Speechreading by Humans and Machines: Models, systems and applications*. Nato ISI Series F150, Berlin: Springer.

Dore, J. (1978). Requestive systems in nursery school conversations: Analysis of talk in a social context. In R. Campbell & P. Smith (Eds), *Recent Advances in the Psychology of Language: Language Development and Mother/child Interaction*. New York: Plenum Press.

Dunn L. & Dunn L. (1981). *Peabody Picture Vocabulary Test, (Revised)*. Circle Pines, MN: American Guidance Service.

Gardner, M. (1979). *Expressive One-word Picture Vocabulary Test*. Novato, California: Academic Therapy Publications.

Geers, A., Moog, J. & Schick, B. (1984). Acquisition of spoken and signed English by pro-foundly deaf children. *Journal of Speech and Hearing Disorders, 49*, 378–88.

Grunwell, P. (1981). *Clinical Phonology*. London: Croom Helm.

Hyde, M. & Power, D. (1991). Teachers' use of simultaneous communication. *American Annals of the Deaf, 136*, 381–7.

Hyde, M. & Power, D. (1992). Teachers' communication with deaf students: An Australian study. *Sign-language Studies, 75*, 159–66.

Kirk, S., McCarthy, J. & Kirk, W. (1968). *The Illinois Test of Psycholinguistic Abilities, Revised*. Urbana IL: University of Illinois.

Miller J. (1981) *Assessing Language Production in Children: Experimental Procedures*. Austin, TX: Pro-ed.

Panagos, J. & Prelock, P. (1982). Phonological constraints on the sentence productions of language disordered children. *Journal of Speech and Hearing Research, 26*, 841–8.

Reynell, J.K. (1977). *Reynell Developmental Language Scales, Revised*. Windsor, UK: NFER-Nelson.

Sacks, O. (1989). *Seeing Voices*. London: Picador.

Stoel-Gammon C. (1982). The acquisition of segmental phonology by normally-hearing and hearing-impaired children. In I. Hochberg, H. Levitt & M. Osberger (Eds), *Speech of the Hearing Impaired: Research, Training, and Personnel Preparation*. Baltimore, Maryland: University Park Press.

Swisher, M.V. (1991). Conversational interaction between deaf children and their hearing mothers: The role of visual attention. In P. Siple & S. Fischer (Eds.), *Theoretical Issues in Language Research. Volume 2: Psychology*. Chicago: Chicago University Press.

Templin, M.C. (1957). Certain language skills in children: Their development and inter-relationships. *Child Welfare Monograph, 26*, Minneapolis: University of Minnesota Press.

Wood, H. & Wood, D. (1992). Signed English in the classrooms: III What gets signed. *First Language, 12*, 125–45.

DEAFNESS, LANGUAGE AND SPEECHREADING: SIGN AND AUGMENTATION

CHAPTER THIRTEEN

Mouth movement and signed communication

Marc Marschark, Dominique LePoutre and Linda Bement
National Technical Institute for the Deaf, Rochester Institute of Technology, Rochester, New York, USA

INTRODUCTION

In a book about speechreading and audio-visual aspects of speech, a chapter on sign language may seem anomalous. The incongruity is more apparent than real, however, because face-to-face communication, regardless of its modality, normally takes advantage of more than just the hands (in sign language) or the mouth (in spoken language). Viewed from this perspective, much of this book serves to demonstrate that during spoken communication, there are other things going on in addition to the "simple" connection between the oral articulatory apparatus of one person and the auditory reception apparatus of another. In this chapter, we consider the possibility that during signed communication, there are other things going on in addition to the "simple" connection between the manual articulatory apparatus of one person and the visual reception apparatus of another.

To ensure that readers do not misinterpret our purpose here or suffer from an unfamiliarity with sign language, we will consider separately below the possible roles of mouth movement in true sign language (here, primarily American Sign Language or ASL) and its more obvious role in simultaneous communication (SC). ASL is a full and formal language with a grammar and morphology all its own. Because it does not parallel English, one cannot be signing fluent ASL and speaking or *mouthing* (producing voiceless word-like elements on the lips) fluent English at the same time.[1] SC may be more familiar to many readers than will ASL. It is what you are seeing when someone (deaf or hearing) signs and speaks at the same time, usually using signed English. It is essential to recognise that the use of hands in SC or signed English does *not* make it sign language. Signed English is an invented hybrid of ASL and English designed to facilitate development of English literacy in deaf children. As laudable as this goal might seem, the theoretical rationale for the combination is dubious (Mayer & Wells, 1996) and raises a host of difficult questions for language, social, and cognitive development (Marschark, 1997).

In order to place the discussion of mouth movements during ASL and SC in the appropriate context, we first consider the possible origins of signed and spoken communication and what we believe to be the universal confluence of hand and mouth in human face-to-face communication. Then, we will examine the occurrence of mouth movements in American Sign Language and simultaneous communication. In those contexts, we will examine when mouth movements occur in conjunction with sign language, their functional roles, and whether their use in fluent, native signers is obligatory or optional, functional or intrusive.

ORIGINS OF LANGUAGE MODALITY

This section provides a brief discussion of the possible interplay of manual and oral articulators in communication as a function of phylogenetic, neuropsychological, and historico-linguistic change. We do not consider at all issues surrounding possible ontogenetic implications of being exposed to spoken versus sign language during childhood, a topic considered at length by Marschark et al. (1997). Instead, we pause to wonder about the form of communication among our early ancestors and the environmental and evolutionary pressures that led to spoken and signed languages as we know them now.

It is now well established that, as humans, we have at least equal potential for the natural acquisition of spoken or signed languages, and that there may even be an advantage for language in the visuospatial modality through the one-word stage of language development (Bonvillian & Folven, 1993; Lillo-Martin, 1997; Meier & Newport, 1990; Siple, 1997). How then does it happen that spoken language is the dominant form of communication for humans who can hear? Although there is considerable debate concerning the origins of sign language use among people who are deaf, there is no doubt that signs have long served a variety of purposes among hearing people in situations where there was no common spoken language (e.g. between Native American tribes), where spoken language would be disruptive (e.g. in the theatre or among would-be thieves), or where it was forbidden (e.g. in monasteries) (for discussion and examples, see Bragg, 1997; Rodda & Grove, 1987, Chapter 2).

From at least the eighteenth century to the present day, various theorists have debated whether the roots of human language are gestural or guttural—whether the first "proto-languages" were manual or oral. Support for gestural origins for language has come primarily from neuropsychological and neuroanatomical sources. For example, the areas of the brain involved in language processing per se differ from those controlling vocal communication in nonhuman primates, and the human vocal tract evolved relatively late (Feyereisen & de Lannoy, 1991). There also is considerable overlap in the neurological and behavioural mechanisms of the manual movements required for gesture and sign, and the oral movements required for spoken language (Kimura, 1975, 1981; McNeill, 1992). Results of a recent study by Hickok, Bellugi and Klima (1996), however, suggest that the neurological processes underlying sign language and non-linguistic hand movements are independent. Thus claims that the dominance of the left hemisphere for language is more a motor than a linguistic phenomenon (Kimura, 1975) seem unfounded. Tzeng and Wang (1984), in contrast, argued that the common neurocognitive roots of language, gesture, and sign might lie in the fine temporal resolution ability of the left hemisphere, a mechanism essential for, and apparent in, production in all three domains. Assuming an early form of gestural communication, the advent of tool use in human evolution (where the right hand/left hemisphere would have controlled tool movement while the left hand/right hemisphere held the object of tool use) would have occupied the hands with other matters, thus creating evolutionary as well as practical pressure for conversion to guttural communication (Paget, 1930).

Human language also has been claimed to have evolved from the kinds of vocal communication used by nonhuman primates. We now know that such productions are not always automatic and there is increasing evidence that primates have a larger vocal repertoire than was previously assumed (for a discussion, see Feyereisen & de Lannoy, 1991, Chapter 1; Gray & Wise, 1959, Chapter 8). Edelman (1992), for example, directly rooted human language in vocal communication in arguing that the of origin of language lies "specifically in the evolution of the vocal tract and the brain centers for speech production and comprehension" (Edelman, 1992, p. 125). Alternatively, Armstrong, Stokoe and Wilcox (1995) suggest that gestural and guttural signals probably both served as the earliest "linguistic units", even if their theoretical orientation favours the gestural modality as the route to syntax and, hence, eventually to language.

Regardless of its evolutionary origins, it is clear that there is a contemporary link between spoken language and the gestures that frequently accompany it. McNeill (1985, 1992) has convincingly argued that speech and gesture derive from the same underlying *verbal* system. In several studies, McNeill and his colleagues have found that gesture and speech bear similar logical and behavioural relations, follow similar developmental courses, and are affected in similar ways following cerebral lesions and in aphasia (see also Kimura, 1975, 1981). Marschark (1994) provided a related analysis involving the relations between gesture and sign language. He examined the functional roles of gestures embedded within sign language productions of deaf children and adults as compared to those embedded within spoken language productions of hearing children and adults. His analysis revealed that gestures produced by deaf individuals can be distinguished from the sign language in which they are embedded in terms of both their privilege of occurrence and their semantic and pragmatic functions, even if the fact that they are in the same (manual) modality make them difficult to distinguish.

Findings like those of McNeill (1992) and Marschark (1994) indicating that manual gestures play an important role in the normal course of both signing and speaking lend credence to views of language origins that entail the involvement of both gestural and guttural communication (Armstrong et al., 1995). While it is intuitively obvious that "oral gestures" also play a role in human communication (e.g. smiling, grimacing), it is unclear whether they would have any specific function within signed communication different than they would within spoken communication. Those of us who sign and are regularly around other signers (with a wide range of abilities) certainly see mouth movements occurring during signing. But what is the role of those mouthings? Are they required or are they fragments of no significance, reflecting the speech training imposed on many young deaf children by hearing parents? How are they related to the needs of the receiver and the abilities of the sender?

THE ROLE OF MOUTH MOVEMENT IN ASL

Since the recognition of American Sign Language (ASL) as a true language in the 1960s, researchers like Baker (Baker-Shenk, 1983; Baker & Cokely, 1980; Baker & Padden, 1978), McIntire (McIntire & Snitzer Reilly, 1988), and Lidell (1986) have described various roles of nonmanual features in ASL. Embedded within this research is consideration of the functions of mouth movements (or mouth shapes) in ASL and, in particular, whether they have linguistic significance or are epiphenomenal actions reflecting only the largely unused speech training of these children. Research on mouthings has been reported for sign languages in Europe by investigators such as Boyes Braem (1990), Ebbinghaus and Hessmann (1996), Schermer (1990), and Vogt-Svendsen (1983). Taken together, these studies clearly indicate that mouth movements can serve a variety of grammatical functions within different sign languages.

One of the more commonly observed uses of mouth movements and other facial actions in ASL is adverbial, indicating the manner of the verb in the phrase. Several common instances of adverbial mouthings are shown in the following photographs. Figures 38 and 39, for example, show the sign DO.[2] In this sign, the hands are moved side-to-side; an accompanying opening and closing of the mouth indicates that the activity involved lesser intensity or effort. Figure 40, in contrast, shows the sign WORK with the lips squeezed together and eyebrows drawn, indicating diligence, care, or deliberation (either mouth shape can be paired with either sign). Figure 41 shows the sign TRAVEL in conjunction with pursed lips, in this case indicating a lack of intensity or effort rather than the reverse; whereas Figure 42 shows the tongue slightly protruding through the teeth in the sign DRIVE, indicating carelessness or lack of deliberation in driving.

Mouth movements in ASL also can serve adjectival functions. In Figure 43, for example, puffed out cheeks coupled with the sign BELLY produce the meaning "big belly". The mouthing serves as an optional adjective in this case, as the signer could have produced the utterance BIG BELLY using the sign BIG instead of the facial modification. In other cases, mouth movements are a mandatory part of adjectival signs. Thus, the handshapes and positions in the adjectival sign FAT *must* be accompanied by puffed cheeks, and those in THIN *must* be accompanied by pulled-in cheeks, as shown in Figure 44.

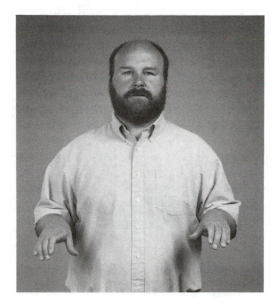

FIG. 38.

FIG. 39.

FIG. 40.

FIG. 41.

FIG. 42.

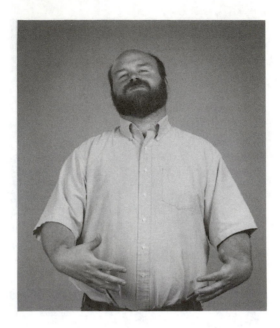

FIG. 43.

FIG. 44.

"Mandatory" here, of course, refers to usage in fluent communication, either by the producer or the receiver. The lack of mandatory features does not mean that the signs will not be understood, and nonfluent, incorrect signing is often comprehended just as English no good? Anyway okay. We, thus, have to decide whether to refer to mouthings as parts of signs or as accompaniments to signs. One kind of evidence that would help to resolve the issue would be the occurrence of signs that mean different things with or without a mouth movement or with one mouth movement or another.

One possible example of this situation lies in the way that mouth movement can be used to differentiate the meanings of the English words "not yet" and "late", which have the same sign in ASL. In the case of NOT YET, there is often a tongue thrust (see Figure 45) that is absent for LATE. This example might indicate a *minimal pair* differentiated by the single feature of the tongue thrust. However, in recent years, we have seen native signers more frequently include the thrust for the meanings of both LATE and NOT YET; thus, its optional versus mandatory status remains unclear (and may be changing). Other cases are not so ambiguous, however, as in the requirement for mouthing in British sign language to distinguish which meaning of the single sign HUSBAND/WIFE is intended (Boyes Braem, Personal Communication, February 9, 1995).

FIG. 45.

Assuming that there is a point at which a sign and a mouth movement form an integrated unit, there is also likely to be a point when one part will become redundant. In such a case, the manual portion of a sign may eventually disappear, leaving only a mouth movement that retains the original meaning of the manual-mouthing combination. This disconnection has happened for ASL in the case of CARELESS, where a tongue thrust between the teeth ("th") can serve either as an adverb or an adjective (see Fischer & Forman, 1980). Another example involves the sign WILLING. Normally, the sign is made with a flat hand moving out from the chest and turning upward, accompanied by the bilabial mouth movement "ma". Within context, however, the manual component can be dropped, leaving only the fully understandable mouth movement (often with accompanying head nod). Similarly, the sign RECENTLY is normally made by moving the cheek and side of the mouth towards a raised shoulder (coupled with an *X-hand* against the cheek). This mouth movement can also occur adverbially, without the handshape, indicating that an event has just happened or is about to happen. Finally, a case where the optional link between sign and mouth movement seems to have become completely disconnected is the bilabial trill, which can accompany signs like MOTORCYCLE and UNRAVEL, indicating rapid and repetitive movement (or the capability for it). The trill now functions as a stand-alone adjective or adverb in the sense that while it must be attached to a referent sign, it does not normally have a signed form (unlike puffed cheeks and the sign FAT being roughly synonymous).

Mouth movements that indicate degree, size, or amount are often used with size and shape classifiers. *Classifiers* are particular handshapes used to represent classes of things or characteristics of objects. The first kind of classifier involves the use of a handshape to represent a particular person or thing already named, indicating actions or directions taken within a particular episode. For example, an upright *1-hand* can be used to indicate a person, and a bent, downward *V-hand* can be used to indicate an animal. Of greater interest here is a second kind of classifier, which functions like an adjective rather than a noun. These are most often used for indicating either shape or size. For example, two *OK* handshapes (*F-hands*) or cupped hands (*C-hands*) moved apart vertically or horizontally are used to denote the size of cylindrical objects, and extended little fingers (*I-hands*) can denote thin filaments or lines (for details, see Marschark, 1997, Chapter 3). Mouth shapes linked to particular classifiers include pursed lips ("oo") to indicate smallness or thinness, puffed cheeks or a "cha" mouthing (often with voice) to indicate largeness, and tightly closed lips ("mm") to indicate sameness or "standard". "Cha" is the only one of these classifier-linked mouth movements that we have seen used as a stand-alone adjective, but it is also the only one that does not appear to have other meaningful occurrences. This situation is similar to that noted for the bilabial trill earlier.

The implications of apparent disconnections between signs and hand-shapes suggest the need for research into unique versus non-unique mouth movements and their possible evolution from being sign accompanied to stand-alone status. To this point, however, we have considered only mouth shapes that appear relatively arbitrary in their lexical linkage. Other mouth movements that occur during ASL production mimic all or part of English words. Generally, the use of such mouth movements is discouraged by native signers as they make the language appear "unnatural" (Padden & Humphries, 1988). However, there are numerous examples of such sign-English hybrids. One common instance of this situation is the sign FINE, usually accompanied by a plosive "f" ("fa"). Partial word mouthing also can be observed frequently in the sign BORING, which is accompanied by a rounding of the lips that occurs in articulation of the word "boring", as shown in Figures 46 and 47; the upper teeth making contact with lower lip in the sign HAVE (see Figure 48); the pressed lips of the "ma" in the production of MAD, as shown in Figures 49 and 50; and the sign WANT being supplemented by "wa", as shown in Figure 51. Figure 52 shows one other kind of example, where multiple repetitions of the sign FOR with the index finger moving out from the forehead accompanied by "fo fo fo" mouthing means "For what reason?" or "Why?" In all of these cases, the mouthing appears to occur most consistently to denote emphasis, but they are not limited to emotionally-laden situations.

FIG. 46.

FIG. 47.

FIG. 48.

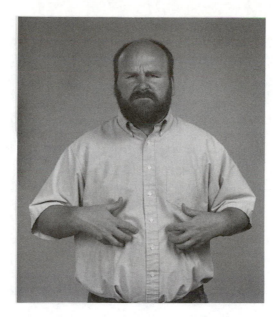

FIG. 49.

FIG. 50.

FIG. 51.

FIG. 52.

Mouthed approximations to English in ASL also have been observed in the signing of deaf toddlers, for example, when HOME and SHARE are accompanied by "om" and "sh", respectively, on the lips and seem to be part of the signs. When and why this occurs in the development of sign language has yet to be studied. McIntire and Reilly (1988), however, suggested that deaf children learn signs and affective behaviours for affective states as *Gestalts*, including both manual and nonmanual gestures, and that the appearance of English words on the lips may be a part of these undifferentiated wholes. In older children and adults, mouth movements frequently accompany fingerspelled English words that have no equivalent in ASL (particularly technical vocabulary) and reflect English pronunciation.

Similar mouthing of words shows up in other situations with varying regularity. Boyes Braem has identified several of these (in German sign language), which she reports can be conditional on context, discourse situation, or even personal style (Personal Communication, February 9, 1995; see Boyes Braem, 1990). One situation she finds to be relatively consistent is in the signing of kinship terms which may be accompanied by mouthed possessive pronouns that are omitted from the signed utterance (e.g. CALL "my" MOTHER). Another regular occurrence is the production of mouth movements (and sometimes a specific sound) accompanying certain idiomatic expressions in ASL. In one interesting case, the sign SUCCESS (also meaning "I did it! Finally!") is commonly referred to as "Pah!" when used as an interjection, because it is often accompanied by both that mouth movement and that (unvoiced) sound when used in that sense.

Beyond being used to augment perception and comprehension of meaning for the producer, mouth movements can be used by the receiver for the purpose of providing conversational feedback without interruption while someone else is signing. Examples of this kind of mouthing include:

1. Rapid, repeated lower lip movement meaning, "interesting new perspective ... tell me more".
2. Rapidly repeated upper lip movement/nose twitch (sometimes with the lip drawn up in the corner) meaning "I understand, go on" or "Yeah, really!"
3. Pursed lips ("mm") accompanied by a slow affirmative head nod and "sad" eyes indicating sympathy or "That's really too bad/sad".

While these examples do not represent all of the functions of mouthing in ASL, they should be sufficient to demonstrate that mouth movements have particular grammatical and lexical functions within ASL. They serve as adverbial and adjectival modifiers, indicate relative time and space in ASL, occur regularly with or in place of certain lexical items, appear on the lips as partial spoken English words, and provide conversational feedback. In other sign languages as well, mouthings can serve to disambiguate signs, establish referents, and substitute for fingerspelling (Boyes Braem, 1990). The full range and implications of sign-mouthing combinations may not yet be clear, but there is enough evidence now to indicate that fluent, native users of ASL acquire the conventions of such linguistic devices early and naturally, and they communicate more efficiently with them than without them. Our observations and anecdotal evidence, meanwhile, suggest that facial expression and mouthings are some of the most difficult aspects of sign language to master as second language learners. To better understand what role mouth movements might play for this larger group of signers, therefore, we now turn to consideration of mouth movement during simultaneous communication (SC).

THE ROLE OF MOUTH MOVEMENT IN SIMULTANEOUS COMMUNICATION

SC is a method of communicating through the simultaneous use of speech with signs, fingerspelling, or both, so by definition, it requires mouth movement (Caccamise & Newell, 1984). As noted earlier, SC usually entails the combination of spoken English and signed English. Although it is not a language, per se (and if anything, it is a form of English, not sign language), some deaf adults who attended SC programs throughout their school years continue to use SC in their day-to-day interactions with colleagues and family, regardless of whether the latter are hearing or deaf. With increasing frequency, however, deaf people who were educated in "oralist" or SC programs are pursuing fluency in ASL and shift to an "ASL register" when conversing with others who are deaf. SC is still used for interactions with hearing families and with acquaintances who have not yet acquired sign fluency. In some cases where it is used by deaf individuals in conversations with hearing peers, SC might not actually be necessary; but many deaf people slip into SC out of habit when they are interacting with hearing people, even when the latter are fluent signers.

SC also can occur in conversations among deaf people and it is not necessary that a conversation be either completely SC or have no SC at all. Within any given interaction, producers can make use of SC for any period of time when they want to provide redundant linguistic codes. In theory, SC should be useful in settings that are visually or acoustically noisy, although most often its use is determined by either limitations in producers' skills or their perceptions of a particular receiver's skills. In either case, mouthing can serve any of several purposes. Most obviously, it provides a visual (verbal) representation of spoken English. In SC, speech and sign complement each other, and there is an implicit understanding that comprehension of the message requires the speech input (Maxwell & Bernstein, 1985). A good speechreader can take whatever is seen on the speaker's mouth, combine it with information from signs, gestures, facial expression, situational cues, and what pieces of a message can be heard and make some sense of it (Kaplan, Bally & Garretson, 1985). Clear and concise lip movements are perhaps the most critical element in this mix, according to both ratings provided by deaf educators (Stinson et al., 1992) and the frequency of effective communication (Mallery-Ruganis & Fischer, 1991).

Mouthing in SC also supports the mapping of meaning onto ambiguous signs. Unlike examples cited in the previous section, the disambiguating mouth movements in this case articulate English words. As noted earlier, single signs in ASL often have several English word interpretations (i.e. *manual homonymy*). Some of these cases involve interpretations that are relatively close, as in the sign NEED, which could be interpreted as "need", "should", "must", or "have to". Others are farther apart, as in the sign HOPE, which is identical to the word EXPECT despite the quite different meanings of the words for native English speakers. Within ASL, context or a single mouth movement will usually clarify which meaning of an ambiguous sign is intended (e.g. HOPE is sometimes accompanied by a rounded ["o"] mouth). Alternatively, it is possible that the structure of the lexicon for native users of ASL is sufficiently different from that of native users of English that such distinctions are irrelevant (see Marschark, McEvoy & Nelson, submitted). In any case, mouth movements associated with sign homonyms specify the producer's intent through the production of a single alternative, just as simultaneous availability of mouth movement can provide important support for comprehension of fingerspelling, especially for less-than-fluent signers.

Mouthing in SC can also function to mark verb inflections for tense and number. In ASL, for example, a head nod is used to express the present, present progressive, or a "state of being", whereas other tenses are marked either by specific signs (PAST or FINISH, WILL) or determined from context. In SC, inflection for number and past, present, and future tenses can be shown on the lips ("walked", "am walking", "will walk") when produced in conjunction with the sign WALK (FINISH-WALK, WALK, WALK-WILL).

SC can involve either voiced or unvoiced speech. Although there is not yet any detailed research on the factors that lead a producer to prefer one form or another (e.g. hearing status/loss of producer or receiver), it appears that the decision is based on the nature of the context (e.g. social versus educational situations) and producer–receiver familiarity. In the latter case, for example, voicing of SC often drops out of communication between members of a couple when they are alone, even if it is maintained when they are among others—whether or not those others are fluent signers. An even more reduced form of SC is seen in the tendency among SC users when they are not voicing to mouth only parts of words. Again, it is unclear when such reduction in mouthing occurs or whether there are any consistent parameters governing it. However, the benefits of adding the acoustic signal to a spoken message in SC are known to extend to almost all receivers, regardless of degree of hearing loss. Erber (1979), for example, reported an increase in speech reception of approximately 30–50% for speechreading plus sound over lipreading alone among individuals who had severe hearing losses and an increase of 1–15% for individuals with profound hearing losses.

In short, mouth movement is obligatory in SC, voicing is not. Although voicing is a significant, independent predictor of comprehension, mouthing alone serves several functions that serve to increase reception of sign language. The reverse is also true, of course, as signing increases the reception of spoken language. The question of which modality "needs" support will be determined by the producer's and the receiver's hearing status, their skills in signed and spoken communication, and features of the communication context. At a lower level of analysis, the relative contributions of speech and sign in SC will depend on the clarity and semantic uniqueness of individual linguistic units. While there has been considerable research concerning methods for improving communication reception in SC and in speechreading alone, the relative contributions of speech and signing during ongoing SC remains in need of clarification.

DISCUSSION

In the dawn of human communication, facial expression and direct action were at some point joined by pantomime, gesture, and vocal communication. It is not necessary here that we reach any conclusions about the relative contributions of gestural and gutteral communication to the eventual emergence of syntax and morphology. What is important is that whichever had the pre-eminent role (if either did), the two remain linked today in the interplay of manual and oral apparatus that are equally able to serve as language articulators. Manual and other gestures have been found to play an important role in the language productions of children and adults who are hearing or deaf (Marschark, 1994; McNeill, 1985, 1992), leading McNeill to suggest that gestures and speech are rooted in a common verbal system. Evidence of the sort presented here provides additional support for McNeill's hypothesis, demonstrating that the mouth and the rest of the vocal tract have semantic and syntactic functions even among individuals who do not use spoken language.

Examples described in this chapter provide evidence of mouth movement serving adverbial, adjectival, and pronominal functions during the production of ASL, as well as allowing the producer to provide emotional prosody-like highlighting to elaborate on a message. In some cases, mouthing is obligatory—particularly those cases where is it used to disambiguate manual homonyms—whereas in other cases, it replaces signs by serving to inflect nouns or verbs. At this point in the evolution of American Sign Language (ASL), some mouth movements have taken on stand-alone adverbial or adjectival status as reductions of signs with redundant information (e.g. the sign and puffed cheeks of FAT). Others are apparently more recent and more limited in their use (e.g. the raised corner of the mouth to indicate recency). There is yet an another class of mouth movements used by receivers to comment on ongoing signed productions (e.g. upper or lower lip twitches), the origins of which are not clear.

Unlike ASL, simultaneous communication (SC) requires mouth movement, by definition, and thus provides more examples as an object of study. The functions of mouthing within SC range from the obvious one of "supporting" less fluent sign language or spoken language skill to the more subtle use of mouthing to indicate tense or number. While SC (signed English and ASL signs) is a tool primarily intended to facilitate the learning of English among deaf children, its lack of language status has done little to reduce its use in a variety of conversational contexts. SC is used in facilitating communication between deaf and hearing individuals, one of whom is less than fluent in the primary language of the other, but it also serves more transient functions during ongoing ASL. Among hearing individuals who know ASL, one often sees signs included for emphasis, but whether these occurrences are accidental or intentionally creative incorporations remains to be seen.

The degree to which mouthing is used in ASL and SC is affected by several factors including degree of hearing loss, age of hearing loss onset, exposure primarily to spoken or signed language during childhood, sign language skill, spoken English skill, and reading ability. For both ASL and other sign languages, the linguistic privileges of occurrence for mouthing have been studied more than the individual differences that lead someone to use mouth movements more or less frequently. Meanwhile, some issues remain elusive. One question that we have not been able to answer is whether ASL has recently evolved to include more mouthing than in previous generations by native ASL signers. In viewing films from the early part of this century of George Veditz, a former president of the National Association of the Deaf, the almost total lack of mouth movement is striking. Was Veditz using some formal kind of "stage signing"? Would he have used mouth movements in social signing? Most of our older deaf informants, unfortunately, cannot remember whether their deaf relatives used mouthing frequently or not. However, we notice that older native signers who are both audiologically deaf and culturally Deaf tend to use less facial expression and fewer mouth movements than younger generations. This could be a reflection of the "oralist" movement in the education of deaf children during the middle part of this century in the United States, but it may indicate that Veditz's lack of mouthing is representative of "early" ASL.

Another issue in need of resolution concerns the partial mouthing of English words in signs like BORING, FINE, and HAVE. We can only speculate on whether they will become necessary components of those signs, perhaps eventually replacing them fully or in part. But, why these signs and not others? It has been observed that in both deaf and hearing children, mouthing occurs frequently in learning to read; and deaf children who are better readers appear to use mouth movement more often. Does this use reflect the impact of phonological decoding processes necessary for reading on expressive language or is there a confound with fluencies and preferences for English or ASL? It is clear that mouth movements and whole-word mouthings serve a number of different functions in sign language, both as a part of ASL and as essential component of SC. While many of these functions have been studied, even more questions remain, and we expect that many of these will be on central issues relating to the nature of language and its variation with language users.

ACKNOWLEDGEMENTS

We wish to thank Sam Holcomb for his demonstrations in Figures 38–52 and Mark Benjamin for his photographic assistance. Correspondence can be sent to any of the authors at the National Technical Institute for the Deaf, 52 Lomb Memorial Drive, Rochester, NY 14623, USA.

NOTES

1. Throughout this chapter, *English* will be used generically to refer to any spoken/written language. Similarly, *signed English* will be used generically to refer to the incorporation of the signs of a given sign language into the grammar of the vernacular. *ASL* will be used generically to refer to any natural sign language, such as British Sign Language (BSL) or Italian Sign Language (LIS). The interchangeability implicit in this last situation does not extend to artificial communication systems like signed English, SEE1, or SEE2, which do not entail the psycholinguistic assumptions of natural languages such as ASL, BSL, and LIS (for a discussion, see Marschark, 1997, Chapter 3). Finally, *communication* will be used to refer to most normal forms of face-to-face communication, ignoring issues related to less evanescent forms such as writing.
2. Upper-case "gloss" represents sign meanings.

REFERENCES

Armstrong, D.F., Stokoe, W.C. & Wilcox, S.E. (1995). *Gesture and the Nature of Language.* New York: Cambridge University Press.

Baker, C. & Cokely, D. (Eds) (1980). *American Sign Language: A Teacher's Resource Text on Grammar and Culture.* Silver Spring, MD: TJ Publishers.

Baker, C. & Padden, C. (1978). Focusing on the nonmanual components of ASL. In P. Siple (Ed.), *Understanding Language through Sign Language Research*. New York: Academic Press.

Baker-Shenck, C. (1983). A microanalysis of the non-manual components of questions in ASL. Unpublished PhD dissertation, University of California, Berkeley.

Bonvillian, J.D. & Folven, R.J. (1993). Sign language acquisition: Developmental aspects. In M. Marschark & M.D. Clark (Eds), *Psychological Perspectives on Deafness* (pp. 229–65). Hillsdale, NJ: Lawrence Erlbaum Associates.

Boyes Braem, P. (1990). *Einfüerung in die Gebäerdensprach und ihre Forschung*. Hamburg: Signum.

Bragg, L. (1997). Visual-kinetic communication in Europe before 1600: A survey of sign lexicons and finger alphabets prior to the rise of deaf education. *Journal of Deaf Studies and Deaf Education, 2*, 1–25.

Caccamise, F. & Newell, W. (1984). A review of current terminology used in deaf education and signing. *Journal of the Academy of Rehabilitative Audiology, 17*, 106–29.

Ebbinghaus, H. & Hessmann, J. (1996). Signs and words: Accounting for spoken elements in German sign language. *International Review of Sign Linguistics, 1*, 23–56.

Edelman, G.M. (1992). *Brilliant Air, Brilliant Fire*. New York: Basic Books.

Erber, N.P. (1979). Auditory-visual perception of speech with reduced optical clarity. *Journal of Speech and Hearing Research, 22*, 212–23.

Feyereisen, P. & de Lannoy, J.-D. (1991). *Gestures and Speech: Psychological Investigations*. Cambridge: Cambridge University Press.

Fischer, S., & Forman, J. (1980). Causative Constructions in ASL. Paper presented at the Annual Meeting of the Linguistic Society of America. San Antonio, TX.

Gray, G.W. & Wise, C.M. (1959). *The Bases of Speech (Third Edition)*. New York: Harper & Row.

Hickok, G., Bellugi, U. & Klima, E.S. (1996). The neurobiology of sign language and its implications for the neural basis of language. *Nature, 381*, 699–702.

Kaplan, H., Bally, S. & Garretson, C. (1985). *Speechreading: A Way to Improve Understanding*. Washington, DC: Gallaudet College Press.

Kimura, D. (1975). The neural basis of language qua gesture. In H. Avakian-Whitaker & H.A. Whitaker (Eds), *Studies in Neurolinguistics* (pp. 145–56). New York: Academic Press.

Kimura, D. (1981). Neural mechanisms in manual signing. *Sign Language Studies, 33*, 291–312.

Lidell, S. (1986). Head thrust in ASL conditional marking. *Sign Language Studies, 52*, 243–62.

Lillo-Martin, D. (1997). The modular effects of sign language acquisition. In M. Marschark, P. Siple, D. Lillo-Martin, R. Campbell, and V.S. Everhart (Eds), *Relations of Language and Thought: The View from Sign Language and Deaf Children*. New York: Oxford University Press.

McIntire, M.L. & Snitzer Reilly, J. (1988). Nonmanual Behaviors in L1 & L2 Learners of American Sign Language. *Sign Language Studies, 61*, 351–375.

McNeill, D. (1985). So you think gestures are nonverbal? *Psychological Review, 92*, 350–71.

McNeill, D. (1992). *Hand and Mind*. Chicago: University of Chicago Press.

Mallery-Ruganis, D. & Fischer, S. (1991). Characteristics that contribute to effective simultaneous communication. *American Annals of the Deaf, 136*, 401–408.

Marschark, M. (1994). Gesture and sign. *Applied Psycholinguistics, 15*, 209–36.

Marschark, M. (1997). *Growing up Deaf*. New York: Oxford University Press.

Marschark, M., McEvoy, C. & Nelson, D. (submitted). Structure of the mental lexicon for sound-related and sound-unrelated concepts in deaf and hearing individuals.

Marschark, M., Siple, P., Lillo-Martin, D., Campbell, R. & Everhart, V.S. (1997). *Relations of Language and Thought: The View from Sign Language and Deaf Children*. New York: Oxford University Press.

Maxwell, M. & Bernstein, M. (1985). The synergy of sign and speech in simultaneous communication. *Applied Psycholinguistics, 6,* 63–82.

Mayer, C. & Wells, G. (1996). Can the linguistic interdependence theory support a bilingual-bicultural model of literacy education for deaf students? *Journal of Deaf Studies and Deaf Education, 1,* 93–107.

Meier, R.P. & Newport, E.L. (1990). Out of the hands of babes: On a possible sign advantage in language acquisition. *Language, 66,* 1–23.

Padden, C. & Humphries, T. (1988). *Deaf in America: Voices from a Culture.* Cambridge, MA: Harvard University Press.

Paget, R. (1930). *Human Speech.* New York: Harcourt, Brace & Company.

Rodda, M. & Grove, C. (1987). *Language, Cognition, and Deafness.* Hillsdale, NJ: Lawrence Erlbaum Associates.

Schermer, T. (1990). *In Search of Language: Influences from Spoken Dutch on Sign Language of the Netherlands.* Delft: Eburon.

Siple, P. (1997). Universals, generalizability, and the acquisition of signed language. In Marschark, M., Siple, P., Lillo-Martin, D., Campbell, R. & Everhart, V.S. (Eds), *Relations of Language and Thought: The View from Sign Language and Deaf Children.* New York: Oxford University Press.

Stinson, M., Newell, W., Castle, D., Mallery-Ruganis, D. & Holcomb, B.R. (1992). Deaf professionals' view on the importance of features of simultaneous communication. *Journal of Rehabilitative Audiology, 33,* 621–7.

Tzeng, O.J.L. & Wang, W.S.-Y. (1984). Search for a common neurocognitive mechanism for language and movements. *American Journal of Physiology, 246,* R904–R911.

Vogt-Svendsen, M. (1983). Positions and movements of the mouth in Norwegian sign language (NSL). In J.G. Kyle & B. Woll (Eds), *Language in Sign: An International Perspective on Sign Language* (pp. 85–96). London: Croom Helm.

CHAPTER FOURTEEN

Touch and auditory-visual speech perception

Michael Oerlemans and Peter Blamey Department of Otolaryngology, University of Melbourne, Parkville, Victoria, Australia

INTRODUCTION

Our understanding of auditory-visual speech perception has reached a stage where the cognitive issues surrounding bimodal perception of hearing and lipreading are relatively well defined. Current debates focus on whether this integration is early (that is before categorisation) or late (after phonetic categorisation), whether lipreading and hearing are encoded in an auditory or amodal code, and whether this code is a prototype representation (Massaro, 1987), an articulatory-gesture (Liberman & Mattingly, 1985) or a direct representation of articulation (Fowler, 1986). One of the main impacts of this debate has been to centralise the notion of speech perception as being multisensory; speech perception is not simply an auditory pheno-menon.

Concurrent with the research in auditory-visual speech perception has been the increasing interest in tactile perception. Generally, the research has focused on defining the structure and characteristics of particular modes of tactile perception (Chomsky, 1986) or the processing parameters of parti-cular tactile prosthetic devices (Clements, Durlach & Braida, 1982) rather than the place of tactile perception in more general speech perception issues (although, see Fowler & Dekle, 1991, for a notable exception). Our interest over the past few years has been the tactile perception of speech; particularly the way speech information from the tactile modality is combined with hearing and lipreading. There is little work available on the psycholinguistics of tactile speech perception. Thus, one aim of our work has been to consider auditory-visual integration as a paradigm case and to use this as a basis for considering tactile speech perception. In this chapter, we are primarily concerned with:

1. The nature of the relationship between hearing and lipreading.
2. What tactile information has in common with these modalities.
3. What evidence there is that tactile information interacts with sight and sound in the same common code.

Our conclusions are necessarily tentative. However, it seems that tactile speech accesses the same kinds of cognitive structures as hearing and lipreading. The extent and nature of combinatorial advantage depends on the relationship of tactile information to hearing and lipreading.

TACTILE PERCEPTION

Tactile perception is not a unitary domain. One way of considering the range of tactile alternatives is the taxonomy presented in Figure 53. Tactile perception is broadly divided into speech- and language-based codes. What we have called language codes encode modes of language which are not directly based on articulation. Global codes, such as tactile versions of sign language, are word- and phrase-based. Molecular codes, such as manual communication, are based on written rather than spoken English. Each of these codes bears some relationship to articulation, but somewhat indirectly.

In contrast, speech-based codes directly encode articulation. TADOMA is a system of tactile perception where the perceiver feels the shapes of the senders'' face. The TADOMA-user places a hand over the face of the speaker with the fingers making contact with the cheeks, lips and throat. Tactile information about the arrangement of the articulators, the passage of airflow and the resonance of the vocal tract is used to achieve perception. The information perceived is not acoustic, but articulatory. It is a non-spectral code because it encodes a direct articulatory signal rather than a signal mediated by acoustic information. As such, it has much in common with lipreading. The spectral codes, including electro-tactile and vibro-tactile prostheses, encode articulation mediated by an acoustic signal. The speaker generates an utterance which is converted into a tactile pattern felt on the skin. The tactile pattern ideally represents the fluctuations of the acoustic waveform produced by the actions of the articulators.

The final distinction, between electrical and vibratory devices, refers to the type of stimulation produced. Vibro-tactile devices transmit the information mechanically; vibratory pads oscillate in response to the speech parameters encoded. Electro-tactile devices provide a tactile sensation by

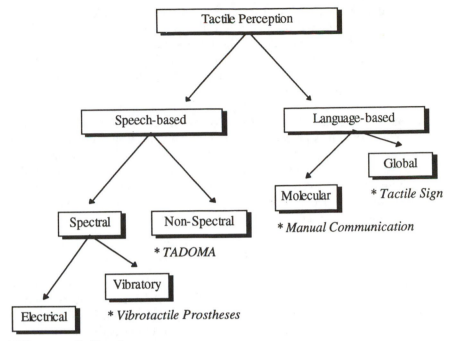

FIG. 53.   A taxonomy for tactile speech perception with selected examples.

means of an electrical current passed through the skin. Although vibro-tactile and electro-tactile devices produce tactile sensations that differ in quality on several perceptual dimensions, it is unlikely that they differ greatly in their potential to convey speech information. However, the speech processing approach adopted, independent of the type of tactile sensation produced, may have implications for the amount and kind of speech information available. Vibratory and electrical prostheses either adopt a feature extraction or bandpass approach. A bandpass approach analyses one or more bands of acoustic information deriving information about amplitude and frequency which are presented directly to the stimulators on the skin. Feature extraction approaches analyse the incoming signal for information about formant frequencies and amplitudes.

The brief descriptions just given highlight a range of variations in tactile signals. These variations have implications for cognitive models of percep-tion. The particular concern of this chapter is with spectral approaches. The device we have most experience with is the Tickle Talker[TM], an electro-tactile device. A microphone converts the acoustic signal into an electrical waveform. This waveform is processed to provide a number of parameters for stimulation on the skin. Like heard speech, and unlike, for example, Morse code, the stimulation is continuous, complex and time-varying. Eight electrodes, located on the sides of the fingers pulsate at rates over 150 cps. The University of Melbourne Tickle Talker uses a feature extraction approach to encode amplitude, fundamental frequency and second formant frequency; amplitude of the signal is coded as intensity of stimulation, fundamental frequency as rate of pulse transmission and second formant information as spatial location of stimulation across the eight electrodes used. Thus, speech is perceived as an array of rapid pulses changing over time and varying in place on the hand. The phenomenological impression is one of gradients of roughness and movements across the fingers. Studies have indicated relatively good multisensory performance is able to be achieved using the Tickle Talker in combination with (residual) hearing and lipreading (Cowan et al., 1987; Blamey et al., 1988).

INTEGRATION

Tactile prosthetic information, at a first glance, is inherently speech-like. This similarity with speech and the fact that the device will most often be used by hearing-impaired populations in conjunction with residual hearing and lipreading means that there are important practical as well as theoretical reasons for understanding how tactile speech may combine with heard and lipread speech. Tactile speech at some level needs to be reconciled with information coming from the residual hearing and lipreading of the perceiver. All studies of tactile speech perception need to include explicit training procedures to familiarise the subjects with the tactile representation of speech. If tactile information cannot be combined with auditory-visual speech, if in fact it competes with this information, it may be more effective to train users of the device unimodally. If tactile and auditory-visual information can be combined, then a training program which exploits the relationships between tactile and auditory-visual speech may be more effective. The question of tactile integration also bears on questions of speech perception generally. Speech perception is multisensory and, as such, theories of speech perception need to be able to accommodate speech input in all its varieties or provide reasons for exclusions.

Integration of information can occur at a number of perceptual levels. Traditionally, information-processing models have defined a number of levels of analysis including feature, phoneme, syllable, word and sentence levels, although models vary as to which of these levels may be psychologically relevant. As a matter of argument, information from different modalities could be integrated at any of these levels. For example, signing and audition both allow word-level identification. Identification of a word presumes access to semantic and syntactic information about the word, so to some extent, at the level of semantic access, signing and audition have an integrated representation. Typically, however, the focus is on integration which occurs before word identification. Recent models of integration have distinguished early- and late-integration models (Vroomen, 1992).

According to Vroomen (1992) early integration occurs before phonetic categorisation. Models such as Summerfield's (1987) vocal-tract filter function or the direct-realist model of Fowler (1986) are examples of early-integration models. Information from each modality contributes to the identification of a phonetic representation. In Summerfield's model, for example, acoustic and optical signals are combined into a common metric. This common metric possesses the information from which word identification can be made. Late-integration models, on the other hand, assume that information from each modality is categorised separately and then a combined representation is formed. Massaro's (1987) Fuzzy Logical Model of Perception (FLMP) asserts that feature values are assigned to auditory and visual contributions to speech perception. These feature values are given a truth value which represents the degree to which a feature conforms to an abstract prototype. For example, auditory and visual contributions to the perception of /ba/ would each represent a degree of "ba-ness" (and a lesser degree of "va-ness", "da-ness" and so on). A match between the feature values for this instance of /ba/ and a prototypical representation of /ba/ yields a measure of goodness-of-fit. If the goodness-of-fit for the prototype /ba/ is greater than that for all other prototypes, /ba/ is perceived.

However, the use of the terms "early" and "late" may be misleading. Positing late integration presumes that integration can occur earlier for a given model. This is not always the case. For example, the only point at which integration can occur in the FLMP is after phonetic categorisation. Perhaps a better description is the more traditional pre-categorical and post-categorical integration.

Tactile speech may be combined with heard and lipread speech pre-categorically, post-categorically or not at all. First, let us consider the case of pre-categorical integration. Tactile speech generates a stimulation pattern on the skin, which corresponds to the sounds, syllables and words produced. This tactile pattern is akin to the auditory mechanical vibrations in the cochlea or the optical stimulation patterns in the eye. In a pre-categorical integration formulation these stimulation patterns are associated with an abstract amodal cognitive representation. Candidates for this representation might be a vocal tract filter function, specifying the source characteristics of the waveform, that is glottal pulses and vocal tract resonances (Summerfield, 1987), or a more general articulatory description (Fowler, 1986). In contrast, post-categorical integration models suggest that an initial analysis of the speech signal is made, usually in terms of features, which contribute to a combined representation (e.g. as in Masaro's FLMP). Tactile information also has the potential to be analysed into a number of tactual features which could then be incorporated into this prototype. That is, each of the level of integration hypotheses could potentially account for tactile speech perception.

However, it may be the case that tactile input is processed in a totally different way from heard and lipread input. Hearing and lipreading are natural codes, available, and probably utilised (Kuhl and Meltzoff, 1984), from early infancy. Tactile speech perception must be taught. Tactile training may necessitate the building of entirely novel representations which are used exclusively for tactile perception. That is, information from the tactile sense may not be combined with other input until a word is identified. The discussion is further complicated by the possibility of differences in the nature of encoding by inexperienced and experienced users. For example, inexperienced users may utilise tactile representations but, given a sufficient amount of experience, may begin to link in this tactile input with available non-modality specific information.

The rest of this discussion will focus on the evidence suggesting that tactile speech perception utilises existing speech information in contrast to the position that tactile speech perception is accomplished through the formulation of a novel and independent representation. There are good theoretical and empirical grounds for suggesting that tactile speech accesses sublexical auditory-visual speech representations.

COMBINING HEARING AND LIPREADING

Hearing and lipreading develop naturally with no direct instruction or tuition. Lipreading ability, in fact, is difficult to teach and learn (Summerfield, 1991) and correlates poorly with a range of perceptual and cognitive abilities (Farwell, 1976). Further, a number of studies have shown that infants as young as four months orient to visually occurring speech information (see Burnham, this volume). On the other hand, tactile speech perception is explicitly taught, although it is not clear whether given a tactile device early enough, individuals might naturally develop tactile perceptual skill. However, to the extent that tactile speech stimuli are a contrived code, integration with other natural codes may not occur.

Hearing encodes articulation mediated by an acoustic waveform while lipreading encodes articulation more directly, by virtue of the visual parameters of articulation such as lip-opening, jaw movement and more general facial transitions. Hearing and lipreading are, therefore, temporally synchronised. Pauses, timing and duration are available both auditorially and visually. Information about manner, place and voicing are available in both modalities, although manner and voicing information are more poorly represented in lipreading. Tactile information provided by electro-tactile and vibro-tactile devices also encode articulation: the acoustic waveform is recoded into a tactile pattern with the temporal speech parameters preserved. These fundamental similarities may allow integration of tactile information with heard and lipread speech.

This temporal concordance has further implications for integration. One of the earliest accounts of the similarities between auditory and visual speech perception, is the changing-state hypothesis (Campbell & Dodd, 1980; Campbell, Dodd & Brasher, 1983). This hypothesis suggests that heard and lipread speech are able to be combined because they both represent temporal information changing over time. In contrast, other visual codes, such as writing or sign language, are spatially organised structures. Campbell and Dodd argue that integration only occurs when both signals change in state over time. Campbell, Dodd and Brasher (1983) showed that auditory-like recency was greater for moving as opposed to still hand signs. Further, the recall of lists of visually presented digits showed recency effects when the digits were revealed in a changing display over time (Crowder, 1986). It is not known whether tactile information shows recency effects akin to hearing and lipreading, although one might expect that it does. Tactile information does vary in time. Generally, the stimulator presents continuous information varying with the frequency and amplitude of the incoming signal. The perceiver has access not only to absolute information about where stimulation occurs and how intense it is but also to information about changing patterns of stimulation and movements from one region of the hand to the other.

Another of the key characteristics of the relationship between hearing and lipreading is its complementarity. Lipreading encodes place of information well and manner less well. Under conditions where hearing is degraded by noise as where there is hearing loss, place of information is eroded whereas manner information tends to be preserved. Therefore, in bimodal perception, lipreading may supplement information which is absent in auditory unimodal perception (Miller & Nicely, 1955). One of the main problems with the complementarity thesis, however, is that under normal perceptual conditions, hearing and lipreading are not complementary. When the auditory channel is clear, hearing can provide all the information necessary for perception. No perceptual advantage is provided by the addition of lipreading.

The complementarity thesis emphasizes two points. The first is about the information available. Hearing is able to encode a complete representation of a stimulus. Under clear listening conditions, information about duration, place, manner and voicing are all available auditorially. At a feature level, each phoneme is able to be uniquely specified. In contrast, lipreading, even under the best conditions, is only able to encode partial information. Even trained perceivers can only distinguish 9 consonant visemes (Walden et al.,

1977) compared to the 26 consonants in Australian-English. Considering phonemes in terms of features, lipreading results in an under-specification which allows confusions between consonants available auditorially. This partial/complete relationship, however, may be one of the reasons why hearing and lipreading are able to be combined effectively.

On the other hand, complementarity is not a thesis about partialness, but about the relative weight of information from both sources. Relative weight may vary according to external conditions such as noise. Relative weight may also have an impact when the overall stimulus is ambiguous. In an ambiguous situation, the relatively greater weight of place information for lipreading may bias auditory perception. Auditory-visual fusion phenomena (MacDonald & McGurk, 1978; Campbell et al., 1990) provide an instance where the partial information of lipreading and the greater weight of place information interact to bias a percept away from what is heard. For example, when presented with a mouth-shape corresponding to /ga/ and an acoustic form corresponding to /ba/, the syllable perceived may be /da/. The overall stimulus is ambiguous because the heard information suggests a fronted stop, whereas visual information suggests a back consonant. The visual information is only partial: /ga/ and /da/ are equally possible alternatives. The auditory information is complete, however, because the overall stimulus is ambiguous, relatively less weight is given to the place information. The combined percept /da/ is, therefore, to some extent, consistent with both the auditory and the visual information available.

Summerfield (1987) suggests that a simple visual-place, auditory-manner hypothesis is untenable given its inability to explain "reverse" McGurk effects. That is, when heard /ga/ is paired with seen /ba/, subjects do not perceive /ba/ but a combination of consonants /bga/. However, in the formulation just given, both auditory and visual sources would provide unambiguous information so the only alternative is a cluster, rather than a fusion. That is, both hearing and vision specify relatively complete articulatory descriptions. The overall stimulus is not ambiguous, rather conflicting.

Partialness is more a continuum in natural spoken language than a discrete category. The notions of partialness and complementarity interact. Table 13 presents some data drawn from a paper by Blamey and Clark (1988), which illustrates this interaction. They investigated interactions between auditory, visual and tactile speech information. Four normally hearing subjects were trained for over 70 hours using the Tickle Talker. They were tested on vowel, consonant and word perception using closed set tasks in each of the modalities, separately and in combination. In order to approximate the results of hearing impaired subjects, the auditory information was degraded by the use of a low-pass filter and the addition of

TABLE 13

The percentage of information transmitted for selected phonetic features in closed set vowel and consonant tasks (after Blamey & Clark, 1988). The data was obtained from an 11 item vowel perception task, a 12 item consonant perception task and a 12 word monosyllable perception task. The predicted values were calculated using an equation which assumes each modality independently contributes a proportion of the information and an error occurs in the combined modality only if the speech feature is incorrectly perceived in each separate modality

| | | *Observed* | | | *Observed—predicted* | |
	Visual	*Tactile*	*Auditory*	*AV*	*AT*	*VT*
Vowels						
Duration	71	49	91	3	1	−4
F1	76	28	33	1	−12	−2
F2	75	51	24	1	−13	−8
Consonants						
Voicing	7	11	79	11	−3	−2
Nasality	27	43	91	7	5	−10
Affrication	70	29	66	5	−6	8
Duration	58	80	38	20	−14	−11
Place	80	20	15	1	−9	−4
Visibility	100	12	24	0	−4	0
A_0	24	25	84	8	−4	−7
High F2	74	59	27	3	−18	−6

white noise. The results were analysed for the percentage of information transmitted, calculated using the method described by Miller and Nicely (1955). Values for visibility (i.e. ease of speechreading) and amplitude information were estimated using a similar method. This was calculated for the unimodal and combined conditions.

Consider first the tactile and visual data in the unimodal conditions. Tactile and lipread stimuli both represent all features to some degree. Clearly, however, some features are represented much more strongly than others. Tactile information represents duration particularly well, and voicing, place and visibility poorly, with all other features occurring around the 30–40% level. Lipreading, on the other hand, represents voicing and some aspects of manner poorly, whereas place perception is good. Both modalities are relatively partial. The third column represents auditory information degraded by the use of low-pass filtering and the addition of noise. Hearing and lipreading are complementary to the extent that features represented poorly by audition tend to be represented well by speechreading. Tactile information with this particular device tends to be like heard information with respect to place information for consonants and vowel features, but not for the representation of duration and some features of manner. As a general statement, then, tactile information is complementary with lip-reading in terms of place perception and some aspects of manner. Tactile information is redundant with hearing in terms of place perception and some aspects of manner.

To summarise: tactile information is structurally similar to auditory and lipread information. Tactile speech prostheses encode articulation. The articulatory information is mediated by an acoustic waveform. This is recoded in a continuous, time-varying spatio-temporal array presented to the skin. Tactile stimuli tend to be partial like lipreading (i.e. speech features are not always reliably perceived). Unlike lipreading, tactile information tends to be redundant with respect to audition. By contrast, lipreading is complementary with both hearing and tactile speech perception.

COMBINING TOUCH WITH HEARING AND VISION

These arguments suggest that we should find good integration of tactile information with lipreading. Similar information is provided by currently available vibro-tactile devices and degraded audition. Consequently, while integration of hearing and touch should occur, the potential combinatorial advantage may be less. Although some aspects of the signal are likely to be better specified, the combined signal does not provide all the information required to identify a phoneme.

Blamey and Clark's (1988) combined results are shown in the last three columns of Table 13. Predicted values were obtained from the unimodal results using a simple formula, which assumes that an error occurs in the combined modality only if a speech feature is incorrectly perceived in both individual modalities. For example, in the case of auditory-visual combination, the proportion of information transmitted (I) in the auditory-visual combination (AV) was predicted as a function of the information in auditory-alone (A) and visual alone (V) conditions:

$$1-I_{AV} = (1-I_A)(1-I_V).$$

The model fit is reasonably good: in most cases, predicting the observed percentage of information transmitted to within a few percent. However, there are consistent differences between the modality combinations. The model underestimates the combined auditory-visual results and overestimates the results for the auditory-tactile and visuo-tactile combinations. This suggests that tactile information is combined less effectively with auditory or visual information than auditory and visual information with each other. Further, the mean difference between predicted and observed values is greatest for the auditory-tactile combination which is the most redundant combination. It is least for the auditory-visual combinations and somewhat greater for visuo-tactile combinations. Although visuo-tactile combination is not as effective as the combination of hearing and lipreading, it is better than combining hearing and touch. It is suggested that one reason for the superior combination is the complementarity of tactile speech with lipreading.

In general terms, the data from this study are consistent with the hypothesis that tactile information can be integrated into a multisensory speech perception process on a similar footing to auditory and visual information. The partial/complete and complementary/redundant characteristics of the relationship help us to understand the relative effectiveness of the particular combination.

THE EFFECTS OF TRAINING ON TACTILE PERCEPTION

The tactile data just reported were derived from subjects trained in the tactile perception of speech in combination with lipreading. It may be that the combination advantage is a direct result of the training approach used. Bimodal training, irrespective of the modalities involved or their relationship, may result in improvements in quality and quantity of bimodal performance. One way to directly investigate this is to consider the effect of different types of training approaches on perceptual improvement. For example, if bimodal training of auditory and tactile information results in greater improvement than an equivalent amount of unimodal training, it could reflect an improvement in the utilisation of information from each individual modality and/or improvement in the utilisation of combined information (i.e. the skill with which information from two separate modalities is combined).

A study of auditory-tactile training by Alcantara, Blamey and Clark (1993) found that bimodally trained subjects experienced no advantage over subjects trained unimodally. In fact, the unimodally trained subjects did somewhat better than the bimodally trained subjects on measures of vowel and consonant performance. The data are consistent with the suggestion that training method is not a factor in auditory-tactile integration. In fact integration appears to occur automatically. This may be a consequence of the redundancy of auditory and tactile information which implies that there is nothing "extra" to be gained by bimodal training.

The converse of this possible interpretation of the data is that complementary combinations (e.g. visuo-tactile combination) may be improved more by bimodal training than by unimodal training. In a recent study, we investigated this directly by comparing a group trained unimodally for 6 hours in tactile perception and 6 hours in visual perception, and a group trained bimodaly for 12 hours on visuo-tactile perception. In a third bimodal (cued) group, subjects were exposed to a bimodal signal, but were simply asked to attend to one or the other condition. This was to counter suggestions that any bimodal improvement was simply the result of more exposure time to each modality rather than the nature of the training.

There was no difference in the perception of consonants between the three groups. However, the bimodally trained subjects showed greater improvements than the unimodally trained subjects on the perception of some vowel features in words. Table 14 shows the mean performance before and after training on two vowel features: duration and first formant frequency. Improvements in perception occurred for the bimodally trained group, but not for the unimodally trained group. Moreover, improvement is not simply the result of more training time in the bimodally trained group. The cued group, like the unimodal group, showed no training improvement. The results are consistent with the idea that bimodal training is required to improve integration of information from complementary modalities.

The differences between auditory-tactile, visuo-tactile and auditory-visual stimuli appear to be larger for vowel stimuli than for consonant stimuli. Differences in improvement over the course of visuo-tactile training were found on measures of vowel perception rather than consonant perception. The finding that vowel features seem to fit with the proposals regarding complementarity and redundancy better than for consonant features may arise from training differences or from the inherent physical properties of vowels.

TABLE 14

Visuo-tactile training data: vowel duration and first formant frequency from the CNC word perception task. The numbers refer to the percentage correct perception of a feature. Standard errors are included in brackets. Pre-/post-training differences which are significant at the .02 level are indicated by an asterisk

| | Percentage correct for features: means and standard deviations | | | |
| | Vowel duration | | Vowel first formant frequency | |
Training approach	Pre-training	Post-training	Pre-training	Post-training
Bimodal	60.8	67.2*	63.0	70.2*
	(8.1)	(7.6)	(10.5)	(11.4)
Bimodal (cued)	68.8	62.5	65.7	63.7
	(6.5)	(7.4)	(8.7)	(12.0)
Unimodal	70.6	68.3	74.4	70.5
	(5.4)	(4.4)	(8.0)	(8.0)

DISCUSSION AND TENTATIVE CONCLUSIONS

There is considerable work yet to be undertaken in tactile speech perception, however, the results are intriguing. Multisensory speech perception exploits the structural and featural characteristics of the modalities to be combined. Auditory and tactile information are able to be integrated because they represent similar sorts of information, albeit encoded by different sensory modalities. The partialness of tactile information and its redundancy allows it to be integrated with auditory and visual information at a sublexical stage. The complementarity of tactile speech with lipreading creates a greater combinatorial advantage than for touch and hearing. The whole combined signal is greater than the sum of its parts. The utilisation of this combined information is improved by specific bimodal training. By analogy, the integration of heard and lipread information is not simply the result of its complementarity. When auditory and visual information conflict, as in the McGurk effect (MacDonald & McGurk, 1978), the partialness of lipreading results in novel perceptions. In normal consistent perception, it is both the redundancy of aspects of each signal and the complementarity of hearing and lipreading overall, which results in an integrated percept. Tactile information also seems to have access to this same common store when trained in isolation. Improvements in tactile-alone performance result in improvements in performance when combined with hearing or lipreading. This combined improvement could simply reflect improvements in tactile perception, without improving auditory perception. The appropriate comparison, that is comparing the level of improvement for auditory-tactile and visuo-tactile training, has not yet been done, however, the arguments suggest that visuo-tactile improvement will be greater than auditory-tactile improvement given the same amount of training over the same period of time.

SUMMARY

The simplest explanation of tactile speech perception using prosthetic devices would suggest that tactile input accesses existing speech representations. Tactile input possesses structural characteristics consistent with both auditory and visual input which would allow such access.

Analysis of the nature of auditory-visual speech perception suggests that visual partialness and auditory-visual complementarity provide the necessary pre-conditions for integration. By analogy, visual-tactile integration should be superior to auditory-tactile integration. Although the amount of available research is limited, our investigations suggest this to be so. Tactile input combines with lipreading because it is like auditory information in terms of a key aspect of its subphonemic structure; it is complementary. Tactile input can result in combined performance improvements.

Consequently, profoundly hearing-impaired users of tactile devices are likely to gain more information from lipreading than residual hearing when combined with a tactile prosthesis. Combined visuo-tactile training should be more efficient and effective than unimodal training. However, the evidence is limited. Further research investigation of tactile prosthetic perception would not only have benefits for our understanding of alternative modes of speech perception, but also of auditory-visual speech perception and what makes hearing and lipreading special.

REFERENCES

Alcantara, J.I., Blamey, P.J. & Clark, G.M. (1993). Tactile-auditory speech perception by unimodally and bimodally trained normally-hearing subjects. *Journal of the American Academy of Audiology, 4,* 98–108.

Blamey, P.J. & Clark, G.M. (1988). Combining Tactile, Auditory and Visual Information for Speech Perception. *Proceedings of the 2nd Conference of the Australian Speech Science and Technology Association Conference.* Sydney, November, 392–5.

Blamey, P.J., Cowan, R.S.C., Alcantara, J.I. & Clark, G.M. (1988). Phonemic information transmitted by a multichannel electrotactile speech processor. *Journal of Speech and Hearing Research, 31,* 620–29.

Campbell, R. & Dodd, B. (1980). Hearing by eye. *Quarterly Journal of Experimental Psychology, 32,* 85–99.

Campbell, R., Dodd, B. & Brasher, J. (1983). The sources of visual recency. *Quarterly Journal of Experimental Psychology, 35a,* 581–7.

Campbell, R., Garwood, J., Franklin, S., Howard, D., Landis, T., & Regard, M. (1990). Neuropsychological studies of auditory-visual fusion illusions. Four case studies and their implications. *Neuropsychologia, 28,* 787–802.

Chomsky, C. (1986). Analytic study of the Tadoma method: Language abilities of three deaf-blind subjects. *Journal of Speech and Hearing Research, 29,* 332–47.

Clements, M.A., Durlach, N.I. & Braida, L.D. (1982). Tactile communication of speech: Comparison of two spectral displays in a vowel discrimination task. *Journal of the Acoustical Society of America, 72,* 1135–7.

Cowan, R.S.C., Alcantara, J.I., Blamey, P.J. & Clark, J.M. (1987). Interim results of open-set speech discrimination with a wearable multichannel electrotactile speech processor. *Journal of the Acoustical Society of America, 82(4),* 1987, 1456–7.

Crowder, R.G. (1986). Auditory and temporal factors in the modality effect. *Journal of Experimental Psychology: Learning, Memory and Cognition, 12,* 269–79.

Farwell, R.M. (1976). Speech reading: A research review. *American Annals of the Deaf, 121,* 19–30.

Fowler, C.A. (1986). An event approach to the study of speech perception from a direct-realist perspective. *Journal of Phonetics, 14,* 3–28.

Fowler, C.A. & Dekle, D.J. (1991). Listening with eye and hand: Cross-modal contributions to speech perception. *Journal of the Acoustical Society of America, 89,* 2910–15.

Kuhl, P.K. & Meltzoff, A.N. (1984). The intermodal representation of speech in infants. *Infant Behavior and Development, 7,* 361–81.

Liberman, A.M. & Mattingly, I.G. (1985). The motor theory of speech perception revised. *Cognition, 21,* 1–36.

MacDonald, J. & McGurk, H. (1978). Visual influences on speech perception processes. *Perception and Psychophysics, 24(3),* 253–7.

Massaro, D.W. (1987). *Speech Perception by Ear and Eye: A Paradigm for Psychological Inquiry*. Hillsdale, NJ: Lawrence Erlbaum Associates Inc.

Miller, G.A. & Nicely, P.E. (1955). An analysis of perceptual confusions among some English consonants. *Journal of the Acoustical Society of America, 27(2)*, 338–52.

Summerfield, A.Q. (1987). Some preliminaries to a comprehensive account of auditory-visual speech perception. In B. Dodd and R. Campbell (Eds), *Hearing by Eye: The Psychology of Lipreading* (pp. 3–51). Hove, UK: Lawrence Erlbaum Associates Ltd.

Summerfield, A.Q. (1991). Visual perception of phonetic gestures. In I.G. Mattingly and M. Studdert-Kennedy (Eds), *Modularity and the Motor Theory of Speech Perception: Proceedings of a Conference to Honor Alvin M. Liberman* (pp. 117–38). Hillsdale, NJ: Lawrence Erlbaum Associates.

Vroomen, J.H.M. (1992). Hearing voices and seeing lips: investigations in the psychology of lipreading. Unpublished PhD Thesis, Katholieke Universiteit Brabant.

Walden, B.E., Prosek, R.A., Montgomery, A.A., Scherr, C.K. & Jones, C.J. (1977). Effects of training on the visual recognition of consonants. *Journal of Speech and Hearing Research, 20*, 130–45.

CHAPTER FIFTEEN

The effect of exposure to phonetically augmented lipspeech in the prelingual deaf

Jacqueline Leybaert, Jésus Alegria, Catherine Hage and Brigitte Charlier Laboratoire de Psychologie Expérimentale, Université Libre de Bruxelles, Brussels, Belgium

INTRODUCTION

From their second year onwards, children born profoundly deaf generally exhibit deficiencies across the board in all activities involving phonological representations based on speech: speech perception and production, oral language development, metaphonological abilities, immediate memory for ordered linguistic stimuli, reading and spelling. This is true not only for children mainly exposed to spoken language, but also for children of deaf parents, for whom sign language is the primary linguistic input. Thus, these underachievements may not be ascribed to a lack of linguistic experience per se. Nor are they due to cognitive deficiences: deaf children are normally intelligent and have at birth the same potential for learning as hearing children. Nor can the visual modality through which they perceive language be responsible. Deaf children exposed to sign language develop, through vision, linguistic competence in sign very similar to that of hearing children in oral language. The most likely explanation, therefore, lies in the under-specified nature of the phonological information deaf children perceive through lipreading.

It is now widely recognised that lip movements involved in the production of speech are automatically processed by hearing persons in normal conditions of listening. The fact that visual speech information influences the automatic processing of auditory information (McGurk & MacDonald, 1976) has led to the conclusion that the lipread signal is dealt with by the brain in a way similar to the auditory signal. These effects compelled theorists to give up the view that speech perception is a purely auditory phenomenon and to postulate that it is bimodal, taking into account both the acoustic and the lipread information (Liberman & Mattingly, 1985; Green, this volume). This suggests that hearing people develop abstract phonological representations, accessible through lipread as well as through acoustic information. The basis for the development of amodal, perceptual representations of speech may occur during the first weeks of life (Kuhl & Meltzoff, 1982; MacKain et al., 1983; Burnham & Dodd, 1996).

Indeed, this perspective suggests that lipreading may constitute a primary input for deaf children to gain information about the phonological structure of spoken language (Dodd, 1966). The main problem is that lipreading, although providing information about some phonological contrasts (e.g. place of articulation), does not afford the perception of all of them (e.g. nasality and voicing; Erber, 1979; Walden et al., 1977). Through lipreading, then, deaf children have access only to phonetically underspecified information. The representations developed from this input are also underspecified with respect to heard-and-spoken language. This may be predicted to hinder deaf children's acquisition of oral language and of all cognitive activities that rely upon phonological representations.

If the development of a phonological system does not depend in any necessary sense on the auditory modality, but rather on the delivery of accurate information about phonological contrasts, one should predict that exposure to systems that deliver well-specified phonological information, by adding visual or tactile information to the lipread signal, would improve the development of phonological skills in deaf children. The aim of this chapter is to examine the effects of one of such system (i.e. cued speech) on deaf youngsters' linguistic and cognitive functioning. The next section provides a description of the system.

CUED SPEECH: A SYSTEM PROVIDING VISUALLY WELL-SPECIFIED SPEECH INFORMATION

Cued speech (CS) was devised by Cornett (1967). In CS, the speaker complements lip gestures of speech with manual cues. A cue is made of two parameters: hand shape and position of execution around the mouth (see Figure 54). The hand can adopt several shapes (eight in the French version of CS) at different positions around the mouth (five in French). Hand shapes disambiguate the consonants and hand positions the vowels. The phonemes are grouped together in such a way that those easy to discriminate by lipreading share a hand shape or a hand position while those difficult to discriminate from each other belong to different groups. For example, a particular hand shape is shared by /p, d, ʒ/, another one by /b, n/.

The consonants

[p]   p (pas)
[d]   d (dis)
[ʒ]   j (je)

[k]
[v]   k (cou)
[z]   v (vu)
      z (maison)

[s]   s (sur)
[r]   r (rit)

[b]
[n]   b (bon)
[ɥ]   n (non)
      w (cuisine)

[m]
[t]   m (maman)
[f]   t (tout)
      f (feu)
      *

[l]
[ʃ]   l (loup)
[w]   ch (chat)
[ɲ]   w (oui, quoi)
      gn (cogne)

[g]   g (gui)

[j]   y (fille)
[ŋ]   ng (parking)

The vowels

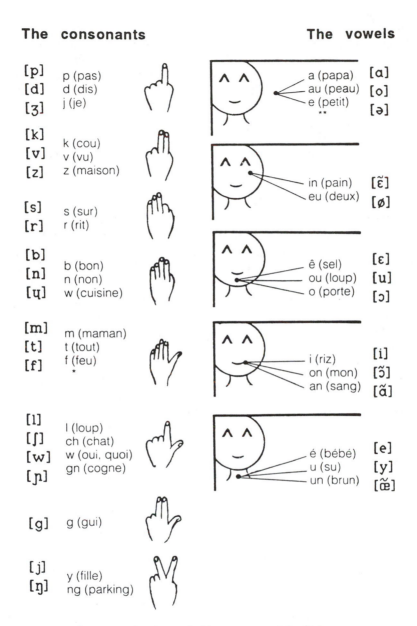

a (papa) [a]
au (peau) [o]
e (petit) [ə]
**

in (pain) [ɛ̃]
eu (deux) [ø]

ê (sel) [ɛ]
ou (loup) [u]
o (porte) [ɔ]

i (riz) [i]
on (mon) [ɔ̃]
an (sang) [ɑ̃]

é (bébé) [e]
u (su) [y]
un (brun) [œ̃]

* and any vowel not preceded by a consonant (arrête)

** and any isolated consonant (sec, prof) or followed by a silent e (lune)

FIG. 54. French version of cued speech (reproduced with authorisation of the Belgian LPC-Association).

285

For the vowels, one place is shared by /i, ɔ̃, ɑ̃/, a second one by /ɑ, o, œ/. Each time the speaker produces a cue (a particular hand shape at a specific position) while pronouncing a CV syllable, he or she is giving visually unambiguous information about this syllable and its constituent phonemes. Syllabic structures other than CV are produced with additional cues. For example, a V syllable is represented by the neutral hand shape (the same one as that used for /f, t, m/, see Figure 54) placed at the position corresponding to that vowel. Syllables with several consonants, such as CVC and CCV, are coded using the hand shape corresponding to the additional consonant at the neutral hand position (the same one as that used for /ɑ, o, œ/, see Figure 54).

It is interesting to note that CS provides a direct help to deaf children for speech reception, but has no direct effect on speech production. Although CS may play an indirect role on speech production, by providing the child with accurate phonological representations, the child's control of his or her verbal productions seems to require some residual hearing which affords him or her possible acoustic feedback. Most of the children exposed to CS are profoundly prelingually deaf and, thus, may gain very little from such feedback. Their speech is, therefore, no more intelligible than the speech of other deaf children (Ryalls, Auger & Hage, 1994). The study of the effects of CS provides an interesting opportunity to investigate how a phonologically well-specified input affects the development of phonological representations in children who cannot tune their speech gestures to acoustic inputs as hearing children can. These children may be subject to a dissociation between speech *production* (based on speechreading and minimal auditory feedback) and speech *perception* (based on speechreading with manual cues that are not used in production). In the next three sections we will summarise the effects of exposure to cued speech on phonological processing, acquisition of morpho-syntax and the development of internal speech.

EFFECT OF CUED SPEECH ON PHONOLOGICAL PROCESSING

Initially, CS was aimed at improving deaf children's speech reception skills. This improvement has been evaluated both for English- and French-speaking children. Nicholls and Ling (1982) studied a group of Australian profoundly deaf children taught at school with CS for at least three years. They found that the speech reception scores of these youngsters increased from about 30% for both syllables and words in the lipreading condition to more than 80% in the lipreading + cues condition. They emphasised that the children's average scores in the lipreading + cues condition were within the range of normal hearing listeners' reception scores of similar material through audition.

Périer et al. (1988) investigated the effect of the French version of CS upon deaf children's reception of oral language. The authors also wished to determine whether children's linguistic background influenced the benefit gained from the addition of cues to lip gestures. Two groups were identified: those who were exposed to CS early and intensively, because their parents used CS (either exclusively or in combination with signed French; see Charlier, 1992) to communicate with them at home, and those who bene-fited from CS later, and only at school, usually from the age of six. The children had to identify sentences presented either by lipreading (LR) or by lipreading + cues (LRC). Although both groups showed better under-standing for sentences presented in the LRC than in the LR condition, the advantage provided by the addition of cues was greater in the early CS-users (from 39% correct responses in the LR condition to 72% in the LRC condition) than in the late CS-users (from 37% to 53%). The differential benefit displayed by the early and the late CS-users suggests that early CS-users are more skilled in perceiving and discriminating the phonetic struc-ture of CS and in identifying lexical meaning automatically. They seem to have developed a mental phonological space where the identity of each phoneme is well-defined according to CS and lipreading, allowing ready identification of linguistic material. On the other hand, the late CS-users who were mainly exposed to spoken language may also have developed a mental phonological space, but in which the perception of CS has not become automatic; thus, different phonemes are probably still under-specified. Therefore, late CS-users have to pay more attention in processing phonological information, even if this information is phonetically accurate.

If early CS-users develop more efficient phonological processing as just suggested, they should be advantaged, compared to late CS-users, especially for processing pseudowords. The fact that early CS-users benefit more from the addition of cues than late CS-users for word processing might be explained by difference of familiarity with the material, the former being more familiar with words presented in CS than the latter. By contrast, pseudowords are unfamiliar for both subject groups. Thus, accurate iden-tification of pseudowords depends of the efficiency of the phonological processor, which depends of the quality of the mental representations of the phonemes. Recent data collected by Alegria, Charlier and Mattys (sub-mitted) indicate that phonological processing is related to linguistic back-ground in CS-users. Alegria, Charlier and Mattys compared early CS-users and late CS-users in written spelling of words and pseudowords, presented either by lipreading (LR) or by lipreading + cues (LRC). They showed that the addition of cues significantly improved spelling accuracy for words as well as for pseudowords in the early group (words: 41.5% of correct responses in the LR condition versus 73.6% in the LRC condition; pseudowords: 17.9% in the LR condition versus 54.9% in the LRC condition) as well as in the late group (words: 47.3% in the LR condition versus 67.4% in the LRC condition; pseudowords: 9.4% in the LR condition versus 32.9% in the LRC condition). The improvement induced by the cues was significantly larger in the early (32.1% for words and 37% for pseudowords) than in the late group (20.1% for words and 23.5% for pseudowords), confirming Périer et al.'s (1988) data. Moreover, the early CS-users were significantly better than the late users at identifying pseudowords in the LRC condition, whereas the two groups did not differ in the LR condition. This strongly supports the idea that the role of CS in early users is to enhance the efficiency of the processing of phonological information.

The analysis of errors also provides some evidence about differences between early and late CS-users' processing of cues. An automatic decoding of the CS signal may cause CS-based confusions. For example, a syllable like /ta/ may be interpreted as /to/, /tœ/, /fo/ or /fœ/, because /t/ and /f/ share the same hand shape and /a/, /o/ and schwa share the same hand position (see Figure 54). These confusions can only be interpreted when occuring in the LRC condition; occurrence of such confusions in the LR condition may be considered as random. Alegria, Charlier and Mattys's data show that early CS-users tended to make more CS-based confusions in the LRC condition (19.5% of their errors) than in the LR condition (5%). In the late CS-users, however, the proportion of CS-based confusions was similar in the LRC condition (11.5%) and in the LR condition (7%). These data suggest that early CS-users take more account of the cues, sometimes erroneously.

One reason why the addition of cues has larger effects in early users than in late users could be that, for the former, the processing of manual cues is an integral part of the speech-processing device. A serial recall experiment was used to investigate this topic. In this task, subjects are asked to reproduce a sequence of items in strict serial order. For just supra-span lists, error rates tend to increase over successive serial positions. However, subjects can usually recall the final item(s), a phenomenon described as the "recency effect". The recency effect consistently appears for spoken, lipread and mouthed lists, but not for orthographic lists, indicating that it results from a phonological code that is not involved in the derivation of phonology from print. This effect has been identified with processes occurring in early speech perception. Dodd et al. (1983) have shown that deaf and hearing teenagers display similar recency effect for lipread lists. This result fits well the notion that lipspeech information is an integral part of speech processing in both deaf and hearing individuals. We explored the possibility that, although the processing of lipread information may be similar in deaf and hearing subjects, the processing of CS information may be different in these two populations. The phonological code involved in speech processing may be derived for deaf subjects from experience of CS, and for hearing subjects from experience of audio-visual speech.

An experiment was run on 11 deaf teenagers, all of whom were early CS-users, and 19 hearing adults, who had learned CS for more than 4 years and who use it on average 18 hours per week. Lists of seven digits were presented to deaf subjects in lipreading (LR), in cues alone (C) and in lipreading + cues (LRC). The hearing adults were given the serial recall task with nine digits and an additional audio-visual (AV) condition was included for them. If recall rate depends on the presentation of stimuli in one's dominant modality of language, better recall rate for LRC lists than for either LR or C lists may be expected for the deaf but not for the hearing subjects. For the hearing, recall rates for the AV lists should surpass those of any of the other lists. Note that, because the set of stimuli was limited to the digits from one to nine, the stimuli were easily discriminable from each other in each of the three conditions.

The data of the early CS-users (see Figure 55, left panel) were submitted to an analysis of variance with repeated measures on type of lists (LRC, LR and C) and positions (one to seven). There was a highly significant effect of type of lists ($F(2,20) = 8.66$; $p < .002$) the LRC condition leading to higher recall rates than the LR or the C conditions. The effect of position was also highly significant ($F(6,60) = 19.32$; $p < .0001$) but did not interact with list type ($F(12,120) < 1$).

The data of the hearing subjects (see Figure 55, right panel) were also submitted to an analysis of variance with repeated mesures on type of lists (LRC, LR, C and AV) and positions (one to nine). Type of lists yielded to a

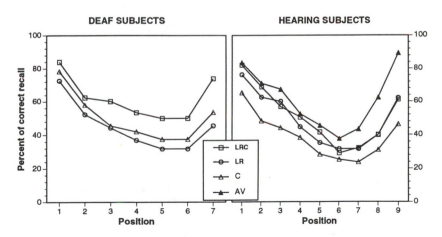

Note: LRC: Lipreading + Cues; LR: Lipreading; C: Cues; AV: Audio-visual.

FIG. 55.   Mean percent of correct responses for deaf and hearing subjects in a serial recall task.

highly significant effect (F (3, 54) = 24.15; p < .0001), the AV lists leading to higher recall rate than the other three types of lists. The position factor was also highly significant (F (8,144) = 33.38; p < .0001). The type of lists by position interaction was highly significant too (F (24,432) = 2.73; p < .0001).

The pattern LRC > LR = C for the deaf subjects and AV > LRC = LR = C for the hearing subjects suggests that CS information is processed differently by deaf and hearing subjects. The higher recall rate for LRC lists than for LR lists in deaf early CS-users suggests that the processing of cues may be part of the early stages of their speech processing device. On the other hand, the lack of difference between LRC and LR conditions in the hearing indicates that they recode both lists in a phonological code derived from experience with audio-visual speech.

It is interesting to note the variations of the recency effect with the type of lists. In the deaf sample, this effect was evaluated by comparing the performance for positions six and seven. The results show significant effects of type of lists (F (2,20) = 6.96; p < .005) and position (F (1,10) = 17.29; p < .005), but no interaction between these two factors (F (2,20) < 1). CS does not lead to greater recency than either the LR or the C conditions. In hearing subjects, the recency effect was evaluated by comparing the mean of recall rates for positions eight and nine to the recall rate for position seven. There were highly significant effects of type of lists (F (3,54) = 16.99; p = .0001), position (F (1,18) = 57.34; p = (.0001) and a significant interaction between these two factors (F (3,54) = 4.27; p = .009). AV lists led to greater recency than the three types of visual lists. Thus, these data are consistent with the notion that the marked recency effect observed in AV lists reflects a number of different components, one being a phonological, modality-independent one, and another being an echoic, modality-dependent one (see Frankish, 1996).

EFFECT OF CUED SPEECH ON LANGUAGE ACQUISITION

The development of phonological knowledge may affect the acquisition of other aspects of language that are particularly dependent upon phonological information, and, more particularly, of morpho-syntactical knowledge. The fact that phonetic factors may contribute to the development of morphological knowledge and to the deficiencies in the use of this knowledge, is demonstrated by different kinds of research: developmental data (Slobin & Bever, 1982; MacWhinney, Pleh & Bates, 1985), but also aphasics (Kean, 1979), children with language disorders (Denes et al., 1987; Leonard et al., 1986) and simulation data (Hoeffner & McClelland; 1993, quoted by Mayberry, 1995).

Although congenitally deaf learners often suffer impairments across the board in spoken language (for reviews, see Swisher, 1976; Mogford, 1988), some studies suggest that the impairment can be selectively greater for aspects of grammatical morphology than for semantic aspects. This may be because morphologically significant features are generally short items, such as closed-class words, or affixes, such as inflexions, attached to content words. They are produced rapidly and with low stress in fluent language. They can be picked up in lipreading, but with difficulty, either because they are affixed to the words' ends (e.g. plural markers in English or French) or because they are short, unaccentuated morphemes (e.g. prepositions and articles). The deaf speaker of a language like French often, understandably, fails to perceive and encode these morphological markers. With such a degraded input, the deaf learner has less opportunity to develop a mastery of the morphological rules.

Hanson and Wilkenfeld (1985) have underlined that the absence of a phonological code should severely hinder the acquisition of morphology in deaf speakers of languages like English. Data provided by Taeschner, Devescovi and Volterra (1988; see also Volterra & Bates, 1989) illustrates this point of view. They reported the case of a congenitally deaf woman who had acquired a high level of competence in spoken and written Italian. Despite achievements in lexical and syntactic competence similar to those of a hearing control, native speaker, she had a specific impairment of grammatical morphology, in particular in the use of free-standing function words. Her morphological deficiencies, thus, cannot be ascribed to a general linguistic deficit, but could be related to underspecified input.

Systems like CS may have a strong impact on the development of morpho-syntactical abilities. CS makes visible through display of the requisite phonological contrasts, the grammatical morphemes that are not easily perceived through lipreading. Early CS-users may, therefore, acquire morphosyntactical knowledge in a way similar to hearing children, and different from that of other deaf children.

Hage (1994; see also Hage, Alegria & Périer, 1991) investigated the relationship between exposure to CS and various aspects of morphological knowledge. In one of her studies, she tested deaf children's productive knowledge of grammatical gender in French. Grammatical gender of French words, although largely unrelated to semantics, can be predicted in some cases on the basis of the phonological characteristics of their ending. Endings like the nasalised /ɛ̃/ sound in (French) "le train" and /o/, as in "le bateau" typically are masculine, while endings like /ɛt/ ("la baguette") or /in/ ("la tartine") typically are feminine. Other endings, like /wɑr/ (as in "la foire" and "le mouchoir") or /ɛr/ (as in "la cuiller" and "le verre") are not systematically associated with one gender and are found in masculine as well as in feminine words. A more reliable syntactic element to identify word gender is the article. Karmiloff-Smith (1979) has demonstrated that normally hearing, French-speaking children have productive control of gender morphology by three years of age. Deaf children, however, generally do not have an extensive knowledge of words' gender. They usually make confusions between masculine and feminine, in their oral as well as in their written production, probably because neither word endings nor articles are easily perceived in lipreading.

Hage (1994) compared the ability to determine gender for familiar and unfamiliar words of two groups of deaf children: early CS-users and orally-educated deaf children who did not use CS. She selected only children who had benefited from early remediation and whose parents were actively involved in the remedial program, in order to rule out any interpretation of the performances of the two groups in terms of differential implication of the parents in the education of their deaf child. The material consisted of 60 words, 30 familiar and 30 unfamiliar. Twenty words had an feminine ending (e.g. in French "la cigarette", "la girouette", "la tartine", "la mezzanine") and 20 had a masculine ending (e.g. "le manteau", "le trumeau", "le lapin", "le troussequin"). The remaining 20 words were gender-unmarked; half of them were feminine (e.g. "la poire", "la foyère") and the other half were masculine (e.g. "le sarcloir", "le verre"). Each word was represented by a drawing. The experimenter showed each drawing to the subject while pronouncing only the picture's name. The subject had to repeat the picture's name and to add the corresponding article. A correct response was attributed if the subject chose the correct gender for the article (e.g. "*la* cigarette", "*le* trumeau").

While the experiment has been run on a larger number of subjects, the data presented here concern only sub-sets of early CS-users (mean age: 10 years, 8 months) and orally-educated children (mean age: 14 years, 10 months), carefully matched on gender-knowledge for *un*familiar *un*marked items. This matching ensures that differences between groups cannot be ascribed to the fact that the words are more familiar to one group than to the other. Both groups had high accuracy rate for familiar words (early CS-users: 97% for gender-marked items and 93.5% for unmarked items; orally-educated: 93.5% for gender-marked and 82% for unmarked items). For unfamiliar, gender-unmarked words, the percentage of correct responses was near chance level in both groups (57% for early CS-users and 56% for orally-educated children), which confirms the unfamiliarity of these items. This makes it possible to interpret the increase of correct responses for the unfamiliar, gender-*marked* words as resulting from the ability to exploit the phonological ending to determine gender. This increase was larger in the early CS group, who achieved 80% of correct responses (increase = 23%) than in the orally-educated children who achieved only 65.5% (increase = 9.5%). Early CS-users seem, thus, to have developed productive morphological knowledge based on phonological information to a greater extent than orally-educated children. It would be interesting to look, in further studies, at the development of morphological knowledge in preliterate deaf children exposed to CS: we predict that they will develop productive knowledge of grammatical gender approximately at the same age as hearing children (i.e. around three years).

EFFECT OF CUED SPEECH ON DEVELOPMENT OF INTERNAL SPEECH

The acquisition of accurate knowledge about phonological contrasts of spoken language may also have important consequences on the use of phonological representations as cognitive mediator for thinking. A large number of studies have indicated that hearing children develop, before learning to read, the ability to make judgements about phonological similarity between words (Cardoso-Martins, 1994; Lenel & Cantor, 1981). Hearing youngsters also use a phonological code for serial order recall, first for spoken items and, at a later age, also for pictures (Hitch et al., 1989; Halliday et al., 1990). Finally, phonological representations are recruited in reading and spelling acquisition, more particularly in the use of phoneme-grapheme correspondences.

Several lines of research indicate that efficiency of the phonological processing is causally related to the use of phonological representations in the three Rs (for rhyming, remembering and reading). The development of phonological awareness in preschool children is influenced by the phonological characteristics of the oral language to which they are exposed (Caravolas & Bruck, 1993; Cossu et al., 1988). Developmental phonological dyslexia, characterised by a difficulty to process new or unfamiliar words, is caused by a phonological processing impairment. This impairment may be located at a central level, with preserved perceptual abilities, as in the case of RE reported by Campbell and Butterworth (1985), or it may concern perceptual abilities (see Masterson, Hazan & Wijayatilake, 1995).

In contrast to dyslexics, the deaf children's problem in this area does not seem to relate to a processing impairment, but rather to a lack of well-specified phonological input. The importance of adequate input for efficient phonological processing is indicated by the study of deafened adults, who show depressed performance in tasks involving access to phonological representations, like rhyme judgement (Lyxell, Rönnberg & Samuelsson, 1994; Lyxell et al., 1996). In the congenitally deaf, underspecification of phonological representations has a negative impact on the development of the three Rs. Preschool deaf children do not have the same opportunity as hearing children to notice the phonological similarities between words. Consequently deaf youngsters' rhyming skills are poor, based on word spelling rather than on word pronunciation, and lag behind those of hearing children (Campbell & Wright, 1988; Hanson & Fowler, 1987; Hanson & McGarr, 1987). Underspecified representations also might cause subjects to avoid phonological coding for immediate memory for ordered nameable stimuli presented visually, and instead to rely on visual storage. As a matter of fact, deaf children fail to show reliable indicators of phonological memory coding, so they show no word length effect in memory for pictures (Campbell & Wright, 1990) and have a reduced immediate-memory span (Conrad, 1979). Finally, they may also avoid use of phoneme–grapheme mappings for reading and spelling, because the relationship between alphabetic orthography and their speech representations is less straightforward than for hearing children. The data show that, although deaf children may exhibit phonological effects in reading and spelling, these effects are less marked than those exhibited by hearing children (Burden & Campbell, 1994; Hanson, Shankweiler & Fischer, 1983; Leybaert, 1993; Leybaert & Alegria, 1993, 1995) and their acquisition of reading and spelling is consequently delayed (Conrad, 1979; Harris & Beech, 1995).

Early use of systems like CS may have a strong impact on the use of phonological representations in the three Rs. CS delivers accurate information about syllables and phonemes of the spoken language. Thus, it gives the child the opportunity to notice the phonological similarities between words and to develop rhyming skills before learning to read. With highly developed phonological lexicon and metaphonological skills, these children should start learning to read and spell in similar conditions to hearing children. The accuracy of their phonological representations for words might also encourage them to use phonological coding for immediate ordered recall of visually presented linguistic stimuli.

Support for these hypotheses was found in several experiments. Charlier and Leybaert (submitted) reported that early CS-users (mean age: 10;1 years) achieved high level of accuracy in making rhyme judgement about pairs of pictures. Their performance was not influenced by spelling similarity, but slightly by lipread/articulatory similarity. They seem, thus, to rely on phonological representations, but give perhaps more attention to the articulatory cue than hearing children of the same age. By contrast, late CS-users (mean age: 12;7 years), like orally-educated children and sign-educated children were poor at rhyming judgement: they were adversely influenced by spelling similarity and lipread/articulatory similarity.

Leybaert (in preparation; see also Leybaert & Charlier, 1996) found that early CS-users (mean age: 9;8 years) achieved the same reading and spelling levels as hearing children at approximately the same chronological age. Most of the spelling errors made by early CS-users were phonologically accurate, meaning that the children started from phonological representations to which they applied simple phoneme–grapheme rules for spelling unfamiliar words. Their spelling development was similar to that of hearing children: at a first stage, they spelled every word by simple phoneme-to-grapheme rule, then they developed progressively a more complex orthographic lexicon. By contrast, late CS-users (mean age: 12;2 years) were delayed in spelling and even more in reading achievement. They made more phonologically inaccurate misspellings. Their performance was determined more by word frequency than by phoneme-to-grapheme regularity, indicating a dependency toward the lexical procedure rather than phoneme-grapheme knowledge.

Furthermore, Charlier (1994; see also Leybaert & Charlier, 1996) found that early CS-users (mean age: 8;8 years) exhibit, like age-matched hearing controls, word length and phonological similarity effects in immediate ordered recall of pictures, indicating that they use phonological coding in memorising series of pictures. By contrast, late CS-users (mean age: 10;9 years) do not show any of these effects, probably because they rely on visual rather than on phonological storage. Finally, the early CS-users had a larger memory span than the late CS-users.

The data summarised in this section indicate that exposure to a well-specified phonological input has a high incidence on the development of phonological representations and their use in rhyming, remembering and spelling. They may also contribute to clarifying the nature of the representations involved in these tasks. In a very influential study, Conrad (1979) proposed a causal model in which the development of internal speech in deaf children is governed by the quality of their speech productions. On the other hand, Gathercole and Martin (1996) recently argued that performance on both immediate-memory tasks and rhyme-detection tasks is underpinned by activated phonological representations resulting from the speech perception process rather than by representations stemming from speech production, as previously thought. The case of congenitally anarthric subjects, who, despite congenital inability to speak, nevertheless show normal word length effects in immediate recall for stimuli presented in pictorial form, unimpaired rhyme judgement (Bishop & Robson, 1989a) and use of phoneme–grapheme correspondences in nonword spelling (Bishop & Robson, 1989b) does not support the notion that speech production mechanisms are critical in the development of internal speech. Our data obtained with early CS-users go in the same direction. Despite limited speech-production abilities, these children show clear evidence of use of a phonological code in short-term memory, rhyming and spelling. As a matter of fact, the correlations between their speech intelligibility and the rhyming accuracy was almost nil (Charlier & Leybaert, submitted). This supports Gathercole and Martin's (1996) hypothesis that the phonological representations activated are not dependent on speech production abilities, rather they result from the speech perception process.

GENERAL CONCLUSIONS

The observations made on children exposed early to CS have important implications for several theoretical and educational issues. First, these data are relevant to the understanding of the potentialities available to deaf people. The fact that early CS-users, despite profound and prelingual hearing loss, behave similarly to the hearing in a number of situations, indicates clearly that it is possible for deaf children to develop phonological representations and inner speech processes.

A second issue concerns the critical conditions for the development of such phonological abilities. The case of early CS-users confirms Dodd's idea that acoustic experience of speech is by no means a necessary condition for the development of internal speech. What seems to be the critical factor is the delivery of accurate, well-specified information about the phonological contrasts of spoken language, independent of the modality through which this information is perceived.

The research reported here also illustrates to what extent a phonological input has wide and important consequences on linguistic and cognitive development. Having the possibility to perceive well-specified phonological information leads not only to the development of an efficient phonological processor, but also to better morpho-phonological knowledge and to the use of internal speech in a number of cognitive activities. These data add weight to the evidence already available concerning the tight relationship between these different domains.

Our interpretations are based on the assumption that the critical variable differentiating early CS-users from other deaf children is exposure to a well-specified phonological input, not to less specific variables like the degree of the parents' involvement in the education of their child, the child's development of linguistic competence and so on. The precautions taken in recruiting our participants (i.e. to select only children whose parents were actively involved in the remediation curriculum; to match the differents groups on reading level) allow us to rule out interpretations in terms of these general variables. With this in mind, it is interesting to consider the origin of the difference between early and late CS-users. These two groups differed in a number of respects. The early CS-users benefitted from CS earlier, more intensively and in both home and school environments, whereas the late CS-users have been exposed to CS later, less intensively and only in school environment. Despite the fact that it is not possible to separate the influence of these three factors in the present data, it seems reasonable to think that initial age of exposure to CS may play a critical role. It has been shown that age of acquisition of sign language determines differences in language-processing procedures (Mayberry, 1995; Mayberry & Eichen, 1991). One explanation of these differences is that early exposure to a formal language favours the development of left-hemisphere specialisation for language (Marcotte & Morere, 1990; Neville, 1991). In our future research, we intend to establish more firmly the effect of age of CS acquisition (i.e. by comparing early and late users of CS at home) on language processing, and, more particularly, on cerebral lateralisation for language.

Finally, the ability of early CS-users to process the visual input conveyed by lipreading + cues might be relevant to current views on speech processing. Theories that account for speech perception in terms of auditory mechanisms or acoustic-phonetic stimulus characteristics per se cannot account for perception of cued speech. Other theories (i.e. the motor theory, Liberman & Mattingly, 1985; the direct-realist theory, Fowler, 1986; Fowler & Rosenblum, 1991) claim that listeners of speech do not hear the acoustic speech signal per se, but recover phonetically significant gestures of the vocal tract that give rise to the acoustic speech signal. Both theories assume that speech perception may involve integration of information from different sources (e.g. the acoustic and the visual one, as in the McGurk effect) when these sources provide information about the talkers' phonetic gestures. This motoric terminology allows us to talk about the perception of speech and of CS in analogous terms. Perception of CS would consist in recovering the phonetically significant gestures, i.e. the combination of lip gestures and manual cues, by integrating information from two visual sources that provide information about the same speech event (for a further discussion, see Alegria et al., 1992).

The case of CS is also relevant to theories of the development of speech perception. According to the motor theory, speech perception is accomplished by an innately specified analysis-to-synthesis mechanism that refers perception of articulatory gestures to production. The perception of CS cannot easily be accommodated to this viewpoint. It is difficult to work out just how speech perception of lipreading + cues implicates access by the perceiver to his own speech-motor system. Early CS-users seldom use manual cues to produce speech and their oral production abilities are far from perfect, perhaps no better than those of other deaf children (Ryalls, Auger & Hage, 1994). It does not seem that the deaf child's perceptual representations "are computed by ... an internal, innately specified vocal tract synthesizer" (Liberman & Mattingly, 1985, p. 26). Early CS-users seem to have a perceptual representation of the oral language phonology, but no corresponding articulatory representation. They provide a clear example of dissociation between input and output speech-lexicons and a further consideration to be acommodated in discussing the dissociation between the child's perception and production abilities (for a detailed discussion, see Studdert-Kennedy, 1991).

Moreover, the CS outcome does not seems compatible with the innateness of the speech decoding mechanism postulated by Liberman and

Mattingly (1985). Arguments against the innate vocal-tract synthesizer have already been raised by Fowler and Dekle (1991), who demonstrated that haptic information about lip movements may influence the perception of acoustic information. They argued that "there is no reason to suppose that selection would have favoured evolution of a synthesizer that anticipated receiving haptic information provided by the hands of a listener" (p. 827–8). The argument that the innate speech mechanism should not be able to decode stimuli such as haptic ones could also be made with regard to artificial gestures like the manual cues.

To conclude, the case of deaf children exposed to CS, together with the case of children acquiring sign language, tell against a view of the child as a preformed adult equipped with specialised linguistic input and output devices, and support the view of the child as equipped with several sensory modalities that are ready to perceive human communicative signals (Studdert-Kennedy, 1991). The child's task is to detect those signals in his or her environment that are linguistically significant. These signals may consist of audio-visual speech or visual language only (as in CS and sign language). The child will develop specialised processing devices for the kind of signal to which he or she is first exposed.

ACKNOWLEDGEMENTS

The research described here has been supported by grants from the Fondation Van Goethem-Brichant in 1989, and by a grant of the Fondation Houtman in 1993. The writing of this paper was partly supported by a ARC Grant "The structure of the mental lexicon: A multilevel approach to the multiple representations of words". We wish to thank Josiane Lechat, who participated in the data collection for various experiments, and Olivier Périer, who actively supported our research work. We are also grateful to the pupils and the staff of various schools in Belgium and France for their cooperation.

REFERENCES

Alegria, J., Charlier, B. & Mattys, S. (submitted). The role of lipreading and cued speech in the processing of phonological information in French-educated deaf children.

Alegria, J., Leybaert, J., Charlier, B. & Hage, C. (1992). On the origin of phonological representations in the deaf: hearing lips and hands. In: J. Alegria, D. Holender, J. Junca de Morais & M. Radeau (Eds), *Analytic Approaches to Human Cognition* (pp. 107–32). North-Holland: Elsevier Science Publishers.

Bishop, D.V.M. & Robson, J. (1989a). Unimpaired short-term memory and rhyme judgement in congenitally speechless individuals: implications for the notion of "articulatory coding". *The Quarterly Journal of Experimental Psychology, 41A*, 123–40.

Bishop, D.V.M. & Robson, J. (1989b). Accurate non-word spelling despite congenital inability to speak: Phoneme-grapheme conversion does not require subvocal articulation. *British Journal of Psychology, 80*, 1–13.

Burden, V. & Campbell, R. (1994). The development of word-coding skills in the born deaf: An experimental study of deaf school-leavers. *British Journal of Developmental Psychology*, *12*, 331–49.

Burnham, D., & Dodd, B. (1996). Auditory-visual speech perception as a direct process: The McGurk effect in infant and across languages. In D.G. Stork & M.E. Hennecke (Eds.), *Speechreading by humans and machines* (pp. 103–115). Berlin: Springer.

Campbell, R. & Butterworth, B. (1985). Phonological dyslexia and dysgraphia in a highly literate subject: A developmental case with associated deficits of phonemic processing and awareness. *The Quarterly Journal of Experimental Psychology*, *37A*, 435–75.

Campbell, R. & Wright, H. (1988). Deafness, spelling and rhyme: How spelling support written words and picture rhyming skills in deaf subjects. *The Quarterly Journal of Experimental Psychology*, *40A*, 771–88.

Campbell, R. & Wright, H. (1990). Deafness and immediate memory for pictures: Dissociations between "inner voice" and "inner ear"? *Journal of Experimental Child Psychology*, *32*, 259–86.

Caravolas, M. & Bruck, M. (1993). The effect of oral and written language input on children's phonological awareness: A cross-linguistic study. *Journal of Experimental Child Psychology*, *55*, 1–30.

Cardoso-Martins, C. (1994). Rhyme perception: Global or analytical. *Journal of Experimental Child Psychology*, *57*, 26–41.

Charlier, B.L. (1992). Complete signed and cued French: An original signed language-cued speech combination. *American Annals of the Deaf*, *137*, 331–7.

Charlier, B.L. (1994). Le développement des représentations phonologiques chez l'enfant sourd: Etude comparative du Langage Parlé Complété avec d'autres outils de communication. Unpublished PhD. Brussels: ULB.

Charlier, B.L. & Leybaert, J. (submitted). Hearing by eye: The rhyming skills of deaf children educated with cued speech.

Conrad, R. (1979). *The Deaf School Child*. London: Harper & Row.

Cornett, O. (1967). Cued speech. *American Annals of the Deaf*, *112*, 3–13.

Cossu, G., Shankweiler, D., Liberman, I.Y., Katz, L.E. & Tola, G. (1988). Awareness of phonological segments and reading ability in Italian children. *Applied Psycholinguistics*, *9*, 1–16.

Dodd, B. (1976). The phonological systems of deaf children. *Journal of Speech and Hearing Disorders*, *41*, 185–98.

Dodd, B., Hobson, P., Brasher, J. & Campbell, R. (1983). Deaf children's short-term memory for lip-read, graphic and signed stimuli. *British Journal of Developmental Psychology*, *1*, 353–64.

Denes, G., Balliello, S., Pellegrini, A. & Volterra, V. (1987). Phonemic deafness in infancy and acquisition of written language. In M. Coltheart, G. Sartori & R. Job (Eds), *The Cognitive Neuropsychology of Language* (pp. 337–49). Hove, UK: Lawrence Erlbaum Associates Ltd.

Erber, N.P. (1969). Interaction of audition and vision in the recognition of oral speech stimuli. *Journal of Speech and Hearing Research*, *12*, 423–5.

Fowler, C.A. (1986). An event approach to the study of speech perception from a direct-realist perspective. *Journal of Phonetics*, *14*, 3–28.

Fowler, C.A. & Dekle, D.J. (1991). Listening with eye and hand: Cross-modal contributions to speech perception. *Journal of Experimental Psychology: Human Perception and Performance*, *17*, 816–28.

Fowler, C.A. & Rosenblum, L.D. (1991). The perception of phonetic gestures. In I.G. Mattingly & M. Studdert-Kennedy (Eds), *Modularity and the Motor Theory of Speech Perception* (pp. 33–59). Hillsdale, NJ: Lawrence Erlbaum Associates Inc.

Frankish, C. (1996). Auditory short-term memory and the perception of speech. In S.E. Gathercole (Ed.), *Models of Short-term Memory* (pp. 179–207). Hove, UK: Psychology Press.

Gathercole, S.E. & Martin, A.J. (1996). Interactive processes in phonological memory. In S.E. Gathercole (Ed.), *Models of Short-term Memory* (pp. 73–100). Hove, UK: Psychology Press.

Hage, C. (1994). Développement de certains aspects de la morpho-syntaxe chez l'enfant à surdité profonde: Rôle du Langage Parlé Complété. Unpublished PhD thesis. Brussels: Free Université Libre de Bruxelles.

Hage, C., Alegria, J. & Périer, L.O. (1991). Cued speech and language acquisition: The case of grammatical gender morpho-phonology. In D.S. Martin (Ed.), *Advances in Cognition, Education and Deafness*. Washington, DC: Gallaudet University Press.

Halliday, M.S., Hitch, G.J., Lennon, B. & Pettipher, C. (1990). Verbal short-term memory in children: The role of the articulatory loop. *The European Journal of Cognitive Psychology, 2*, 23–39.

Hanson, V.L. & Fowler, C.A. (1987). Phonological coding in word reading: Evidence from hearing and deaf readers. *Memory and Cognition, 15*, 199–207.

Hanson, V.L. & McGarr, N.S. (1987). Rhyme generation by deaf adults. *Status Report on Speech Research, S-R, 92*, 137–56.

Hanson, V.L. & Wilkenfeld, D. (1985). Morphophonology and lexical organization in deaf readers. *Language and Speech, 28*, 269–79.

Hanson, V.L., Shankweiler, D. & Fischer, F.W. (1983). Determinants of spelling ability in deaf and hearing adults: Access to linguistic structure. *Cognition, 14*, 323–44.

Harris, M. & Beech, J. (1995). Reading development in prelingually deaf children. In K.E. Nelson & Z. Réger (Eds), *Children's Language* (pp. 181–202). Hillsdale, NJ: Lawrence Erlbaum Associates Inc.

Hitch, G.J., Halliday, M.S., Dodd, A. & Littler, J. (1989). Development of rehearsal in short-term memory: Differences between pictorial and spoken stimuli. *British Journal of Developmental Psychology, 7*, 347–62.

Hoeffner, J.H. & McClelland, J.L. (1993). Can a perceptual deficit explain the impairment of inflectional morphology in developmental dysphasia? A computational investigation. *Child Language Forum, 25*, 38–49.

Kean, M.L. (1979). Agrammatism: A phonological deficit? *Cognition, 7*, 69–84.

Karmiloff-Smith, A. (1979). *A Functional Approach to Child Language*. Cambridge, England: Cambridge University Press.

Kuhl, P.K. & Meltzoff, A.N. (1982). The bimodal perception of speech in infancy. *Science, 218*, 1138–41.

Lenel, J.C. & Cantor, J.H. (1981). Rhyme recognition and phonemic perception in young children. *Journal of Psycholinguistic Research, 10*, 57–67.

Leonard, L., Sabbadini, L., Leonard, J. & Volterra, V. (1986). Specific language impairment in children: A cross-linguistic study. *Brain and Language, 32*, (2), 233–52.

Leybaert, J. (1993). Reading ability in the deaf: the roles of phonological codes. In M. Marschark & D. Clark (Eds), *Psychological Perspectives on Deafness* (pp. 269–309). Hillsdale, NJ: Lawrence Erlbaum Associates Inc.

Leybaert, J. (in preparation). The effect of cued speech on the development of deaf children's spelling.

Leybaert, J. & Alegria, J. (1993). Is word processing involuntary in deaf children? *British Journal of Developmental Psychology, 11*, 1–29.

Leybaert, J. & Alegria, J. (1995). Spelling development in deaf and hearing children: Evidence for use of morpho-phonological regularities in French. *Reading and Writing, 7*, 89–109.

Leybaert, J. & Charlier, B. (1996). Visual speech in the head: The effect of cued speech on rhyming, remembering and spelling. *Journal of Deaf Studies and Deaf Education, 1*, 234–48.

Liberman, A.M. & Mattingly, I.G. (1985). The motor theory of speech perception revised. *Cognition, 21*, 1–36.

Lyxell, B., Arlinger, S., Anderson, J., Bredberg, G., Harder, H. & Rönnberg, J. (1996). Verbal-information processing capabilities and cochlear implants: Implications for pre-operative predictors of speech understanding. *Journal of Deaf Studies and Deaf Education*, *1*, 190–201.

Lyxell, B., Rönnberg, J. & Samuelsson, S. (1994). Internal speech functioning and speech-reading in deafened and normal hearing adults. *Scandinavian Audiology*, *23*, 179–85.

McGurk, H. & MacDonald, J. (1976). Hearing lips and seeing voices. *Nature*, *264*, 746–8.

MacKain, K., Studdert-Kennedy, M., Spieker, S. & Stern, D. (1983). Infant intermodal speech perception is a left hemisphere function. *Science*, *219*, 1347–9.

MacWhinney, B., Pleh, C. & Bates, E. (1985). The development of sentence interpretation in Hungarian. *Cognitive Psychology*, *17*, 178–209.

Marcotte, A.C. & Morere, D.A. (1990). Speech lateralization in deaf populations: Evidence for a developmental critical period. *Brain and Language*, *39*, 134–52.

Masterson, J., Hazan, V. & Wijayatilake, L. (1995). Phonemic processing problems in developmental phonological dyslexia. *Cognitive Neuropsychology*, *12*, 233–59.

Mayberry, R. (1995). Mental phonology and language comprehension, or what does that sign mistake mean? In K. Emmorey & J. Reilly (Eds), *Language, Gesture, and Space* (pp. 355–70). Hillsdale, NJ: Lawrence Erlbaum Associates Inc.

Mayberry, R. & Eichen, E. (1991). The long-lasting advantage of learning sign language in childhood: Another look at the critical period for language acquisition. *Journal of Memory and Language*, *30*, 486–512.

Mogford, K. (1988). Oral language acquisition in the prelinguistically deaf. In D. Bishop & K. Mogford (Eds), *Language Development in Exceptional Circumstances*. Edinburgh: Churchill Livingstone.

Neville, H.J. (1991). Whence the specialization of the language hemisphere? In I.G. Mattingly & M. Studdert-Kennedy (Eds), *Modularity and the Motor Theory of Speech Perception* (pp. 269–95). Hillsdale, NJ: Lawrence Erlbaum Associates.

Nicholls, G. & Ling, D. (1982). Cued speech and the reception of spoken language. *Journal of Speech and Hearing Research*, *25*, 262–9.

Périer, O., Charlier, B.L., Hage, C. & Alegria, J. (1988). Evaluation of the effects of prolonged cued speech practice upon the reception of spoken language. In I.G. Taylor (Ed.), *The Education of the Deaf: Current Perspectives, Vol 1, 1985 International Congress on Education for the Deaf*. Beckenham, Kent, UK: Croom Helm, Ltd.

Ryalls, J., Auger, D. & Hage, C. (1994). An acoustic study of the speech skills of profoundly hearing-impaired children who use cued speech. *Cued Speech Journal*, *5*, 8–18.

Slobin, D. & Bever, T. (1982). Children use canonical sentence schemas: A crosslinguistic study of word order and case inflections. *Cognition*, *12*, 229–65.

Studdert-Kennedy, M. (1991). The emergent gesture. In I.G. Mattingly & M. Studdert-Kennedy (Eds), *Modularity and the Motor Theory of Speech Perception* (pp. 85–90). Hillsdale, NJ: Lawrence Erlbaum Associates.

Swisher, L. (1976). The language performance of the oral deaf. In H. Whitaker & H.A. Whitaker (Eds.), *Studies in Neurolinguistics (Vol 2)*. New York: Academic Press.

Taeschner, T., Devescovi, A. & Volterra, V. (1988). Affixes and function words in written language of deaf children. *Applied Psycholinguistics*, *9*, 385–401.

Volterra, V. & Bates, E. (1989). Selective impairment of Italian grammatical morphology in the congenitally deaf: A case study. *Cognitive Neuropsychology*, *6*, 273–308.

Walden, B.E., Prosek, R.A., Montgomery, A.A., Scherr, C.K. & Jones, C.J. (1977). Effects of training on the visual recognition of consonants. *Journal of Speech and Hearing Research*, *20*, 130–45.

Author index

Subject index